AN INTRODUCTION TO NIGERIAN
TRADITIONAL ARCHITECTURE

VOLUME ONE

Northern Nigeria

First published in 1990 in Great Britain
by ETHNOGRAPHICA Ltd.
19 Westbourne Road London N7 8AN
and in Nigeria by
The National Commission
for Museums and Monuments
Onikan, Lagos

ISBN 0 905 788 26 5

ACKNOWLEDGEMENT

*An Introduction to Nigerian Traditional
Architecture* Volumes 1-3 were printed
under provision of the European
Development Fund to whom the co-
publishers express their gratitude.

AN INTRODUCTION TO NIGERIAN
TRADITIONAL ARCHITECTURE

VOLUME ONE

Northern Nigeria

Z.R. DMOCHOWSKI

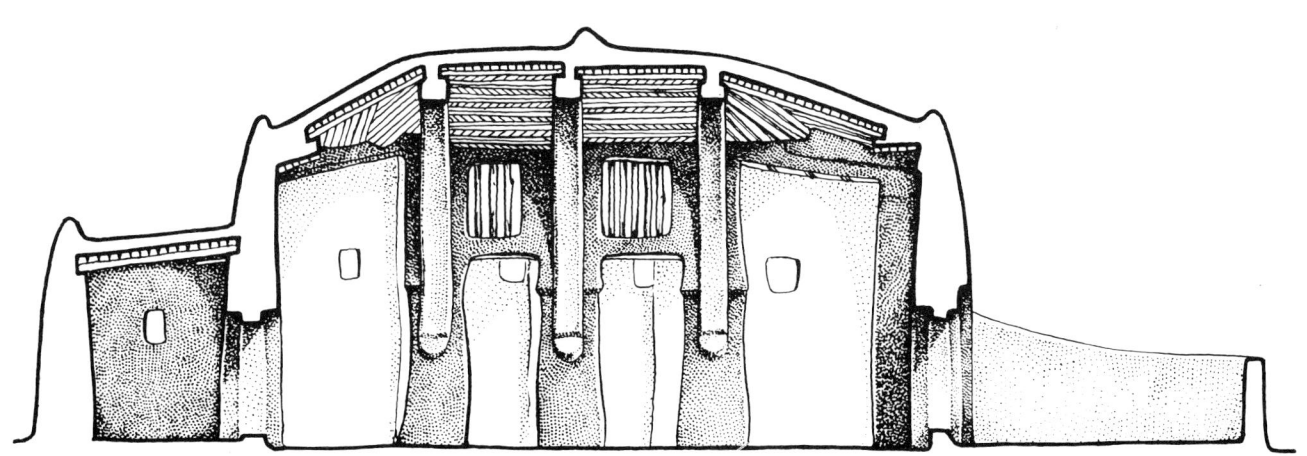

ETHNOGRAPHICA

in association with

THE NATIONAL COMMISSION FOR MUSEUMS AND MONUMENTS

1990

Preface to the Series

The purpose of this book is to fill the gap which exists in the record of one of the essential elements of Nigerian cultural achievement, namely Nigerian architecture.

Architecture is neither a purely artistic nor an exclusively technical activity. Its aim is to provide a material frame for the major part of human life: for work and rest, for religious, social and artistic activities. In order to achieve this end, the work of architecture – the building – must be strong to assure reliable shelter. It also must be well planned, to provide for comfortable use of its component parts. Finally, it must satisfy a demand always inherent in the human mind, for aesthetic satisfaction: for that elusive, precious quality called beauty.

Thus a building is not an end in itself, but rather a means to an end, which is to satisfy the material and spiritual needs of the people for which it is created. As a natural result, among all the arts architecture is the most firmly linked with human life and reflects its dynamics most faithfully.

In consequence, all over the world familiarity with the architectural achievements of one's country, an understanding and appreciation of its traditions and development through the ages, it now almost universally considered to be an elementary means towards the formation of national consciousness and self-assertion. The aim that is sought by these means is to create deference and regard, and finally love, for one's own traditions. Such true love, Leonardo da Vinci said, is the daughter of true knowledge. The word love is unfortunately seldom used by scholars. But architecture is devised by architects, and no good architecture can originate without respect and love on the part of the society for which it is created – a society which is conscious and proud of its own culture.

From love of the human heritage there is just one step to accepting its values as a starting point in the creation of modern cultural forms, forms which grow out of, or evolve from, the society's own cultural past.

This statement involves the conception of labour, of human effort, resulting in the creation of new and better human surroundings, both material and spiritual.

The differentiation between the material and spiritual aspects of life was popular some years ago but must not be accepted too literally nowadays; and perhaps particularly when dealing with architecture, one of the major elements of human culture. Certainly buildings satisfy physical needs – security from animal and human foes, and protection from the elements – all these are material requirements. But buildings are improved only by the influence of spiritual and intellectual factors: the organised collaboration of men; progress in social understanding and knowledge of technology; the creation of ideological and religious convictions. All these are almost standard aesthetic incentives. Thus fostered in the process of its development, architecture creates constantly escalating standards of human desires which lead, step by step, to improved conditions of social life.

It is important to emphasize the word 'social' because every idea, principle or technological method, as well as every moral attitude or doctrine (these are the organic elements of culture) is valid only in the context of an appropriate social organisation. Each must have conscious support within the society.

This support must be based on the observation of facts from the past and in turn should lead to observable results. In other words, it should be inductive and able to be experimentally tested. The resulting conclusions, strictly defined and therefore accessible to any students, can be used to predict the consequences of specified intellectual attitudes, and lead to the improvement of social life.

This all seems to indicate a general rule that no individual achievement, spiritual or material, can enrich the national culture unless it is supported by society as a whole. In cultural endeavour the vision of a noble task, as long as it remains just a theory detached from life, does not matter. What matters are visions and ideas turned by a willing society into a cultural reality of observable facts. And this rule applies very strongly indeed to the dynamics of architectural creation.

Efficient labour, conscientious planning and the support of a society which comprehends and appreciates its own achievements and develops them, constantly and lovingly, are elements of architectural creation time tested over many years of social experiment and development.

There is reason to believe that the present generation, and especially the creative citizens of the countries that are now evolving most eagerly, would profit by being acquainted with certain theories created and experiences gained not long ago by trail and, sometimes, by error.

It is natural that the developing nations are going through revolutionary changes in very many aspects of life: scientific, economic and social. This is of course a truism, but it should be remembered that it is not the first time that momentous changes have occurred in the flow of human affairs. Let us recall at least one such period, which has certain similarities with the present, namely the Europeans era called the Renaissance. It well illustrates the dynamics and rules of cultural and architectural achievement in a positive context.

The 15th century Renaissance period witnessed a fundamental reversion from mediaeval ways of life. The fall of Byzantium altered the network of the old economy; new trade routes and new continents were discovered. New technologies contributed to the rapid material growth of the cities and states, and to the creation of new nuclei of economic and political power. Simultaneously, prodigious changes developed in intellectual attitudes. Mediaeval mysticism gave way to new trends of thought, considerably influenced by classical ancient philosophy. This, largely forgotten in the west but preserved in Byzantium and brought from there by Greek scholars, filled the peoples of the Italian city-states with respect and admiration for the glorious past of their own land. They never achieved the security of Pax Romana, but the certainly enjoyed the considerable wellbeing of the Quattrocento's Italian city-states. Acquainted with the rediscovered treasures of classical literature, surrounded by the still-imposing monuments of classical architecture, they decided to equal the ancients in material and intellectual standards. This trend was regarded as a re-birth, a renaissance of the traditional values. However what actually happened differed greatly in its sociological context, and in many cases also technologically exceeded the ancient patterns.

Symbolically enough, the people who intended to repeat the classical criteria erected as one of the first renaissance buildings neither a Roman circus nor an ampitheatre, but a children's hospital—the Florentine Ospedale degli Innocenti. Later on, Michelangelo, erecting St Peter's basilica, crowned it with a dome which was originally to follow the cast of the Roman Pantheon: but he did much more than that. The dome of the Pantheon was erected on a circle of massive walls some 23 metres. St Peter's dome is supported by four pillars at only four points and is over 80 metres high. The dome of the Pantheon is a solid cast of brickwork and mortar – the dome of St Peter's is a sophisticated living organism, erected from two concentric shells of thousands of voussoirs, each stone block individually shaped.

These are only two examples of the Renaissance phenomenon, but I think they are typical of its spirit. The people of the Italian Quattro- and Cinquecento were creating new values of their own modern culture, on the basis of the old one.

'Strength, commodity, beauty' – these are the three qualities enumerated by Vitruvius in his treatise *De Architectura Libri Decem*.' He wrote it in 27-23 B.C., summing up the professional knowledge and wisdom and also the practical experience of the Greek and Roman specialists. He did not limit himself to a comprehensive analysis of public and private buildings, but devoted large sections of his work to subjects he considered to be related to architecture, namely philosophy, music, meteorology, astronomy and engineering. Vitruvius' work was brought to Italy by Byzantine scholars and at once became the object of thorough and enthusiastic study. It was published in Rome circa 1486. All the same, this happened a year later than the publiction of an Italian treatise, 'De Re Aedificatoria' by Leone Battista Alberti. This Renaissance master, although full of reverence and affection towards his Roman forerunner,

nevertheless developed and modernised some of his designs by presenting projects of his own.

Vitruvius' *Libri Decem* remained a classic source for exhaustive study for many years to come, but Alberti's ideas were readily accepted by his contemporaries. This happened, as it was bound to happen, because the whole of Renaissance society was enthusiastically eager to take part in a common effort to build a modern reality in all aspects of life, in the same way as Alberti developed designs which had their roots in Vitruvius' *De Architectura*.

All over the country, libraries, academies and schools were founded by those in power, and the Renaissance movement was constantly fed with scholarly research, study and creativity.

The magnificence and splendour of the period appears still more impressive because it ran simultaneously with bitter and bloody competition between the leading families of the cities, and the cities themselves. The Renaissance period was certainly not peaceful; but the Renaissance idea succeeded because it enjoyed the almost unanimous backing of all classes of people, who were proud of their past and proud of their own progress. They were led by men of talent, who were able and willing to act in a free, independent way. Both the leaders and the masses were men of courage, and emboldened by the magnitude of their ideas, they were ready to fight for them.

When Raffaello Santi was appointed by Pope Leo X to produce an inventory of ancient buildings which were to serve as quarries providing stone for St Peter's Basilica, he prepared instead a comprehensive treatise on 'Roma Antica,' based on careful study and detailed surveys of classical monuments. He wrote: 'Since every man is bound to honour and esteem his parents and his country, he should even more devote his humble powers to rescue this, what has been saved from the comon heritage of all the men of Christianity.' Yet it was the same Raffaello who, when the time came to plan the extension of St Peter's Basilica, produced designs of weightlessness which in structural courage far surpassed any ancient pattern.

This culture-building was enhanced by the very important fact that in resurrecting the traditional they were dealing with values that belonged to their own country, that represented their own cultural heritage. The inhabitants of the Appennine Peninsula felt at home when continuing in creative way the Roman tradition of their own land.

There are many definitions of architecture. I think one of the most notable was made by the late Maitre Auguste Perret. It speaks of architecture as technical activity performed by a poet. This is a very good definition: but another great man, the poet T.S. Eliot, said that poetry has the kind of value that perishes when translated into a foreign language. Perhaps here there is one more reason to believe that true architecture, creative architecture, cannot be copied from foreign patterns. It must grow out of its own roots, be expressed in its own language.

A large group of people claim that art is international. This sounds reasonable and attractive, but many half-truths sound just as reasonable and attractive. I believe that art, like every other cultural achievement, cannot arise in a void. Its background, its soil, must be its own – that of its own people. Only then will it grow healthy and beautiful. Only in this way can it reach the highest level of artistic achievement and become universally appreciated and universally accepted. Nigerian carvings and bronzes have been admired as masterpieces of international art ever since they became internationally known, and as recent discoveries have proved, Nigerian art has a two thousand year old tradition of development. Nigeria is an example of what happens everywhere. When art reaches the highest level, it becomes the proud possession of all mankind. In this sense, and in this sense only, art is international.

I trust that in due time Nigerian architecture will attain this level. If this is to be accomplished, the roots of the nation's building craft as well as the triumphs of Nigerian developed architecture should be made known and popularized. At present it is a real tragedy that although during the last decades very many learned treatises have been produced about Nigerian art, Nigerian architecture has been treated as a marginal item, if at all.

As I said in the first paragraph of this Preface, the purpose of this book is to make known those achievements of Nigerian architecture with which it was the author's privilege to become acquainted. The title, *An Introduction to Nigerian Traditional Architecture* is purposely restricted. There is no doubt that a comprehensive treatise on the subject is a work to be done by Nigerian scholars: preferably by the combined effort of architects and geographers, anthropologists, ethnographers, art historians and sociologists.

But before such a book is written, the 'Introduction' will provide future writers, and present-day readers in particular, with the basic material for any further architectural research.

The book contains, first and foremost, several hundred architectural drawings: plans, sections, elevations and isometric cut-out projections. It also contains a selection from several thousand photographs. All the buildings thus presented were recorded during the period 1958-1966. Many of them do not exist any more, and it is only in this way that they will be remembered.

In order to build up this corpus of reliable surveys I had to train a group of young Nigerians. They were eager to work, but most of them had only basic education; it was necessary, therefore, to combine their training with actual survey in the field. When organising this I adapted the methods I had used previously for many years in Poland before 1939 when surveying and researching Polish traditional architecture. This involved the use of certain basic instruments and techniques, some of them our own, developed at the Warsaw School of Architecture, in particular the method of modifying plane-table survey for measuring horizontal projections and three dimensional triangulations for sections and elevations. I shall always remember with respect the wholehearted efforts of my Nigerian assistants in carrying out this hard, pioneering work.

Thus over one thousand six hundred precise measured

drawings were made, records of monuments, large and small, of traditional architecture in the Nigerian Federation. Depending on the size and complexity of the building concerned, the number of measurements taken varied from a few dozen to a few thousand.

Between 1965 and 1972 most of the survey material was drawn to scale, inked and prepared for publication at the Gdansk Technical University in Poland.

The material of the book is introduced topographically, and arranged whenever possible in typological groups (for example, mosques of the Sokoto pattern), according to plan, construction and form. An attempt was made to analyse the buildings in relation to their geographical and social background. I am aware that this aspect is not always treated in proportion to its anthropological importance. But my main task was to produce a reliable architectural survey, which I expect will be further analysed by specialists in various fields.

The first impression of Nigerian architecture is its great variety, an obvious consequence of geographical factors and the ethnic diversity of Nigeria's population. The characteristics of architectural design were determined by the natural conditions of a given area, most of all by the climate and the building materials available.

Climatic conditions imposed two basic necessities: thermal insulation and ventilation. Each of these needs was met in many ways. For instance in the north, walls of great thickness were adopted; the Edo and Tiv developed ingenious ways of profiling building façades in order to keep large parts of them in shade but at the same time increase the radiation of heat accumulated by the walls in the daytime; the Igbo often insulated their houses with very thick, grass-thatched roofs.

Ventilation, and often cross ventilation as well, was provided by the Tiv; and the Igbo sometimes erected lattice-like walls resulting in a constant flow of air in the interiors. These are only a few examples – more details can be found in relevant paragraphs of the book.

The social philosophies of Nigerian cultural centres influenced both religious and secular architecture. The moslem mosques of the north, however grand and elaborate, were nevertheless designed merely as places of communal prayer. In the south, the shrines sheltered sacred objects or symbolised supernatural beings. Similarly, Hausa palaces were intended solely as residences and quarters for administration and social ceremonies. In the south the palaces of Edo and Yoruba rulers fulfilled further requirements: being residences of sacred kings of divine descent, they were the focal point of religious rituals, the object of mystical awe. Among the Igbos, Obu houses were similarly conceived, although in a very different context.

Geographical location determined another major factor in building craft: the materials available. The two main constituents of Nigerian building fabric are building earth, always carefully processed, and timber. The building earth differs greatly in quality, from the excellent clay of Benin and many Habe-Hausa areas to the sandy soils of large parts of Igboland, which forced builders to adopt wattle-and-daub constructions.

Even more varied are the timbers used in different areas of the country, from the famous *Iroko*, a very hard wood from the rain forest, to *Gongola*, palm ribs, which are rather fragile but beautiful in their colour and texture.

Migrations of ethnic groups undoubtedly affected the creation of new architectural forms. In Imuaroli village in Onitsha, the Benin origin of the people partly influenced local planning, though not architectural composition. Sometimes emigrants developed designs quite different from those typical of their country of origin: in Abuja for instance builders abandoned most of the forms of their original Habe-Hausa art. At the same time they adopted elements from far-away Nupe buildings, probably as a result of trade connections.

The varied social structures influenced the organisation of the building trade. In the main cultural centres of the north, well organised professional guilds were prevalent, as also among the Edo and the Yoruba. In Igboland, practically everyone was able to build a house. Almost everywhere decorative architectural elements such as mouldings and carvings were the exclusive domain of respected groups of artists.

The varied characteristics distinguishing individual buildings in Nigeria prevented the adoption of a standardised scheme of classification. The criteria for analysis had to be modified, in keeping with the physical and cultural features of the environment. Nevertheless, despite the diversities in Nigerian architecture, some common characteristics are to be found in practically every area of the country, irrespective of the size and substance of the fabric.

Perhaps the most striking feature is the competent practice of the art of significant forms in space; a clear understanding that building is a three-dimensional art. It is tempting to assume that the sense of rhythm, so obvious in Nigerian music and drumming, found material expression in the design of Nigerian buildings; from the tiny but beautiful huts of the Jaba tribe to the monumental mosques and residences of the mighty. The word rhythm is often used by architectural designers, and there are many similarities in approach to both musical and architectural composition.

Another common characteristic is the technological perfection obtained in spite of the relative fragility of building materials and the simplicity of the working tools. This is the result of a thorough understanding of the qualities of the materials used, and of skills developed and improved by many generations of builders great and small.

This being said, the heterogeneity of the Nigerian architectural achievement must be presented, at least in general outline.

In the north, the Habe-Hausa method of building dominates. It is best represented by the sophisticated architecture of the mosques and great residences. Among mosques, Zaria's Masallaci Juma'a is the foremost achievement, but no lesser virtues are to be found in many Habe-Hausa palaces of the Emirs and of the city-states' aristocracies. Both groups, using basically the same principle of bold frame construction, made in timber-reinforced loam, differ in spatial composition as they imaginatively fulfil their particular, differing functions. In their beautiful interiors, pillared, domed or roofed on ornate compositions of brackets and ingeniously made bracketed-arches, the Hausa builders demonstrated not only their craftsmanship, matured during centuries of steady development, but also their excellence in shaping splendid forms in space.

Another great northern school of building art was created by the Nupe. It is outstanding in the monumentality of the Etsu-royal palaces, and in the perfect proportions as well as the exquisite moulded decoration of domestic architecture.

Monumentality is also dominant in the palaces of the ancient kingdom of Benin and the afins of the Yoruba rulers. There exists a certain similarity in the plans of both, since their network consists of a number of linked courts, each surrounded by a ring of verandahs in front of a ring of rectangular rooms. Within this general scheme, the differences are considerable. Benin courts, rather closely built, have a more secluded patio-like character, and the heavy pillars supporting the verandah roofs are at present made of loam. The afin courts, occasionally much larger, have the character of courtyards and the verandah posts are sculptured compositions, usually of two human figures one perched on top of another. These caryatids (atlantes) are among the highlights of Yoruba sculptural art. However an outstanding quality of the afins and even more of the Benin palaces, is their excellent planning. The palaces of Benin chiefs are much more than just domestic quarters. With their ceremonial pillared halls and numerous altars for worship they serve as places for official gatherings and religious rites. The three basic functions of life are fully provided for. The result is a mature, truly functional design in which the personal, the social and the sacred aspects are mirrored in the carefully thought out plan. The proportions of the interiors are suited to their purpose, and the general serenity of the conception is appropriate for a building that is partly ecclesiastic in its bearing.

The Igbo peoples originally were not unified politically, and they consisted of several groups and sub-groups. There are therefore considerable cultural differences among them, and the body of their architectural monuments possess a great number of types, varied in function, plan, construction, outer form and decoration. In the religious division alone, there are shrines to the ancestors like the famous temple of the Ndi Ezera clan; votive shrines, called Mbari houses, with their profusion of sculptural images; and meeting halls, Obu houses, of various types, used for religious rites as well.

Igbo domestic architecture contains an enormous quantity of variations, from the two-storied, complex houses of the Aros to the see-through buildings of Nri-Awka, and the beautifully ordered compounds of Umuaroli. There are buildings that are roofed on loam-made walls, or on posts, set outside the walls, or in the thickness of the walls, or inside the walls. There are roofs made with such exquisite skill that their texture of palm ribs and grass serves by itself as an architectural adornment. And the innumerable patterns of carved doors or carved wooden panels – patterns that never repeat themselves and must be counted by the thousand – almost symbolise the immense variety of Igbo architecture.

These are the three important architectural groups, but the qualities of many others are certainly of no lesser value; for example, the Tiv with their timber pillared, circular halls (*Ate*) of extremely delicate and ingenious wall construction; the mosques and city houses of Ilorin; the ornate buildings of Abuja; and the multitude of small hill tribes whose structures, serene and functional, are shaped with such a consummate excellence that many of them, analysed in their three-dimensional whole, appear as beautiful abstract sculptures.

The book will thus provide the reader with reliable records of as many Nigerian buildings as the author was able to see, measure and analyse. Unfortunately not all areas of Nigeria could be studied during six years of intensive exploration and fieldwork.

Nevertheless, the book will supply scholars with fairly comprehensive material to work upon; it will provide the general public with the knowledge of important cultural achievements of talented people, with an appreciation of buildings which otherwise would probably remain unnoticed or forgotten.

This book is dedicated primarily to the architectural youth of Nigeria. They should seek inspiration from the glorious past of their building art. Through the intense study of the functional planning, remarkable construction and splendid form created by their ancestors, they will develop an instinct, an almost subconscious capacity for shaping space in a way that would be their own continuation of the work done by their forbears.

They should not repeat the ancient patterns, nor copy them in any revivalist attempt. They should act as did the courageous designers of the Italian Quattrocento, inspired by the old national achievement, yet fully aware of being in the service of their contemporaries. In the same way the present day Nigerian architects should fulfil their duties to the 20th century Nigerian society which is their own. Accepting tradition as the starting point of their creative, independent thinking, they should evolve in steel and concrete, glass and aluminium, a modern school of Nigerian Architecture.

Contents

Contents (continued)

1 Hausa Building Technology

Pl.1.1 ZARIA. The 'bicycle' house.

Introduction

HISTORICAL BACKGROUND

The Hausa form a large group of mixed blood and various physical types, linked by language, by Islamic faith and by a common way of life. Hausaland comprises much of Northern Nigeria outside the 'Middle Belt' and Bornu, the territories north of Kano and Katsina Provinces, and north and west of Sokoto; it is said that it extends into the Niger Republic, Dahomey, Togo and Ghana.[1] Hausa legends speak of Bayajida, a refugee prince from Baghdad, who after numerous and romantic adventures reached Daura.[2] There he killed the dragon Kia, who prevented access to a source of water. The prince married Queen Daura, and adopted the title Sare Kia, the vanquisher of Kia.[3] His direct descendants founded the seven Hausa *bakwai*, the 'legitimate' states of Daura, Katsina, Kano, Gobir, Rano, Biram and Zaria. His seven illegitimate sons founded Zamfara, Kebbi, Nupe, Gwari, Yauri, Ilorin and Kwararafa.

The reliability of the Bayajida legend is debatable. It is of a later date than the actual formation of Hausa society, which probably happened at the beginning of the first millenium AD, when nomad Berber tribes subjugated the grasslands and their indigenous Sudanese peasant population, an area extending from Kanem in the east to Gao and Ghana in the west and beyond.[4] The invaders mixed with the autochthons, and began to create petty units, sometimes consisting solely of immigrants, sometimes of natives, and sometimes of ethnically mixed agglomerations. A number of small chiefdoms arose, mainly engaged in agriculture around their walled cities, which became centres of trade and industry. For centuries they carried on mutually destructive wars. However, 'the first formative period of Hausa history really ended in 1350, a year after Ali Yaji began to reign at Kano. By then all the main Hausa states had been established'[5] (1359 AD), and missionaries brought the Muslim religion first to Kano and Katsina. Later on Islam reached Zazzau and Daura. Under the influence of Islam a system of public revenue, a judiciary and an administration based on Muhammadan law was introduced. The city states grew in power and wealth, by controlling the trans-Saharan trade routes, by slave raiding, by industrious cultivation of the land adjoining their cities, and by developing the crafts of smithing, weaving, dyeing, tanning and leatherworking. Even so, the Hausa states were constantly invaded and often subjugated by powerful neighbours. Early in the sixteenth century Mohammed Askia of Songhai captured Katsina and Zaria, and then Kano. According to the *Kano Chronicles*, Kano, Katsina 'and all the towns as far as Kwararafa and Nupe' were conquered about 1580 by the martial Queen Amina of Zazzau (Zaria). The end of the century opened a period of ravaging wars between Kano and Katsina, when the armies of the two city states invaded and plundered one another's territories in a constantly changing pattern of success. At the beginning of the seventeenth century Kano, Zaria and Katsina were invaded by the Jukun people, who in the second half of the century, had established the powerful empire of Kwararafa. In 1734 Kano succumbed to Bornu, and paid tribute up to the time of jihad.

The jihad was led by a Fulani scholar, Shehu Usman dan Fodio, who launched his revolution of religious and social reforms, followed by the military conquest of the Habe kingdoms, and culminating in the creation of a Fulani empire. Fourteen of his best lieutenants were each given a flag as an emblem of their authority as Muslim governors of the fourteen states.

'The seven important flag-bearers were to take over Kano, Katsina, Zaria, Bauchi, Adamawa, Nupe and Ilorin. Six others were to possess the less important Gombe, Kazaura, Daura, Hadejia, Missau and Katagum. The fourteenth was for Bornu, but this mission was never completed. All these were to be independent commands, though acknowledging the supremacy of the Sarkin Musulmi in Sokoto.[6] After Shehu's death the relations between the courts were strained for a time, but finally, in accordance with Shehu's will, the eastern emirates paid tribute to Sokoto, the western emirates to Gwandu.[7]

Throughout the nineteenth century rebellions and civil wars disrupted the Fulani imperium. Consequent upon the weakening of religious fervour came military decline. The early pioneering spirit was overcome by luxury, intrigue and the ruthless search for slaves, which caused devastation and economic deterioration. The British conquest was initiated by the Royal Niger Company with the capture of Bida and Ilorin in 1897 and then of Zaria, Kano and Sokoto. In 1903 all the Fulani provinces came under British domination, which lasted until 1960.

[1] 'An Introduction to the History of Hausaland', *Nigerian Field*, Vol. XXXI, No. 1/1966.

[2] The following is a version of the legend, one of many; it was presented to me in manuscript by Mallam Bukari Musa, Madakin Daura, and subsequently much abbreviated. In any case it seems inconsistent, and should be regarded simply as an interesting myth.

[3] The commonly used Hausa word *sarki* (chief) is said to be an abbreviation of *Sare-Kiya*.

[4] S J Hogben and A H M Kirk-Greene, *The Emirates of Northern Nigeria*, London 1966, p. 82.

[5] M G Smith, *The Beginnings of Hausa Society AD 1000-1500/The Historian in Tropical Africa.*

[6] S J Hogben and A H M Kirk-Greene, *op cit, passim.*

[7] F de F Daniel, *Journal of the African Society*, XXV, 1925-26, pp. 278-83.

Building Materials

Hausa building materials fall into three groups:

Rocks and products of natural decay and disintegration, alluvial deposits of earth, laterite, etc;

Plants: trees and shrubs, their leaves and byproducts as extracts or ashes and, thirdly, metals.

The builders know the various building materials available in their areas, especially the properties of different trees, shrubs and plants, both wild and cultivated. They are also well acquainted with the properties of building earth.

Building earth is processed with water and different additives, and is employed in a number of ways. In the more primitive buildings it is used as plaster on a structural frame, made of timber and creepers, cornstalks, reeds and grasses. Plaster is also used in thick beds set between layers of broken stone. In more sophisticated constructions building earth serves as the material for making *tubali*, sun dried bricks.

Building earth which has a large clay content can be baked. Baked bricks are not used traditionally by the Hausa, but occasionally layers of broken pots set between beds of mortar are used by the natives of the north-eastern areas (linked with the Hausa sphere of influence).

In common with the rest of the country, the two basic building materials used by the Hausa are building earth and wood. The earth is for making mortar and plaster and the sun-dried building elements called *tubali*.

Birji

The earth of which both mortar and *tubali* are made is called *birji*. It is dug out from the *kududdufi*, the borrow-pit carefully chosen by the builder, since the *birji* varies considerably from town, and even from pit to pit. Before the decision is made, samples are taken from a depth of between one and two metres. Some *kududdufi* are over seven metres deep. In Kano reddish, or rather sanguine-coloured earth (*jan birji*) is considered superior to yellow. Daldy has said, that in general the earth of Niger and Benue provinces contains a higher percentage of fines than that of Sokoto or Hadejia.[8] In Kano, when brought from the pit, the *birji* is not uniform in colour or consistency. Most of it is brought from the pit in large lumps hard enough to resist a fall of one metre. Usually there is also a certain amount of gravel-sized lumps and loose coarse-grained sand.

The colours of *birji* vary considerably within the same lump – from sepia and indian red to burnt-sienna and sienna, the second and third colours prevailing. The *birji* is first broken into small particles with adzes and shovels. From then on the processing is quite different, depending on whether it is to be used for tubali, mortar or plaster.

Tubali and mortar

For *tubali* the broken *birji* is wetted, spread flat and trampled by foot until it reaches the consistency of thick paste. It is left for a couple of days to dry and then wetted and trampled again before being formed into *tubali*. When the quality of *birji* is inferior, it is mixed with grass (*datsi*) the colour of dusty straw. *Datsi* is used dry and is broken into small pieces by rubbing one bundle of it against another. (Plate 1.3.)

The actual manufacture of *tubali* occupies three men: a carrier who brings the material from the heap in his headpan, a small boy who makes *churi*, and the *tubali*-maker himself.

Working *churi* is usually the first step in the career of a builder, as distinct from being the builder's labourer. (An old master builder, Mallam Aminu Tudun Wuzurci, told me that at the age of seven, working *churi* was his first duty when his father, himself a builder, decided to teach him the trade. He was then, he remembered, not paid at all, only beaten.)

The *churi* maker sits on the ground with the heap of wet *birji* between his outstretched legs; he detaches from the mass a lump, about 30 centimetres in diameter, rolls it twice towards him, squeezes it from both sides into a solid loaf and throws the *churi* thus formed to the *tubali*-maker, who squats nearby. He begins by rolling the *churi* on the ground as a baker kneads his dough, using fine sand instead of flour to prevent sticking. He then shapes his material first into a short cylinder and then into a double cone, thick in the centre and pointed at both ends. This he lifts in both hands about half a metre from the ground and then throws it down with one hand in such a way that one of the pointed ends flattens against the earth. The fairly loose particles of *birji* contract violently and the final shape of the *tubali* is formed – one is tempted to say – in an organic way. The molecules of the *birji* adjust themselves during this short moment of impact to the natural stresses working between them. About a fortnight later, when the *tubali* are dry, the molecules will be immobilised in this position – within their conical, slightly bulging, static shapes. The *tubali* is thus almost pre-stressed. (Plates 1.4 & 1.5).

---

[8] A F Daldy, *Temporary Buildings in Northern Nigeria*, Public Works Department of Northern Nigeria, Technical Paper No. 10, 1945.

Pl.1.2. Breaking up building earth.

Pl.1.3. Adding grass to birji *for strength.*

Tubali were generally made in the vicinity of the building site and under the supervision of the master-builder. In Kano however there were specialists, who earned their living by producing *tubali* for sale. In 1960 many of them worked at the base of Dalla Hill; another site of production was near Jakara Pond. The latter were considered inferior to and sold at half the price of the former. Mischlisch notes that the original price for a single *tubali* was one cowrie, while a Dalla *tubali* cost two cowries.[9]

Conical-shaped *tubali* were the only type used in Kano. In Katsina these were the commonly used type, but *tubali* of a different shape and consistency were used. To make them even the poorest surface layers of soil were consumed, which when mixed with water were moulded into lumps about 15 centimetres in diameter. Their consistency was poor, but their purpose was limited to that of a filler in the wall structure. The structural function was performed by plaster, carefully processed from *kasa* of the highest quality. It formed a strong

[9] A Mischlisch, *Uber die Kulturen in Mittel-Sudan*, Berlin 1942.

Pl.1.4. Making tubali.

Pl.1.5. Tubali *drying in the sun.*

shell around each *tubali*, and in the body of the wall created a three-dimensional structural network, rather like the complex of wax cells in a honeycomb. The *tubali* within each cell became resistant to compression, and formed a reliable structural composite. The concept was fundamentally different from that in Kano, where reliability resulted from the homogeneous nature of the *tubali* and plaster, which were both made from *birji* of the same quality.

Birji is processed in three different ways as a binding material and as plaster.

Mortar is prepared from the same *birji* as the *tubali*, only the process of consecutive breaking, wetting, trampling and drying is repeated more than twice. When *birji* is of very high quality, some builders consider it unnecessary to add horse-manure to it. It is nevertheless a common practice for the trampled *birji* to be covered with a layer of horse-manure and left for about three days, with more water poured on daily. The heap is then wetted and trampled again, the mixture covered with another layer of manure and the process repeated about four times over a period of two to three weeks. Instead of manure, *datsi* grass either fresh or dried is occasionally used. Both methods are adopted for the best quality work and this mortar is used both for binding the *tubali* and as a first coat of plaster, the base for *makuba* plaster.

Another kind of mortar is prepared from very dark, blackish earth mixed with *datsi*. This is used mainly for cementing the bracketed ribs supporting the domes of Hausa buildings.

Plaster

The most generally used plaster for covering walls is *makuba*, which derives its name from the fluid, *makuba*, with which the red building earth is mixed. *Makuba* is made from the fruit pods of the locust bean tree (*Parkia filicoidea*) (Hausa name: *dorowa*). The *dorowa* pods, which are about 2 centimetres in diameter and about 30 centimetres long, are processed in various ways. In Kano only the pods are used: they are grated into ragged strands which are soaked in water. After a few days the mixture produces a gelatinous, viscous liquid, which is poured onto the red building earth and carefully mixed with it. The preparation has a much looser consistency than mortar. When freshly made and spread on the walls, it is a bright sienna or sanguine colour. It begins to darken after a few hours, and becomes Vandyke with a tint of indian red, when

completely dry and hard. In Bida the beans and the pods together are soaked in water, then removed from the thickened liquid, dried and fired. The ash is mixed with the liquid, and this mixture is added to the red building earth to form the plaster. In areas where the *dafara*[10] or wild vine plant (*Vitis pallida*) grows its extract improves the waterproofing qualities of the *makuba*, and protects it from attack by termites. *Makuba* has great plastic properties, and lends itself particularly to the making of moulded decorations on the inner and outer surfaces of walls.

Another type of plaster is called *laso*. It is a waterproof cement made from three ingredients: *katsi*, *gashin jima* and *dafara*.

Katsi is a by-product of indigo dyeing, a deposit which forms at the bottom of the dyepits, still a part of Hausa townscapes, in which the locally woven cotton is given its deep indigo-blue colour. The liquid indigo is a dilution of *shuni*, an extract from the *baba* plant, which is sold in the form of cones or lumps. As the dye loses its effectiveness, a dense deposit, *babbarkiya*, is formed at the bottom of the dyepit. The *babbarkiya* is formed into small flat cakes (in Zaria) or into lumps (in Kano). These are dried and fired, after which they are pounded into a very fine light grey powder called *katsi*, which is the main constituent of *laso*.

---

[10] In Katsina the plant called *loda* (*Rogeria adenophylla*) is sometimes used.

Pl.1.6. KANO. Indigo dye pits.

Pl.1.7. Firing the babbarkiya *which is then pounded to powder.*

Pl.1.8. Forming indigo deposits (babbarkiya) *into flat cakes.*

Pl.1.9. Katsi *powder.*

Pl.1.10. Laso *waterproof plaster on the roof of a house.*

Gashin jima consists of goat hair mixed with the grease scraped from the inside of previously soaked skins.

Dafara is obtained from the root of the wild vine, named *dafara.* The roots are pounded with stones into a soft pulp onto which water is poured, and the viscous solution thus obtained is mixed with *gashin jima* and *katsi.* The mixing is repeated twice a day for ten days.

The hair in the *gashin jima* mechanically improves the stoutness of *laso,* the grease gives it waterproofing qualities and the *dafara* gum serves as a binder, making *laso* a hard, weather-resistant cement. It possesses an important quality: the same rate of expansion as the loam from which the wall is built. In consequence the layer of plaster adheres strongly to the surface of the wall and lasts for four or five years. *Laso* was most often used in those parts of the building which required the greatest degree of waterproofing – on the surface of flat or domed roofs, on the parapets of walls, and on *zanko.*

Chafe Plaster

Chafe is made from black earth to which a glutinous fluid is added – the latter is obtained in Bida from *makuba* beans which have been pounded and soaked in water, and further in the north from the acacia tree *gabaruwa.* The surface of the walls is covered with this black substance, and then sieved gravel is gently pressed into the partly dried plaster with a flat tool. Before it hardens finally the surface is incised with geometric patterns; lastly it receives two coats of *gabaruwa* and two of *makuba.*

Chafe lasts for many years without maintenance; it is mainly used in Emirs' palaces where decorative plasters are used in the interiors. One of them consists of small pieces of quartz set in gum arabic and is called *dada kyau.* It reflects the light in prismatic colours. Another plaster includes mica particles and gives silvery reflections. When yellow pigment is added, the reflections have a rich golden hue.

Timber

The best timber used in the north is obtained from the trunk of the male palm tree, locally called *deleb* or *giginya* (*Borassus flabellifer*). The outermost layer of the trunk is extremely hard, in contrast to the softer centre. It is sliced into narrow rods lengthwise and radially towards the centre of the trunk, which gives each piece its trapezoid cross section, about 10 x 6 centimetres, occasionally more. The builder decides the length of the pieces according to his needs. (Pl. 1.11.)

These timbers are commonly called *azara* (*izara* in Katsina, or *kyemmi* in Sokoto). They are heavy and so rigid that they remain unpalatable to termites, and resistent to decay for many years. Their uses are wide-ranging. They serve as a wooden reinforcement, strengthening the structure of walls and pillars of loam; they make sophisticated frame constructions, beams, brackets and corbels; they create a framework within archlike structures; and they serve as elements carrying flat and domed roofs.

Kirya and *goriba* (Dum palm) wood is used in Katsina to make planks. In Bornu, *goriba* wood is used constructionally. Hard planks are also made of *kawo* (*Afzelia africana*), of *kainya* or *kaiwa* – 'ebony' tree (*Diospyros mespiliformis*).[11]

The most popular roofing material is *gongola*, the mid-ribs of the *tukuruwa* palm (*Raphia vinifera*), reaching 10 metres or more in length. They are orange in colour, turning brownish-grey with age, and have a pleasant, eggshell sheen.

For rafters *kurna* wood, fairly hard and supposedly immune from white ants, is used.

The fronds of palm trees provided various materials for building purposes. The fronds of the *giginya* palm (called in Hausa *gazari* or *karinkgifinya*), were especially favoured. They were used for thatch, and the leaf-veins of the young fronds provided good fibre for binding. Ropes of great strength were produced from twisted bark from the roots of *dakwora* (*Acacia senegal*). Strong ropes, *kista*, were also produced from the inner layers of the bark of the *kuka* (baobab) tree. For binding the rafters of grass-roofed houses, the extremely tough stems of the *fara geza* (*Combretum micranthum*) were used.

The ashes of timber were often used as an insulating layer spread on top of flat roofs, and infusions from pods or roots served as waterproofing materials.

[11] H V Lely, *The Useful Trees of Northern Nigeria*, London 1925.

Pl.1.11. Cutting azara

Reeds and Grasses

Cornstalks and reeds are commonly used building materials. In recent years they appear mostly in minor buildings, especially outside cities, but before the 19th century large town residences were also erected in this way. Barth mentions them frequently. In the 'town of Yelkaza, province of Mashena', the residence of the Governor Mohammed 'was situated in the middle of the town, and consisted altogether of reed work . . . he came out of the interior of his reed house into the audience hall, which likewise consisted entirely of reed work, but was spacious and airy'. Similarly in the settlement of Bundi near Alamay he saw the residence of Ghaladima Omar, where 'the house of the Governor, consists entirely of reed work . . . The mats (*lagara*) which surround the whole establishment are of very great height, at least fifteen feet, and of considerable thickness, made of a peculiar reed called *sugu*, and being sustained by long poles, and kept in a good state of repair'.

Cornstalks were even more popular than reeds as a material for making walls, and the majority of buildings in old Hausa towns were built in this manner; only the residences of the nobility were made in wood and building earth.

The roofs of buildings made of cornstalks or reeds were supported on forked poles (*gofa*), frequently made from *marike* saplings, or the stems of *kasfiya* or *cham* trees.

The pagan tribe Ngizim of Fika, conquered by the Bolewa, originally built exclusively using cornstalks and grass (such buildings were called *casta* by the Ngizim). Only the chief's residence in Fika was a solid building with massive walls. It was a unique structure of broken pots bound with building-earth mortar.

Pls.1.12. & 1.13. Making zana *matting.*

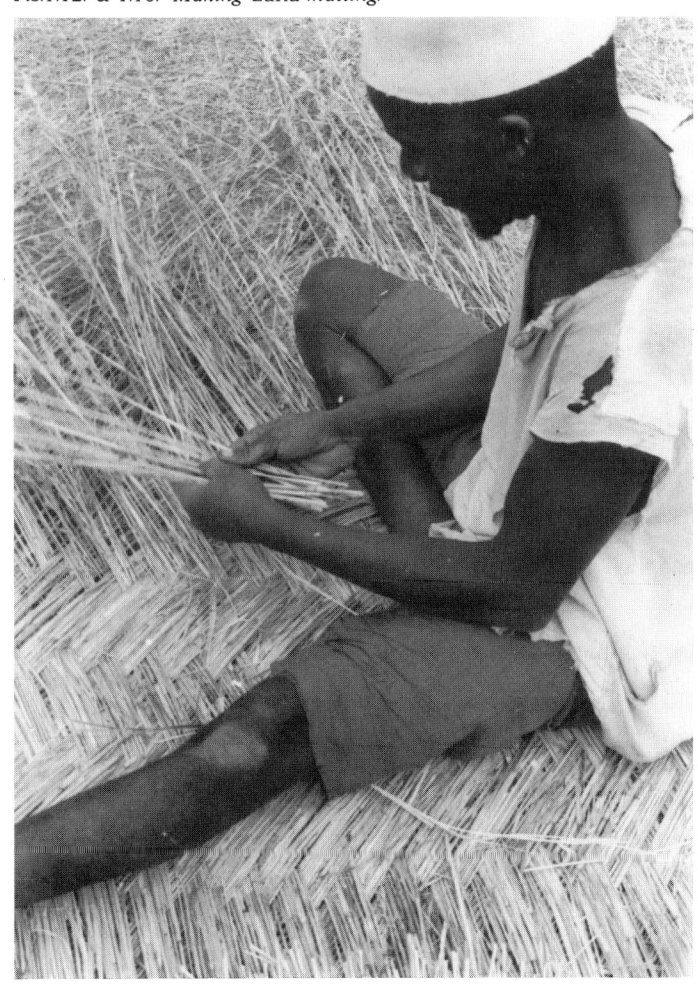

Pls.1.14 to 1.16. JOS-BAUCHI ROAD. Grass fencing reinforced with cornstalks.

Pls.1.17. to 1.19. KATSINA. Grass sheds near Kofar Waziri.

Pls.1.20 to 1.24. Stages in the construction of a roof for a circular building (type 1).

Pls.1.25 to 1.27. Roof construction for a circular building (type 2).

Burnt bricks

Burnt bricks were in use in the Bornu caliphate from the end of the fifteenth century up to the middle of the eighteenth century.[12] Burnt-brick building first started with the erection of the Garu Kime palace, and then the foundation by the Kanuri of their Bornu capital, the city of Birni Gazargamu. 'The first who built it was our lord the Amir ul-Muminin and Sultan of the muslim Ali B Dunama'[13] (1476-1503). 'The walls of the town are . . . partly formed of clay and partly of brick.' The king's palace was surrounded by high walls and formed a kind of citadel. In 1823 in many places the walls were still standing in large masses of hard red brickwork from 3 to 4 feet in thickness and 16 to 18 feet in height. 'The abode of the sultan covers a great extent of ground, and is entirely built of brick, this is much superior to the brick of our country, its fine texture and external surface have a fine gloss.'[14] This description was confirmed by Barth: 'the principal buildings consist of baked bricks'. He also recorded that the principal mosque, formerly built of thatch and then of clay, was finally re-erected in brick.[15]

Another site of brick buildings was the walled palace of Gambaru, built for the Sultan Idris Alooma by his mother in the sixteenth century.[16] It became 'the chosen residence of the late and former Sultans of Bornu : the ruins now standing give proof of the buildings have been of a princely kind : the walls of a mosque more than 20 yards square are still visible . . a private mosque appears also to have been attached to the sultan's residence; the buildings were all of brick.'[17]

The brickwork was praised by Barth: 'I did not expect to find the workmanship so good. The bricks are certainly not so regularly shaped as in Europe but in other respects they seemed quite as good.' He also mentioned a 'tolerably well preserved building evidently part of a mosque at the south eastern corner of the wall'.[18]

In 1920 a more detailed description ran: 'The vast palace which is all that remains to be seen, was an oblong building of about 250 yards by 150 yards. The walls are of burnt brick. The bricks are red and hard but not very regular in shape. The thickest parts of the walls are four bricks length, and the laying of the bricks rather shows that all the workers were not equally skilled. For mortar clay was used. The walls still stand in places to the height of about 8 feet.' He concluded that the brickwork formed yards for keeping horses, or gardens. 'A great palace in the form of a house did not exist . . . and no doubt many of the occupants of the palace lived in round huts with mud walls and grass roofs.'[19]

In the years that followed the ruins of both Birni Gazargamu and Gambaru were plundered, and the bricks are said to have been used in the palace of Machena.

Yet another brick palace was erected, presumably by Galadima, the semi-autonomous overlord of western Bornu, around 1630, at Birni Nguru. Some seventy years later a brick palace was built in the nearby village of Waro.

Gashargomo and the chief towns of the adjoining provinces were famous for their baked bricks.[20]

The last of the known Bornu palaces of this group is said by J E Lavers to be at Lergum, 'just to the west of Geidam of mai Muhammad B al-Hajj Harmdun (ca 1731-47)'. If this palace was indeed built by Muhammad it would suggest that the use of burnt brick was continued until much later than has been generally assumed'.[21]

Stone

Stone was not often used for building in Nigeria. In the north, the best known structure in stone is the massive wall of Surame, capital of Kebbi, west of Sokoto. It was built about 1516 on the orders of Kanta, the sarkin Kebbi, surrounding his capital city. According to tradition all the Hausa states conquered by Kanta had to participate in this enormous task. The surviving walls, which I visited in 1962, were over 8 metres high, were built from roughly dressed stone, laid in regular courses, and almost vertical. The clefts were filled, according to C K Meek, with laterite gravel and red plaster. (see Plate 1.28.)

Meek also recorded 'rather remarkable stone bridges . . . in the Ba-Ron district of Bauchi province'. They were 'built in granite slabs carefully fitted to each other, the interstices being filled with earth. Built-up from the river bed – leave two, three or more openings for passages of water. Arches [sic] formed by placing a long flat stone over two upright stones. The bridges are built concave to the flow of the stream, and are carried into the bank for 20 or 30 feet on either side. The one at Batura is 50 yards long, 5 feet wide and 10 feet deep. They are of great strength and must have stood for many generations. The Ron natives of the district say they were found when they came to the country four generations ago'.[22]

Hausa builders occasionally used rough stone for the foundations of their loam structures. In Kano stone was quarried at the bottom of Dalla Hill.

Various tribes, especially those living in the hills, also found it natural to use stone in their walls. In the houses these were formed from pieces of weathered or broken rock, with the clefts wedged with small pieces of stone and filled with earth plaster. The fences between the outermost houses of the compounds were formed by dry stone walls. (Plate 1.29.)

[12] J E Lavers, *A Note of Birni Gazargamu and 'Burnt Bricks' sites in the Bornu Caliphate*. This paper, presented to the 4th Conference of the West African Archaeologists, provided the material for the compilation of the following paragraphs.

[13] *The Brief Divan*, published by H R Palmer in Bornu, Sahara Sudan, London 1936.

[14] D Denham, J Clapperton and W Oudney, *Narrative of Travels and Discoveries in Northern and Central Africa in the years 1822 and 1824*, London.

[15] H Barth, *Travels and Discoveries in North and Central Africa . . . in the years 1849-1855*, London, reprint 1965.

[16] W J R Hallam, 'An Introduction to the History of Bornu', *Nigerian Field*, XXV, no. 4, October 1970. The article is illustrated with an excellent photograph of the 'ruins of the palace . . . on the Yobe river'.

[17] Denham, *op cit.*

[18] Barth, *op cit.*

[19] F W H Migeod, *Through Nigeria to Lake Chad*, London 1924, pp. 226-7.

[20] J M Freemantle, *A History of the Region comprising the Katagum Division of Kano Province*, Journal of the African Society, 1911.

[21] J E Lavers, *op cit.*

[22] The Antiquities Commission mentions two more causeways near Bokkos: *forof* and *tading*.

The walls of living huts were also erected with courses of broken stones set between thick layers of earthen plaster. All hill peoples used dry stone retaining walls to raise their terraces for cultivation.

A comprehensive account of stone building in the Sukur kingdom in Adamawa Province is given by A H Kirk Greene. Stone architecture includes the royal compounds, 'surrounded by a six to eight feet high wall built up of unmortared stones... two enormous monoliths... one... about twelve feet high, the other eight, with a circumference of perhaps fifteen feet, as well as a causeway... almost two miles in length... which even now ranks as a feat of engineering'.[23]

A very particular stone structure, a cairn of rough stones, was erected by the victorious army of the Emir of Bauchi, Yakubu I, as a memorial of the submission of the pagan tribes of Panshanu Hill. Still standing at the foot of Panshanu Pass, it is known as the *kwandan kaya*.

[23] A H M Kirk-Greene, in *Nigerian Field*, Vol. XXV, no. 2, 1960.

Pl.1.28. SURAME. Surviving stone walls.

Pl.1.29. JOS PLATEAU. Dry stone walls between buildings.

Pl.1.30. Restoring a city gate.

Iron

Knowledge of iron-working in the western Sudan is very ancient – it goes back as far as the last centuries BC and must have been well developed at the very beginning of Hausa culture. Kano became one of the main Hausa centres of iron smelting, and tradition maintains that it was founded by iron workers of the Abagazana tribe; it is certain that for centuries iron workers played a vital part in establishing the economic power of the city. Until the beginning of the twentieth century it was customary for Kano blacksmiths to mine and smelt iron at Lafiaro, to the east of Kaita. 'The iron ore was found six or seven feet down and to get it "wells" were dug to the ore levels and then extended sideways as the ore was excavated. Huge furnaces of clay six feet high were built on the site and charged with alternate layers of ore and wood charcoal. The fire, once started at the bottom, was controlled by blocking or opening four vent pipes upon which the furnace stood.'[24]

The most impressive Hausa iron products were their famous city gates, made of long strips of hammered metal joined together on sturdy frames and set on pivots instead of hinges (Plate 1.30).

Otherwise iron was used for complementary items, mostly for nails, which anyway were only seldom required by traditional builders. Among these, nails with decoratively worked iron heads were usually applied to the rails of the outer doors of houses.[25]

[24] C Graham, 'Some Sketches of Katsina from the Past', *Nigerian Field*, Vol. XXXIII, No. 1/1968.
[25] A comprehensive study of the blacksmithing of the Birom tribe of the Jos Plateau is given by Hamo Sassoon in his 'Birom Blacksmithing', *Nigeria Magazine*, No. 74/1962, pp. 25-31.

Pls.1.31 to 1.33. Restoring a city gate.

Building Tools

The tools used by Hausa builders to handle their homely materials were few and of a simple kind. The factory-made steel headpan replaced the baskets and calabashes formerly used and is now an almost universal vessel for carrying *tubali*, mortar and plaster.

In the 1960s, locally made adzes and axes were still more popular with traditional builders than imported pick-axes and axes. They consist of a wooden handle and an iron blade. The favourite wood for making handles was *makarfo* (also called *kariye gatari*: 'break the axe') a common bush tree of excessive hardness. The timber for the handle was a carefully selected part of a trunk cut out on both sides of an outgrowing branch. The branch, trimmed to the desired length, served as a handle. The forked part of the trunk was worked into an egg-like form serving as the head of the handle, into which the blade was set. The flat wedge-shaped blade was elongated by a narrow projection with a sharp point. This projection was driven into the head of the handle, and its form ensured it was firmly wedged inside the head when the tool was used. The weight of the head added momentum to the stroke of the tool.

The main difference between the adze and the axe was the position, horizontal and vertical respectively, of the cutting edge. Usually the blade of the axe was narrower but thicker than that of the adze.

A lighter type of adze was made from an elongated piece of metal, one end of which formed the blade. The other, rolled into a cylinder, served as a mount for the handle (a widely forked branch served to make the handle). One limb cut off close to the fork, had the blade set into it, the other, longer limb, inclined at an angle, was used as the hold.

Scaffolding was not often used. The whole process of working at the top of the building was done from ladders, rather flimsy affairs made of bamboo and midribs of palm leaves, bound together by ropes or by strips of roughly processed leather. Such ladders were used when completing ceilings, both flat and domed, and especially when plastering the walls of the rooms inside and outside, including their moulded decorations. When plastering particularly high outer façades, for instance of fortified city walls, the ladders were usually strengthened by an additional, axial stile, set fast to the middle of each scale.

Building Construction

Tubali Walls

The fact that despite the simplicity of building materials and tools traditional Hausa architecture reached its final mature excellence was due to the decisive human factor: the quality of Hausa building men.

The behaviour of a traditional Hausa builder was purposeful, economical of effort and competent – obviously the result of long training in accordance with firmly established standards of professional efficiency. I noticed this in Kano when observng a single man at work, and even more in the co-operation of a team of three men or more. They proceeded quietly, with a clear mutual understanding and therefore in almost complete silence.

The walls of most Hausa dwellings were built on foundations. The depth and thickness of the foundations varied considerably, the deciding factor being the dimensions of the walls to be built upon them. Since the site for a building was carefully selected, the quality of the ground had to be taken into consideration only occasionally, and then the trench for the foundations was dug so as to get below the loose topsoil.

The cross section of the foundations was usually an extension of the footing of the wall. In Katsina ,however, I was told that the foundations of large buildings consist of two parts: at the base was a footing six *tubali* thicker than the wall itself and two layers of *tubali* high. The footing projected by two *tubali* on each side beyond the upper part of the foundation. The thickness of the wall itself was further reduced by one *tubali* on each side. This would mean, for example, that a wall 1.5 metres thick would have a footing ten *tubali* thick and the upper part of the foundation would be six *tubali* thick. The foundations of certain buildings were laid by specialists and reached considerable dimensions. For instance, Kofar Sauri at Katsina had foundations twenty-two *tubali* thick.

The depth of the foundations varied from 45 centimetres to 'the height of a man's chest'. (There was a special term, *gaba*, used to indicate the depth – not the width, which was based on the dimensions of a man with his arms spread.)

Foundations were sometimes laid using broken stones instead of *tubali*. In Kano there existed a special group of workers who broke up stones at the foot of Dalla Hill. The price of a stone was twenty or more times that of a *tubali*.

The physical fitness of the craftsmen and labourers who erected the walls was striking. It permitted them to work in strained positions for the sake of greater efficiency, and this was obviously the result of long training.

The labourer laying *tubali* on the wall (*bango*) squatted with his feet flat on the ground giving both support and balance to his body. His calf was compressed against his thigh, so that his buttocks were within an inch or two of the ground. Thus his centre of gravity was lowered and it was easier for him to catch and handle the heavy *tubali* without losing his balance and with the greatest economy of movement. He caught the *tubali*, which was thrown up by his assistant above the place being worked on, his arm carried it over to the right place and he set it into the wet mortar with a wobbling movement. This procedure was possible only as long as the wall erected remained low. Once it grew so high that the *tubali* had to be thrown up in the air in order to reach the hand of the bricklayer, the rhythm and movement changed completely. The bricklayer sometimes retained his squatting position but more often he sat on top of the wall as if on a horse. When the wall reached a height of 3.5 metres or more, the throw required considerable strength. The bricklayer caught the *tubali* in mid air, rather like a tennis player his spare ball, and at once it was in the right position, that is, with the top of the cone inside his palm. The momentum of the *tubali* carried the bricklayer's hand higher up, until his arm was stretched full length. This gave him a proper grip, and permitted him to reverse direction without much effort, throwing the *tubali* down hard from above his head, with its flat base landing right in its proper place, one among the many in long rows running parallel to the face of the wall. When the whole layer was completed in this way, outstanding *tubali* were adjusted: and it was proof of the craftsmen's skill that very few alterations were needed. Occasionally the relative position of *tubali* was changed in order to compensate for the irregularities of their form.

The greatest care was given, naturally, to the outermost and innermost rows of *tubali*, since these determined the shape of the wall face. When approaching the corner of the building, the *tubali* layer made a break in the row about one metre from the corner. Very carefully, with both hands, he fitted the corner *tubali* in place and then completed the row. If the remaining space could not be filled evenly with *tubali*, one of them was usually placed bottom up, its pointed top wedged downwards between the others. (Plate 1.34).

The layer of *tubali* thus completed presented a fairly regular, three-dimensional pattern of conical shapes fitted close to each other at the bottom, and gap-toothed at the top, with empty spaces that were almost a negative in voids of the positives of the *tubali* in solids. These voids had now to be filled with earthen plaster and, clearly, the resulting interlock of the two basic elements comprising the wall – the *tubali*-brick and the mortar – was extremely thorough.

Pls.1.34 and 1.35. Laying tubali *to form a wall.*

Mortar too was placed by the builder mainly by throwing. The lump of mortar served to him from the ground was usually disposed of in two powerful throws, the second correcting the first. The internal *tubali* of the wall were plastered first, leaving the outer rows bare. Then the builder worked somewhere else for a while and came back when the central part had dried a little; only then did he plaster the wall surface. This was done with the greatest care, and began with the usual throw from above, but was followed immediately by a forceful horizontal pressing of mortar from the outside of the wall towards its centre. When the empty spaces between the *tubali* were properly filled, the next handful of mortar covered their outer faces completely and was smoothed vertically downwards for about 25 centimetres; thus a thin layer of mortar was spread onto the surface of the previous layer of *tubali*, sealing the two neatly together. (Plates 1.36 & 1.37).

The greatest asset of this construction lay in the positive-negative system, which made a well balanced *tubali*-mortar compound of each layer. Thus the interlocking of the two elements was developed to the full.

Considering the homogeneity of the *birji* (the material from which both *tubali* and mortar were made) it may be said once again that within the narrow limits of traditional technology a perfect solution was reached in the erection of walls.

Conical *tubali* were the only kind used in Kano. In Katsina another type, of a different shape and consistency, was used as well. The poorest surface layers of soil were mixed with water and moulded into lumps about 15 centimetres in diameter. They had only a slight consistency, but their role was limited to that of a filler. The structural function was served by the plaster, which was very carefully processed from *kasa* of the highest quality: it formed a strong shell around

Pls.1.36 and 1.37. Plastering over tubali.

each *tubali* and created a three-dimensional structural frame within the body of the wall.

Its function was not unlike that of the wax parts of a honeycomb. The *tubali* within each shell became resistant to compression, thus creating a reliable structural complex. It differed fundamentally from the Kano principle, where reliability resulted from the homogeneous nature of *tubali* and plaster, which were both made from *birji* of the same quality.

In Sokoto too, where the building earth, called *buri* or *turda*, is of poor quality, local *tubali (unku)* were used although they had no structural value. As in Katsina, the strength of the walls was ensured by the network of high quality mortar, made from a light grey clay called *laka*. It was dug out of pits in marshy ground east of the city.

When the cost of the building was not the main consideration, and when the walls were to be high, particularly in two-storeyed buildings, horizontal bracings made from *azara* grids were set within the walls. Each bracing consisted of two layers of timber: a bottom one of short timbers set transversely across the wall and an upper one of longer rods, laid longitudinally. These grids were usually fixed at about one metre and again at two metres above the ground.

The walls decreased in thickness towards the top through the reduction, one by one, of the number of *tubali* used in their cross section. The first reduction was usually made at the height of a man's breast, the second at his full height, and so on. In consequence the walls were strongly tapered, which added to their stability. Their thickness varied greatly. The walls of Hausa palaces were often about six *tubali* thick (ie. about 90 centimetres) at ground level, but in some cases they were twice as thick – as, for example, the outer walls of entrance gates, the *zaure*. This was done to create an impression of strength and opulence rather than from constructional necessity. It is worth noting, however, that in some buildings excessive thickness of the outer walls resulted from yearly rendering of their surfaces with new layers of plaster. This process, repeated for decades, added several strata to the original cast and created imposing masses of solid masonry.

When the height of a wall was so great that the tapering reduced its thickness too much, the uppermost part of the wall was often protruded towards the interior on brackets set into its thickness. These brackets supported beams, *tauyi*, which overhung the lower part of the wall. The effect thus created was like a cornice around the walls of the room, and allowed their cross section to be increased to the appropriate thickness.

On rare occasions the walls were strengthened on the outside with a slightly projecting buttress rather like a pilaster (*dogari*). The part these played in the construction is indicated by their other name, *mataimakin al'amudi* (*mataimaki* = helper), because they were almost always erected when the original walls began to crack.

Above roof level the wall was crowned with a continuous parapet (*rawani*) which surrounded the building. The dimensions of parapets differed, and their construction was adapted to their size. For example when two *tubali* high, the parapet was two *tubali* thick at the bottom and one *tubali* thick at the top. A larger parapet would have two layers two *tubali* thick with a third layer of *tubali* laid horizontally, lengthwise – the roundness of the cross section of the top *tubali* completed the tapering of the whole. A large parapet would have two layers of double *tubali* laid vertically at the bottom, then two layers of double *tubali* laid horizontally, lengthwise, and a top layer of single vertical *tubali* which formed the crest – all lavishly plastered over with *laso*.

At the corners of the building the parapet was emphasised with thick-set finials, *zanko*, not unlike the acroterion of classical pediments. *Zanko*s were also rythmically spaced along extended parapets, as well as on the edges of the canopies (*gemu*) which overhung the outer doors of buildings.

Pl.1.38. Erecting a zanko.

Pl.1.39. Erecting a zanko.

The form of the *zanko* has evolved greatly during the last fifty years. Photographs taken at the beginning of the century showed that the *zanko*s were flat and had a shape that would have fitted within an obtuse triangle. Somewhat higher and more slender *zanko*s became popular in the years that followed; they would have fitted within an equilateral or even an acute triangle. These lasted until the 1960s, when the increasing use of cement radically changed their shape. They became still slimmer and were shaped like a pointed leaf, or even a spearhead.

Doorways

Doorways in Hausa houses were of two kinds. Outer doorways were closed by wooden (or, in major palaces, by single iron) doors. These hung on pivots, rarely and only recently on hinges. Inner doorways, which allowed passage between adjoining rooms, were doorless and occasionally screened with grass-plaited curtains.

Outer doorways were generally rectangular in shape, with a horizontal lintel; this was a wooden beam supported at each end by an abutment, usually the end of the wall which flanked the opening, or sometimes a pair of jambs, which were thicker than the wall. (Plate 1.47).

The length of the flat lintel-beams was restricted by their limited resistance to bending, which could lead to breaking. Lintel-beams could be made longer if the timbers were thicker, or used double. But a lintel more than two *azaras* thick was considered uneconomical. (Fig.1.1).

The breaking of a beam, if it occurs, happens in the middle, but breaking results from bending, which usually begins above the support. In order to avoid breaking, bending must be prevented, and to achieve this the beam must be strengthened above the abutment. When wooden rods were to be used for a beam, the simplest way was to put another short

Fig.1.1 Detail of lintel beam in doorway.

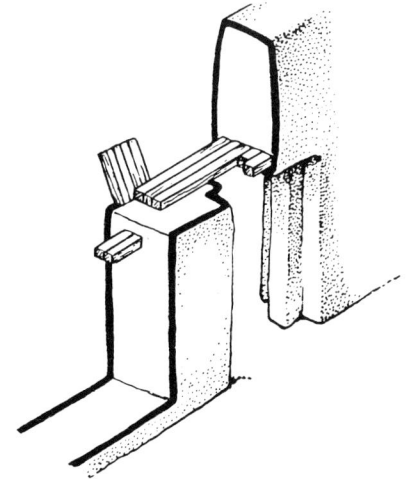

Pl.1.40. A hide covered door.

Pl.1.41. KANO. No.30 Garke Street. Door covered with strips of iron.

rod immediately under the abutment, and this both strengthened the beam where it tended to bend, and of course also shortened the span of a single rod. Thus the bracket in its most elementary form was born. Its natural development was by multiplication; that is, beneath one short bracket another was placed to give it support.

Such strengthening of the beam by brackets made it possible to increase the span and was to be seen in many settings. It was cantilevered when above a door or window. When supported by a pillar, brackets were symmetrically balanced on top of the pillar; but in every case, their strength was conditioned by their resistance to bending above the point of support.

Doors (kyaure) were made from a few vertical planks (gizago) held in position by rails (mafiyadi), set on each side into a stile (kafar). All these were fixed together with nails (kusa), which had wide, frequently decoratively shaped, heads. One of the kafar often served as the pivot for the door. Usually it was made of azara, the lower end revolving in a stone socket (dustin kofa), the top end held in place with an iron mariki.

Doors in Katsina were closed with a pair of short chains (sarka).

Occasionally the outer surface of a door was covered with horse's hide, or narrow strips of iron. (Pls. 1.40 & 1.41).

A typical doorless entrance consisted of two parts. The lower part was rectangular, and this was covered by a semi-circular arch (kandame) the diameter of which extended about 30 centimetres beyond each of the jambs. Thus on top of the jambs two small shelves were formed (ma'ajin fitilla); they were suitable places to put oil lamps (fitilla). The kandame rested on a hidden internal frame, which was almost the same width as the thickness of the wall. The frame was made from two symmetrical slabs of azara, set in grooves hacked out of the bottom of the proposed arch; their upper ends reached its apex. In the next stage, the walls on both sides were erected level with the apex, and then a horizontal beam, as wide as the thickness of the wall, was laid on the walls and the diagonal azaras. The trapezoidal form thus produced carried the upper part of the wall, and maintained the plaster forming the arch in position. (Pls. 1.42 – 1.45).

This device was additionally strengthened when it was set

in a wall of considerable thickness. The frame of the arch consisted of only a few rods, and was placed along the longitudinal axis of the wall (in the middle of the wall's thickness). Thus it was recessed from the two faces of the wall, ie. it was put between two shallow niches, which were covered with a horizontal beam of *azaras* extending through the whole thickness of the wall. The cross section of the composite thus formed resembled a T-beam, and once again securely upheld the weight of the wall above the door.

Infrequently, when the floor of the room was not raised above ground level, the lower part of the doorway was barred with a threshold (*dangarama*) which prevented the entry of rainwater.

There were usually copings above outer doors. These were called *gemu* and they rested on supports (*kahwan karo*).[26] The *gemu* protected the doorway from the rain. They projected some distance in front of the wall above the opening, tapered strongly in their upper part, and usually reached the crowning parapet. Above all however they were a decorative element in the façade, emphasising the entrance to the building. Almost invariably the *gemu* were flanked by a pair of *zanko* and very often covered with moulded decoration. (Pl. 1.47).

[26] The word is apparently appropriated from the tailor's vocabulary, where it means 'a narrow piece of double-thickness material on each side of the centre piece back and front in the upper part of the gown'. Revd G P Bargery, *A Hausa-English Dictionary*, London 1934, p. 527.

Fig.1.2.*Azara* construction in an arched doorway.

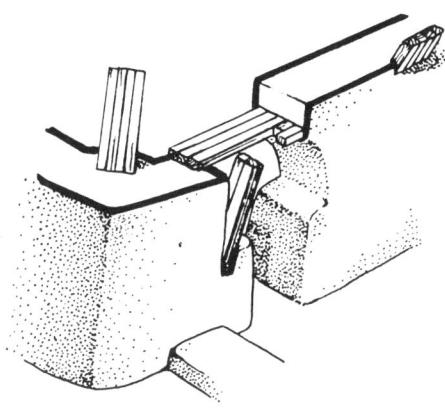

Pl.1.42. Arched doorway (kandame).

Fig.1.3. Detail showing a bracket and its counterweight.

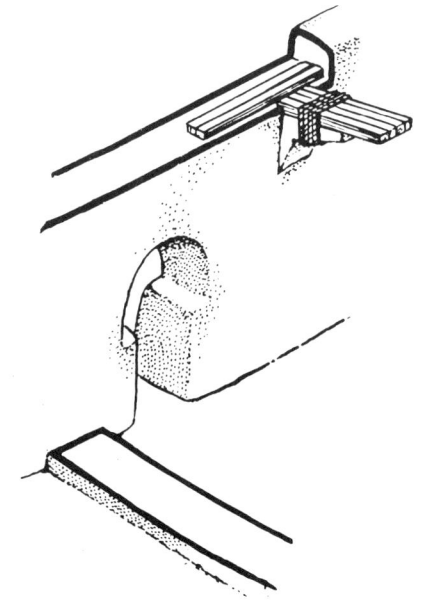

Pls.1.43 to 1.45. Stages in the construction of an arched doorway.

Pl.1.46. KANO. Windows of a house in the market square.

Pl.1.47. KANO. Gidan Makama. Door and window.

Windows

The windows in old Hausa buildings were simple openings almost always set in the uppermost part of walls on the lee side of the building, which were less affected by driving rain. In spite of their small size the windows were sufficient to let in some of the brilliant outside light, and at the same time they provided ventilation. Most often their shape was an elongated upright rectangle, although in more elaborate buildings they were often topped with an arch, *kandame*; or with a triangle, which gave the whole the form of an arrowhead. Inside wider rectangular windows were set grilles of vertical *azaras*, occasionally plastered to a baluster shape (Plate 1.47). Or the rectangle of the window was filled with a decorative lattice-work of thin boards, intertwined and profiled in such a way as to give the effect of an arabesque design (Plate 1.46).The triangular windows of Nupe palaces also deserve mention. They were filled with a network of triangular or hexagonal divisions made of wooden rods and then plastered. There was

an interesting effect from the brightly lit trelliswork, contrasting with dark voids, which probably inspired the almost arabesque patterns introduced later when the use of cement permitted elaboration of the idea. Also among the Nupe, small windows above the outer doors were filled by screens of imported tin, cheap but perforated into very pretty tracery. For further discussion of Nupe architecture see Volume II, Chapter 3.

Floors

Floors (*dabe, debe*) were usually laid by women. A surface of laterite about 3 centimetres thick was put on top of a layer of beaten earth. Laterite is the brittle red clay found on top of the ground, and contains iron or iron oxide.

In Katsina *dabe* were made from building earth. This was sprinkled with gravel, then watered and beaten with a tool called *madabi*, a thick, slightly curved branch, flattened a little on the outer side. When it was dry the floor was further hardened with *makuba*, which however was used in a different way than for plaster. Powdered *makuba* pods were spread onto the floor surface and water was poured over them.

Pillars

Pillars, as a rule used by Hausa in their interiors, have a structure similar to that of the walls. Pillars that are square in plan are called *al'amudi*, those with a plan of a cross, *ginshiki*. They supported flat roofs in rooms of large dimensions. In other instances they provide support for a pseudo arch, as in the more sophisticated interiors.

Al'amudi are battered towards the top and have capitals which are wider than the top of the pillar and trapezoidal in outline. Since the whole effect bears a certain similarity to the pestle used by women for pounding corn (*tabarya*), this type of pillar is called *al amudi mai tabarya*. The top of each capital is extended horizontally on two, or on all four, sides by short brackets made of *azaras*, set symmetrically and balanced. The latter device forms a cross. These brackets support the beams (*tauyi*), whose outer ends are laid on corbels set into the walls, or simply on the walls themselves.

In the royal palace of Katagum a very special kind of post impressed visitors: 'The pillars that supported a room over the western gate were superior to any I had seen in central Africa; they were formed of the trunks of the palm-tree, fashioned into columns, with rude pedestals and capitals of no inelegant appearance, all encrusted with clay.'[27]

[27] Denham, Clapperton, Oudney, *op cit*, Vol. II, p. 251.

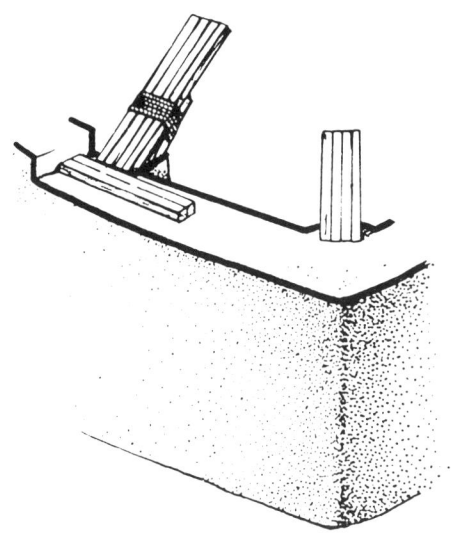

Figs.1.4 & 5. Corbel with *mashim fidi* counterweight.

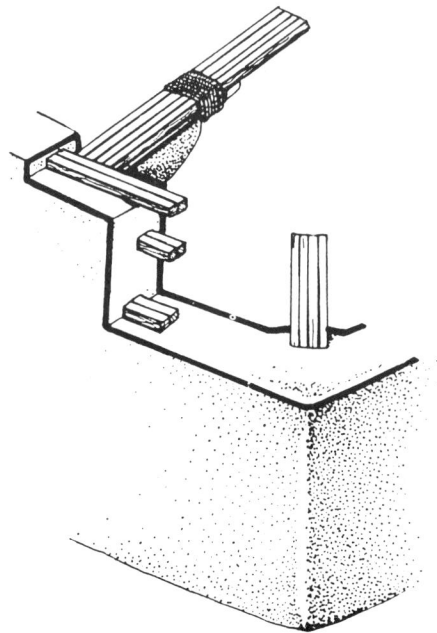

Brackets and Corbels

A simple bracket of rods laid horizontally was greatly strengthened if the end of the bracket was additionally supported by a diagonal member, set with its lower end at some distance below the abutment; and this can be considered as the beginning of the logical development of the bracket.

In order to differentiate it, let us call this new item a corbel. The corbels were made usually of four layers of *azara* rods, cantilevered and set obliquely in the wall. Each rod was called *kafar guga*, each layer *kafin kafa* (where *kafi* means the fixing and securing of rods from which an arch is made, and *kafa* means erect, establish, set-up, fix).[28] The first layer jutted out at a very sharp angle — it formed a support for the three subsequent layers, each leaning towards the wall at a steadily reduced angle and projecting further out.

Brackets and corbels were never built out of single *azaras*. Anything from three to six *azaras* laid in a row gave the bracket both the desired strength and a satisfactory appearance.

The setting of four consecutive tiers, *kafin kafa*, was synchronised with the building of the layers of the wall, into which the corbels were set.

The first tier, about 30 centimetres wide, made usually of 4 *azaras* laid on edge, jutted out at a very sharp angle. It was set almost vertically into the wall, in such a way that its upper end stood out about a third of a metre above the wall so far erected. At this level of the wall was mounted the lower part of the second tier. Half of its length (about 65 centimetres) overhung the top of the lower tier, and its angle was more inclined towards the horizontal. The two tiers were then bound fast with rope, and the wedge-shaped space between them was filled with *tubali* and special plaster. Above the base of the second tier, at right angles to it, short *azaras* (*mashim fidi*) were laid along the axis of the wall. The *mashim fidi* when plastered provided a counterweight for the overhanging part of the tier. Next, the wall was built up to a level about 30 centimetres below the top of the second tier. Subsequently, the same process was repeated, with further tiers mounted so that each projected still further out, and the angles at which they were inclined were steadily reduced. The last tier in consequence was almost horizontal. This top layer of cantilevered *azaras* projected towards the centre of the room, thus making the horizontal span of the beam (*hadin kafa*) no more than the desired length of 3 metres. The *azaras* used for this purpose (*biko*) were about 10 metres long and not only spanned the corbels but usually also covered the crowns of the two opposite walls. (Fig. 1.9; Pls. 1.48 – 1.49).

The beams, about 25 centimetres thick, were bound together with rope. The angularities of the corbels were then plastered over to form a quadrant or a quarter-ellipse in outline.

[28] Revd G P Bargery, *A Hausa-English Dictionary*, London 1934, pp. 528 and 524.

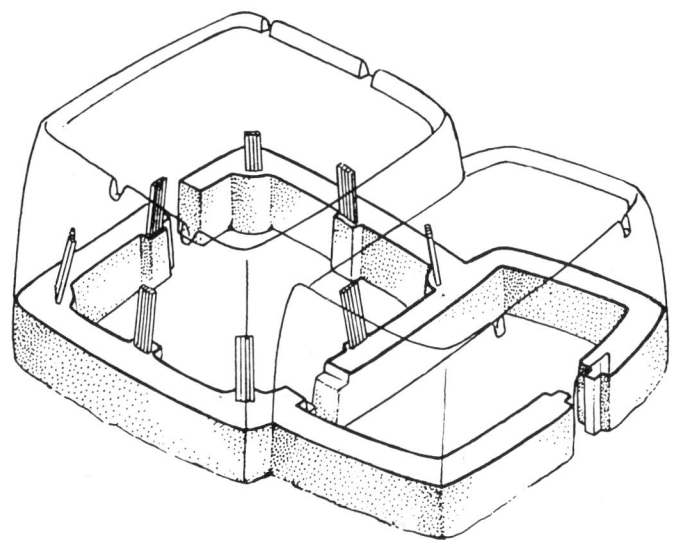

Figs.1.6-8. Kano. Gidan Makama. Roof construction
of eight corbels.

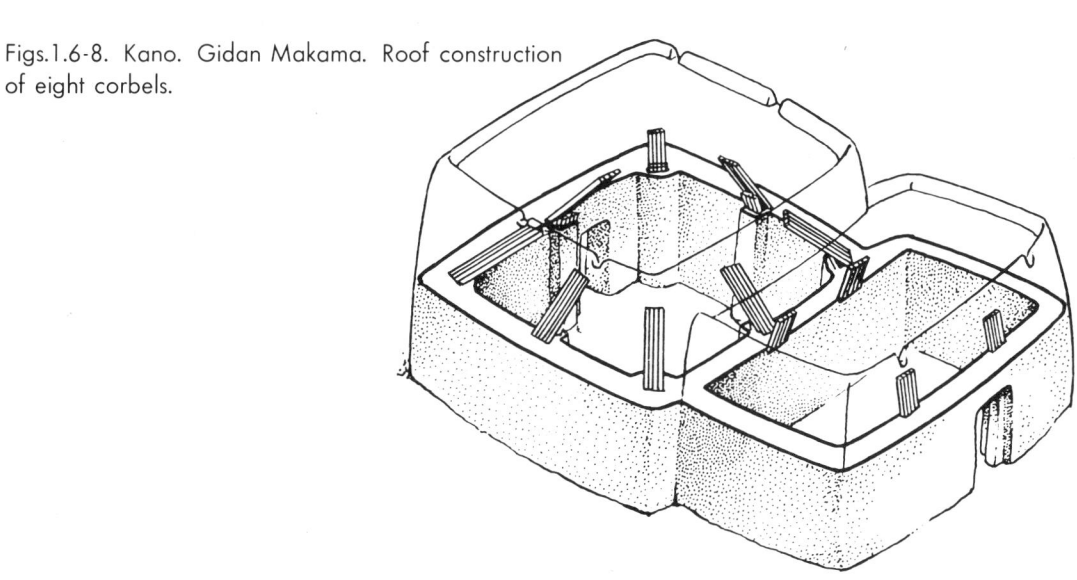

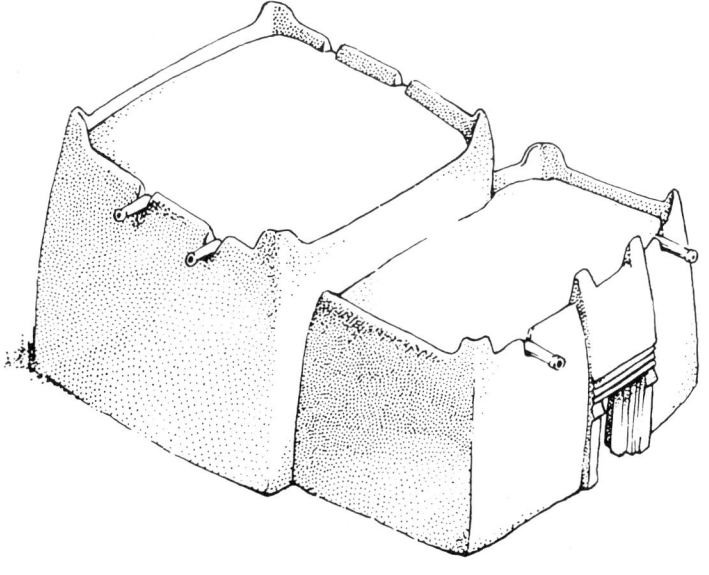

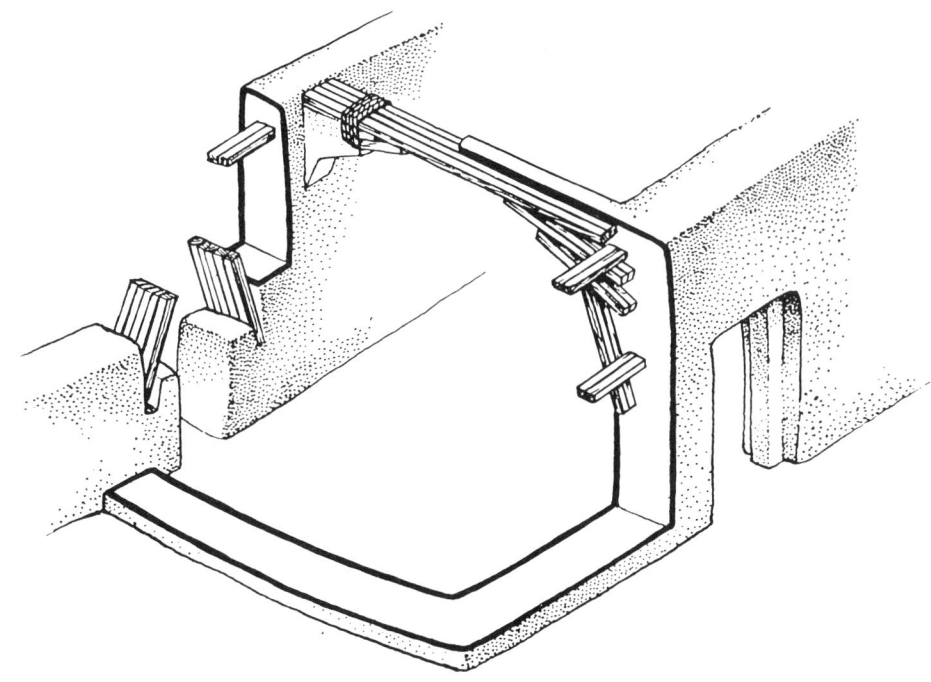

Figs.1.9-12. Kano. Gidan Makama. The construction of corbelled 'arches' which support flat roofs. (The roofs are covered with *zana* matting and waterproof plaster.)

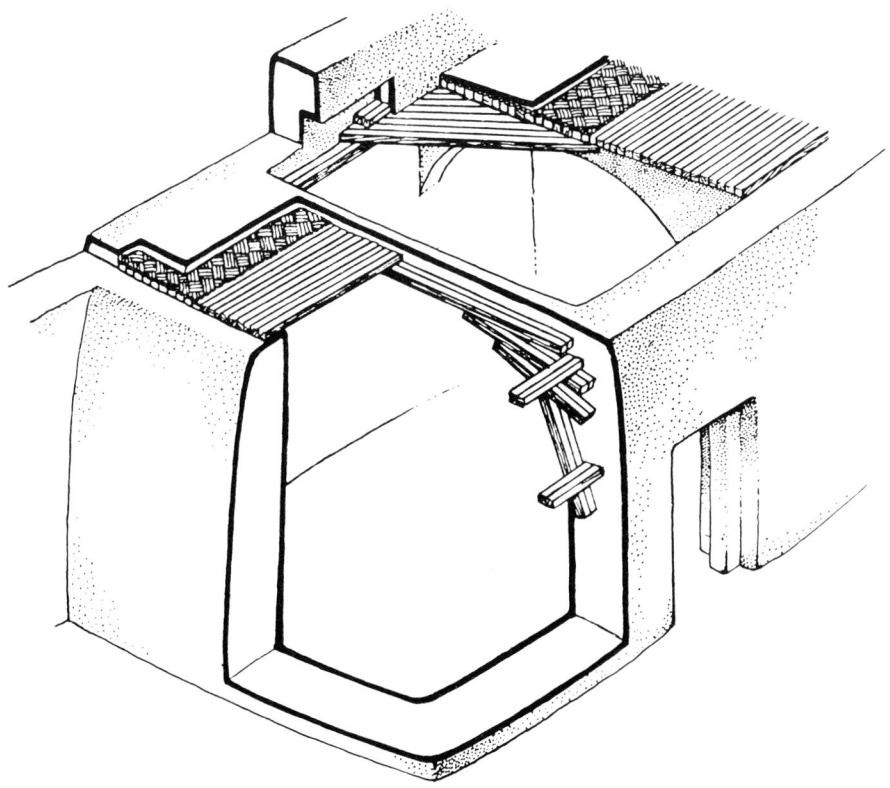

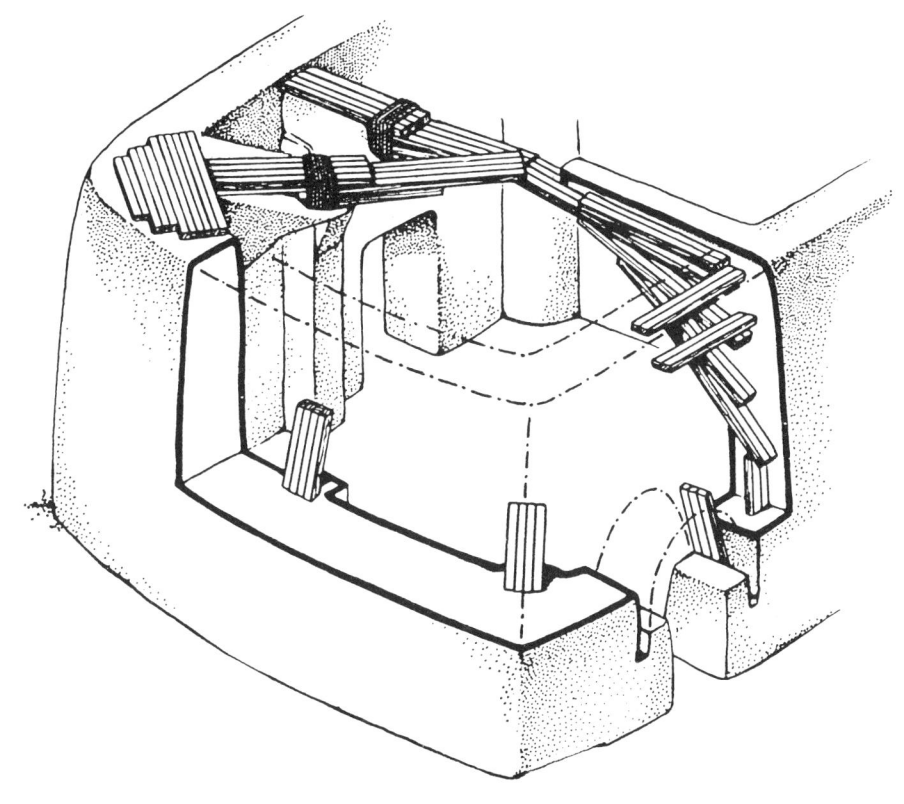

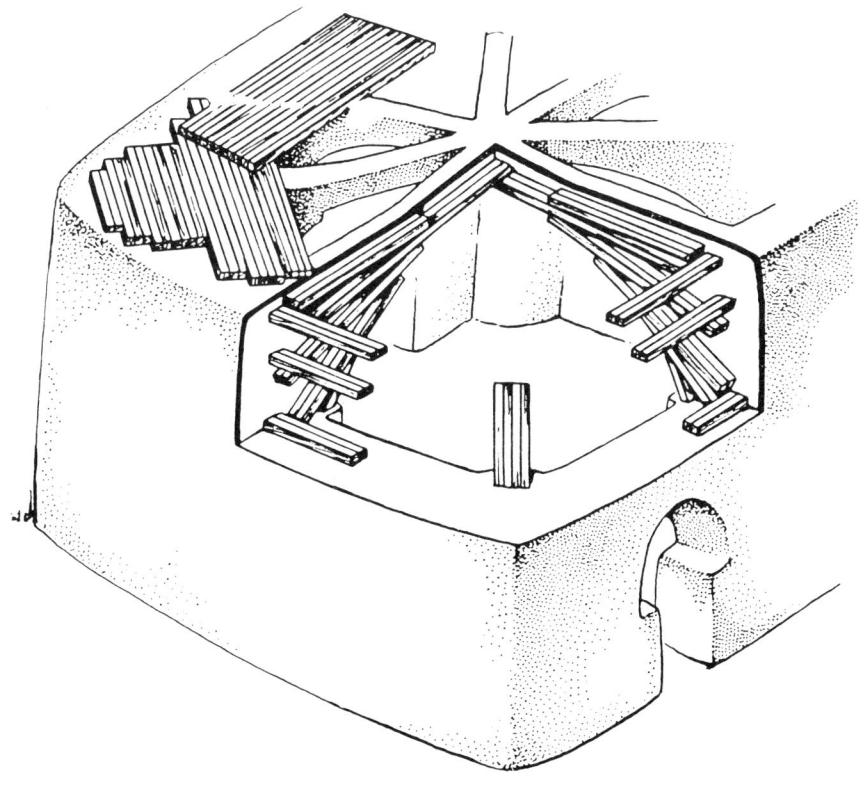

Pls.1.48 & 1.49. Stages in the construction of a cantilevered arch.

Corbelled beams of this type were placed at about 1.8 metre centres; they supported the closely laid joists which spanned them. There was a gap of up to 3 centimetres between each joist. The flat surface thus obtained was finally covered with layers of mats and plastered to form the waterproof roof (Fig. 1.10).

Bracketed construction was developed further by the increasing use of corbels, to a point where the horizontal element of the beams was greatly reduced, or even rendered unnecessary. The final stage in this process occurred when the brackets met in the centre of the roof; in other words, the series of corbels, stepped forward and upward along the tangents of the arches which rested on opposite walls, met in the apex (*daurin guga*) of the arch-shaped multi-angular frame. In such constructions there was no need to join fast the two component parts, because each corbel was structurally self-supporting. It is true that they were tied with rope at their apex, but only to immobilise them both, before they were finally combined by plastering. After plastering both corbels assumed the appearance of a uniform arch (*baka*), which

Pls.1.50 & 1.51. Stages in the construction of a cantilevered arch.

structurally was the reverse of a stone or brick arch, in which the voussoirs (truncated wedge-shaped blocks) are locked in position by a keystone, in the very place where the Hausa pseudo-arch has no structural purpose. (Figs. 1.11 & 1.12.)

More sophisticated buildings had an additional strengthening of *guntun azaras*, squeezed between the main tiers of *kafi*. When made by the best builders, using the best materials and taking the greatest care, the *baka* could reach a span of over eight metres. Furthermore, *baka* were used in closely set pairs, as for example in the *zaure* of the Katsina palace (Pl. 2.7) or

in the Zaria Masallaci Juma'a (Pl. 2.5.). In addition to strengthening the structure, such arches enriched the plastic composition.

In the simplest composition of a room, a corbelled *baka* might be used singly to support the ceiling of an elongated interior. A square interior could have a ceiling support by two such *baka*-arches set crosswise, or by four, set perpendicularly and diagonally inside the square room. A four *baka*-arch construction was by itself a very impressive device indeed. To join the eight component corbels together, all uniformly shaped, over the optical centre of the room, at the properly chosen height, and under the correct angles requires a complete mastery of craftsmanship. And this was by no means the boldest attempt to enrich the interior – there were rooms with not merely four, but ten *baka*-arches, springing from the four corners of the room, and then from four points on each of the four walls, and joined together in a central apex.

To emphasise how correctly the Kano builders qualified the structural basis of their formal compositions, the nomenclature concerned with them is worth noting.

The pseudo-arch, the complex of coupled quadrantal corbels was called *bakan gizo*, meaning the rainbow, a name that is suggestive of shape, not of construction. But – and this seems to me quite remarkable – rooms containing *bakan gizo*'s were never named according to the number of *baka* arches, but according to the number of corbels that made them. Thus a room containing, for example, six *bakan gizo*'s was called '*soro ne daurin guga kafa goma sha biyu*' meaning 'building roofed on twelve corbels, centred in *daurin guga*'.

The organic character of Hausa corbelled *baka* permitted a number of solutions, sometimes purely utilitarian, sometimes adorning architectural composition. When one of the walls was pierced by a door on the axis of one of the perpendicular *bakuna*[29] or if it was desired to keep the wall plain for any reason the *baka* parallel to it was set fairly near to the plain wall. The cross-wise *baka* was reduced to part of its full span, and this *talkalmin kasa* was set into the centre of the former, complete *baka*. (Fig. 1.13 & 1.16.)

In large, square rooms the roof came to be supported by a grid of *bakuna*, which sprang from all four walls of the interior. When two *bakuna* only were used four square panels were created as supports for the roof. A pair of *bakuna* springing from each of the opposite walls formed nine square panels. In rectangular interiors three (seldom more) *bakuna* were set in the longitudinal walls and the curve of the longer *bakuna* looked like a much extended semi-ellipsoid. For structural reasons the shorter *bakuna* always supported the longer ones.

In more extensive houses it was common for the inner walls between adjoining interiors to carry *bakuna* on both sides. In such cases, the *bakuna* were almost always not set opposite each other; this was apparently done so that the corbels of one *bako* should not interfere with those of the other. However, the *mashim fidi* used in such cases were sufficiently long to reach and counterweight the corbels of both *bakuna*.

Bakuna were often used in pillared interiors. The simplest method was an interpretation of a flat-roofed pillared room (as in Fig. 1.25.) or in Kafin Madaki mosque (Fig. 2.25.), with this difference: the flat beams were supplanted by *bakuna*. This arrangement gave way to varied designs, of which one of the best was applied in the *zaure* of Katsina Palace, where the possibilities of corbelled construction were exploited to produce an ingenious spatial composition.

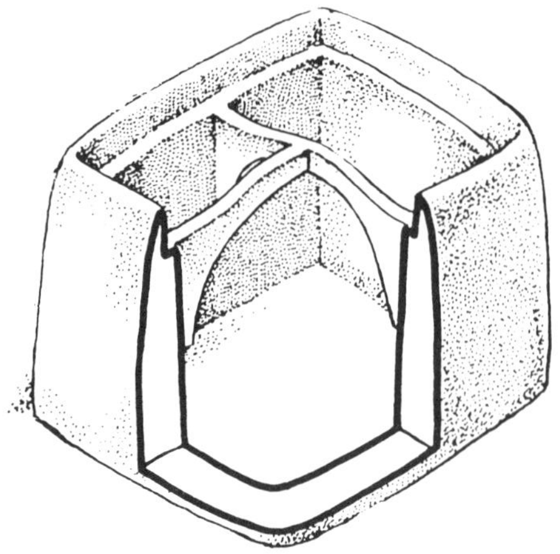

[29] *Bakuna*: plural of *baka* (in Katsina = *bakankuna*).

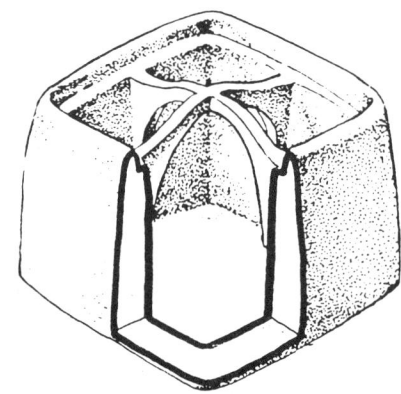

Fig.1.13. The construction called *takalmin kasa*.

Fig.1.14. Square interior roofed with two crossed baka (*bakan gizo*).

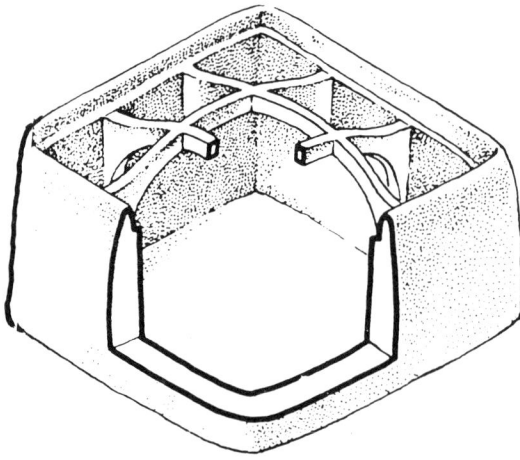

Fig.1.15. Square interior roofed with four crossed baka arches.

In some cases these essentially structural devices were elaborated by the multiplication of closely set *bakuna*, establishing a rhythm of accented reverberations which continued down to the floor, giving the walls a plastic texture composed of protrusions and recesses of equal width (see Pl. 5.10). A purely decorative purpose was fulfilled by setting within the structural panels additional ribs forming geometrical patterns.

Bakuna usually sprang from the place where the top of the first corbel protruded from the surface of the wall. Originally (up to the end of the nineteenth century) this protrusion was supported by a sunk-in pillar. Since the column had no structural importance it was abandoned, but the *baka* was protruded downwards, giving it a slightly horseshoe configuration. Conscientious builders supported these protrusions with a bracket of *azaras*, set into a narrow horizontal groove hacked out of the wall.[30] (Pls. 1.52 – 1.55.)

All the types of cross-arched roofs were called *daurin guga*, and in consequence of their shape they provide support not to flat but to domed roofs (*tuluwa*).

[30] In Sokoto it was customary to set a base at the foot of each *bakuna* (made of a pair of crossed *azaras*). Daldy, *op cit.*

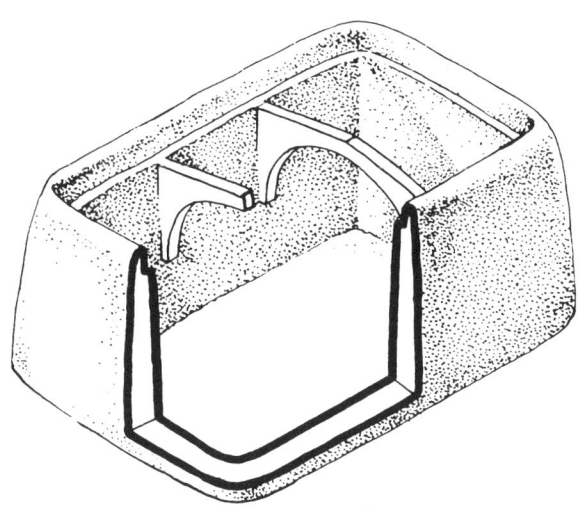

Fig.1.16. Rectangular interior roofed with two parallel baka.

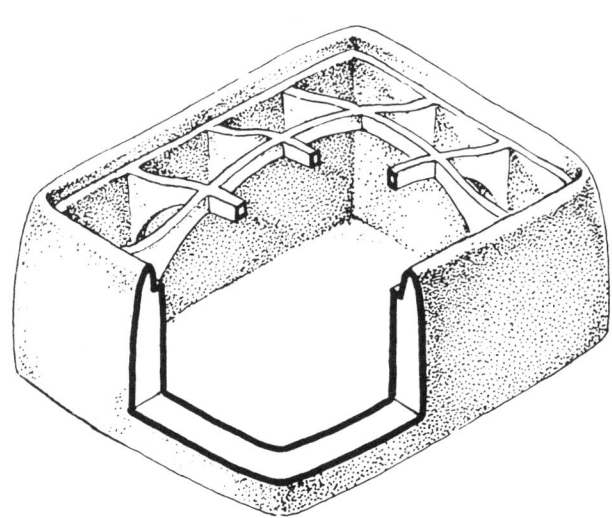

Fig.1.17. Rectangular interior roofed with a grid of crossed baka.

Pl.1.52. Stages in the construction of a domed roof.

Pls.1.53 to 1.55. Stages in the construction of a domed roof.

Flat roofs

The popular view that houses which are rectangular in plan and have flat roofs were introduced south of the Sahara through Islam, should not be accepted without reservations. Ter Engerstrom observes that it is likely that this 'terrace' type was introduced independently and long before Islam; but he also considers as possible the influence of settlement architecture between the Sudan and Egypt.[31]

This hypothesis seems to be too strongly inclined towards the formerly popular method of finding the origin of building forms and constructions in the influence of other cultures. Alien authority is, in my opinion, only one of many factors in the dynamics of progress in architectural development. Certainly a dominant role is always played by the ingenuity and skill, and the creative ambition, of native builders working in the context of their own national culture. The history of European architecture provides a massive bulk of proof to this effect, and there is no reason to assume that things went contrary to this natural trend in Hausaland or in any other region of Nigeria.

It is reasonable to consider that flat-roofed rectangular buildings appeared independently in Hausa countries. The basic principle of their layout is so simple and elementary that it certainly could have been, and was, conceived in even the most primitive circumstances, in Hausaland or elsewhere. Surely it did not need to be obligated to others. For example, the hypothetical 'early form of hut' with a flat roof supported on posts (obviously referring to regions with small rainfall) as given by Bannister Fletcher, is merely one attempt at reconstructing this elementary form.[32] Engerstrom was struck by the fact that in the areas around the Upper Niger, 'the terrace style is generally applied among a number of predominantly fetishistic population groups and tribes such as the Dogon, Samo, Bobo, Lobi . . .' A similar type of flat-roofed building also appears in east Africa. In Tanzania I saw the buildings of the Gogo tribe, which had a rectangular plan and were covered with a ceiling-roof made from a flat slab; this was supported on numerous forked posts (sombiri), placed outside the walls as well as on the axis of the interior. On them was laid the elements of the roof's wooden substructure: booms, makapa, laid crosswise on them; and finally a raft of thin branches, walo, the immediate underlay for the thick roof slab, which was made from a mixture of cow dung and the outer shells of anthills (irongo).

The flat Hausa roofs, supported not on timber posts but on walls of building earth, have an inner structure which is similar, though often more developed. There is no need to link them to the buildings of Upper Niger, or Tanzania, or any other country. The device is so simple, so elementary, that it does not seem reasonable to claim its dependence upon foreign influence.

Again, as in many attested cases, similar geographical conditions and similar technological possibilities gave rise to analogous forms and constructions. With the passage of time, technology improved, and the social demands made upon builders increased.

The roofing of Hausa interiors of various sizes and shapes prompted a number of different solutions, from the simple to the complex, always subject to the growing skill of the builder and the quality of his materials. Resulting from centuries of experience, Hausa people have found that the maximum span between supports for azara timbers should be about two metres, and for cheaper and less resistant types of timber, about 1.5 metres.

The span of both rectangular and circular buildings was therefore limited at first to these dimensions, and the ends of the joists rods rested on the tops of the walls.

Larger buildings were required, however, and the simplest way of roofing large rectangular interiors was to reduce the span by placing brackets on one or both sides of the room. (The brackets were flat topped projections made from one or more layers of rods set in rows.) Jutting out horizontally from the walls, the brackets supported tauyi, wooden beams running parallel to the walls. In this way the span of the timbers forming the roof was reduced to the required dimensions. (Figs.1.18 – 1.20).

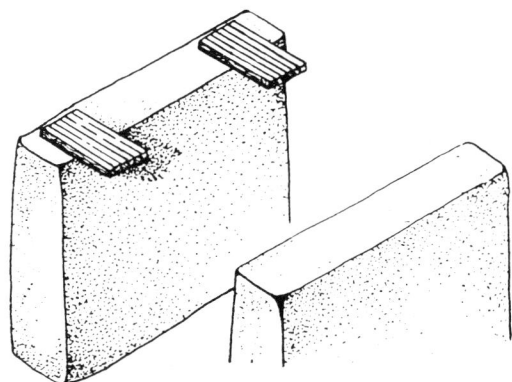

Fig.1.18. Azara brackets.

[31] Ter Engerstrom, Origin of Pre-Islamic Architecture in West Africa, 'Ethnos', Vol. 24, Stockholm 1959.
[32] Sir Bannister Fletcher, A History of Architecture on the Comparative Method, London 1943, p. 85.

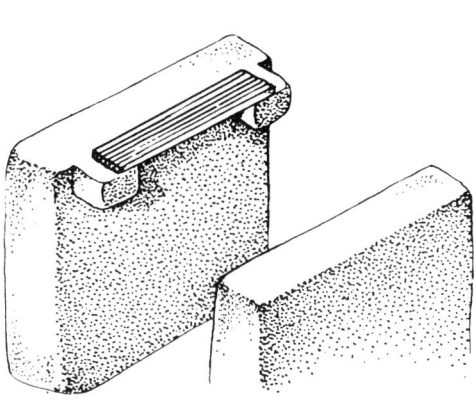

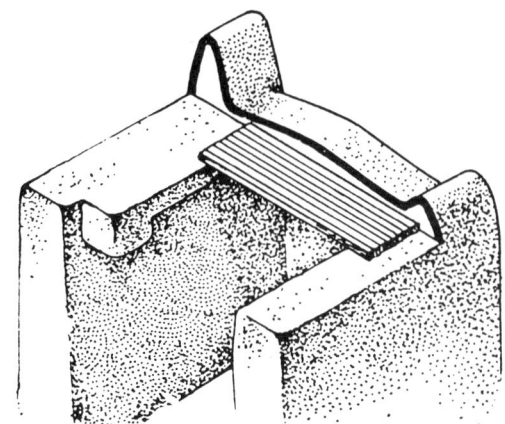

Fig.1.19. *Tauyi* beams, formed by laying *azaras* on top of brackets parallel to the walls.

Fig.1.20. Crosswise *azaras* laid on top of *tauyi* to form the roof.

Another method of roofing interiors wider than 2 metres was to lay diagonally-fitted triangles of *azaras* in the four corners of the room. On top of the triangles, parallel to the two opposite walls, two further layers of *azaras* were placed, *tauyi-* fashion, reducing the span of the top crosswise *azara* joists to the desired length. This method was used in both rectangular and square interiors (Figs. 1.21 & 1.22). The different levels of the individual layers and especially the rhythmical display of *azaras*, set in four directions, transformed the flat roof into a pleasing three-dimensional composition; in consequence the builders increased the number of superimposed layers above purely structural needs. They created in this way a decorative pattern culminating in the centre of the ceiling, the apex of the whole, which was several thicknesses of *azara* above the first, bottom layer. This

structure provided a support for the slightly domed exterior surface of the roof, which the rainwater could run down.

Brackets made of *azaras* laid horizontally always had a width of three or more pieces of timber, and equally were two or more layers thick — the lower layer projected about 45 centimetres from the wall and supported the upper one(s) which projected about 90 centimetres. This type of support was frequently to be found in city gates, and carried not *tauyi* running parallel to the walls, but strong beams (*doki*) going across the width of the gate, at 2 metre centres. These beams divided its area into a number of bays and allowed *azara* joists to be laid on the beams, parallel to the axis of the gate.

In large interiors the above methods were not adequate and internal pillars (*alamudi, ginshiki*) had to be introduced to support the beams of the roof. The capitals of these pillars

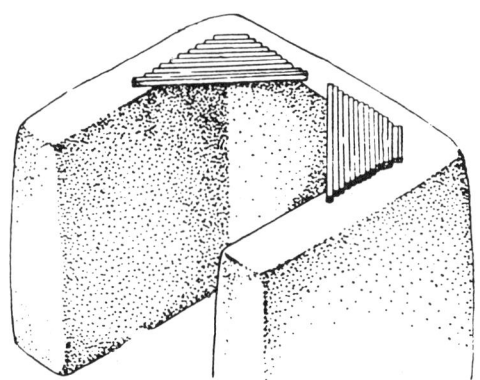

Fig.1.21. *Alwatika* (triangle) of *azaras* laid diagonally across a corner.

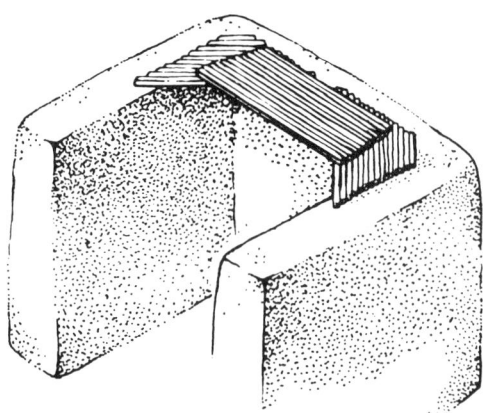

Fig.1.22. *Alwatika* support for *tauyi*.

were topped with brackets that were not cantilevered like those set into the thickness of the wall, but, being made of longer rods, projected over both sides of the pillar. Thus they balanced the weight of the two opposite beams. This device was evolved by setting crosswise two such symmetrical double brackets, in order to support four beams, set at right angles to one another. The crosswise timbers overlapped, thus one pair of symmetrical brackets was always one *azara* higher than the crossing pair. The pillars supporting such brackets were often not square but crosslike in plan.

There were many ways of waterproofing flat roofs. The most frequently used material for joists was rods of *azara*, which provided both an attractively textured ceiling (*rufi*) and a base for the heat-insulating and rainproofing slab of the roof. Immediately over the *azaras* was an overlay of *zana* mats, plaited from *zana* grass; or a course of neatly arranged cornstalks or straw; or, when there was the danger of termites, of twigs of the *makarfo* plant which are very strong, as well as being resistant to termites. This overlay prevented the plaster (*kafar rufi*), which constituted the next level of the slab, from leaking through the gaps between the underlying *azaras. Kafar rufi* was carefully prepared from very smooth *kasa* (building earth), and laid about ten centimetres thick. When completely dry and hard, *kafar rufi* was covered with *babbarkiya*, a pale grey earth found in waterholes and borrow pits as a dry, fine powder. *Babbarkiya* was sprinkled to form a layer about fifteen centimetres thick, then compressed with bare feet to solidify its consistency, and left in this condition until the end of the harmattan. The early, light rains moistened the upper level of *babbarkiya*, forming a hard shell on top. It was desirable that the bottom of the deposit remained in its original powdered state, keeping the roof dry and properly insulated.[33] Another well known waterproof coating was *laso* .

It was important to provide the roof surface with a slope to carry the rainwater towards the parapet. This was best done by appropriately inclining the *azaras*, not by changing the thickness of the waterproof slab above them. The parapets were deeply chased to contain long rain-gutters, or rather rainvalleys (*indararo*) running perpendicular to the parapet. They used to be made in burnt clay by specialists and were shaped rather like cannon barrels. In more modest buildings they were carved out of wood – but they always protruded far beyond the walls, to prevent the outflowing rainwater from damaging the façade of the building. (See Kafin Madaki; Pl. 5.60 & 5.61).

Large flat roofs were occasionally divided by a grid of low internal parapets into rectangular panels: a central parapet formed the ridge, and each panel sloped gently towards the outside.

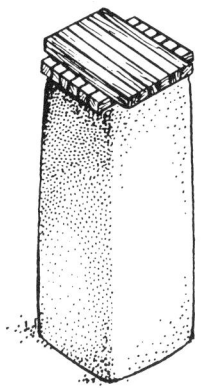

Fig.1.23. Pillar with brackets forming the capital.

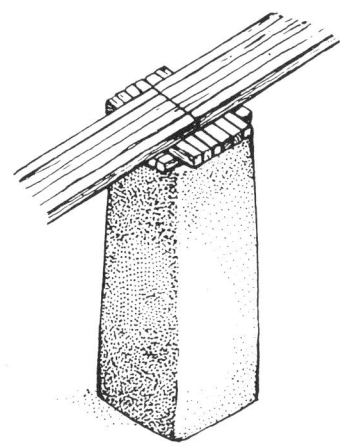

Fig.1.24. Capital supporting ceiling beams.

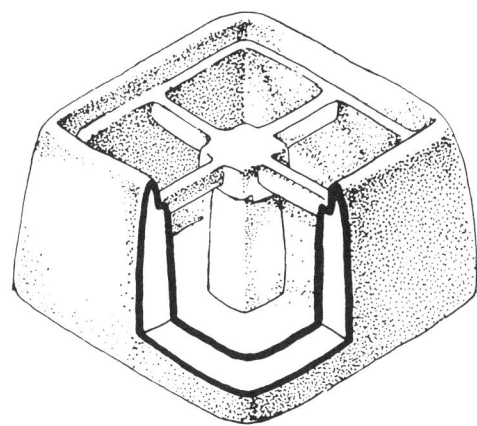

Fig.1.25. Isometric of a pillar supporting a flat ceiling.

[33] Some of the above information was provided in 1974 by Mallam Iro Shehu, Dipl. Law, Ahmadu Bello University. According to Daldy, *babbarkiya* was a sandy red earth which dried quickly and was therefore useful for urgent repairs.

Pls.1.56 & 1.57. Laying azaras *to form a flat roof.*

Pl.1.59. Building a parapet.

Pl.1.58. Plastering over zana *matting laid on top of the* azaras.

Pl.1.60. The roof completed.

Pl.1.61. Erecting a zanko, *the decorative finial on a building.*

Domed roofs

The structure of the *tuluwa* combines a number of the elements described in the paragraph on flat-roofed square or rectangular rooms.

The simplest *tuluwa* covered a square or almost square interior and was supported by *daurin guga*.

The crown of the walls at the four corners of the room was covered with triangles of diagonally laid *azaras* (*tauyi*). On top of these were laid beams about 30 centimetres wide, also called *tauyi*, although they ran not diagonally but parallel to the four walls – rather like those supported by horizontal brackets. The apex of the crossed *baka*[34] was plastered and next covered with four triangular layers of *azara*. The layers were necessarily triangular, and were set parallel to the walls of the room. Thus the upper support for the final layer of the dome's joists was created. The joists filled the four triangles framed by the *baka*, and the bottom of the *azara* joists were set either on the crown of the walls or on the perpendicular *tauyi*.[35]

More elaborate *tuluwa* might be supported by four *baka*, two of them parallel, and two diagonal, to the walls of the interior. The basic principle was similar to the two-*baka* structure, although the corner triangular *tauyi* might sometimes be supported by decoratively moulded pillars set into the walls. Karl Kumm's photograph of a room in the palace of the Emir of Kano shows a dome supported by ten *baka*.[36]

A probably unsurpassed composition of six *tuluwa* set on a sophisticated construction of walls, piers and twin *baka*, a monument of Nigerian ecclesiastical architecture was the Zaria Masallaci Juma'a. Attached to it was a square building, the Sharia Court, topped by six *bakan gizo*. The imaginative roofing of the Zaria Massallaci equalled the masterly structure of the building itself.

Tuluwa were rainproofed with considerable ingenuity. To begin with the dome's construction, the *bakuna* and *tauyi* were combined into an organic whole, the outer edges of the *tauyi* being inserted into the top layers of the *bakuna*. The joists of the *rufi* were set radially from the apex, in the same way as in two-*bakuna* type. The waterproofing of the dome was not much different from that of flat roofed rooms – although necessary amendments had to be made according to the convexity of the dome. Instead of flat and stiff *zana* mats, much more flexible *asabari* mats were used, made chiefly of strong grass (*tsaure*). The mats were laid in such a way as to keep the stalks parallel to the curvature of the dome, and were usually fixed together at the apex with thin vines. The consecutive layers of *kasar rufi* and *barbakiya* or *katsi* waterproofed the structure much better than on flat roofs, since the rain water ran off the dome surface fairly quickly. (See Plates 1.64 to 1.82 for domed roof construction.)

---

[34] In Katsina the word *kafa* was used, as well as *baka*. It properly described the structure of two multi-layered corbels, as it means 'the foundation'.

[35] A F Daldy explains that, 'by this means most of the weight of the roof is transferred to the beams near the walls: to lay the azaras horizontally would transfer the weight to the arches'. A F Daldy, *op cit*.

[36] K Kumm, *Hausaland to Egypt*.

Pls.1.62 & 1.63. KANO. The rebuilding of Gidan Makama. Construction details.

Pls.1.64 to 1.70. KANO. The rebuilding of Gidan Makama.
Stages in the construction of a domed roof.

Pls.1.71 to 1.76. KANO. The rebuilding of Gidan Makama. Stages in the construction of a domed roof.

Pls.1.77 to 1.80. KANO. The rebuilding of Gidan Makama.
Stages in the construction of a domed roof.

Pls.1.81 & 1.82. KANO. The rebuilding of Gidan Makama. Matting covering roof azaras. The underlay for plaster.

Pl.1.83. KANO. Gidan Makama restored. Part of the palace, showing completed domed and flat roofs.

Pls.1.84 & 1.85. KANO. Gidan Makama. Applying the final layer to the walls: a waterproof plaster called makuba.

Pl.1.86. Decorative surface of a Hausa building.

2 Muslim Religious Architecture

Birnin Kebbi
Jega
Argungu
Katsina
Bebeji
Zaria
Kafin Madaki
Gurin
Ilorin
Lagos
Wusasa

Introduction

Monumental ecclesiastical architecture in Northern Nigeria consisted almost exclusively of Muslim mosques. They were not conceived as temples, which meant that, unlike most religious buildings in the world, they did not enshrine holy sacraments or sacred and ritualistic articles. Their purpose was clearly expressed by the Arabic word *mesgid* (mosque): they provided the faithful with a place for submission to Allah, for prayer and communal reading of the holy Koran. This naturally determined the general lines of the architectural planning, which reflected the philosophical motivations of the Muhammadan designers. On the other hand, since in the early years the services of mercenary architects from the countries converted to Islam were used, local cultural traditions were adapted to new religious purposes. Islam developed from Persia and Syria, through Egypt and North Africa up to Spain, and finally in the Turkish empire and in India. A number of individual styles were created, and an abundance of architectural monuments of the highest order arose in the various areas where Islam became the leading religious and political force.

The Nigerian *massallatai* belonged to this great family of religious buildings. True to type they fulfilled the basic demands of religious doctrine and at the same time developed their own particular character.

There was a great variety of types – from simple roofless enclosures providing a place for common prayer to magnificent buildings whose structural perfection and compositional excellence put them into an exclusive group of classical monuments; the word classical being used to express the ultimate achievement possible within given technological limits.

Sokoto was the centre from which the doctrines of modern Nigerian Islam spread through Usman dan Fodio and his disciples and adherents. The architectural forms developed there had a major influence on the development of Islamic architecture from the nineteenth century onward. The mosques recorded on the following pages were based almost without exception on the severe but extremely functional concepts developed by the spiritual heirs of the Fulani jihad. This can be seen even in the most sumptuous works of sacral architecture erected after the jihad – as for example in the famous Massallaci Juma'a in Zaria. Only in exceptional cases, probably as a result of the balance of political power, did Nigerian mosques depart from the Sokoto pattern of composition.

It would require a more comprehensive study and thorough research in the field to discover examples of original pre-jihad Habe ecclesiastical architecture, of which as for example in Katsina, merely the remains were to be seen at the beginning of the twentieth century.

A good description of the old Sokoto mosque was given by Captain Clapperton, who in April 1824 witnessed the erection of the building. It had a rectangular plan, was orientated, and was 24 metres long. There were two doors in the eastern wall and in front of the western entrance a square room served for ritual ablutions. Seven rows of pillars, seven in a row, carried 'arches' supporting the joists of the flat roof. The joists carried 'slender spars placed obliquely from joist to joist' and were covered with a thick layer of clay. This description fits the characteristics of the structure presented in this chapter, with one exception. Clapperton tells us that 'the pillars were of wood plastered over with clay, and highly ornamented.' If this assertion were accepted literally it would mean that the 'master builder . . . a native of Zeg-Zeg'[1] did not rely on the admittedly poor quality of Sokoto building earth and decided to adopt the unusual device of plastered wooden posts instead of the commonly used *azara*-reinforced *tubali* pillars.

[1] Whose father acquired in Egypt a smattering of Moorish architecture and left him all his papers, from which he derived his only architectural knowledge.

Birnin Kebbi Mosque

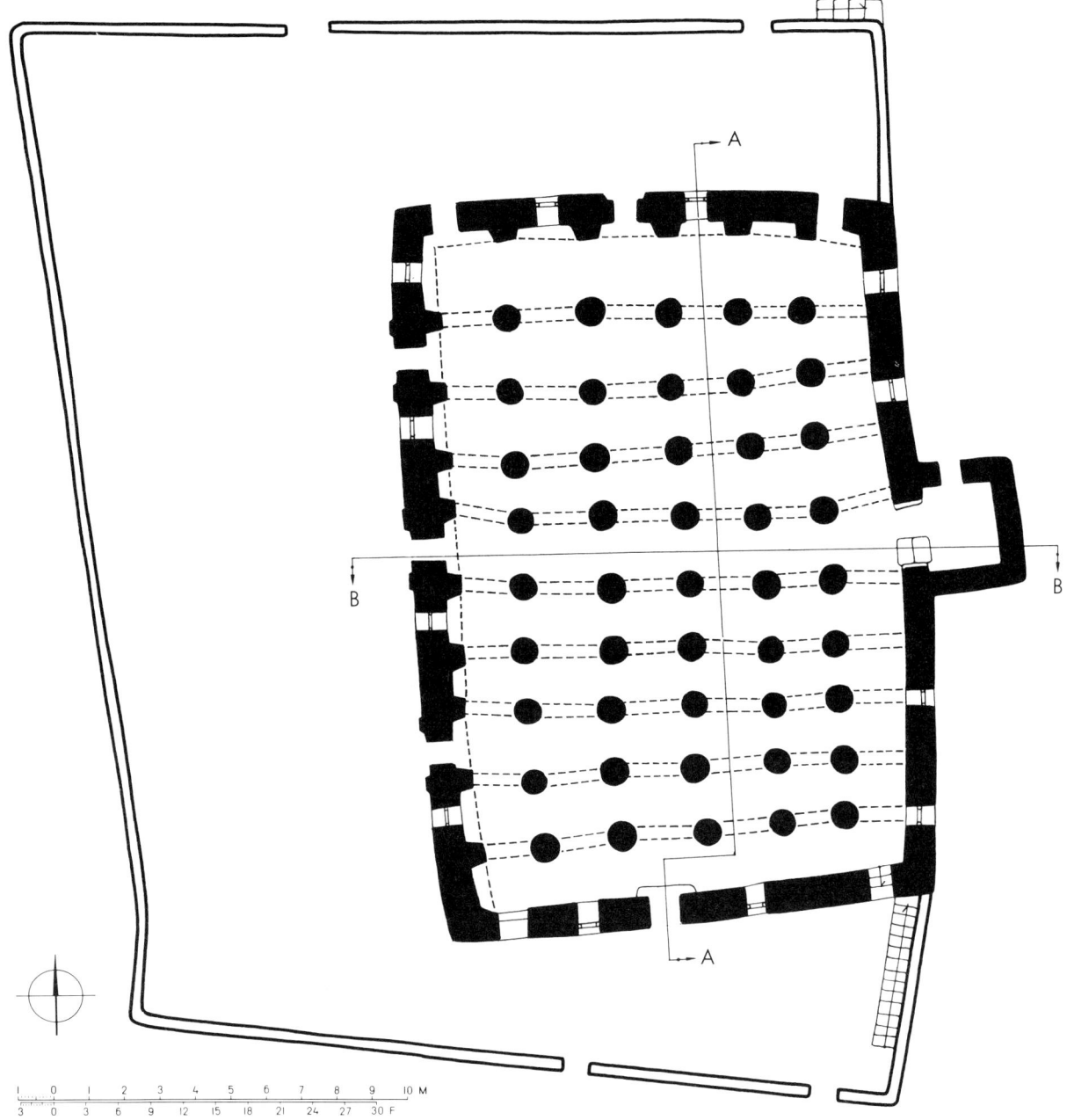

Fig.2.1. Birnin Kebbi Mosque. PLAN

The founders of Birnin Kebbi left their original capital and settled in Argungu, where they established a new kingdom which was never subdued by Fulani conquest. Birnin Kebbi was attacked and burned in 1805 by the forces of Abdullahi, and was surrendered to him some eight years later by Hodi, the ruler of Kebbi. In 1826 he revolted and was killed. Kebbi's struggle continued throughout the century. There was a period of eighteen years of Fulani domination followed by a further uprising, a new peace treaty and subsequent revolt, during which Sarkin Kebbi, Samaila Samo (1883–1915) was credited with burning ninety walled towns of the Fulani.[2]

[2] *The Emirates of Northern Nigeria*, pp. 250, 251.

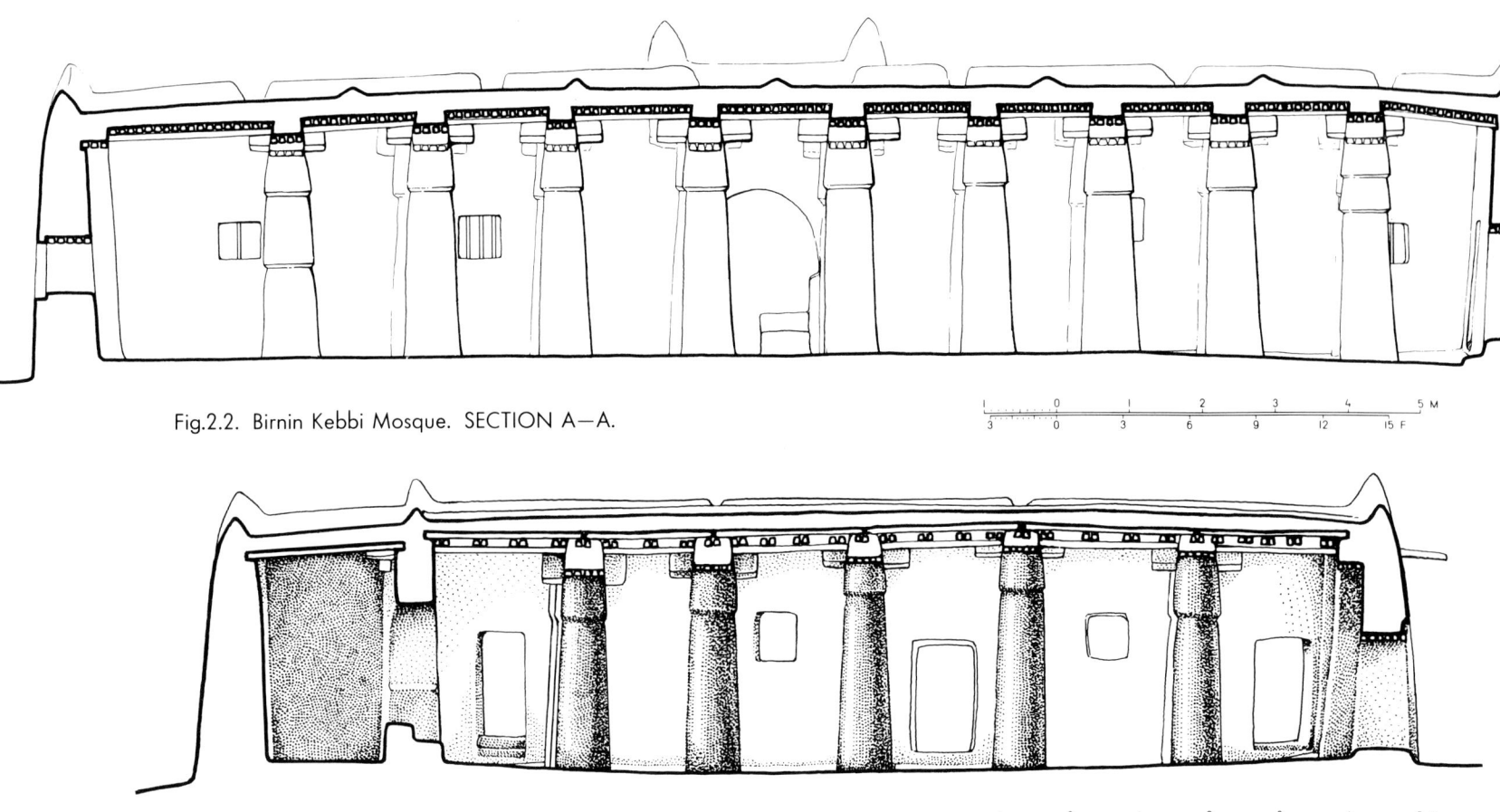

Fig.2.2. Birnin Kebbi Mosque. SECTION A—A.

Fig.2.3. Birnin Kebbi Mosque. SECTION B—B.

In spite of the political disturbances, the Fulani cultural influence played an important part in the life of the city and made an obvious imprint on the design of the Masallaci Juma'a. Its plan also corresponded to Clapperton's description of Sokoto mosque, as well as to the plan of the mosque at Jega.

There are two basic differences in the design, however. First of all, the main axis with the *mihrab* at its E end is much shorter than the N-S axis − a far more functional arrangement than at Jega, providing an easy approach towards the rows of sitting places facing the *mihrab*.

The other difference is the shape of the pillars, which were cylindrical and topped with a typical head, *al' amudi mai tabarya*, (see p. 1.29). The main E-W axis on which both the

mihrab and the main W door were situated, was additionally accentuated by a slightly wider span between the *al'amudai*. There were only three doors in the W and N walls and only one in the centre of the E wall. On the other hand, there were a number of windows all round the building − probably they replaced the original doors. The *mihrab*, projecting from the E wall, resembled that of Jega, and also had a door in its N wall leading outside the complex. Steps to the corner of the roof, from where the *ladan* chanted his invocations for prayer, were set along the SE portion of the perimeter wall. As in Jega the perimeter wall enclosed the U-shaped *haraba* courtyard, from S, W and N. There were two entrances in each of the S and N walls.

Jega
Old Mosque

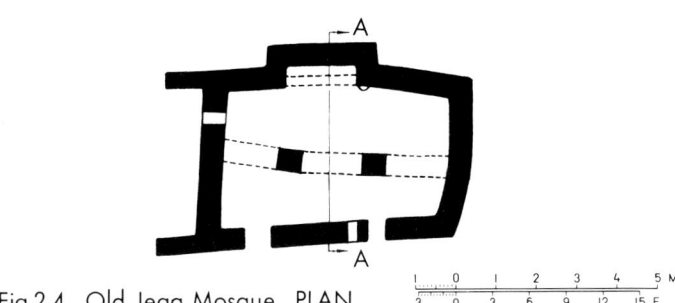

Fig.2.4. Old Jega Mosque. PLAN

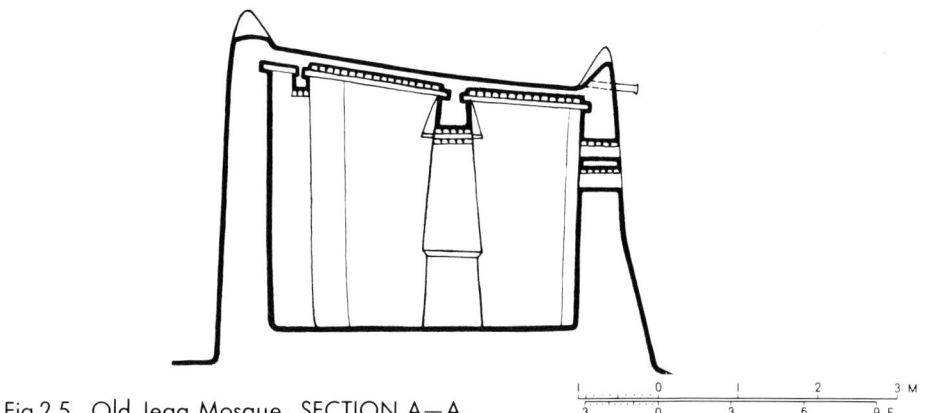

Fig.2.5. Old Jega Mosque. SECTION A—A.

Jega and Birnin Kebbi were two cities within the Fulani sphere of influence, both almost equidistant from Sokoto (some 134 km. SW), and their mosques were similar to the old Sokoto mosque as described by Clapperton.

Of the two cities, Jega on the river Zamfara was the more prosperous, because of its position on the NS–EW crossroads and as a trade centre between the regions of the northern savannah and southern forests. It was founded during the reign of Abdullahi dan Fodio (1808–28) by Buhari, who made his submission to Abdullahi, and this probably determined

the design of the mosque, causing it to follow the Sokoto pattern.

The building was erected on a rectangular plan, its flat roof supported by six rows of square pillars, *ginshiki* (meaning having the plan of a cross with very short arms). They were set seven in a row, which meant that the N–S axis was longer than the E–W – rather an unusual arrangement. The *mihrab*, projecting from the centre of the E wall, had a slightly trapezoidal plan and a door leading N outside the complex. The three remaining walls, S, W and N, were all pierced by a

Jega
New Mosque

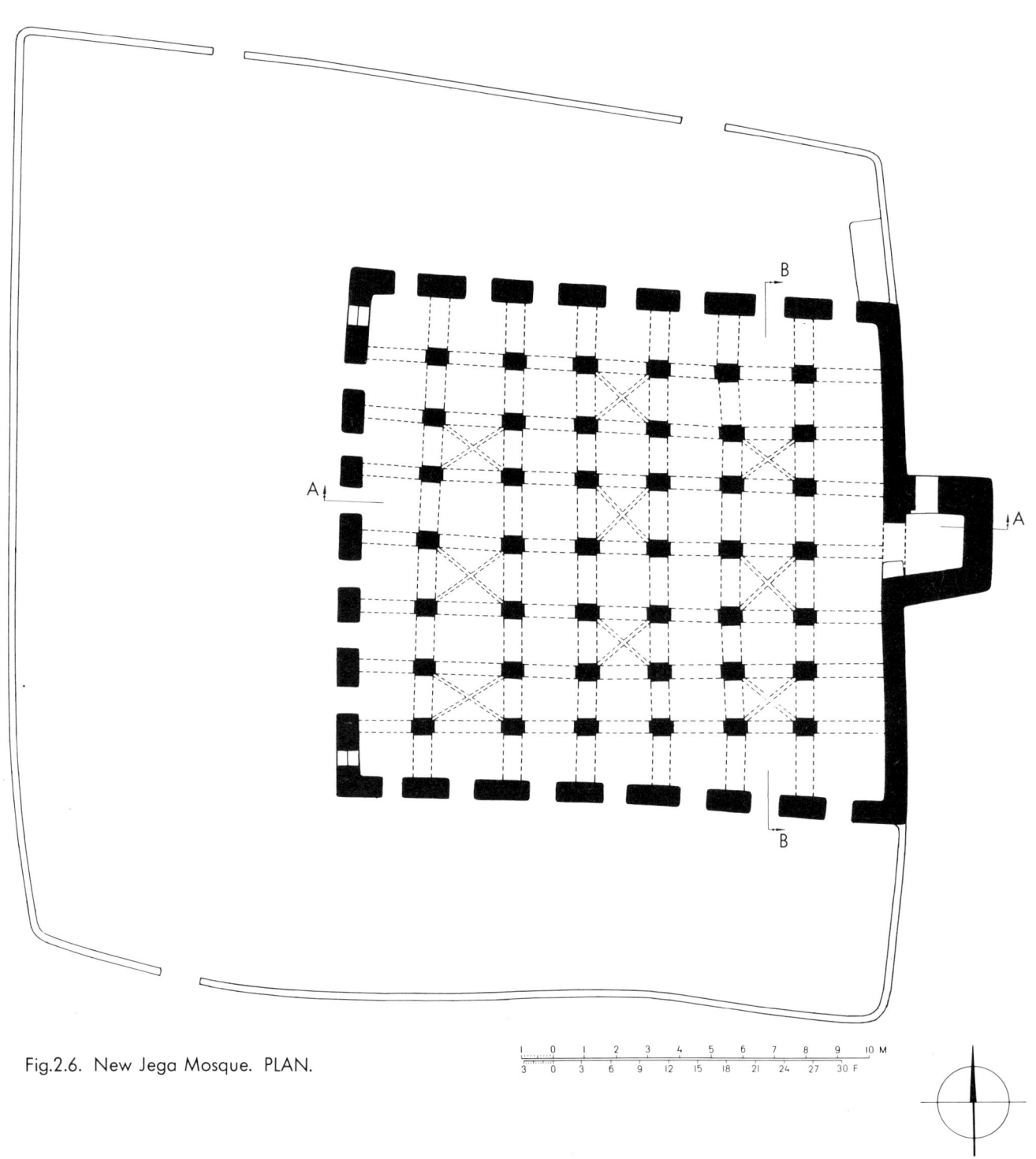

Fig.2.6. New Jega Mosque. PLAN.

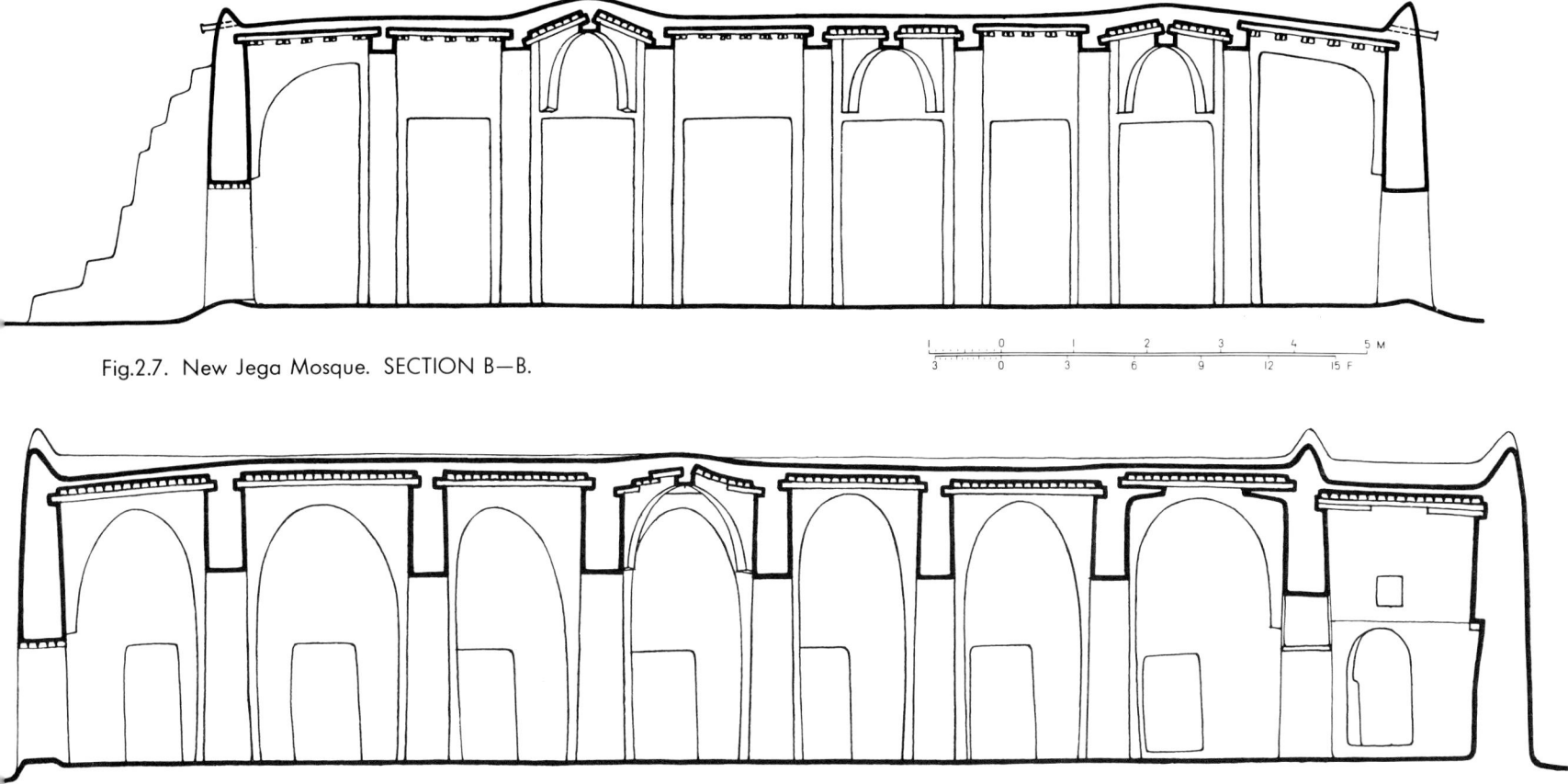

Fig.2.7. New Jega Mosque. SECTION B—B.

Fig.2.8. New Jega Mosque. SECTION C—C.

number of doors, at the ends of the passages between the pillars, thus giving the people easy access as well as providing good cross ventilation.

As in a number of mosque plans, the axial line of pillars faced the central part of the *mihrab* doorway – perhaps the purpose of this was to provide a view of the lectern from a greater number of seating places.

The span between the E—W pillars varied between 1m. and 1½m., and thus kept well within the accepted safe span of 2 m. for flat beams. The span between the N—S rows of pillars, where the sofitt was carried on corbelled *bakuna*, was extended in some bays more than two metres. Some of the bays had a more elaborate overlay, made from rib-like crossed *daurin guga* (*daurin* = tying, *guga* = crosswise). There was a certain system in their disposal – three such bays were set in each of the seven rows of bays, so that each ribbed bay was surrounded by eight plain ones. Further, the second and sixth rows of panels began at the S side of their row; the fourth, the

central one, at the N side. The central panel of this row was specially emphasised by having a more elaborate *bakuna* which supported a shallow dome. The *mihrab* to the E of this asymetrical axis had a ceiling slightly lower than the rest of the mosque and was partitioned by a bracketed arch from the rest of the interior.

Along the N and S walls of the building the bays were covered with flat beams, resting on brackets from the outer walls on one side and supported by complementary pillars on the other.

As was the custom, the building was surrounded on three sides, N, S and W by a courtyard, *haraba*. The perimeter walls, *ginin haraba* were broken by two entrances on the N side and one on the S. As mentioned above, the *mihrab* had a door of its own, set in a particularly massive wall. On the NE corner of the building, along the inside of the perimeter wall, ran a steep clay staircase leading to the corner of the roof from which the *ladan* called the faithful to the devotions in the mosque.

Argungu Mosque

The last of the group of four mosques surveyed in the NE part of the Sokoto area was Argungu Masallaci Juma'a. Although only 60 miles from Sokoto it differed entirely both in plan and spatial composition from the three mosques previously described. It is tempting to assume that the independent spirit of the Argungu people prompted the city's builders to reject the standardised Sokoto/Fulani design. Like the people of Abuja, the Argungu people, although they had abandoned their former capital of Kebbi, retained their political and cultural independence in the face of the Fulani jihad. Several attempts to conquer their new city were repelled with great losses to the attackers, and although the constant warfare impoverished the emirate, Argungu developed a strong Habe nationalism, to the extent of banishing the Fulani language.[3]

The architectural composition of the Argungu mosque made full use of the traditional Habe/Hausa framed structure and its dexterously-shaped interior was quite at variance with the serene simplicity of the Sokoto pattern.

The roughly square outline of the outer walls contained in the centre a practically independent fabric of three pairs of solid square pillars forming an inner structural quadrangle. Each pair of opposite pillars was linked by a lofty *bakan gizo*, and three of them provided a spectacular frame for the mihrab at the end of the E–W axis. The pillars, divided at half their height by *tabarya* capitals, reached the top of the central quadrangle. In their lower part they were separated by two narrow passages, and in their upper part by two grilled windows. Horizontal *azara* beams above the pillar capitals and above the windows stiffened the structure in an E–W direction on both its sides. Most probably they also served as *mashim eidi*, counterweighting the bracketed layers of *azara* which formed the frame of the arch-like *baka* (see p. 32).

The apexes of the three *bakuna* were raised about 1 metre above the tops of the six internal pillars, thus shaping the roof above the central quadrangle into a waggon vault. The spaces above the ambulatory were covered with sloping roofs running down from the ridge of the central dome towards the outer walls of the mosque. Two large entrances and two windows were set in the W wall of the mosque, and there were four more windows in the S wall.

The *haraba* was reduced in Argungu to a rather small rectangular courtyard directly in front of the W wall of the mosque; the remaining façades were left unprotected.

[3] Hogben and Kirk-Greene, *The Emirates of Northern Nigeria*, pp. 249-51.
P L Monteil, *De Saint Louis à Tripoli par le Lac Tchad*, Paris 1895, pp. 248-55.

Fig.2.9. Argungu Mosque. PLAN.

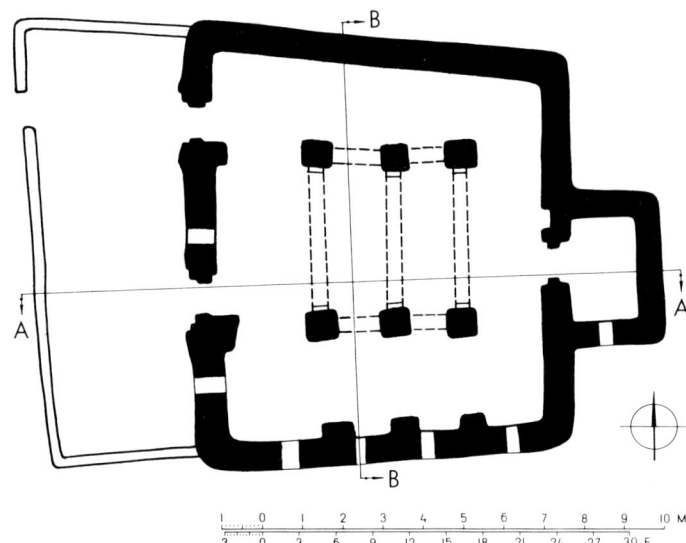

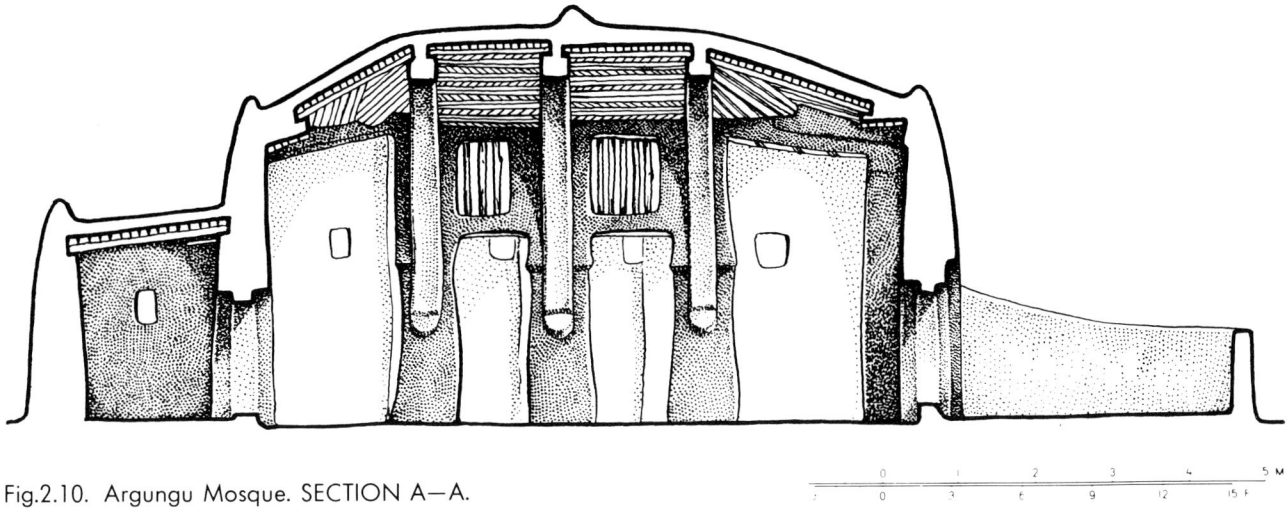

Fig.2.10. Argungu Mosque. SECTION A—A.

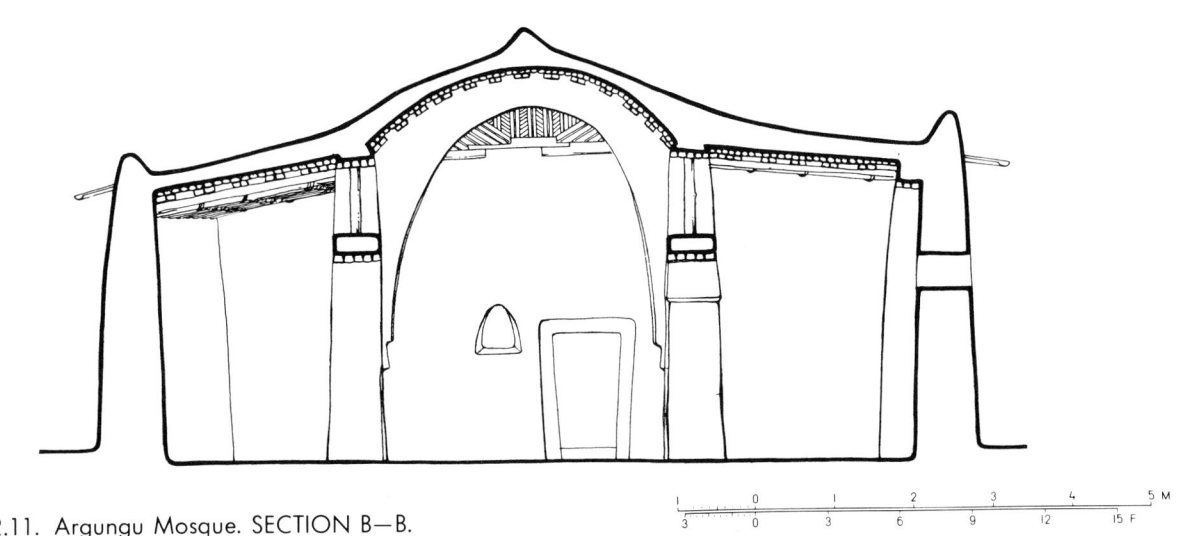

Fig.2.11. Argungu Mosque. SECTION B—B.

Katsina
Habe Gobirau Minaret

What was known in 1959 as the Katsina Habe Gobirau minaret consisted of a much dilapidated pillar enclosed within a structure of three superimposed blocks.

Pl.2.1. KATSINA. Habe Gobirau Minaret. N. façade.

The central pillar, eroded into an indefinable shape, was the last remnant of the *hasumiya*, presumably a minaret, which originally stood by the west end of a mosque. This mosque was said to have been built over three hundred years ago but was later entirely demolished.

In 1927, on the instigation of Mr F. de F. Daniel, the Emir decided to protect what was left of the *hasumiya* by erecting an outer encasement for it.[4] (Pl. 2.1).

The structure was massive in appearance but very well proportioned. It had a large block of solid masonry as a base and on the north and east sides of this was a flight of steps. The steps, which had a wavy battlemented parapet, led to the terraced top of the bottom block. The middle block was built on its vertical axis; it was narrower than the base block, thus leaving a passage around, which was protected by a parapet with a few merlons on each side and *zankos* at the corner.

At the top of the eastern flight of steps a door led to a chamber inside the middle block. This chamber had a door in each of its four walls, and in the centre was visible the middle part of the *hasumiya*, built in a rough loam containing a large amount of gravel.[5]

Above the first two flights of steps, that is on the north and east sides of the building, there were two more flights, leading to the uppermost block. For structural reasons its plan was only a little smaller than that of the one below, leaving no room for a passage around it; but the recession of the walls sufficiently accentuated the three-part composition of the building.

The top block of the edifice was entered through a door in its eastern wall. The interior was entirely occupied by a staircase winding around the uppermost part of the *hasumiya* – each step bound it to an outer wall, thus stiffening the whole structure. The block was covered with a dome which was pierced by the finial-like end of the *hasumiya*. (Pls 2.3 & 2.4).

The Habe Gobirau minaret, although not an ancient building, deserves appreciation not only for its considerable architectural merit, but also as a successful attempt to preserve an ancient Katsina structure to which a number of local traditions and memories were attached.

[4] Dept of Antiquities File No 7017. G Graham, 'Some Sketches of Katsina from the Past', *Nigerian Field*, Vol. XXXIII, 1968, p. 88.
[5] The same kind of loam, I noticed, was used for the city walls of Katsina.

Pl.2.2. KATSINA. Habe Gobirau Minaret. Interior, showing the roof above the staircase.

Pl.2.3. KATSINA. Habe Gobirau Minaret. East facade.

Pl.2.4. KATSINA. Habe Gobirau Minaret. South facade.

Bebeji
Mosque

Bebeji, some 48 km. SW of Kano, was one of the many walled towns surrounding the emporium. When taken by the British in 1903 (Aliu [Abu] was then Emir) its fortifications were still in good order.

According to Department of Antiquities' records, the mosque was said to have been started around 1770 and to have been erected in three stages. Its northern part was rebuilt in the 1950s. The striking irregularities of the plan, and to some extent of the architectural details, certainly confirm the heterogeneous history of the building.

It seems reasonable to suppose that the massive eastern wall flanking the *mihrab* (orientated ENE) was the oldest part of the fabric, together with two rows of irregular bays running NNW–SSE. Probably there were only three bays in a row at the beginning, which seems to be indicated by the height of this portion, as shown on the section (A–A). Nevertheless it should be noted that five irregular bays in the E corner of the

building were of equal height to the two rows of bays just described.

The five further rows of bays running NNW–SSE which ended in the solid front wall with its two main doorways, were more or less uniform in character. Their rather low and sturdy *tabarya al amudai* carried the low flat roof on bracketed horizontal beams, contrasting with the *bakuna* arches of the older section. Only the easternmost row of bays displayed the well-known device of the half-*bakuna* (*talkamin kasa*) which counteracted the stresses of the *bakuna* in the older part of the building.

The SE and NW walls of the Masallaci had two and three doors respectively. A narrow staircase between the front doors led to the roof platform of the *ladan*. The *haraba* courtyard surrounded the mosque on two sides only, from the NW and SE, and was accessible through two circular *zauruka* serving for ablutions.

Fig.2.12. Bebeji Mosque. SECTION A—A.

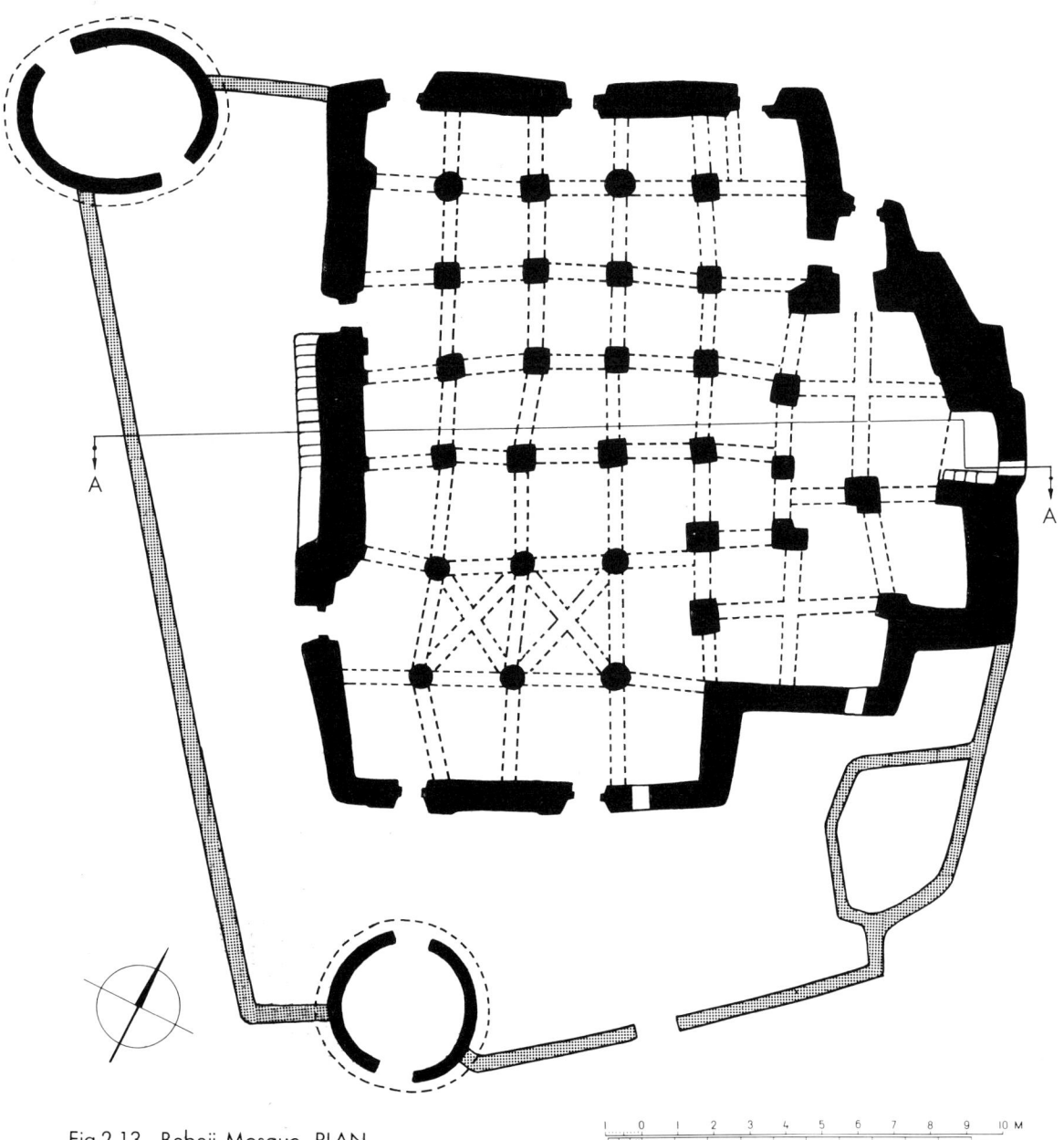

Fig.2.13. Bebeji Mosque. PLAN.

Pl.2.5. ZARIA. Masallaci Juma'a North aisle facing East.

Zaria
Masallaci Juma'a

The Masallaci Juma'a in Zaria, the main hall of which is called *Uwar Masallaci*,[5] was erected during the reign of Abdulkarim (1834–46)[6] of the Fulani Katsinawa dynasty – the first Fulani-installed king, who ended the centuries-old Habe autonomy of Zazzau. The decision to build the mosque was made, significantly enough, on the advice of Muhammed Bello, Sultan of Sokoto (1817–37), and with his moral and material support. It was on his orders that charge of the endeavour was assigned to the famous Sokoto master builder Mallam Mikhaila, who enjoyed the honourable title of *Babban Gwani* (Supreme Expert) and also *Kakan Magina* (Grandfather of the Builders). Mikhaila arrived in Zaria with his children and grandchildren and was generously received by the Sarki, who gave him a hundred slaves as labourers. He also provided him with a ward near the city market place, and this site remained the family residence until recently, retaining the name Babban Gwani Ward. Babban Gwani's slaves were settled in a ward, *unguwa bayan*, south of the mosque. They stayed there after the building was completed and remained in charge of its maintenance under the supervision of Mikhaila's sons and grandsons.

It is not clear when Mallam Mikhaila was posted to Zaria. It is likely that he did not start the work immediately on his arrival. To design a *masallaci* so elaborate, and, as will be seen, to readjust standardized forms into a new spatial composition, required some time. The creative process involved the concurrence of a mature aesthetic imagination and technological mastery; and the conclusions reached during this period of incubation needed to be precisely defined before even the foundations of the building were delineated on the ground.

In the meantime, Mallam Mikhaila's sons undertook a number of minor jobs in the city – another way of preparing for the major task.

It is the consensus[7] that Mallam Mikhaila designed and erected the whole Masallaci complex: the main hall; the surrounding *haraban masallaci* with its wall, *ginin haraba*; and the three gates on the north, west and south sides (*kofar masallaci arewa, yamma* and *kudu* respectively).

The building completed, Zaria was visited by the Sultan of Sokoto, Muhammadu Bello, who inspected the Masallaci and considered it to be 'excellent, with nothing to be altered or improved.' If this story is correct it would suggest the approximate date of completion of the Massallaci, haraba and zauruka as before 1837, which was the year of Sarkin Bello's death.

It is not clear whether the courthouse, *majalisa-na-sharia* (a court of law and justice) standing at the north-east corner of the mosque was erected by Mallam Mikhaila himself, or by his sons. It is traditionally accepted in Zaria that the old master did nothing more in the city than the mosque itself; so it is probable that the court house was built by his sons. Furthermore, I was told that the court house was erected during the reign of Abdulkarim, i.e. before 1846.

It is known that Mallam Mikhaila established a dynasty of builders, the members of which for many years bore his honourable title, Babban Gwani. This ended when Mallam Balarabe was too young at the time of the death of his father Ismaila, the last Babban Gwani of Zaria, to inherit the title; Balarabe and his descendants were known as *Sarkin Magina*.[8]

The Zaria Masallaci may certainly be considered as the most noble achievement of Nigerian ecclesiastic architecture.

[5] This was translated for me as 'Mother Masallaci'. (According to the Revd G P Bargery, *Uwar Daki* = a woman to whom a man looks for advice and help; *Uwargida* = the head wife.)
[6] S J Hogben & A H M Kirk-Greene, *The Emirates of Northern Nigeria*, pp 223-414.
[7] Informants: Jibrin Sarkin Magina, Sarkin Ladane, Mallam Muntaka, Sarkin Gwarin Masallaci, Mallam Jibirilu.
[8] Ismaila and Balarabe erected their splendid residence. Some members of the family were noted for their physical fitness: Labaran Menungoto never climbed down a ladder but always jumped.

Pl.2.6. ZARIA. Masallaci Juma'a in 1963. West facade.

Its spatial composition was most impressive and imaginative, and the structural skill of its designer has never been equalled in any other mosque in the country. The architect applied practically every device ever used in the most developed constructions of Northern Nigeria, enriched them with a number of his own creations and combined them in a serene, logical whole. Even taking for granted his complete mastery of the building craft which had been developed for generations and was displayed in the best monuments of Habe/Hausa/ Fulani architecture, there is still the probability that Babban Gwani, true to his appellation of distinction, possessed some

professional secrets of his own. His mastery in shaping a harmonious and impressive form is obvious to everyone. But what is not obvious is that he used some technical devices of his own in the processing of the building material. Today only a few remaining examples of similar processes exist. The use of *dorowa*, *dafara*, *cabaruwa* and various grasses seem to be the last vestiges of the old science. It is probable that in this way he succeeded in erecting the surprisingly bold fabric, a cohesion of strict Fulani planning and artistic licence in spinning a complex web of stanchions, arches, ribs and domes.

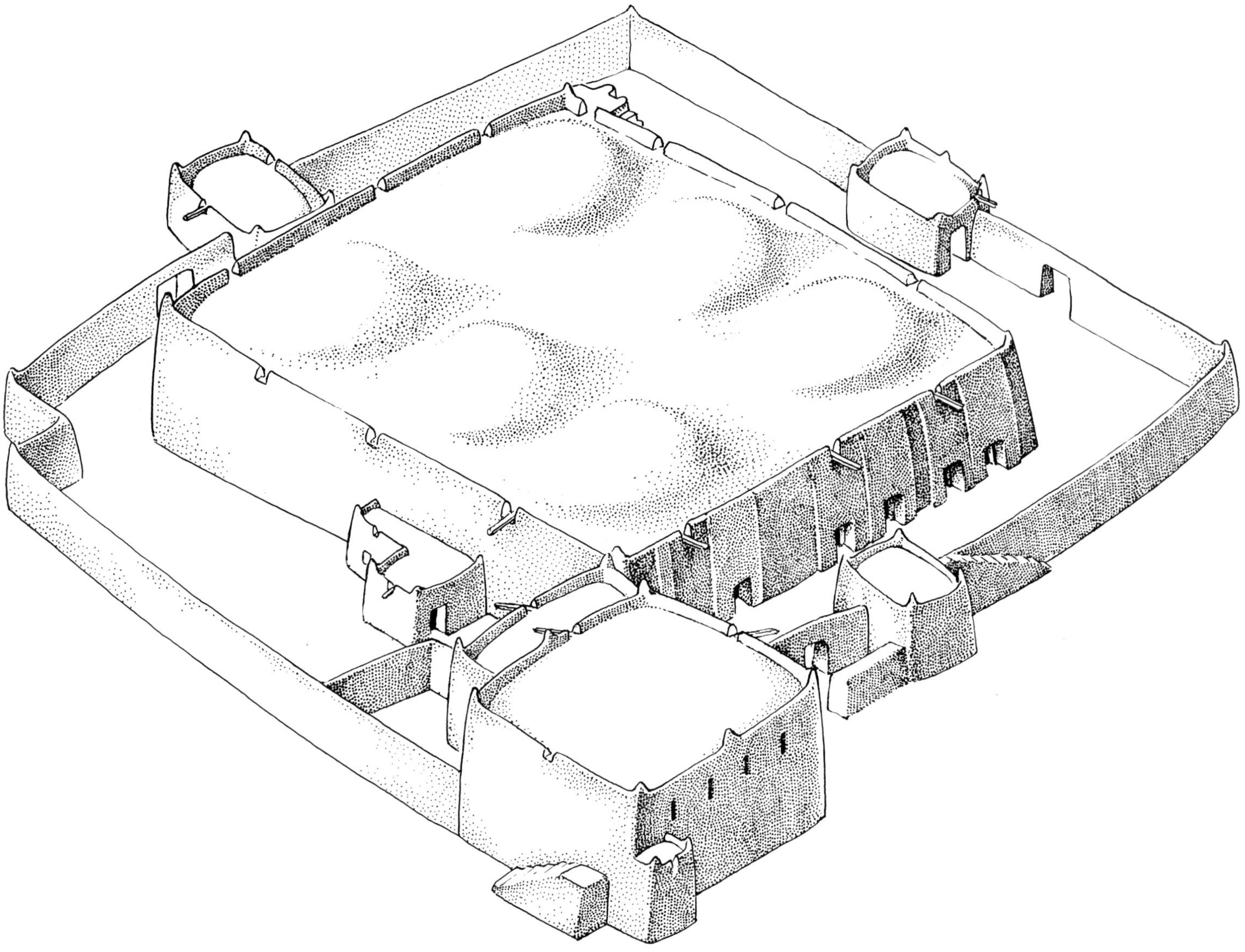

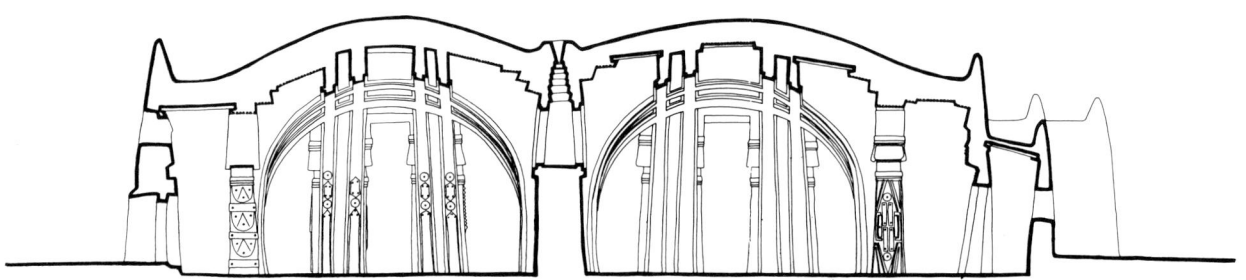

Fig.2.14. Zaria. Masallaci Juma'a. ISOMETRIC

Fig.2.15. Zaria. Masallaci Juma'a. SECTION A—A.

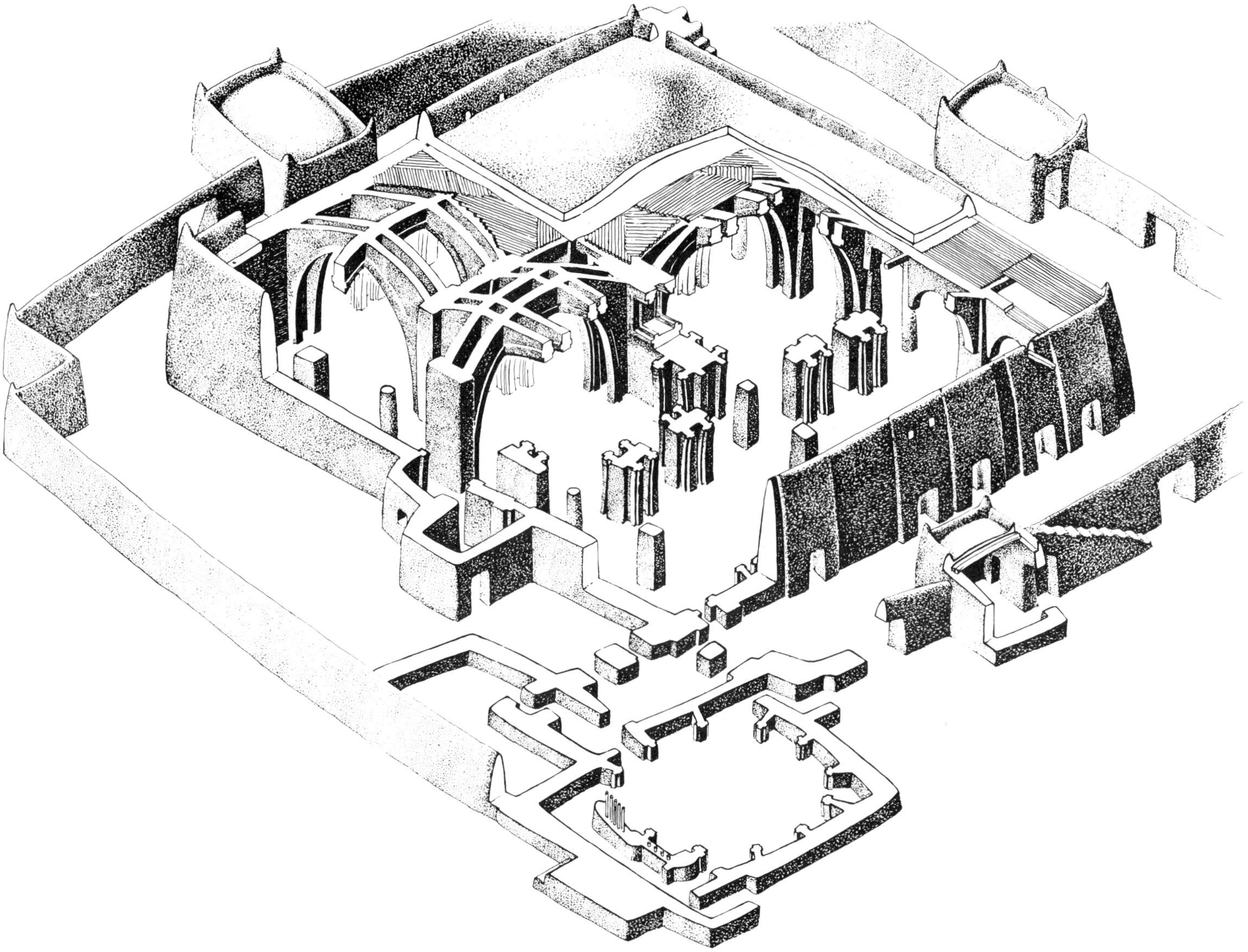

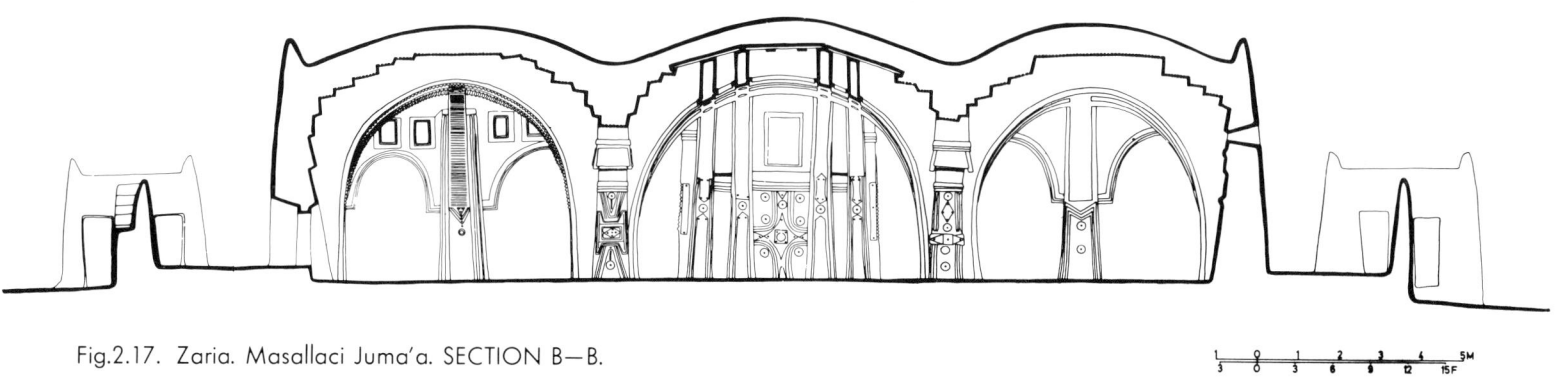

Fig.2.16. Zaria. Masallaci Juma'a. ISOMETRIC OF INTERIOR.

Fig.2.17. Zaria. Masallaci Juma'a. SECTION B—B.

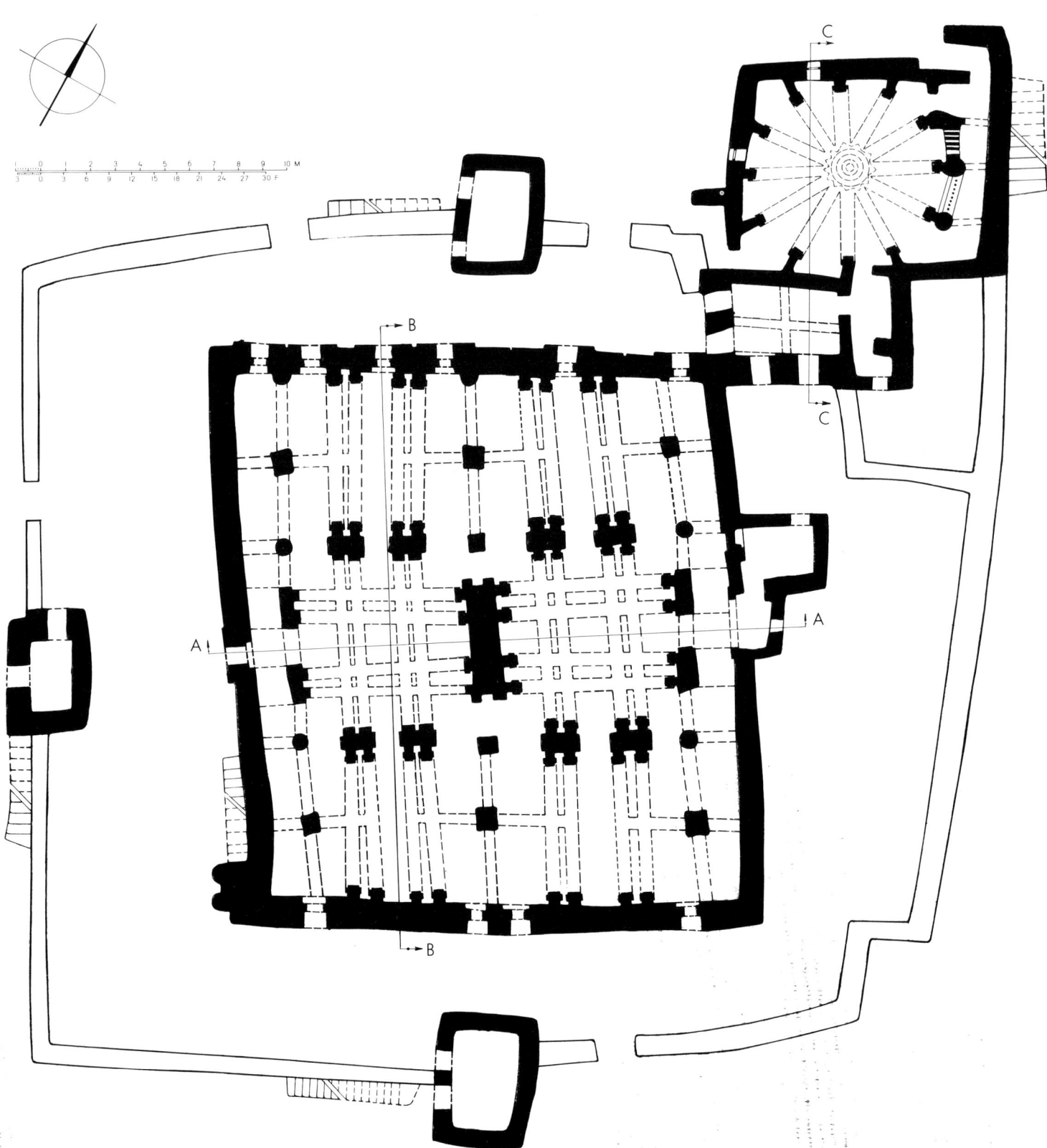

Fig.2.18. Zaria. Masallaci Juma'a. PLAN.

Mallam Mikhaila's design combined two concepts. The initial conception followed the pattern of the old Sokoto mosque, as described by Captain Clapperton,which became the model for other monuments in this group. All of these had flat roofs supported by a grid of quadrangular bays supported in turn by pillars and walls.The passages between the rows of pillars running N–S provided sitting places for the congregation facing the *qibla*. Babban Gwani revolutionized this concept by converting the traditional flat roof into an elaborate complex of six shallow domes. Once such a bold decision had been made, it led him to arrange the whole body of roof-bearing stanchions into a number of diversified piers, pillars and columns. The basic task was to establish a set of major piers, aided by pillars and columns, in order to establish six quadrilateral bays supporting the domes. The bays were arranged in three lines running E–W. There was a central nave with the *mihrab* in the centre of the *qibla* wall, and a door at the opposite end. The nave was flanked by two aisles. The rectangle of six bays was separated from the E and W walls by narrow passages.

The architectural value and structural wisdom of Gwani Mikhaila's design can be appreciated only by careful study of every part of the building. What follows is an attempt to elucidate the matter as far as analysis makes it possible, without actually dissecting the amazing fabric created by the ancient master.

Piers were the fundamental elements carrying the *daurin guga*, the arched cross structure of the domes. The plan of each pier was rather unusual – it consisted of a rectangular core and was developed on its longitudinal sides by twin attachments. It must be remembered that the contours as shown on the plan were measured and drawn almost at floor level; therefore they do not give a full picture of the three-dimensional structure unless analysed in conjunction with the N–W and S–E sections of the building. This will be done below.

Sixteen such massive piers provided the basic though not the only set of supports for the six bays (*sahu*)[9] of the roof and of the framed design of the whole structure. The piers were set in four rows running N–S, each row containing four piers lined E–W. The piers of the two central lines were freestanding; those in the two outer lines were embedded in the N and S walls. Each of the four N–S rows was spanned across the whole width of the building with three *bakan gizos*. As already signalled on the plan, they had an unusual construction, being formed not of single but of twin, corbelled *baka*; these ran parallel to each other at a distance of some 4 to 12 centimetres. This arrangement not only increased their stability but lightened their appearance.(Pl. 2.5.)

The *bakan gizos* ran all the way down to the floor, where they curved slightly inwards, horseshoe fashion. This device was not unique in old Hausa architecture. It was used, for instance, in the interiors of the Emir's palace in Daura and Katsina and, with some alterations, in Gidan Makama in Kano.

The two central lines of E–W piers were flanked, almost symmetrically, by *bakan gizos*. Their oblique pressure was therefore counteracted and safely transmitted to the ground. The stresses of the outer *bakuna* in the side aisles were taken by piers, themselves strengthened by the walls in which they were embedded.

In other words, a substantial part of the roofing system consisted of sixteen piers, joined together in N–S rows of four with twin *bakan gizos*. Their stresses were counter-weighted by the two central lines of piers and balanced by the outer piers and by the weight of the thick N and S walls. This, as mentioned above, constituted the basic cadre (scheme) of the fabric; but it did not suffice to create a quadrilateral network of bays for the six domes. The two central bays, with a wider span and facing the *mihrab*, needed to be more elaborate structurally and decoratively.

In order to achieve this, Gwani Mikhaila introduced six more piers along the central axis of the building. Right in its centre he erected another two, joined together by an ingenious artifice: a ventilating shaft, with large rectangular outlets on the E and W in its upper part, it was a chimney-like channel, open to the sky. The whole feature, consisting of two piers linked by the shaft, had the semblance of a massive wall. It filled almost the whole width of the central nave, leaving only a narrow passage on each side. (Fig. 2.17 & Pl. 2.13.)

The piers flanking the shaft were almost identical to those between the central nave and the side aisles. Opposite them four more piers were erected in pairs – one near the *qibla*, the other near the west gate. They thus outlined the two rectangular central bays of the mosque. In this way the grid of eight twin *bakan gizos* with their respective supports was created, and the frame for the two central domes made complete.

The E–W *bakan gizos* had the same, slightly horseshoe shape as the N–S ones. They crossed each other just under the apex of the *tuluwa*, but somewhat below, thus forming quadrilateral panels in the centre of each bay. The corbelled structure of the *twin bakuna* was obviously helpful in such an arrangement, but its execution required great skill. Undoubtedly it was considered no mean achievement by all the professionals concerned. Perhaps to emphasise this, both apex panels were accentuated by special refinements: trellises of decorative ribs (Pl. 2.7.).

Both aisles of the mosque were almost identical in design. Their basic elements were the same as in the central nave – actually a continuation of the N–S *bakan gizos*, which in their twin castings ran the whole width of the building. However, the spatial composition of the nave and of the aisles was entirely different.

Each of the aisles was divided into two bays, but instead of the massive double-pier-block on the N–S axis, each was divided by a single pillar; (Pls. 2.9 & 2.10). Similar pillars delimited the edges of the E and W bays. Their appearance was if anything even more picturesque than the central nave.

[9] *Sahu* means literally 'a row', which seems to indicate, as often happens in Hausa builders' vocabulary, the compositional function of every item in the design.

Pl.2.7. ZARIA. Masallaci Juma'a. Decorative panel in one of the central bays.

Full use was made of the structural possibilities of the *bakuna*. The central pillar supported four *bakuna*, springing at a height of 1.80m. and each supported on a short horizontal bracket (*dungu*). This resembled the method customary in Sokoto, where a base for each *bakuna* was made from crossed *azaras*. It is worth noting that it was introduced by Mallam Mikhaila at the same time as the horseshoe *bakan gizos* in the central nave.

The curvatures of the *bakuna* were skilfully adapted to compositional necessities. The E–W corbels, called *maburgi* in this arrangement, joined the apexes of the twin N–S *bakuna* and their radii were therefore about equal. The E–W *bakuna* had a different purpose both structurally and sculpturally. Their span was about half that of the main *bakan gizos* and their apexes were proportionately lower. In the W aisle, where the ratio was almost exactly $\frac{1}{3}$ to $\frac{2}{3}$, the wall erected above the *bakuna* was lightened by three windows, the transoms of which supported the *azaras* of the *rufi*.

The superstructure of all the *bakan gizos* was used to reduce the span of the *rufi*'s coffering. This was done by projecting the upper parts of all the external and internal walls inwards. First, layers (*denni*) of *azaras* were laid between the two *bakan gizos*, projecting from the wall below. The 180 cm. length (nearly 6ft.) known to be a reliable span for *azara* timber, was never exceeded. Another layer of short *azaras* was laid on top of this, at right angles to the wall. Thus a bracket was formed which supported the upper layer of slightly

battered masonry, up to where the next bracket provided a further protrusion (Figs.2.16 & 2.17.)

Except for the two central panels of the main nave, the remaining coffers were filled with *azaras*, usually in one of two ways.[11] The simple way was by laying *azaras* parallel and close together. A more elaborate method was to fit triangles (*alwatika*) of *azaras* into the corners of the rectangular panels. Further layers (*tauyi*) of *azaras*, running E–W, were placed on top of these. The procedure was repeated several times, and this increased the convexity of the domes.

The six bays were flanked on the E and W by narrow passages. It was there that the external supports of the two central lines of stanchions were placed: four cylindrical columns.

The *qibla* wall of the E passage had a wide decorated portal to the *mihrab* with an entrance to an antechamber on the N and further access to the Emir's palace. At the other end of the central axis there was the main door, for men only. In the S corner of the W wall an outer flight of steps, *babban matakali*, led to a small platform from which the evening call for prayers (*magariba*) was chanted.

There were six doorways in the N wall and four in the S, providing good cross ventilation and sufficient lighting of the interior.

[10] Cf. paragraph on flat roofs.

Pl.2.8. ZARIA. Masallaci Juma'a. View of the central bay looking North.

Pl.2.9. ZARIA. Masallaci Juma'a. The North aisle.

Pl.2.10. ZARIA. Masallaci Juma'a. The North aisle.

Pl.2.11. ZARIA. Masallaci Juma'a. Pilaster. Detail.

Pl.2.12. ZARIA. Masallaci Juma'a. West central bay, looking East.

Pl.2.13. ZARIA.
Masallaci Juma'a. The vent-
ilating shaft between the West
and the East central bays.

Pls.2.14 and 2.15. ZARIA. Masallaci Juma'a. Pillars.

The spatial merits of the Masallaci in themselves made it an outstanding architectural monument. The exterior displayed only its monumental forms. Inside, the same merits were enriched by bold and imaginative decoration moulded in plaster.

At the same time care was obviously taken to ensure that the surface embellishment should not distract attention from the architectural qualities of the building. If anything, it emphasised the structural values of the design. In accordance with strict Muslim principles, human and animal images were prohibited as decorative subjects and only geometrical motifs provided themes for a variety of patterns. Another characteristic

of Mikhaila's decoration was the three-dimensional, almost sculptural quality.[11] Most of the decorations were made by superimposing several layers of patterns and the resulting reliefs, not a linear treatment, determined the design (Pls. 2.14 & 2.15).

The central pillars of the aisles had a square outline and the corners were profiled with vertical incisions, while the central parts were moulded concave (Pl. 2.9). The variety of other patterns, as shown in the photographs, proved that the severe

[11] A similar approach was independently used in the distant country of Nupe. (See Volume II Chapter 3).

Pls.2.16 and 2.17. ZARIA. Masallaci Juma'a. Pillars.

limits imposed on the artist's imagination did not impoverish the final effect.

To emphasise the architectural importance of the *bakan gizos* they were embellished in a particular way: their soffits were profiled, chevron-like (Pl. 2.10.).

The sculptural character of the decoration of the Masallaci and the multitude of variously lighted surfaces was originally enhanced by a slightly glittering coating made from a thin solution of powdered mica. This was used in a most discreet way and deserves comment for at least two reasons. First, it was characteristic of Gwani Mikhaila's restrained approach to the problem of adornment. Secondly, by 1960 only a few remaining traces permitted appreciation of the excellent handiwork; they disappeared completely a few years afterwards. What is hardly noticeable in some of the photographs is that the flat surfaces were intagliated herringbone fashion with the fingertips in the wet plaster. When this hardened, it was painted with mica solution and left to dry. Only then was the final, masterly touch given to the surface. It was gently scratched so that the glittering mica was rubbed off the edges of the incised patterns, leaving a delicate brownish-red network on the silvery background.

Pl.2.18. ZARIA. Masallaci Juma'a. The south haraba and zaure kudu (South gate).

The courtyard, *haraba* surrounding the Masallaci, was entered through three gatehouses. They were orientated and named accordingly: *zaure yamma* (western);[12] *arewa* (northern), and *kudu* (southern). There were four more gateways, mere gaps in the perimeter wall, called *kofar taimoko* (assisting gates). All the *zauruka* were roofed with a flat, corniced terrace with an external flight of steps for the *ladan* to call for daily prayers (Pl. 2.20). The doors of the *zauruka* were always set so as to prevent a view into the *haraba*. Each *zaure* contained a number of large water pots (*randan rua*) for ritual ablutions (*alwala*).

The NE corner of the *haraba* was filled by the large block of the *Kafin Lema Shari'a* court. It was linked to the mosque by a rectangular antechamber and a small passage, which permitted claimants to enter the mosque and swear to the truth of their case. (Pl. 2.19.).

The planning of the court building itself was purposeful,

with its functional system of communicating doors and passages. The main hall, appropriately for a place of judgement, was very impressive yet severe. Its interior, almost 7 metres high, was lit by a few narrow slits at the top of the walls. A very elaborate *daurin guga*, cross arched roof, was composed of six *bakan gizos*, i.e. of twelve corbelled *kafar guga*, half *bakan gizos*. The *kafar gugas* sprang from rectangular piers at floor level; they were set radially towards the centre and were profiled in the same way as the piers of the mosque – not unlike modern T-shaped steel beams. The apex of the *daurin guga* was decorated with a circular boss, projecting in a few stepped circles and linked by triangles on the vault-ribs which created a starlike pattern.

[12] *Zaure yamma*, the main gatehouse, was as a rule used by men only, but on Fridays old women and widows were permitted to say their prayers there, and occasionally also in the *haraba* (Informant: Mallam Jibirilu, Sarkin Gwarin Masallaci).

Pl.2.19. ZARIA. Masallaci Juma'a. The North haraba, *showing the* mihrab *on the left with the* Shari'a *court in the background.*

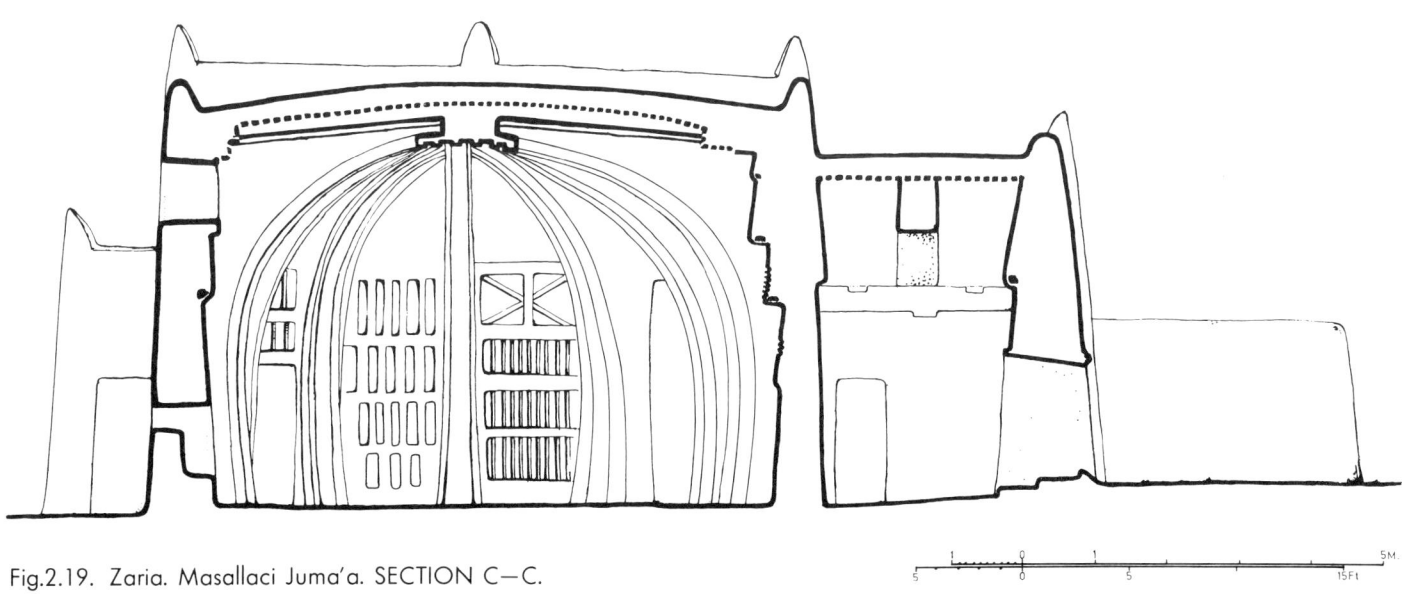

Fig.2.19. Zaria. Masallaci Juma'a. SECTION C—C.

Pl.2.20. ZARIA. Masallaci Juma'a. The East haraba

The planning of the court's interior was carefully devised. A U-shaped corridor provided the Emir with passage from his palace to the E part of the courtroom; nearby the *Sarki's* throne against a partition wall was the seat for the chief judge, *Babban Alkali*. Behind this, screened by a massive partition grille, was a place reserved for women; they entered from the E *haraba* through the antechamber, as far as possible from the male attendants. By the centre of the S wall, between two piers, sat the court scribes (*maga takarda*). In the SW corner of the room a screened passage led to the entrance for the witnesses and attendants. The accused stood in the NW corner of the room, far from the doors.

As mentioned before, the authorship of the *shari'a* cannot be firmly established. Undoubtedly it did possess all the characteristics of Babban Gwani Mikhaila's artistry: design competence and structural mastery. If not the personal achievement of the old Master, then it was proof of his influence, exercised on his sons and descendants.

It is a real disaster for Nigerian culture that the Zaria Masallaci Juma'a, a great monument of Nigerian architecture, was partially razed to the ground, and what remained of it encased in cement blocks, altering it out of all recognition. It is to be hoped that the above paragraphs, the excellent

measured drawings in Professor J.C. Moughtin's article in *Savannah*,[13] and numerous survey drawings and photographs in the archives of the Federal Department of Antiquities, will serve not only to document the past, but as an inducement to creative thinking by Nigerian architects of the present day.[14]

[13] J C Moughtin, 'The Friday Mosque, Zaria City', *Savanna*, Vol I, no 2, December 1972, pp. 144, 144A. See also sketch by J C Moughtin of 'roof vaulting plan' in Geoffrey J William's 'The Juma'a (Friday) Mosque, Zaria City, *Savanna*, Vol I, no 1, June 1972, p. 104.

[14] On the basis of the comprehensive survey of the Zaria mosque, made in 1961, 1962 and 1963, I projected an exact copy of the mosque, the *haraban* and the courthouse as one of the main features of the Museum of Traditional Nigerian Architecture in Jos. Following accepted practice in the preservation of ancient monuments, I decided to strengthen the traditional structure with a reinforced concrete frame and R.C. shell domes, all covered with traditional materials: loam and *azara* timber. *Azaras* were also to be used as an intermediate layer over the concrete columns and beams in order to insulate materials having different rates of expansion. An elaborate design for the R.C. framework was made by Professor S Oleszkiewicz, Head of the Department of Civil Engineering, Ahmadu Bello University, Zaria. In 1972 deep foundations for the main hall, the perimeter wall and the N and S *zauruka* were completed. In 1974 Alhaji Baba Galadima, the Principal Superintendent of Monuments, who took over the management of MOTNA from me, supervised the erection of the courthouse. Lack of funds stopped the work, but it was resumed recently.

Pl.2.21. ZARIA. Masallaci Juma'a. The Shari'a *court, seen from the North East.*

Kafin Madaki
Mosque

Fig.2.20. Kafin Madaki Mosque. PLAN.

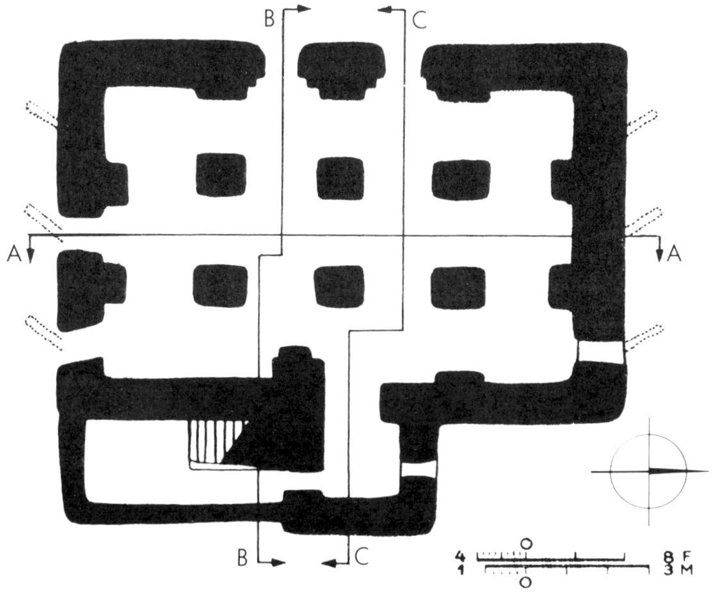

The town of Kafin Madaki was erected some 45 km. N of Bauchi on the orders of Ibrahim (1845–77), second Emir of Bauchi. The walled town, founded by Ibrahim's madaki,[15] who was named Abdulkadir (d. 1897), was to provide defence (*zaman ribatsi*) against the inroads of the Ningi.[16]

According to Department of Antiquities' records, the mosque was erected in 1859, the first monumental building of the new town, a year before the magnificent residence of the Madaki was begun nearby.[17]

In 1958 the mosque complex consisted of two parts – the mosque itself built in loam and timber, and the forecourt on its W side, the *haraba*; it had a solid fence of loam and was partly covered with a flat trellis-like roof, a rather unusual variation of a standard component.

The mosque consisted of a rectangular room with a flat roof supported on three pairs of stout pillars which divided the interior into three aisles running NW and facing the deep annex of the *mihrab* at the centre of the *qibla*, the E wall. There were two doors in the W wall of the building, giving access to the passages between the NS lines of pillars, and two doors in the S wall, on the axes of the E and central naves. The *mihrab* as usual projected in its entirety beyond the E wall of the building, but the projection was further expanded towards the

S by a small walled courtyard approched from the *mihrab* and containing steps leading to its roof-platform, for the *ladan*.

The structure of the pillars conformed to the well-known *al amudi mai tabarya* type, whose capitals, extending about 5 cm. on all four sides, were made from consecutive layers of short *azaras*. The *alamudai* carried brackets, once again laid crosswise, but extending about 30 cm. further out, called *gemu*. On top of these came a rectangular, horizontal frame of beams, *tauyi*, containing six *azaras* each. The *tauyi* were further supported by brackets in the W and E walls, and by two pairs of pilasters on the N and S walls. This frame supported the ceiling, *damatsa*, an arrangement of parallel *azaras* set closely together. This was the bottom part of a rather elaborate flat roof system.

---

[15] *Madaki*, an important official title and office, second or third in order of precedence to the *Sarki* (Emir): Revd G P Bargery, *A Hausa-English Dictionary*, Oxford University Press, 1934.

[16] Hogben and Kirk-Greene, *The Emirates of Northern Nigeria*, Oxford University Press, London 1966, p. 461.

[17] Mallam Ahmadu Jermai, Sarkin Gini Madaki, told me in January 1964 that as a young man of 22 he assisted in 1894 with some work on the mosque. I personally witnessed a thorough overhaul of the masallaci's roof construction in 1958.

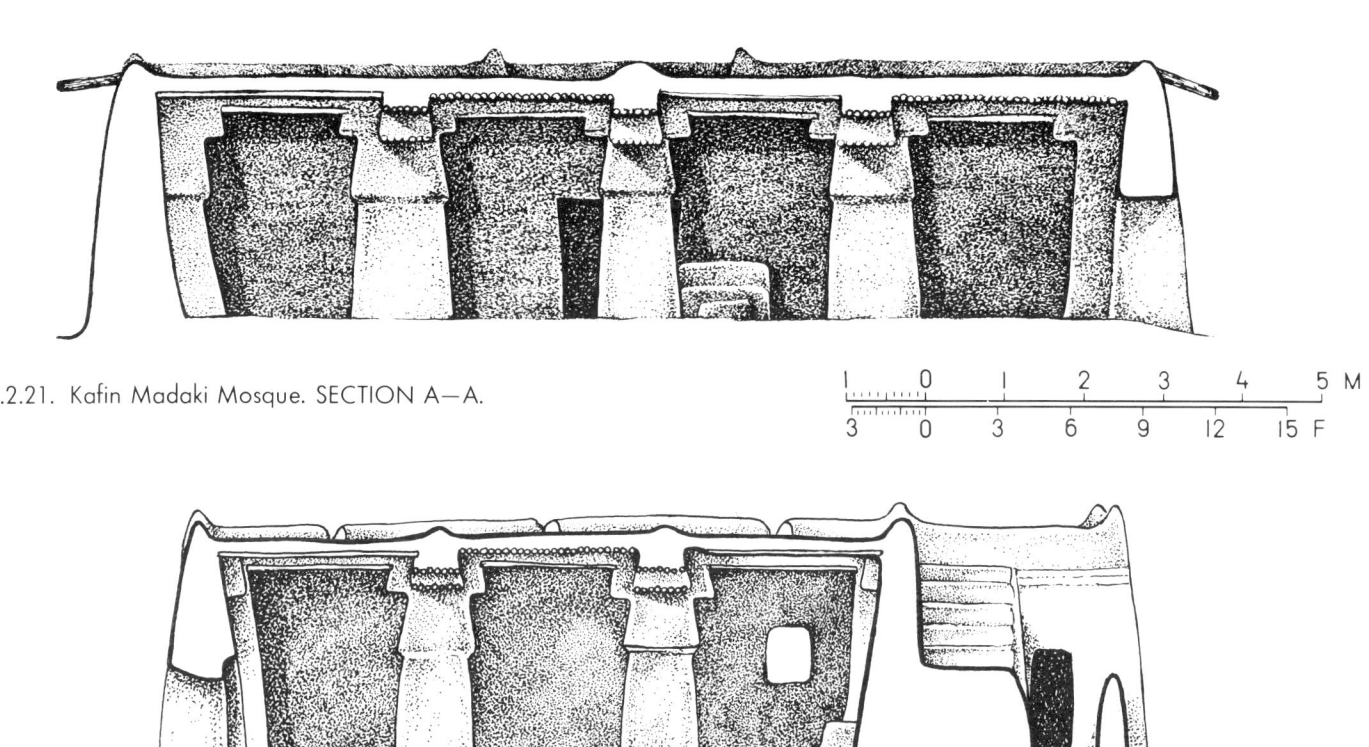

Fig.2.21. Kafin Madaki Mosque. SECTION A—A.

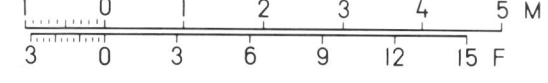

Fig.2.22. Kafin Madaki Mosque. SECTION B—B.

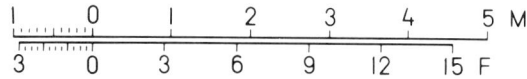

Fig.2.23. Kafin Madaki Mosque. SECTION C—C.

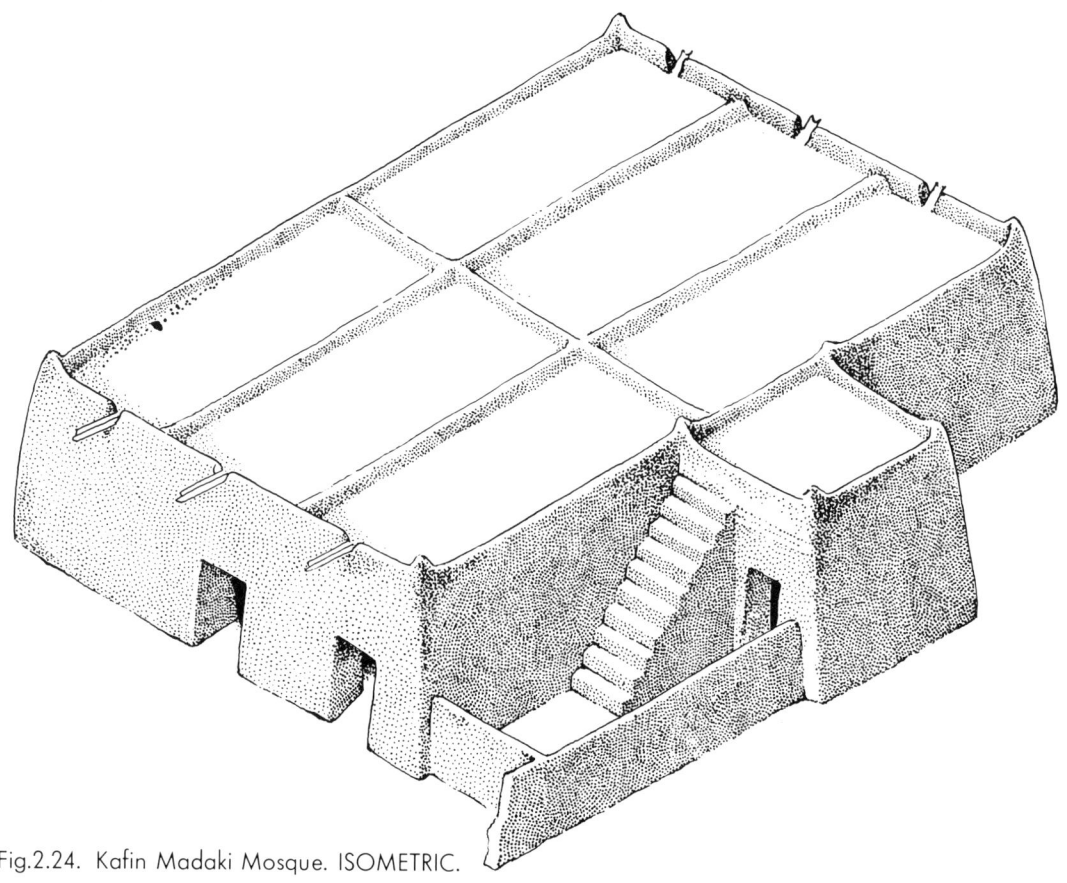

Fig.2.24. Kafin Madaki Mosque. ISOMETRIC.

The *azaras* in each of the twelve ceiling bays were arranged in a chequered pattern. This having been done further layers of plaster were moulded on top of the *tauyi*, covering the edges of the ceiling panels. Next, *zana* mats were laid inside the rectangles thus created; the mats prevented the loam that was spread on them (to a thickness of about 3 cm.) from penetrating between the *azaras* of the ceiling. (Fig.1.10., Pl.1.58.) When hardened the loam was covered with another layer, of wood ash, (*toka*) to a depth of between 30 and 60 cm. (500 baskets of *toka* were used for the purpose). On top of the ash, laterite (*marmara*) was spread in a layer about 10 cm. thick. This, when thoroughly wetted, pounded and soaked, with *makuba* liquid, provided a waterproof seal over the heat-insulating layer of ash.[18]

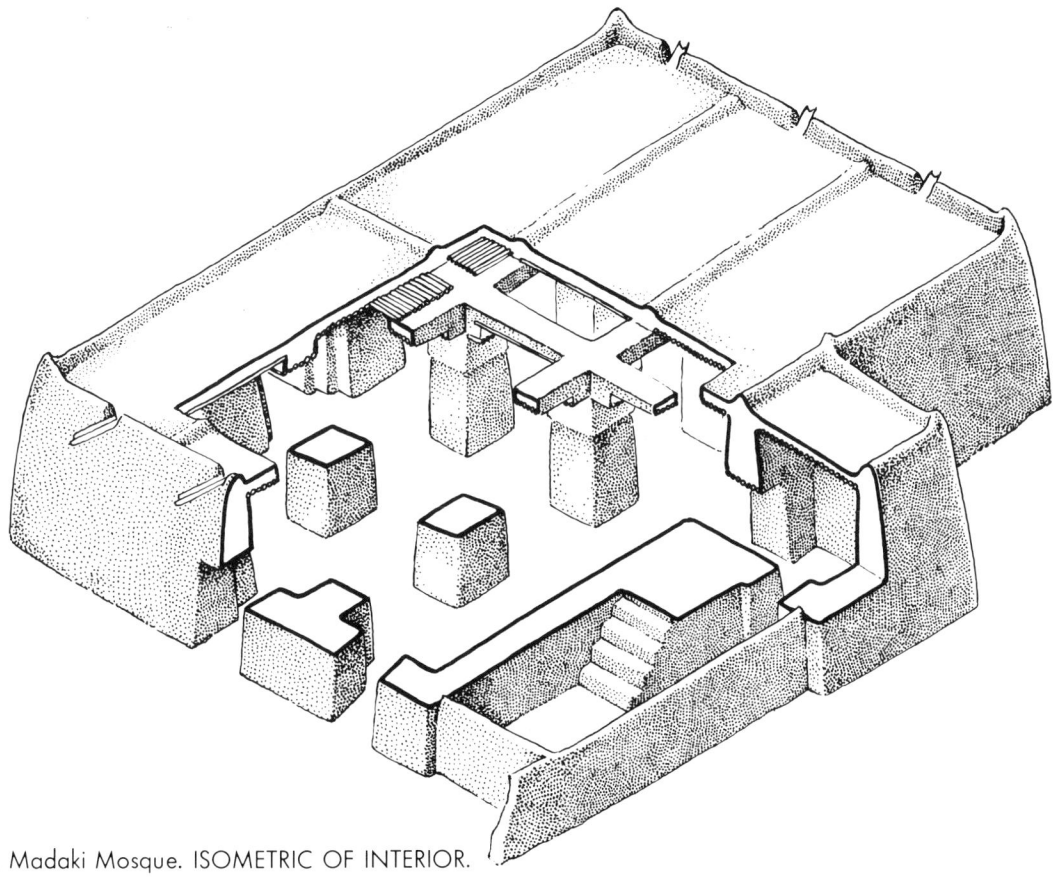

Fig.2.25. Kafin Madaki Mosque. ISOMETRIC OF INTERIOR.

The courtyard, *haraba*, had clay walls on three sides, and was covered on its W side with a pergola-like, flat roof of *zana* mats. It was supported by four rows of forked posts, eight in each row. These carried a grid of two superimposed layers of branches, crossed above each post and running EW and NS respectively. The posts were about twice as high as the perimeter wall, and the mats overhung the edges of the grid, reaching down to the top of the walls on the N, W and S, and leaving the E side open towards the masallaci. A number of beautiful large palm trees provided additional shaded areas within the *haraba*.

[18] Dept of Antiquities File T F 128/C5B.

Pl.2.22. KAFIN MADAKI. View of the mosque.

Pl.2.23. KAFIN MADAKI. The mosque in 1958, when the roof was reconstructed.

Pl.2.24. KAFIN MADAKI. Roof azaras *prior to plastering.*

Gurin
Julurde Jambare

Gurin, which was established at the beginning of the nineteenth century, for twenty years headquarters of the Fulani kingdom of Adamawa. It houses a masallaci unique in its construction and spatial composition. Generally, it could be classified within a group of open-space, roofless praying grounds, which are fairly common all over the Muslim countries (another example is the revered Ilorin Masallaci Danni). Among these, the Gurin Masallaci was outstanding in size, building material and structure. Its most impressive characteristic, however, was the almost ritualistic organisation of its maintenance. This, to my knowledge, was unequalled by any religious building in Nigeria.

The plan of the complex, a much elongated rectangle, was based as was customary on a short EW axis with the *mimbar* (*mihrab*) at the centre of the *qibla* side. Four doorways lead to the interior: *damugal woila* on the north, *damugal fombina* on the south and two symmetrically placed doorways in the

western, *hirange*, wall. The mosque is surrounded on the E, W and S by an outer, U-shaped courtyard, entered from the east on both sides of the Masallaci. There is still another entrance to the courtyard, at the W side of its northern fence, leading to a trellis-roofed rectangular stall: *danki jodugo* (stall for sitting), reserved for religious meetings of the senior members of the community. At the N end of the W wall a number of water pots were placed for ritual ablutions (Pl. 2.28.)

The mosque itself consisted of two parts. The main structure was covered with a flat roof, supported by a multitude of forked posts (*nopije*) made of rough studs of various timbers: *kojole, kulaje, kohe, kokobal* or *banwal* – the last one considered as the best. The *nopije* were arranged in long rows running N–S and divided the interior into a number of narrow aisles. These were covered with a network of two layers of crosswise laid joists, *gafe*, and these in turn were thickly covered with cornstalks (Pls. 2.25 & 2.27.)

Pl.2.25. GURIN. The sheltered central part of the mosque.

Pl.2.26. GURIN. The sheltered central part of the mosque.

To the W of this sheltered part of the *julurde* extended an open part of the complex. Shaped again as an elongated rectangle, it was about the same size as the former. Two doors were set by the ends of its western wall.

The structural method of the walls of the *julurde* could be considered as a development of popular, cornstalk walls of many northern cornstalk buildings. The distinction resulted from the size of the fabric and from the refined quality of craftsmanship.

The walls of the whole complex were made solely of cornstalks, set vertically and providing a screen of generous thickness. Perpendicular stalks were stabilized by three rows of twin horizontal belts. Each belt contained about twelve cornstalks, fastened in long bunches with *balami* cords. Three pairs of such twin belts, tightened together across the verticals, strengthened the lower half of the wall; the upper remained erect by itself.

Pl.2.27.GURIN. Detail showing the rows of forked posts and their roofing.

Pl.2.28. GURIN. Ablution pots against the West wall of the courtyard.

Pl.2.29. GURIN. Doorway with its high jambs.

The doorways were accentuated with jambs, each made of clusters of several dozen cornstalks, rising considerably above the crown of the walls (Pl. 2.29). In order to embellish the entrance, but also to strengthen the jambs, they were fastened with several coils of neatly-folded cords held together, chevron fashion, with diagonal bindings. (Pl. 2.30)

The remarkable feature concerning the mosque, apart from its architectural value, was the method and organisation of its maintenance. Obviously this was determined by the fragility of materials used, but also by punctillious Muslim custom. The whole cornstalk construction was entirely rebuilt every year. To achieve this, the *wakili* (district head) gave orders to all his people to collect the best of their cornstalks for the yearly reconstruction. The collection was usually completed in January, and in May the seasoned material was used for the restoration. The best craftsmen were employed to fulfil the task – to keep the *julurde jumbare* a proper expression of the community's devotion and of its local pride.

Pl.2.30. GURIN. Detail of door jamb.

Pls.2.31 and 2.32. GURIN. Details showing construction of walls.

Ilorin
Masallaci Juma'a

The main mosque of Ilorin, called the Friday Mosque, is also called Masallaci Jimoh.[19] It was erected some time before the last decade of the 19th century, since, according to information provided by the *imam*, it was already enlarged at this time with a spacious *haraba* on its W side. The original grass-thatched roof was replaced in 1932 with corrugated iron sheets. The building was surveyed in December 1962.

The plan of the mosque had rather unusual proportions – two rows of pillars, fifteen in each row, divided the interior into three long aisles running N–S. Each aisle contained sixteen roughly square bays covered with flat timber ceilings. On the axis of the central pair of pillars stood the *mihrab*; it occupied the width of almost two bays, and, as usual, formed a recess in the E wall. Immediately to the S of it a door led to the E aisle; it served the Emir, who had the place of honour in front of the *mihrab*.

The unusual proportions of the much elongated interior created compositional possibilities that were exploited by the architects with truly artistic skill. The view along each aisle, which had sixteen bays, each separated vertically by a frame formed by the floors, walls, pillars and ceilings, and visually reduced by the depth of perspective, made a striking impression on the onlooker (Pl. 2.33). This was further enhanced by the consummate composition of the vertical framing of each consecutive bay. The pillars of the two central rows had a restrained decoration – their only unusual feature was a fairly sharp tapering. But the imaginative system supporting the ceiling provided the Ilorin Masallaci with a particular architectural valour unique in this group of Nigerian buildings.

[19] Jimo is a name given to a girl born on Friday (G B Bargery, *op cit.* p. 503).

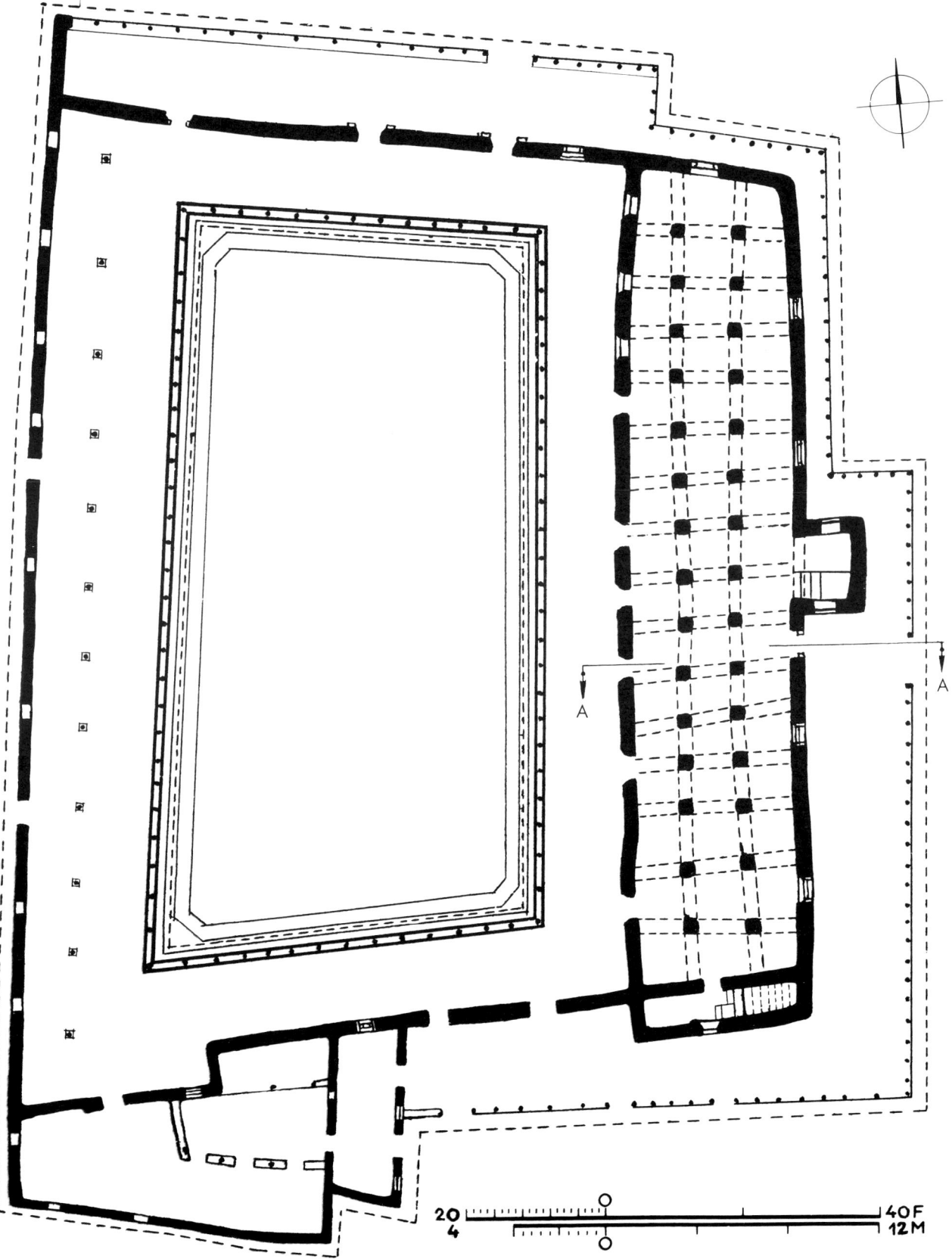

Fig.2.26. Ilorin. Masallaci Juma'a. PLAN.

Pl.2.33. ILORIN. Masallaci Juma'a. View North along the length of the West aisle.

Pl.2.34. ILORIN. Masallaci Juma'a. Detail of the roof construction in the West aisle.

Fig.2.27. Ilorin. Masallaci Juma'a. SECTION A—A.

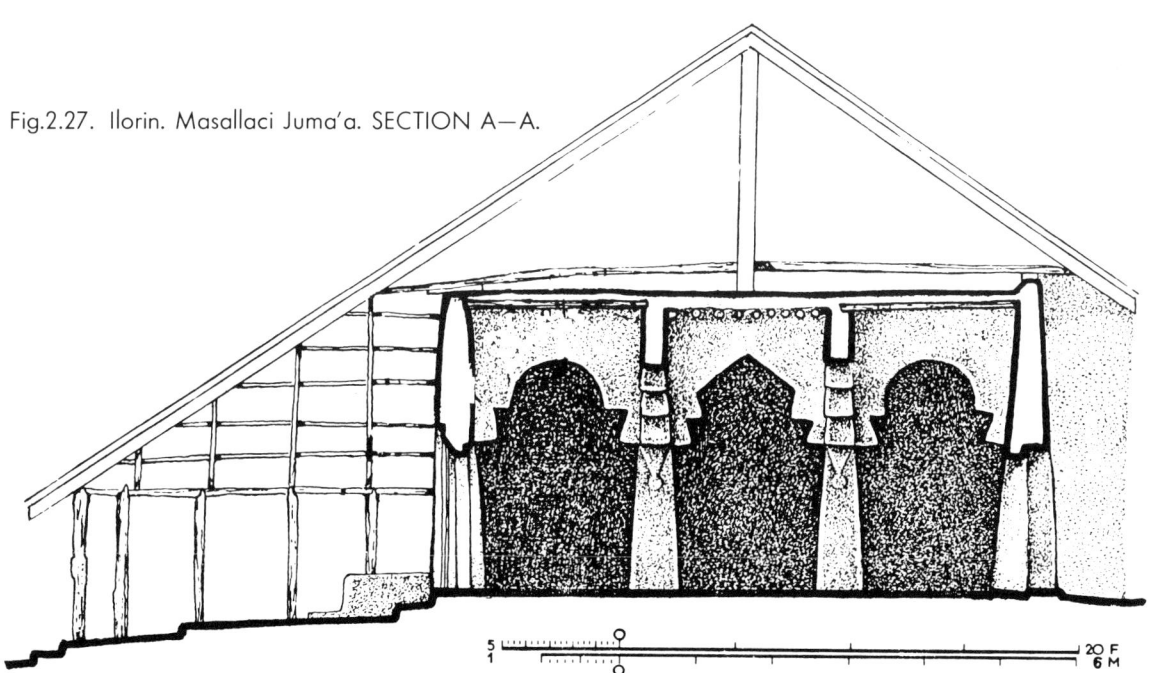

Pl.2.35. ILORIN. Masallaci Juma'a. Interior, looking South East from the central aisle.

Pl.2.36. ILORIN. Masallaci Juma'a. Interior, looking towards the mihrab.

First of all, the two NW rows of pillars were linked at the top by beams, each supported on three equidistant, stepped brackets (Pl. 2.34). This in itself considerably enriched the upper part of the interior. The SE lines of pillars were linked in a more diversified and therefore more sophisticated way. The four pairs of pillars on the south and seven pairs on the north end were bound together with horizontal beams supported on simple brackets at each end, the brackets resting on the walls and on the respective pillars. The remaining four pillars in the proximity of the *mihrab* were richly moulded. The side aisles were provided with semicircular, bracketed *bakuna*, the central aisle with a triangular, rafter-like system of supports. Both devices supported girders running E–W and carrying the uppermost slabs of masonry and the ceiling joists. The latter were not of *azara* but of stout, fairly straight rods of timber, and were laid at a distance roughly equal to their diameter. They were covered with patterned mats. The joists over the central aisle were all laid from N to S, and over the side aisles from E to W. The joists over the mihrab were laid herringbone fashion, the sharp points directed E. By the S wall of the

mihrab there was the usual short flight of steps leading to a little rostrum for the Imam. Another flight of steps, separated by a partition wall, was erected at the S end of the building; it provided access to a small platform which served for a minaret.

The roof construction seen in 1962 was corrugated iron sheets, and was obviously the successor to the original.

Since the bays were not very spacious, being about 180 cm. square, and the profiles of the *bakuna* were massive, their appearance from below, with the sharp contrast of light and shadow on their multi-angled surfaces, provided a magnificent display of three-dimensional composition(Pl. 2.37.) The interior was lit by nine doors in the W wall; they were placed irrespective of the position of the inner pillars, and consequently some of the *bakuna* overhung the lintels of the doors.

Compared with the magnificent architectural interior, the remaining parts of the Masallaci were rather an anticlimax; except, perhaps, for the size of the *haraba*. Like the mosque itself, the *haraba* did not resemble the typical Fulani plan. It consisted of a very large enclosure, slightly trapezoidal in

Pl.2.37. ILORIN. Masallaci Juma'a. Part of the West aisle , looking North East.

*Pls.2.38 and 2.39. ILORIN.
Masallaci Juma'a. East and West
verandahs respectively of the
mosque courtyard.*

shape, whose narrower side ran the whole length of the mosque. It was surrounded with a clay wall on the N, S and W; the W wall contained two doors and eight windows with decorative wooden grilles. There were also doors in the N curtain wall as well as in the S; the two doors in the SW corner gave access to the womens' room and ablution chamber, both of which were roofed over.

The enclosure had a lean-to roof on three sides – in front of the mosque and on the N and S. On the W side was a saddle roof with a much larger span, its ridge supported by a row of sturdy posts. Along the centre of the enclosure ran a row of beautiful trees. Thus the W façade of the mosque was sheltered by a roof forming part of the verandah which surrounded the large enclosure; all the remaining walls of the building had other outer verandahs of various forms serving different purposes. On the E side there was a verandah covering the façade of the Masallaci; it was fairly wide from the *mihrab* towards the S, in the direction of the Emir's palace; N of the *mihrab* it narrowed to a passage of a mere 1.25m. or so, just giving access to the much wider verandah along the N wall of the great enclosure and sheltering the four doorways leading to the inner verandah. On the S side the outer verandah ran towards the roofed ablution chamber and women's room, as mentioned above.

The great W enclosure, both in size and character, was again a unique feature in a Nigerian mosque. It contained some of the characteristics of other *haraba*, but its spaciousness and the ornamentally elaborated windows in its otherwise blank surface had more in common with some of the magnificent examples in the Middle East.

Ilorin
Masallaci Katibi

This modern mosque, dating from 1934, was representative of a small group of similar and contemporary buildings. It combined in an interesting way the essential requirements imposed by religion with conditions imposed by the city environment, and, most important of all, it was an attempt to develop traditional forms as far as traditional technology permitted.

The building materials were all local. Building earth (*ama* or *oro*) was dug out in the vicinity of the site, after removal of a thin layer of topsoil. It was mixed with grass (*koriko*) and water, and used immediately for the erection of walls in layers of standard height and thickness. No foundations were built because the bearing capacity of the ground was considered sufficient. The roof sheets were laid on laths (*ira*) and rafters (*eke*) supported on wall plates (*iraile*) for which *ake ebo* wood was used for preference. The building was erected on sloping ground, so its platform changed height from a few centimetres to more than 70 centimetres.

The building formed a compact whole and had a rectangular plan; it was covered by a single roof of corrugated iron sheets. It was, in 1962, the achievement of two builders, both deceased at the time of the survey. The main interior of the mosque and the verandah, which was originally surrounded with simple loam pillars, were built by Mallam Bakare, who lived in a house named Ile Kura. His work was completed by Mallam Kuranga, who replaced the original pillars of the verandah with stout posts decoratively crowned with bulbous capitals, bearing some resemblance to the verandah of the Yoruba Afin Akure (c.f.Vol.II). It was covered with a very high entablature – if the word can be applied to a completely individual composition of structural elements, aiming at the effect of an almost traceried screen, which was decorative but sufficiently sturdy to carry the solid crown of the wall and the wall plate of an iron roof. The ways in which the main vertical pressures were concentrated along the axes of the pillars; the voids between the pillars which were relieved by tracery work

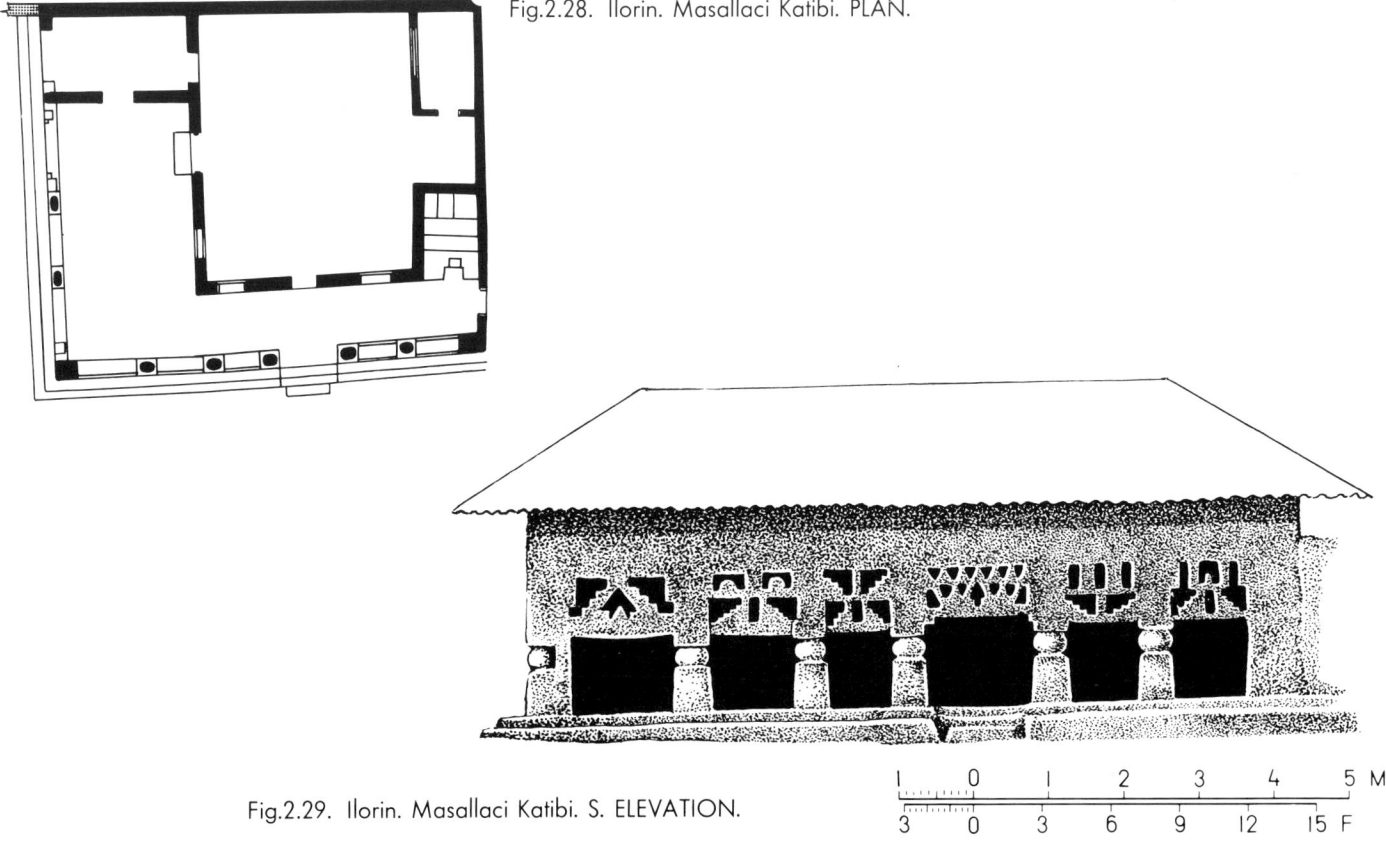

Fig.2.28. Ilorin. Masallaci Katibi. PLAN.

Fig.2.29. Ilorin. Masallaci Katibi. S. ELEVATION.

Pl.2.40. ILORIN. Masallaci Katibi. View of the mosque from the South West.

above; and the wooden framing of the tracery which directed the stresses towards the most resilient parts of the transome (*wakun*) below – all this proved Mallam Kuranga's complete mastery of structural craft. I was told that in the great archway, parts of the wooden frame were bent ('like a bow, *orun*'), using freshly-cut bamboo (*aparun*) from the river. (Pls. 2.40 & 2.41).

The main interior of the mosque, with the *mihrab* properly orientated, was enveloped by additional parts of the structure in the most economical way. There was a large verandah on its

Pl.2.41. ILORIN. Masallaci Katibi. The West facade.

W façade and a narrower one on the S – both uniform in general rhythm of composition, but varied in decorative detail. The wealth of decorative patterns and the excellent proportions of the generous archway of the front entrance, were beautifully accentuated by the contrast of their brightly-lit surfaces against the dark background of the anterior of the verandah. At the NW corner of the verandah there was an ablution chamber with three doors conveniently placed and a number of copper taps for running water.

Lagos
Masallatai

Pl.2.42. *LAGOS. Masallaci Olosun. The King Street facade.*

Pl.2.43. *LAGOS. Masallaci Olosun. The* mihrab.

The numerous mosques of Lagos form a distinct group of Muslim religious architecture. Late in the fifteenth century the city became one of the trading centres of Portuguese merchants, and in the mid-nineteenth century became a British colony. The Lagos mosques therefore reflect a Nigerian interpretation of foreign forms. They are strongly influenced by Brazilian, colonial versions of Portuguese architecture, and since most of them date from the late nineteenth century. British and Dutch motifs of the period are equally apparent.

Pl.2.44. LAGOS. Masallaci Juma'a. View looking North West.

Pl.2.45. LAGOS. Masallaci Juma'a. The South facade.

Pl.2.46. LAGOS. Masallaci Juma'a. The South end of the West facade.

Pl.2.47. LAGOS. Masallaci Juma'a. The North facade.

Wusasa
Roman Catholic Church

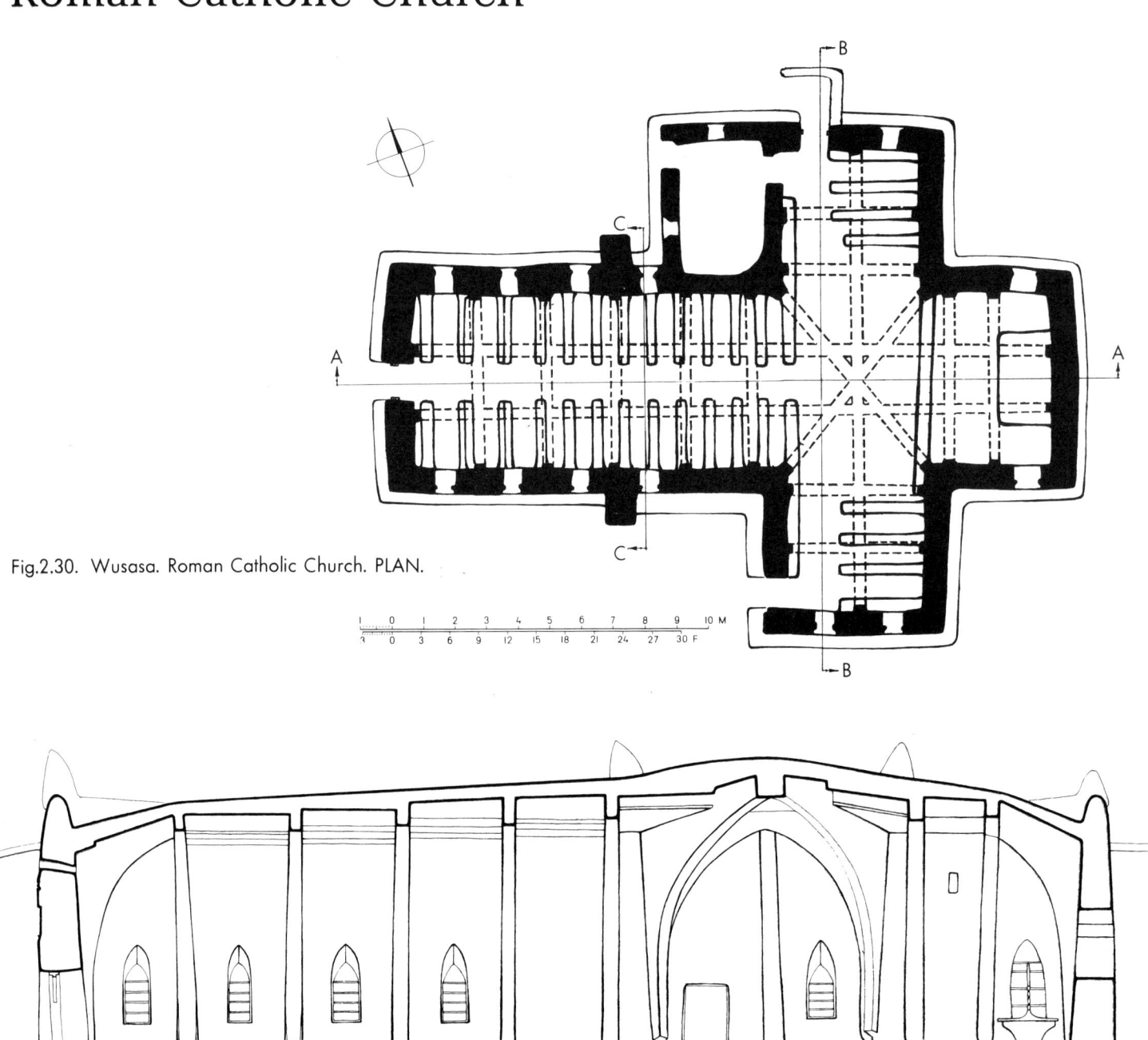

Fig.2.30. Wusasa. Roman Catholic Church. PLAN.

Fig.2.31. Wusasa. Roman Catholic Church. SECTION A—A.

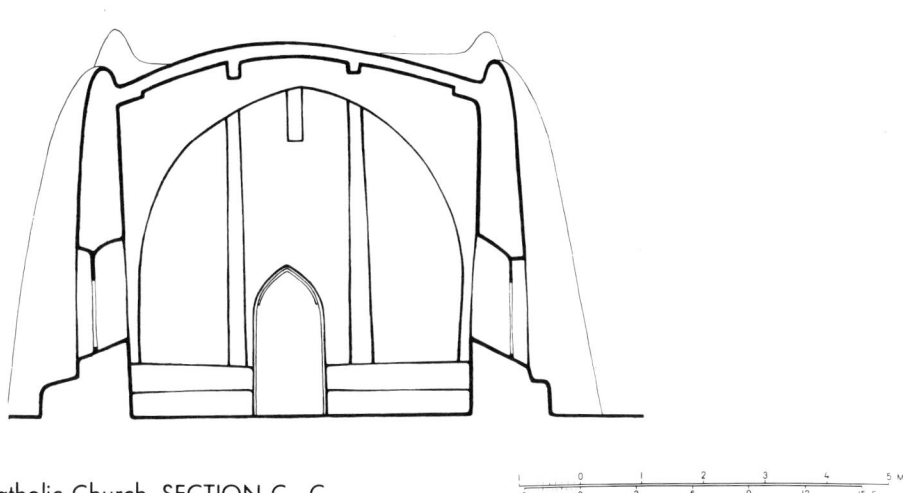

Fig.2.32. Wusasa. Roman Catholic Church. SECTION C—C.

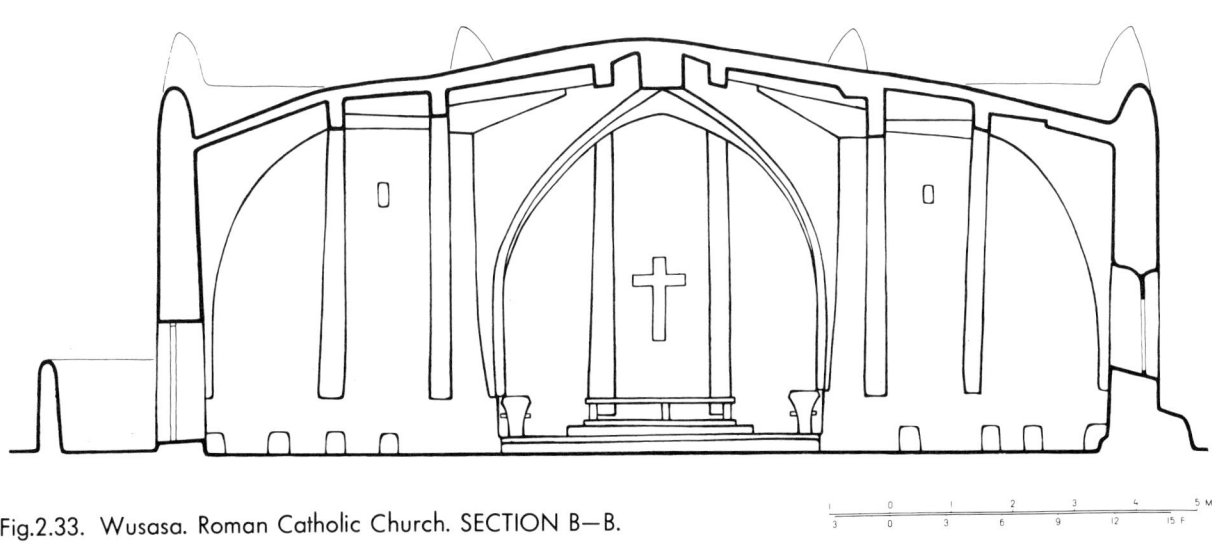

Fig.2.33. Wusasa. Roman Catholic Church. SECTION B—B.

Pl.2.48. WUSASA. Roman Catholic Church. Interior.

Pl.2.49. WUSASA. Roman Catholic Church. Exterior.

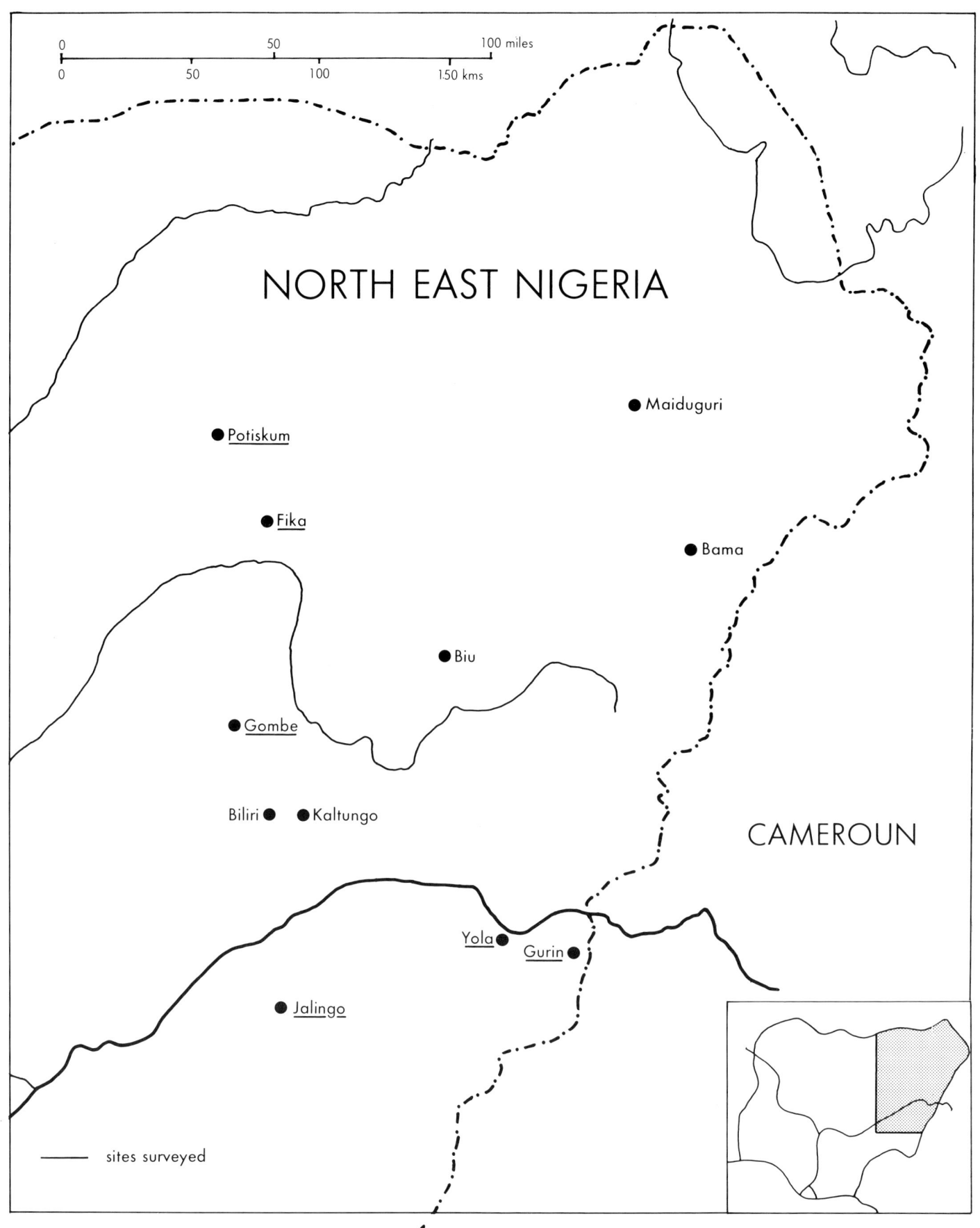

NORTH EAST NIGERIA

● Maiduguri

● Potiskum

● Fika

● Bama

● Biu

● Gombe

Biliri ● ● Kaltungo

CAMEROUN

Yola ● ● Gurin

● Jalingo

——— sites surveyed

SECULAR ARCHITECTURE OF NORTHERN NIGERIA

3 *Architecture of the North East*

Potiskum
Fika
Gombe
Jalingo
Yola

Pl.3.1. POTISKUM. Emir's Palace. Central bay of the kofar zaure.

Potiskum
Emir's Palace

Potiskum was founded by Bauya, Chief of the Ngizim people, and Moi (king) of Fika, on the site of an old Karekare town, captured previously by Bauya's grandfather.

The old town was built up with three types of hut:[1] *casta*, with cornstalk walls; *salam*, where walls were replaced by a screen of *salam* mats (*zana* in Hausa); these two had a roof frame made from cornstalks. The third type, called *riyak*, had a wooden roof frame. All three types were never plastered. The roof construction was based on a ring (*dinglis*) made of bundles of cornstalks bound together with a cord of bark from the *Apsawu* plant. *Dinglis* was supported by a circle of forked posts (*tika*) of *anum* or *hagda* wood. *Tapsar* grass was used for thatching; long mats of grass were bound with *gabiwa* (*rama* in Hausa) string. The mats were laid spirally from the eaves upward, and sewn to the roof frame with a thatching needle (*gizir*). A stick was inserted into the top of the roof frame and the uppermost layer of thatch-mats was fastened around it and tied with cord. On top of this a pot would be placed to waterproof the apex.

Among the cornstalk houses of the town only the ruler's residence was built with fireproof material: the house of Mai Agudum, Chief of the Ngizim. It had a most unusual structure. The walls were erected using pieces of broken pottery (*nguma*) placed in layers (*gina*) and plastered on both sides. Usually a new spread of plaster was applied every year, considerably increasing the thickness of the wall (Pl. 3.10).

When the Bolewa came to Potiskum from Fika, they introduced a new method of wall building, with layers of processed earth, roughly 30 centimetres thick and 45 centimetres high; though the thickness depended on the wealth of the owner. Finally, the Hausa type of structure was introduced.

In 1924, the Moi of Fika, Alhaji Muhammadu Ibu Idrissa, moved his headquarters to Potiskum, which became the administrative centre of the Fika emirate.[2]

The façade of the old palace was screened by new buildings and a tower, on the axis of which stood the original gatehouse (A) *kofar zaure*, facing W. (Fig. 3.2).

This rectangular building (*soro*) was over six metres high and was covered with a flat roof the outer surface of which was slightly convex to drain off the rainwater. A lofty internal frame supported the roof. The structure consisted of four stout, cylindrical pillars carrying a grid of horizontal beams (*molu*) forming the ceiling. Each pillar was divided into three sections of about the same height. The two lower ones, each slightly battered, formed the shaft of the pillar, and the uppermost, the capital. The beams linked the opposite walls and were supported by pillars with slight brackets; thus the ceiling was divided into nine bays. The central bay was the largest (Pl. 3.1). In order to reduce the span of each bay the corners were filled with triangles of *azaras*, laid diagonally. On top of them, parallel to the beams, were placed further layers of *azaras*.[3] On top of these in each ceiling bay were laid pairs of thick *azara* rods, at about 25 centimetre centres; their direction was changed in each bay. On top of these again, in herringbone pattern, were laid short sticks of wood, about 0.5 to 1 centimetre thick, and about 30 centimetres long. For these split pieces of *jar* wood were preferred; they were very hard and unpalatable to termites (*torom*).[4] A layer of building earth covered the *jar*, then a layer of ash was put down as insulation against heat and damp; and finally a waterproofed surface of building earth.

[1] Informants: Mallam Baba Galadima and the Emir's son, Mallam Maina Abali.
[2] The Emirate's population, due to numerous migrations, is heterogeneous. There are four major groups: the Bolewa, Ngamo, Karekare, Ngizim, and a number of other tribes. (J E Lavers, *The History and People of Fika Emirate*, New Nigerian Special Supplement, 23 December 1972.)
[3] This is a typical Hausa construction,
[4] This device was introduced from Fika, where besides the *Jar* wood, branches of a small bush plant called *Redde* were also used.

Pl.3.2. POTISKUM. Emir's Palace. The North door of Room F.

Pl.3.3. POTISKUM. Emir's Palace. View of Room F.

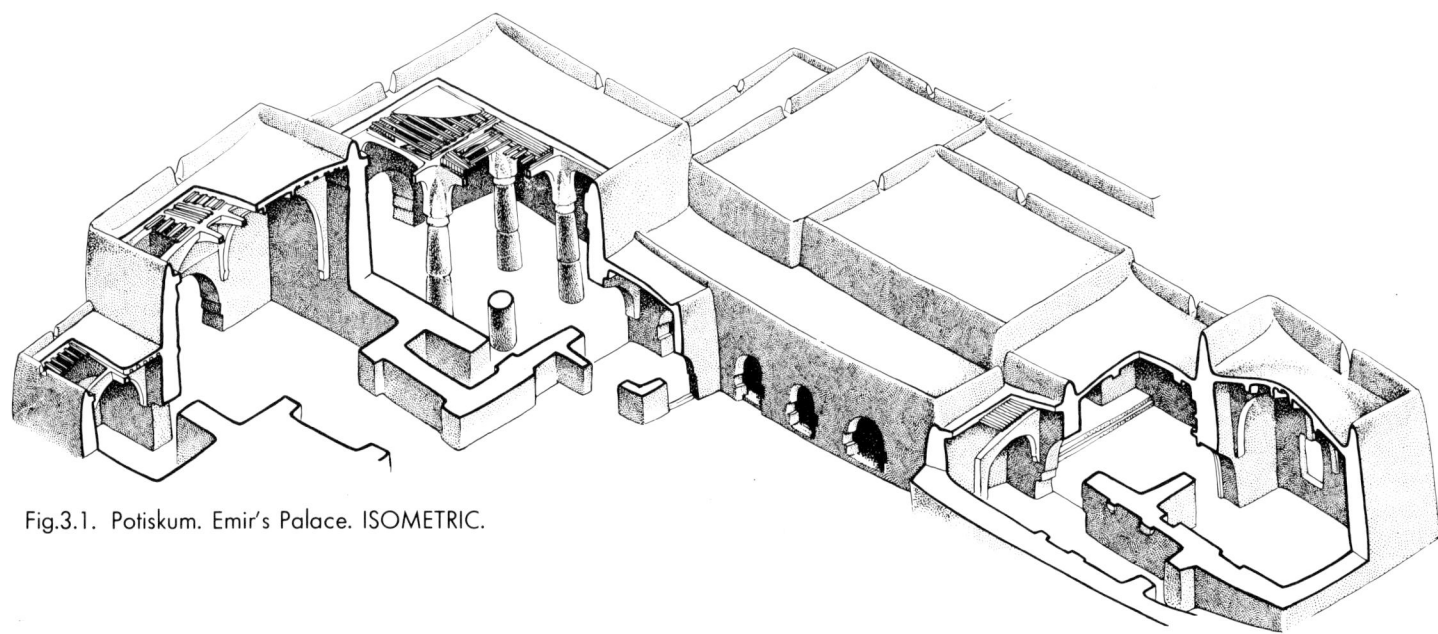

Fig.3.1. Potiskum. Emir's Palace. ISOMETRIC.

Opposite the main doorway there was a passage to a small square porch. It had four large openings, one on each side; they were arched and shaped in the particular style of Potiskum (Fig. 3.5). The opening to the N led into a narrow passage which linked a verandah (C) on the E and an antechamber (D) on the N which provided access to the main apartments of the palace. On its longitudinal (E-W) axis there was a row of three rooms. The first (E) was covered with a flat roof, with three longitudinal beams supported by three *bakan gizo*s and covered in a fashions similar to that in *kofar zaure* (Fig. 3.3). Three doors opened the room onto the outer verandah – the rectangular central door was flanked by two arched ones. The next room (F), had a *tulluwa* dome on a frame of four *bakan gizo*s; their soffits were profiled with a number of overlapping projections (Pl. 3.3). The large, arched doorway (Pl. 3.2), led to a small, narrow and rather dark room (G) with *bakuna* which had a rather unusual form, that of an almost pointed arch. The last room in this row (H) was the highest in the whole palace complex and had a dome supported on an elaborate grid of four corbelled *baka* half arches which sprang diagonally from the four corners of the room and perpendicularly from four points on each of the four walls, making ten *bakan gizo*s altogether.

In the NW corner of room (E) a doorway led to a square chamber (I), most of which was filled by a quarter-turn staircase going up to a small attic room (Pl. 3.8). A door under the second flight of steps led to a small cubicle (J) (Fig.3.4); and a door in the NE corner at the foot of the staircase opened on to a corridor leading E to the outside and to the door of the northernmost room of the palace (K). Here, two pairs of *bakuna* sprang from each of the opposite walls, forming nine panels in the domed roof. The most unusual feature of the palace was the fireplace, set in the centre of the N wall. It had a funnel topped by a chimney above the parapet crowning the walls of the room.

Pl.3.4. POTISKUM. Emir's Palace. View of kofar zaure.

Fig.3.2. Potiskum. Emir's Palace. PLAN.

Pl.3.5. POTISKUM. Emir's Palace. Interior view of kofar zaure.

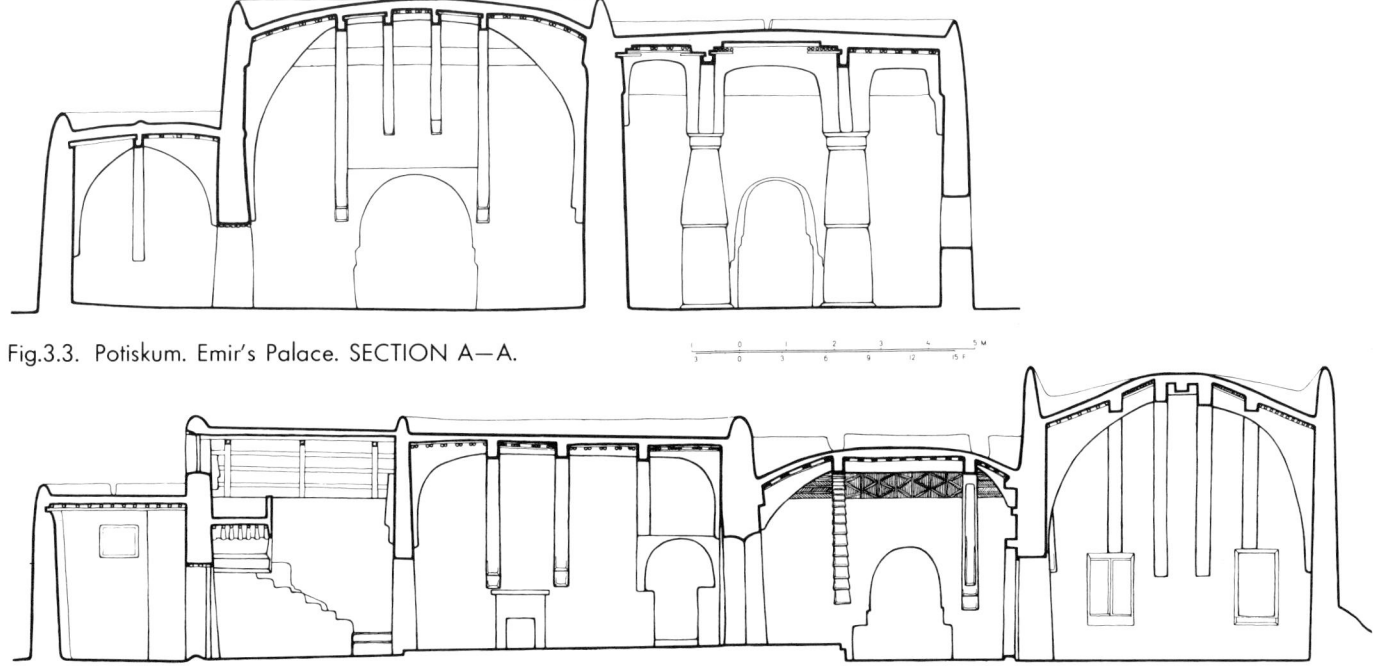

Fig.3.3. Potiskum. Emir's Palace. SECTION A—A.

Fig.3.4. Potiskum. Emir's Palace. SECTION B—B.

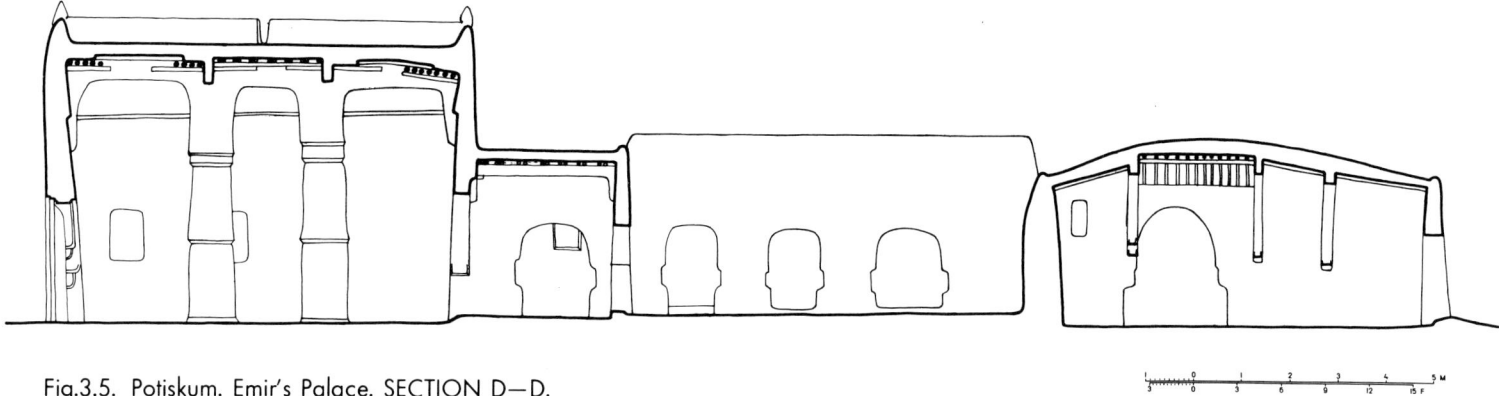

Fig.3.5. Potiskum. Emir's Palace. SECTION D—D.

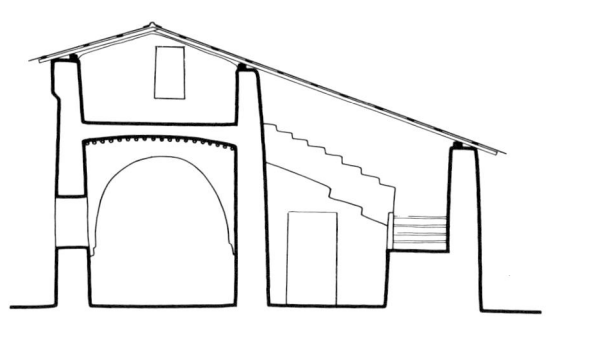

Fig.3.6. Potiskum. Emir's Palace. SECTION C—C.

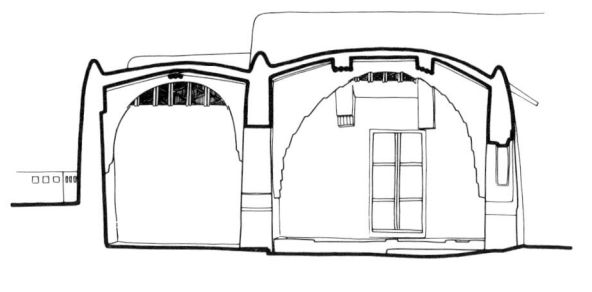

Fig.3.7, Potiskum. Emir's Palace. SECTION E—E,

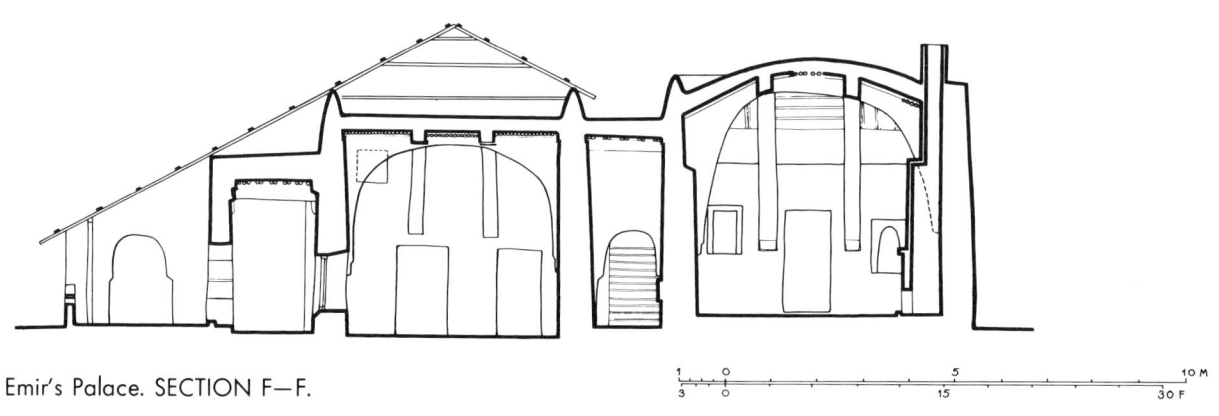

Fig.3.8. Potiskum. Emir's Palace. SECTION F—F.

Pl.3.6. POTISKUM. Emir's Palace. Room B.

Pl.3.8. POTISKUM. Emir's Palace. View of the stairs in Room I.

Pl.3.7. POTISKUM. Emir's Palace. Room E. (South wall).

Fika

The town of Fika is built around the Daniski Hills. The area was originally inhabited by the Ngamo people, but they were forced out by a group of Bolewa, who built themselves first a fortified settlement on the rocks, and then a new one below. A long line of rulers of Daniski, later known as Moi, was then established.

Early in the nineteenth century the Bolewa left Daniski and moved to Fika.[5] The settlement was surrounded by a walled suburb and the town itself had a very high wall with double ditches, wrote Dr Overweg, companion of Henry Barth.

The present writer visited Fika in May 1964, assisted by Mallam Baba Galadima. At this time little was left of the former palace of the Moi.

Mallam (later Alhaji) Baba Galadima and Mallam Maina Abali of Fika provided me with the information on which the following paragraph is based.

The massive city walls were called *ganua*. The Moi's palace was erected inside a rectangular perimeter wall during the reign of Moi Buraima (1805-1821). It was preceded by a large courtyard, *bayi*, where stood the houses of the servants, *jebbe*. The *bayi* was entered through a circular gatehouse. Nearby was a large boulder, on which the Emir sat when distributing arms to his subjects before they went to war. Next to *bayi* was *jura*, a courtyard for the Moi's old wives; when separated, they lived in small huts of their own.

The perimeter wall of the palace, *sandiram*, was entered through the gatehouse, *matira tinja*.[6] Outside the gate a pillar called *tubali* (not to be confused with Hausa tubali bricks) still stood. It was two metres high and was built with stones brought from Daniski. It served as a flogging post for convicted criminals.

Behind the *matira tinja* was the large front court of the palace, the *gafuya*. The palace itself, the *Pai Boni Moi*, was completely ruined in 1964 and only the remaining fragments of the structure permitted the location of two of the original interiors. The first *soro*, to the right of the main entrance door, was that of the *masaya*, the chief messenger of the Emir. The door leading to the *masaya*'s apartment had a very special design. It was a wide aperture, divided by a central post, which was circular, and tapered so strongly that it looked almost like a slender cone. On top of it, supported by two *azara* beams, a transom was mounted in loam; it was conical in section and probably carried the beams of the ceiling. This type of pillar was, I was told, typical of Bolewa buildings; its form was perhaps influenced by the Kanuri.

A door similar to the one described led to *soro minda*, the

room of the royal princes. When married, they moved to houses of their own.

The loam used in the palace was processed in a special way: to the usual mixture of building earth and water, honey was added – a special gift from the people of Gadaka village to the Moi.

All the rooms of the palace were completely dark and had to be lit with oil lamps. Ventilation was provided by narrow slits in the upper part of the walls.

Food was served according to the rank of courtiers, who ate in different groups in separate *soros*: for instance, the Madaki ate in the *matira tinja*.

Near the ruins of the palace a burial ground, *bei mbalu*, was founded, on the site of the former stables. The graves of the following rulers of the Bawa royal family were seen there: Moi Buraima (1805-21); Moi Adam (1822-42); Moi Disa (1843-56); Moi Ismaila (1866-70); Moi Aji Gimba (1881-82); Moi Disa (1902-22).[7] A *zonge* tree (*adua* in Hausa) was planted behind each grave.

The houses of the Bolewa of Fika were round, with conical thatched roofs, or rectangular, with flat roofs. The standard building materials were building earth, timber, cornstalks and grass. In addition, granite stones were used for foundations.

Building earth (*janga*) was usually dug out of three pits (*uyo*). One was outside the perimeter wall of the compound and two were inside (that was also the case in the Moi's palace). The *janga* was mixed with water, stored in a heap covered under grass, mixed again after two days and used for building without any additions. This was acceptable because the quality of the local building earth was very high. However, for plaster (*yabu*) dried and broken grass (*rusho*) was added. The lumps of plaster (*sheddu*) were dipped in water before being applied to the walls. A special kind of plaster was prepared for the Moi's palace, made from red (*dai*) clay, called *jangan-dai*.

[5] J E Lavers, *The History and People of Fika Emirate*, New Nigerian Special Supplement of 22 December 1972; *The Bolewa of Fika*, Nigeria Magazine No. 51, 1956, p. 340.
[6] *Tinja*, the equivalent of the Hausa Madaki, although a commoner, was the most important personage next to the king. He was the representative of the people and chief adviser of the Moi. (Meek, *Tribal Studies in Northern Nigeria*, London 1931, Vol. 2, pps. 289, 290.) *Ibidem*: the very complex system of titled members of the royal house, male and female, is described.
[7] Another royal family, the Mama, was extinct.

Pl.3.9. FIKA. Emir's Palace. One of the ruined interiors.

Walls (*garu*) were built in layers (*gali*). There were no strict rules about the height of walls; on average nine to ten *gali* were used. The walls had no cornices, either inside or outside, but they were occasionally strengthened with buttresses. I was told that a house could be built in a few days.

A description of the thatched conical roofs would be identical to what has been said of Potiskum town. The flat roofs were laid on horizontal beams (*molu*).[8] When the span of the beam exceeded a structurally acceptable length, it was supported by pillars. *Molu* were made from three to five *bagur*

(*azara* in Hausa) and then plastered. No brackets or corbels were used. Joists of *azara* rods were placed at right angles on top of the *molu*, with short pieces of timber covering the gaps between them (see also Potiskum flat roofs). On top of an insulating layer of building earth (*janga*) and ash (*buto*) went a waterproof cover of *sibi*. *Sibi* was made in a similar way to *katsi*, out of dye-pit sediment; but when dry, it was not baked, only pounded into powder. The other method of sealing the

[8] *Molu* literally means to 'carry on the back'.

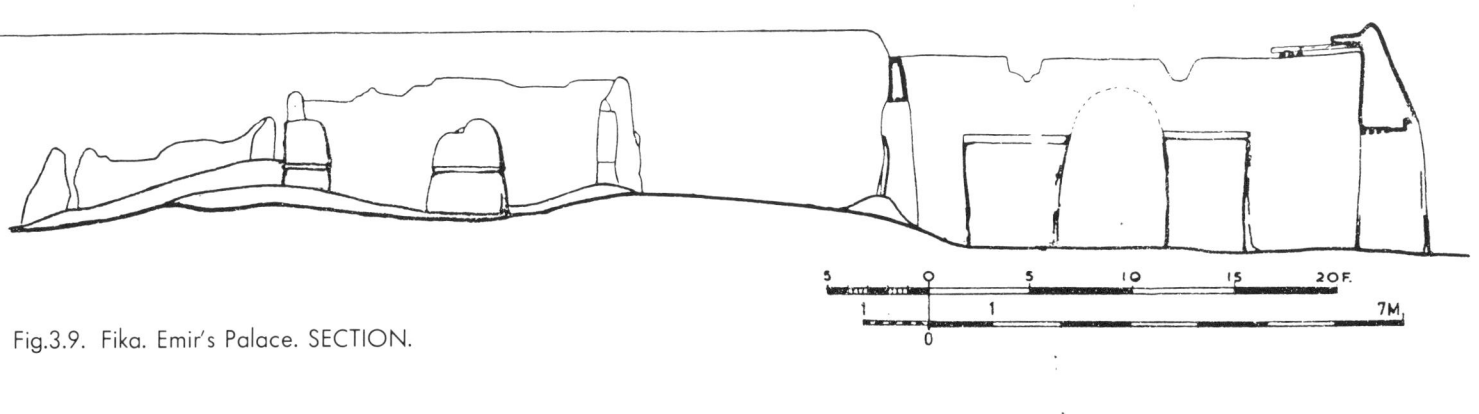

Fig.3.9. Fika. Emir's Palace. SECTION.

Pl.3.10. FIKA. Emir's Palace. Detail showing wall construction of potsherds and plaster.

roof was to use processed building earth; this ,however, was apparently not reliable enough, and had to be covered additionally with *janga* or *laka* (clay) plaster.

The floors were laid with *ka-ka-shaki* building earth — gravel. The work was done by women, and was accompanied by drumming and singing.

Decoration of the walls was done with the hand and fingers in the plaster when it was still wet. Four basic colours were used for painting the walls: the white, *petila*, was white chalk (*pendele*), found in the hills; the yellow, *bulbul*, was from the hills again; the red, *dai*, was from powdered earth; and the black from the ashes of *jember* (*rama* in Hausa) stalks burnt after removal of the bark. An extract from the pods of the

locust bean tree, *dampara* (*makuba* in Hausa) was sometimes added to improve the quality and colour of the plaster.

Stone (*gusho*) was occasionally used, especially in pillars; it was selected in the hills, and bound with the usual mortar of building earth.

The oldest building shown to me in Fika was a small rectangular shrine. It contained a special charm, which was thought to retain protective powers as long as a donkey did not enter the shrine. Consequently Moi Buraima banned donkeys from the town. I was not permitted to visit the shrine either. The original entrance was supposed to have been through an underground tunnel and the name of the shrine had to remain secret to strangers.

Compound of Mallam Madaki

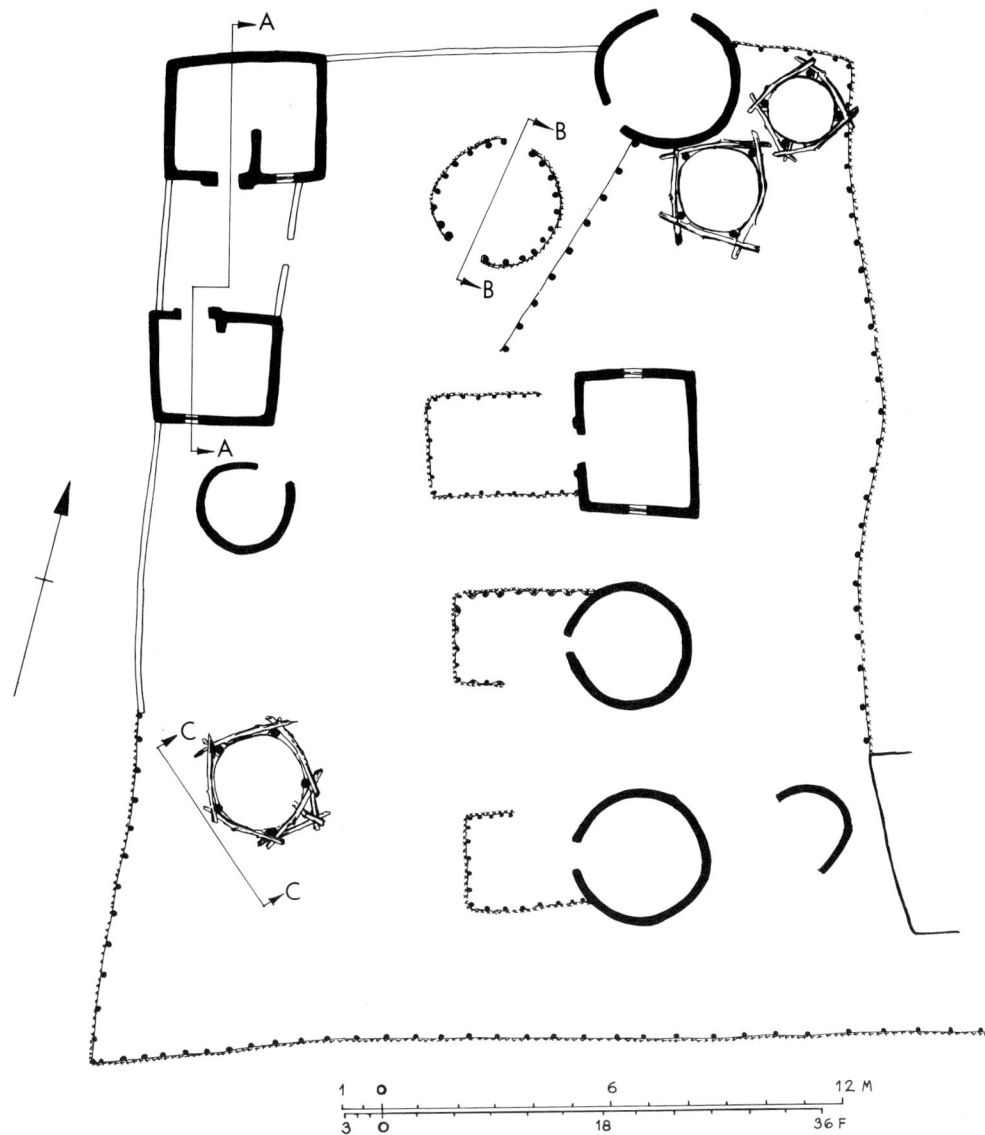

Fig.3.10. Fika. Compound of Mallam Madaki. PLAN.

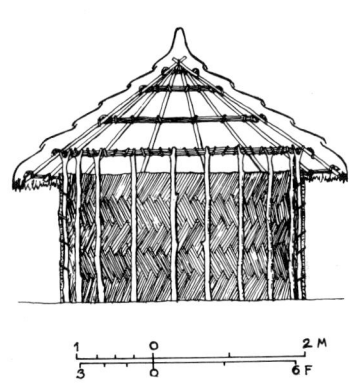

Fig.3.12 SECTION B—B.

Fig.3.13. ELEVATION C—C.

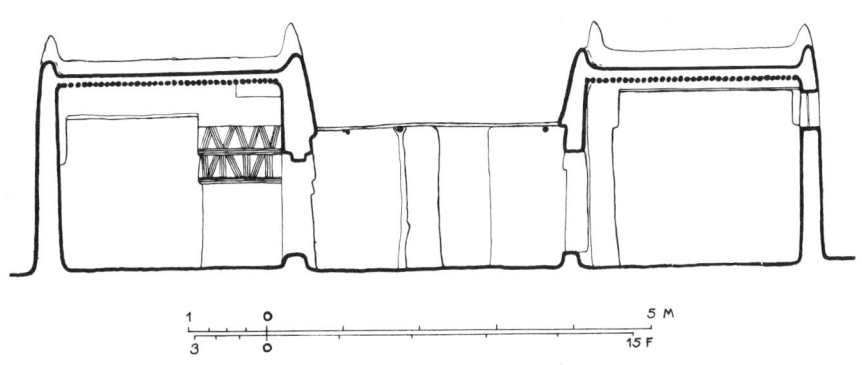

Fig.3.11. Fika. Compound of Mallam Madaki. SECTION A—A.

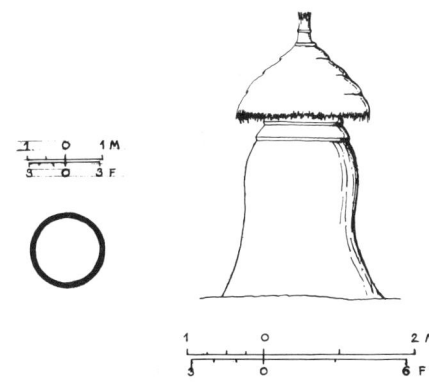

Fig.3.14. Granary. PLAN. ELEVATION.

Gombe
Emir's Palace

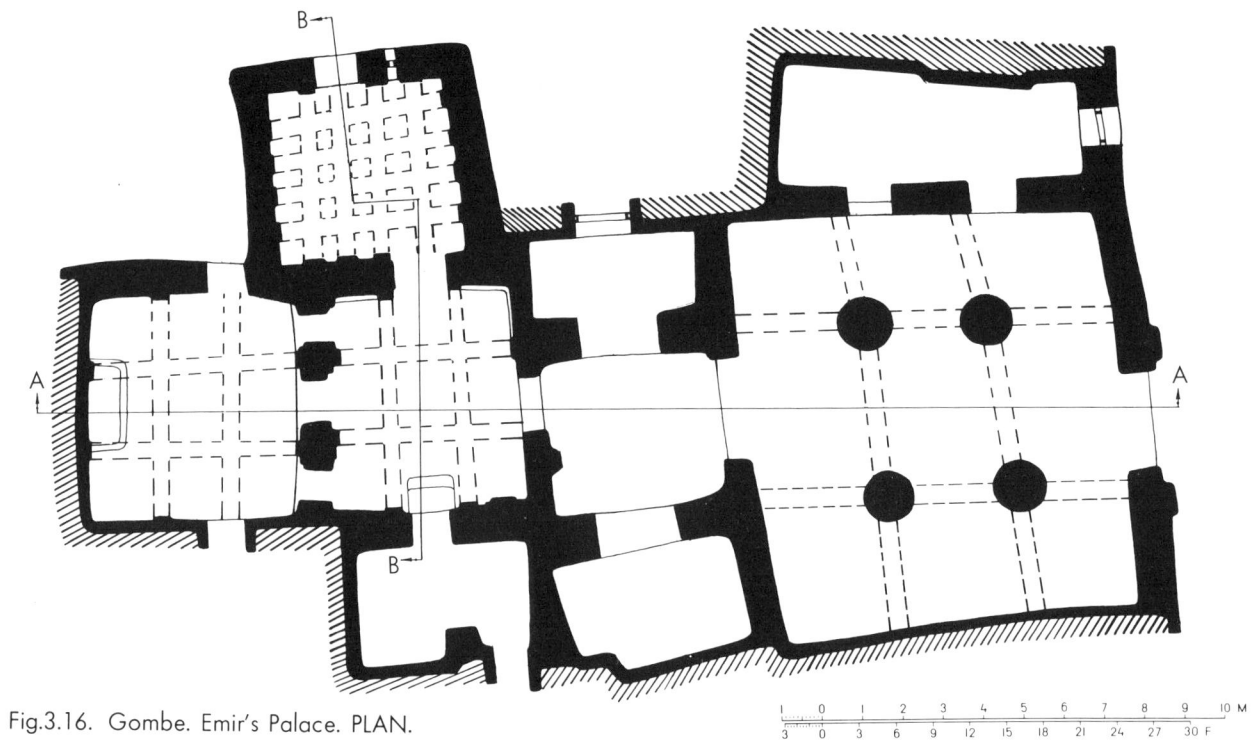

Fig.3.16. Gombe. Emir's Palace. PLAN.

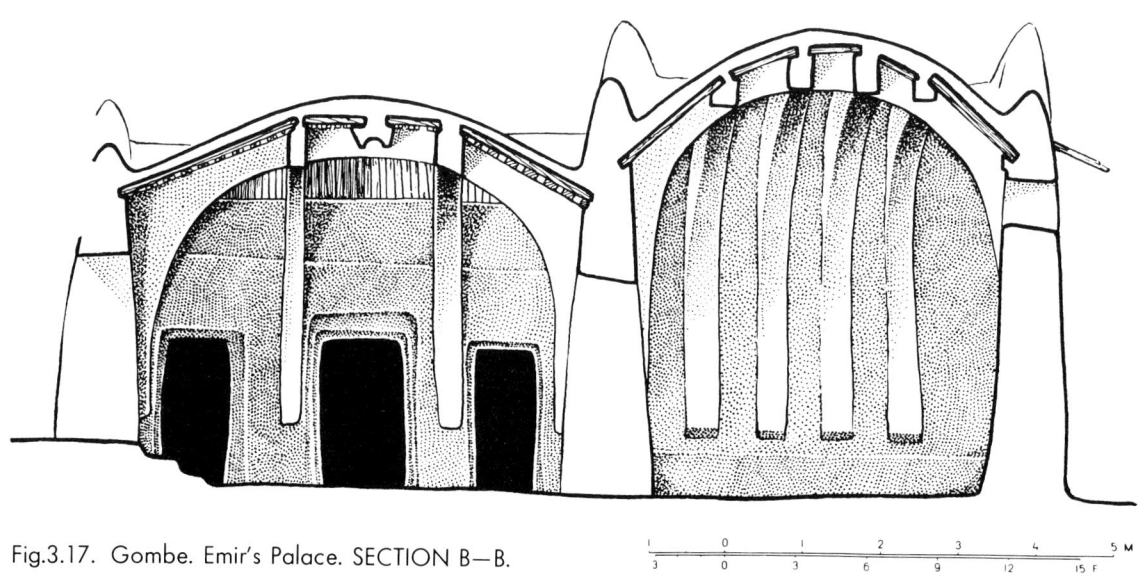

Fig.3.17. Gombe. Emir's Palace. SECTION B—B.

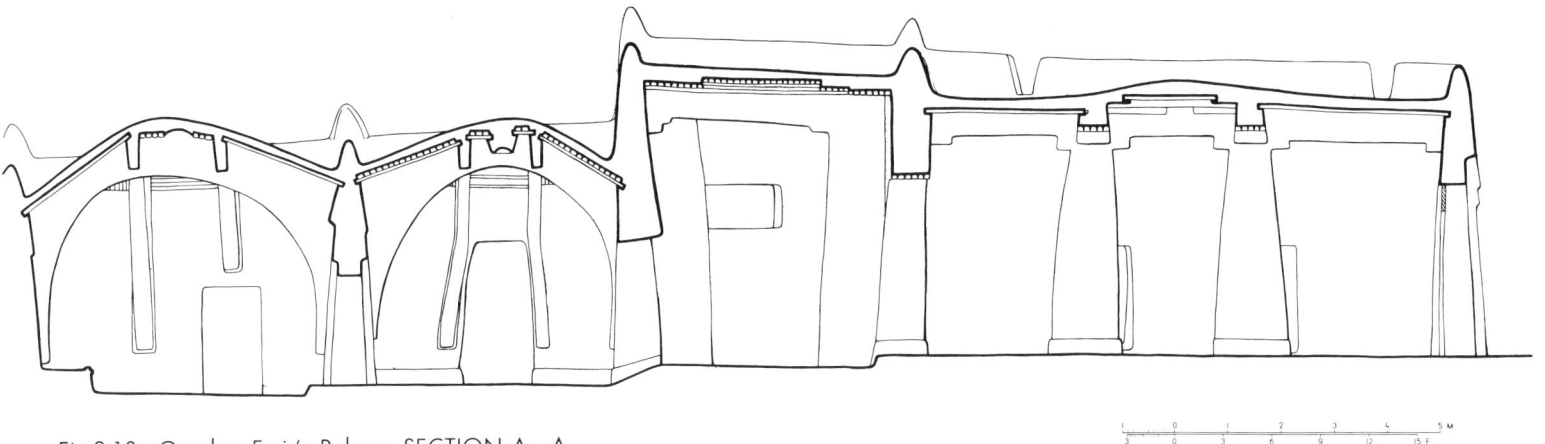

Fig.3.18. Gombe. Emir's Palace. SECTION A—A.

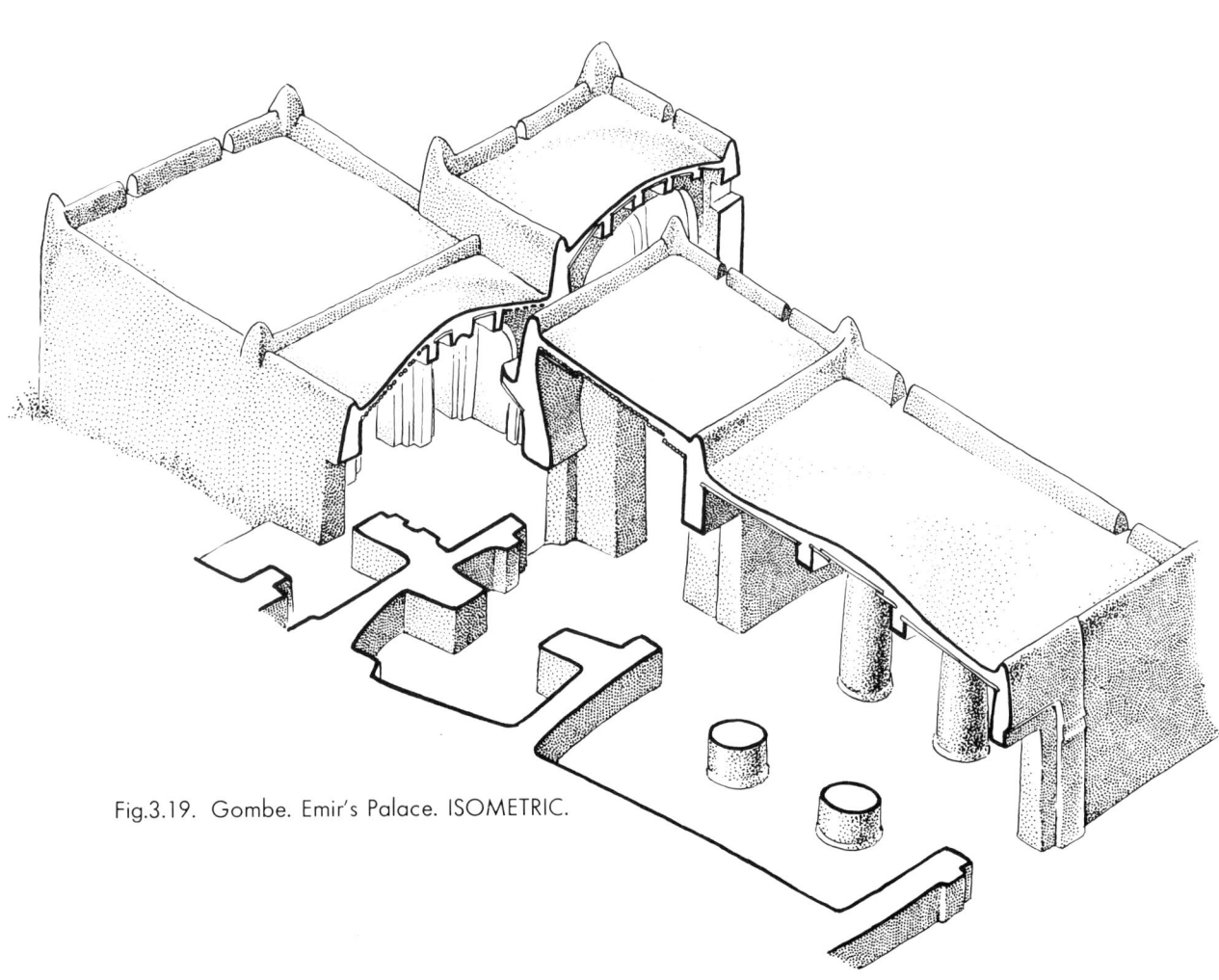

Fig.3.19. Gombe. Emir's Palace. ISOMETRIC.

Compound of Chief Gadam

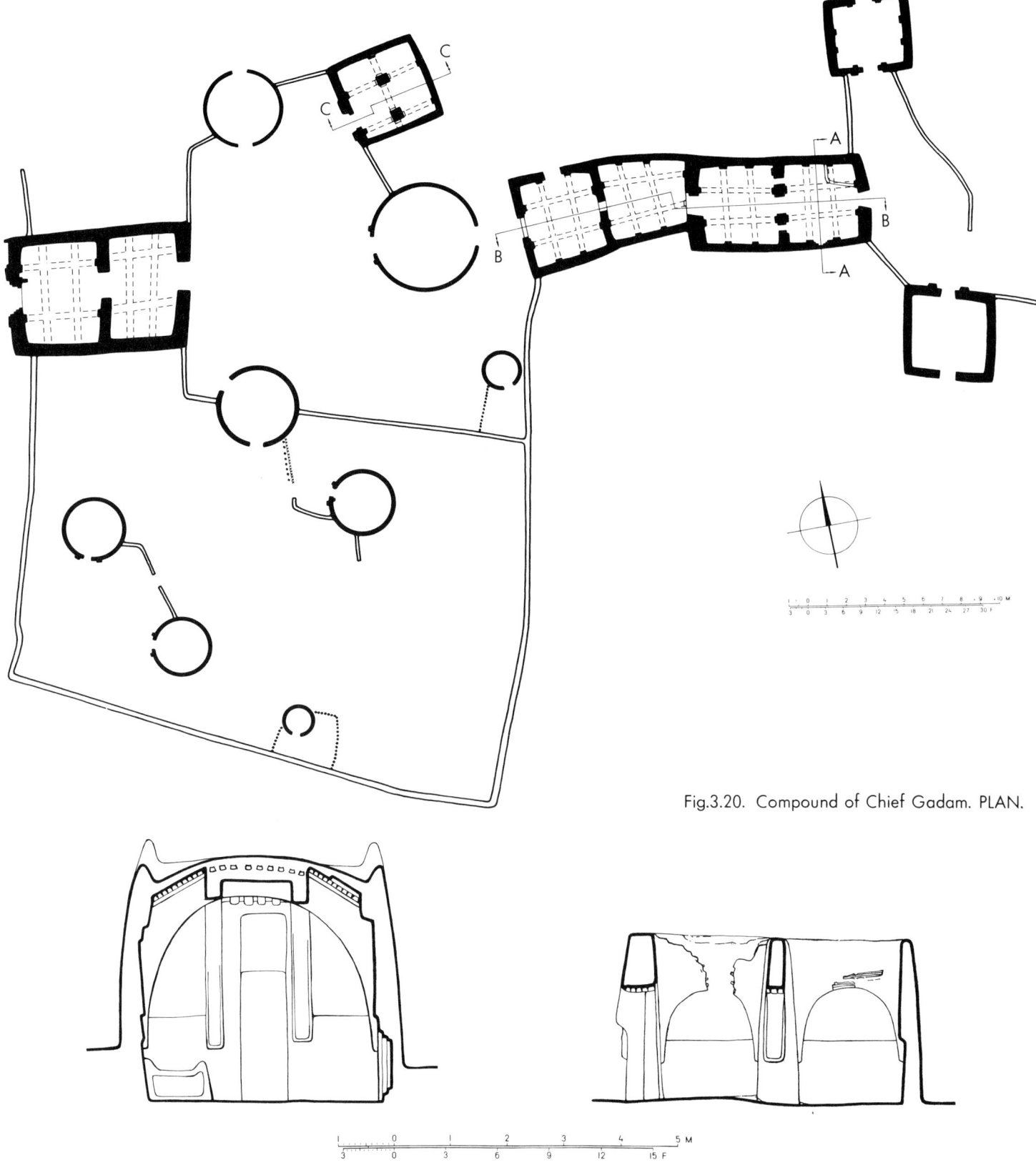

Fig.3.20. Compound of Chief Gadam. PLAN.

Fig.3.21. Compound of Chief Gadam. SECTION A—A.

Fig.3.22. Compound of Chief Gadam. SECTION C—C.

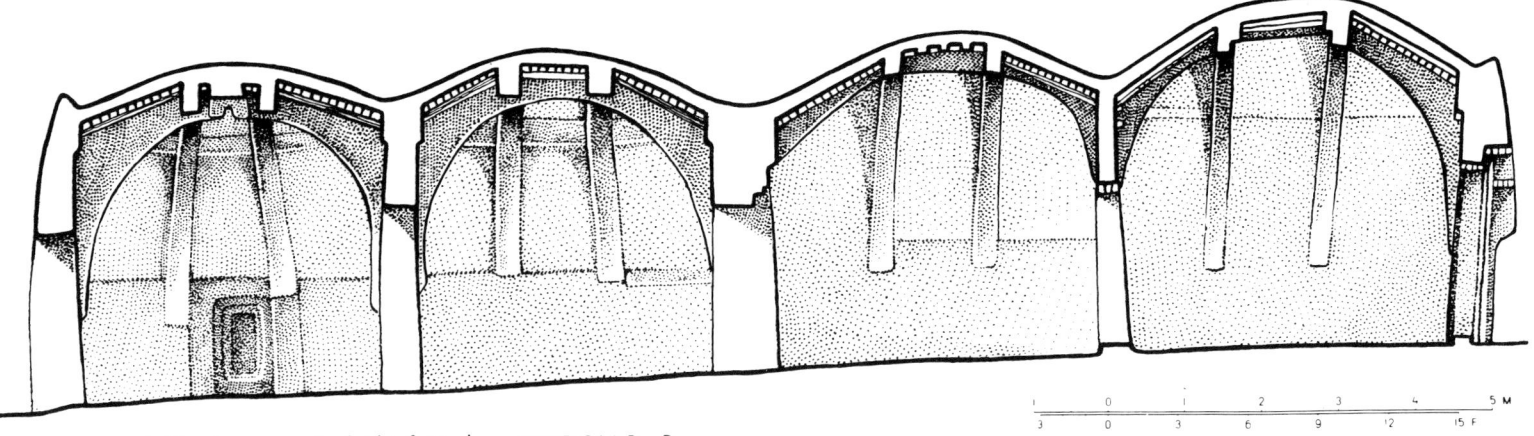

Fig.3.23. Compound of Chief Gadam. SECTION B—B.

Compound of Lamalio Lanwang

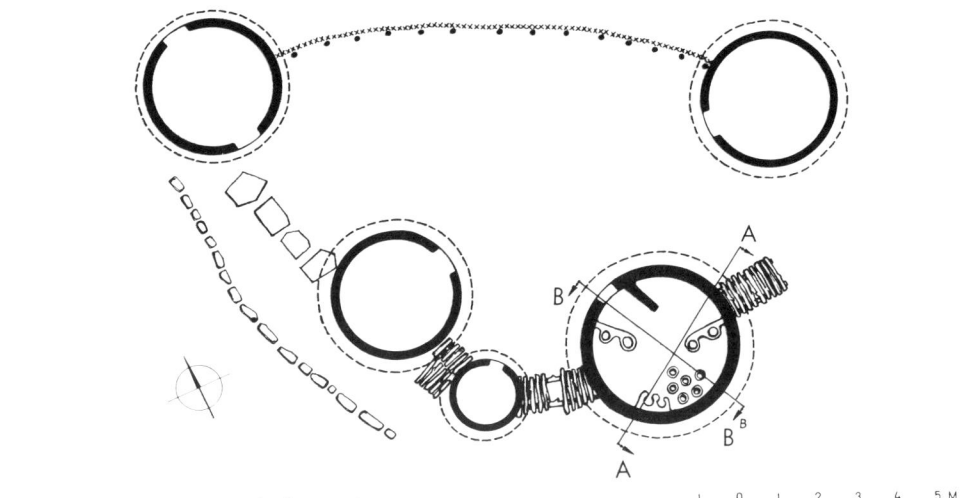

Fig.3.24. Compound of Lamalio Lanwang. PLAN.

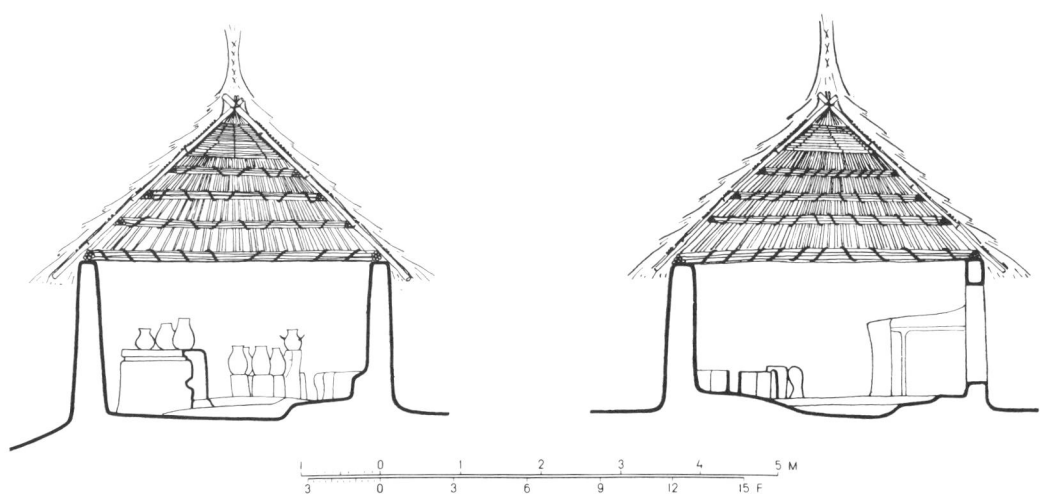

Fig.3.25. SECTION A—A.

Fig.3.26. SECTION B—B.

Deba Palace

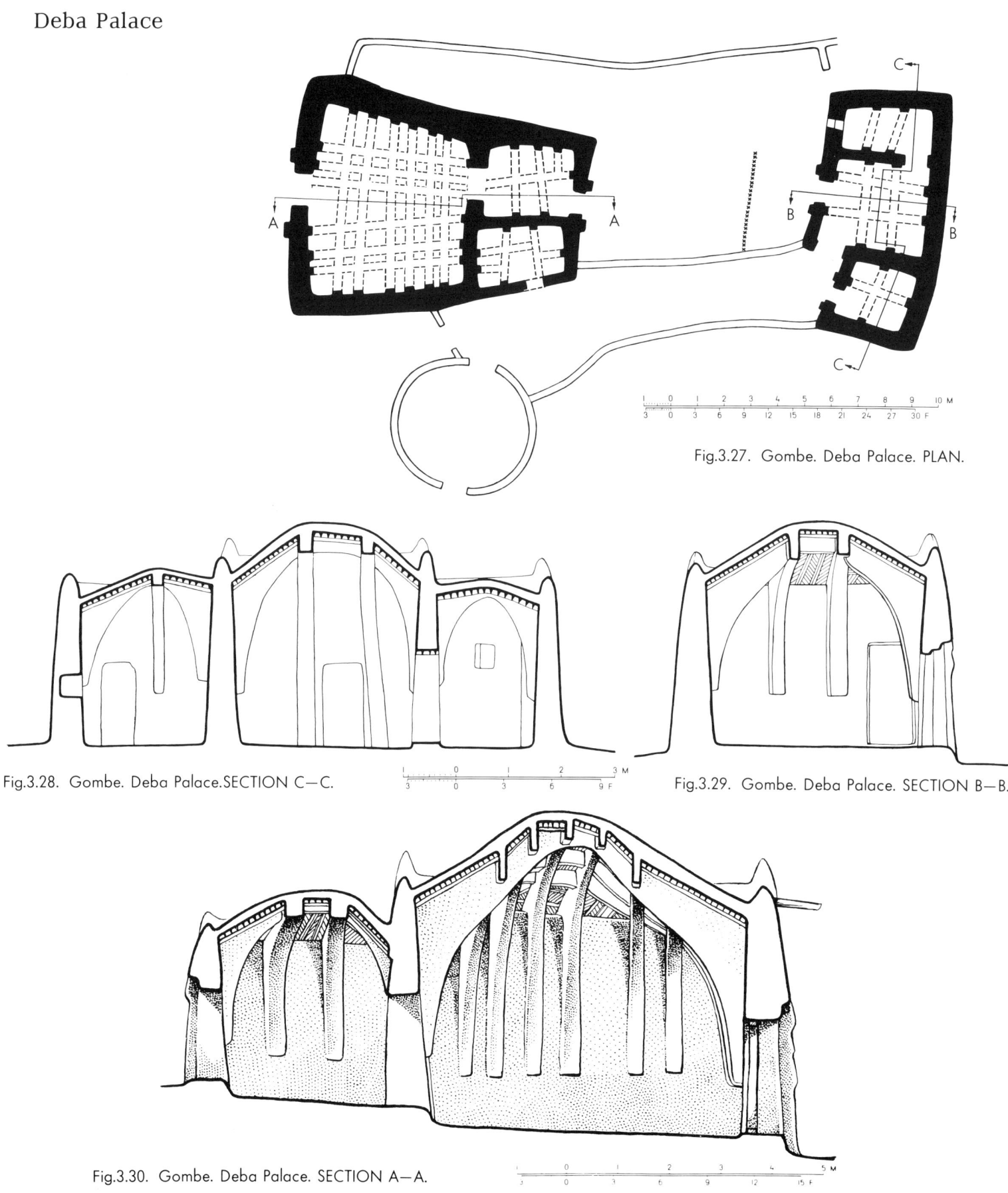

Fig.3.27. Gombe. Deba Palace. PLAN.

Fig.3.28. Gombe. Deba Palace. SECTION C—C.

Fig.3.29. Gombe. Deba Palace. SECTION B—B.

Fig.3.30. Gombe. Deba Palace. SECTION A—A.

Jalingo
Emir's Palace

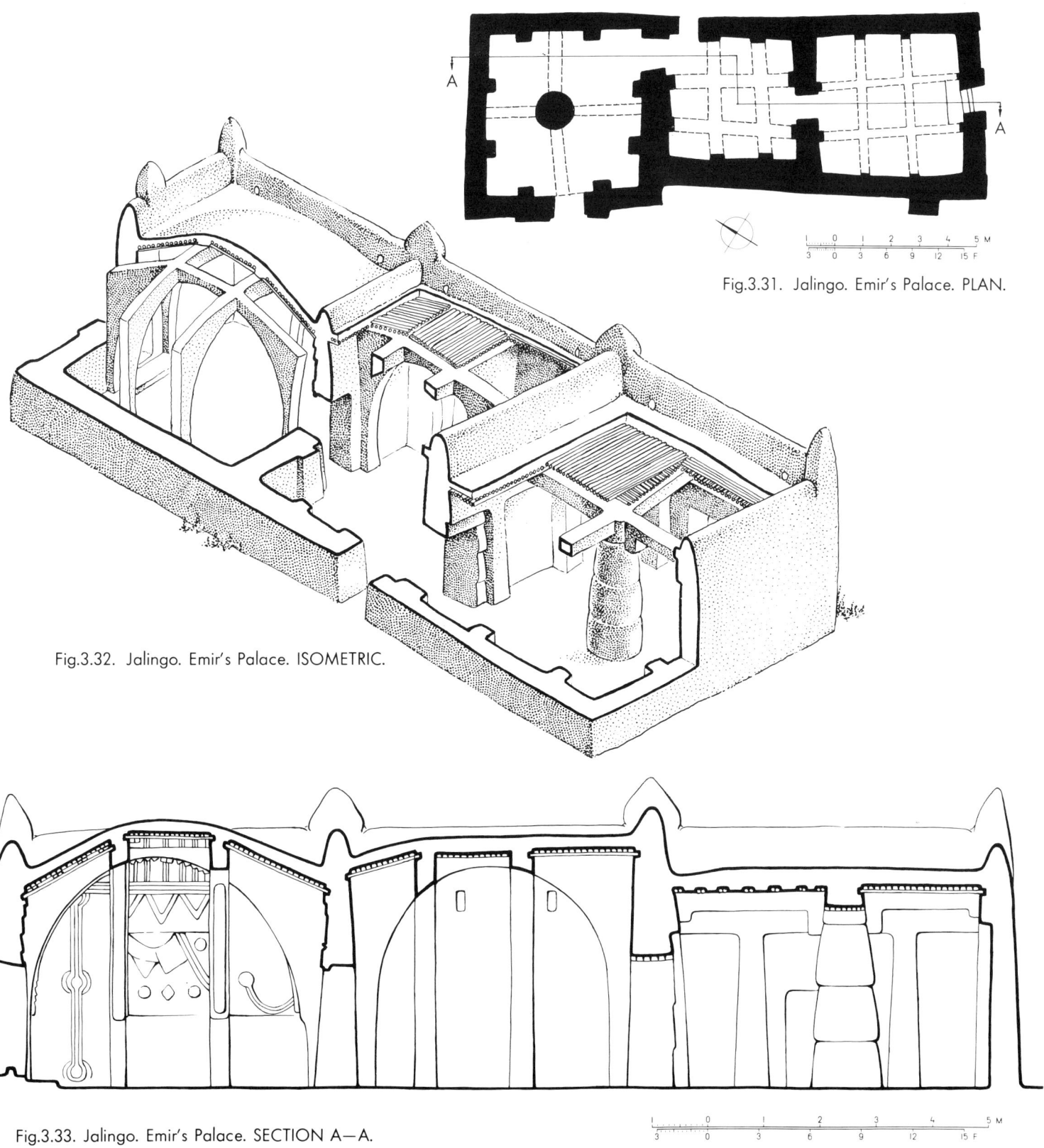

Fig.3.31. Jalingo. Emir's Palace. PLAN.

Fig.3.32. Jalingo. Emir's Palace. ISOMETRIC.

Fig.3.33. Jalingo. Emir's Palace. SECTION A—A.

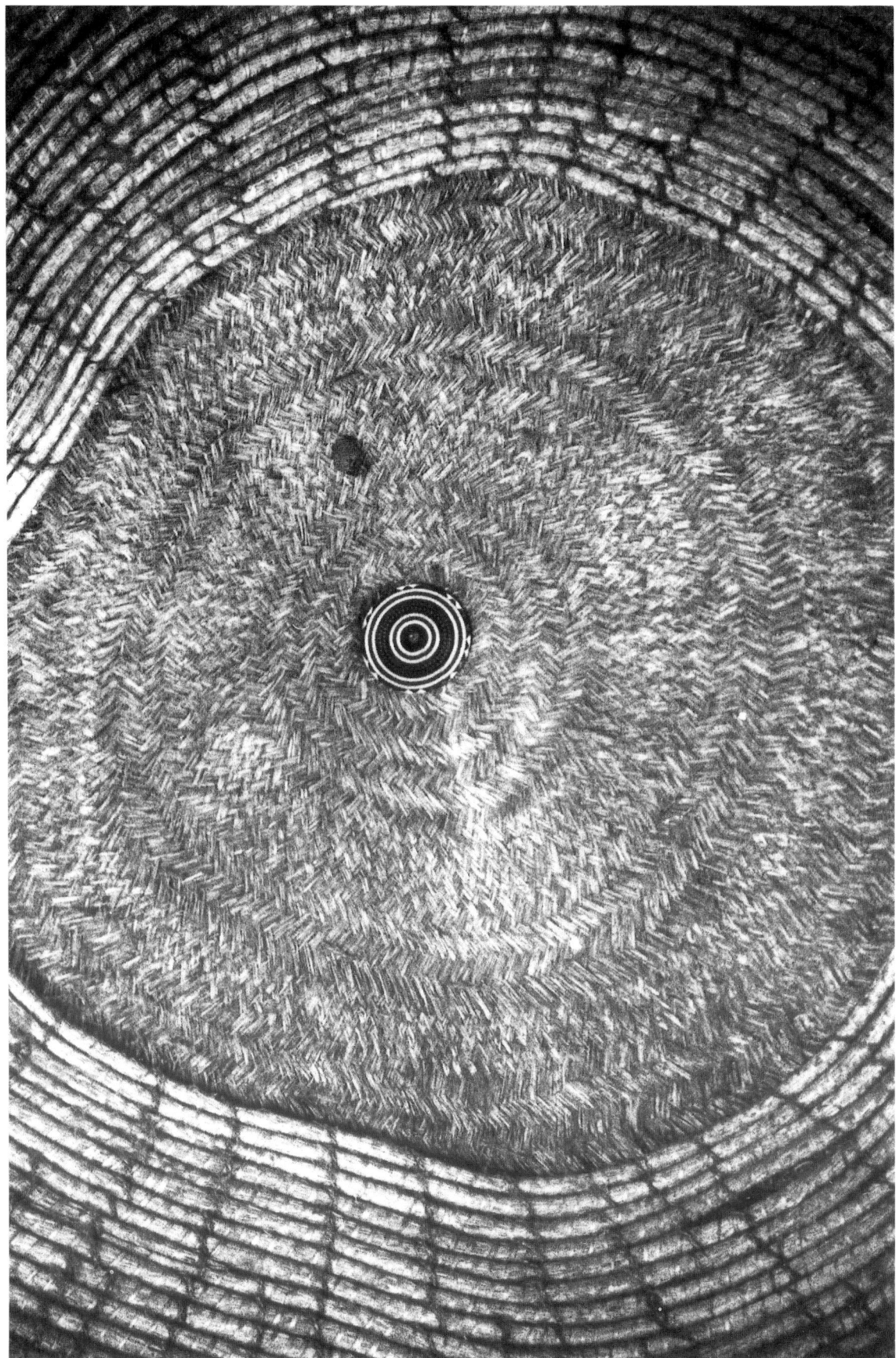

YOLA. Compound of the Sardauna. Matting in the roof apex.

Yola

HISTORICAL BACKGROUND

Yola, which is the present capital of Gongola State, formerly Adamawa Province, is one of the few areas where Fulfulde/ Fulani is used as the everyday language.

The Fulani race, quite distinct from the negroid peoples, became the object of a number of controversial theories concerning their origin. All of these take into account their unusual features: lighter skin, thin lips, narrow nose and long, straight hair.[9]

The earliest Fulani migration into the eastern region of Northern Nigeria was recorded circa 1200, but it was only at the beginning of the 19th century that Ardo Modibo Adama founded a Fulani kingdom, called, after his name, Adamawa. For the first twenty years Adama's headquarters was Gurin (mentioned by Denham), from where he moved to Ribadu. Finally, in 1841, he founded Yola as his capital and became the first Emir (*Lamido*)[10], 1806-48, of Adamawa Kingdom.

Heinrich Barth visited Yola during his travels,[11] when Lamido Laval ruled the Emirate. Barth described Yola as a large open space built up mostly with conical huts among spacious courtyards or cornfields. The huts were built 'with clay walls, and thatched'. Only a few of the houses were rectangular and flat-roofed. Of these the Lamido's residence, Lamorde, stood 'on the west side of a small open area, opposite the mosque'. It was 'covered with a flat thatched roof a little inclined on one side'. Barth entered the palace through the spacious *zaure*, called *segifa*, the flat roof of which was 'supported by square pillars'. The main reception hall, where Barth was introduced to Lamido Lawal had a 'stately, castle like appearance'. The interior 'was rather encroached upon by quadrangular pillars two feet in diameter, which supported the roof, about 16 feet high and consisting of a rather heavy entablature of poles'. The little sketch attached to this description shows a façade not unlike some of the present-day mansions in Yola, as for instance the Sardauna's residence.

I carried out an architectural survey of Yola in 1973 with my Department of Antiquities team. I was introduced to His Highness the Lamido of Adamawa on the advice of Mallam Joda, the Federal Minister of Education; thanks to his kindness the Alhaji Bakari of Yola gave me the assistance of the Sarkin Gini, Salimu Magini Yola, and Mallam Sambo Abubakar Wambai, as well as the owners and family members of the compounds surveyed. They provided me with comprehensive information on which the following paragraphs are based.

Wall Construction

Walls in Yola were built from *tubali* bound with mortar. Both *tubali* and plaster were made in the same manner, from building earth (*lope*) taken from selected pits far away from the building site. To crumbled and watered *lope* was added grass or rice leaves (*gene marori*) chopped up with an axe (singular: *sagdere*. plural: *chaddeje*). A pile of this mixture was covered with grass until the next day, when more water and grass was added. After this the processed earth (*lope yabade*) was ready for making *tubali* (singular: *tamre lope;* plural: *tame lope*). The work was arranged as follows. Five men dug the *lope*, ten men brought the water, five mixed the water and *lope*, cut the grass and added it to the mixture, and two to five men made the *tubali*.

The *tubali* were made in three shapes. The originally conical form was replaced in the 1950s by a round one which was easier to make. Sometimes the *tubali* were shaped like a loaf, and laid flat.

Walls were built without a footing on foundations an arm-length deep. The walls were in tiers, each four *tubali* high; they were all plastered, but the plaster between each tier of four *tubali* was much thicker than between each layer of *tubali*. The bottom tier was four *tubali* high; the next one, three; the next, two; and the top tier, one *tubali* high – it usually formed the parapet around the flat roof. This general principle was adhered to in rectangular buildings. In circular structures, as for example in the entrance gate *jauleru* (*zaure* in Hausa) of Muhammadu Mustafa's compound, the walls were three *tubali* thick at the base and two at the top.

Occasionally walls were reinforced with external pilasters by adding an extra thickness of *tubali*. The bottom tier in perimeter walls was five *tubali* high.

[9] A H M Kirk-Greene, *Adamawa Past and Present*, London 1958.
S J Hogben and A H M Kirk-Greene, *The Emirates of Northern Nigeria, op cit,* p. 429, *passim.*
[10] C O Migeod, *Gazetteer of Yola Province*, compiled from material supplied by S H P Verekar, Esq., and Captain E A Brackenbury, Lagos 1927.
[11] Heinrich Barth, *Travels and Discoveries in North and Central Africa . . . in the years 1849-1855.* London 1857-8, Vol. 2, pps. 485, 490, 501.

Roof Construction

Circular buildings (*sudu*) with walls of *tubali* were covered with a roof construction formed by a frame of *azaras* (*lochi-dubbe*) arranged in a cone. Between them were sometimes inserted bamboo sticks (*lochi kewe*). The cone rested on a ring (*tekkere*) made from coarse grass *kalwal* (the same as used for *zana* mats) set on the crown of the wall and tied with *balamji* rope. *Tekkere* was made on the ground as a continuous roll, then it was raised with the aid of scaffolding inside the house to the crown of the walls and formed into a ring, the ends overlapping by 60 centimetres. The conical frame of *lochi* was stiffened on the outside by numerous rather slender rings (*bilori*) of *kalwal* grass, the same as was used for *tekkere*.

At half its height the cone had a thick ring (*gangawal*) on the inside, made from thin stems (*kole*) closely bound first with *balamji* rope and then with a decorative plait, *boggol*, made from *sodornde* grass. Above *gangawal* a type of basketwork was mounted inside the cone; it had about twenty rings (*murdaka*) of *tappo* grass, bound round with strips of *rama* bark.[12] Above this ring the last element but one was made of *iware* grass. Finally the apex of the cone was covered by a horizontal circle, *mbedu* or *bedel*, a round mat made by women and used for serving food. *Mbedu* consisted of several spirals of *sodornde* grass, bound with coloured *chochodi* grass so as to form rich patterns. (Pls. 3.16 & 3.17)

Thatching

When the roof construction was completed, poles were placed upright around the walls of the building at a distance of 1.3 metres; they were higher than the walls and were linked horizontally at the top, which created a scaffolding, although a flimsy one. On it in a circle stood the five men who laid the thatch; a sixth man passed the rolled up grass mats to them on a stick (*titorgal*). The best kind of grass was called *bodaji*, a cheaper sort, *vome*, and the cheapest, *sodornde*. The grass was sewn with thin thread, *tappo*, into a long mat (*ware*; plural: *ba'e*).

These mats were laid spirally, with the bottom part of the grass stems downwards. The first layer of thatch consisted of four thicknesses of mats, one on top of the other. The next layer was three mats thick. From then on up to the middle of the roof single layers were wound in a spiral with a small overlap. A step was formed in the middle of the roof by placing four layers of mat on top of one another; then the same process as in the lower half was repeated. The step enriched the appearance of the thatch, but more importantly it increased the momentum of the rainwater running down its surface. The simplest finishing of the thatch involved the tight binding of the topmost spirals of mats with *balamji* rope above the apex of the roof frame; finally a clay pot was placed over the binding, protecting the most fragile part of the thatched roof.

However, another method was often applied, far more elaborate and using the best kind of grass, *titiji bodeji*. A man sat astride the apex of the roof and carefully adjusted the position of the topmost spiral of matting. Then he grasped a handful of grass and bound it with *balamji* rope about three centimetres below the grass-heads, where the stems are more flexible. This first handful of grass was the starting point – then every 30 centimetres along he bound another handful, joining them together around the apex of the roof construction in a stiff circle. Two centimetres higher up the next binding was wound around the whole, and the ends of the grass were bent into the ring thus created. A plug of grass was pressed into the centre to firm and tighten the top. Next a kind of net was pulled over the top to keep the whole together. This process of finishing the apex (*lamsal*) is described by the verb *lamsol*.

Finally the apex was covered with *malapare* or *lupare*, a sort of conical basket woven from *uware* grass by men specialists. The bottom of *malapare* was strengthened with *balamji* rope to prevent expansion. Openings were made above it in six or eight places and similar *balamji* ropes were threaded through the holes. The *balamji* pierced the thatch, was bound to the *lochi* inside, and then threaded back to the outside again; and this sewing process was continued all round the holes of the *malapare*. Three sticks were driven diagonally downwards into the apex of *malapare* and an inverted pot placed over them. The pot was filled with grass so that it would remain securely in position.

RECTANGULAR BUILDINGS

Adada

Rectangular buildings were thatched in a similar way to round ones, though naturally they had a different roof construction. The main elements were rafters (*noppije*) of *kojole* timber, bound in pairs, trestle-like. The ridge beam (*pilal*) was laid above their crossing, and four or five battens (*pile*) were fixed on each side of the roof. When the walls were sufficiently thick the rafters were set not on wallplates but into openings cut diagonally into the crown of the walls.

---

[12] *Rama*, widely used in the North, was made from the bark of the plant called *Gabai* in Yola. Before use *Rama* was softened in water.

Pls.3.11 and 3.12. YOLA. Thatching with grass.

Compound of the Sardauna, Mallam Muhammadu Mustafa

This compound was originally the residence of the Waziri of Yola. When surveyed it still represented one of the most evolved complexes of the town. Characteristically, it occupied quite a large area, contained within an irregular polygon (Fig.3.34). It consisted of two main parts: an entirely separate pair of residences for the Sardauna in the SW part of the site; and a series of courtyards in the W, N and E, containing round *jauleji* (Fulani) (*zauruka* in Hausa) and living houses.

A *zaure* (singular: *jauleru*) led to the public part of the Sardauna's residence: it was a round building with an outer portal facing W and second door at an obtuse angle to it, facing SE, which led into the interior of the compound. Such a change of direction was customary and hid the view into the compound from the street. This end was achieved even more effectively by an additional visual barrier – there was a porch behind the second door with a wall which completely screened the interior of the compound. (Figs. 3.35 & 3.36).

The outer door had a threshold (*damugal*) and a transom of three *azaras* (*tinde damugal; tinde* = forehead). To the right of this door was place for the gateman (*gaga*) where visitors also waited for the master of the house; he sat on an easy chair to the left of the entrance.

Jauleru was covered with a conical roof and its construction was as described previously except for the apex, which was lined with basketwork (*mbedu*) resembling *zana* matting.

The first courtyard (*babal*) past the *jauleru* was sometimes used by the master and his honoured guests as an eating place. The surplus food was given to the servant boys (plural: *machchube*; singular: *machchudo*).

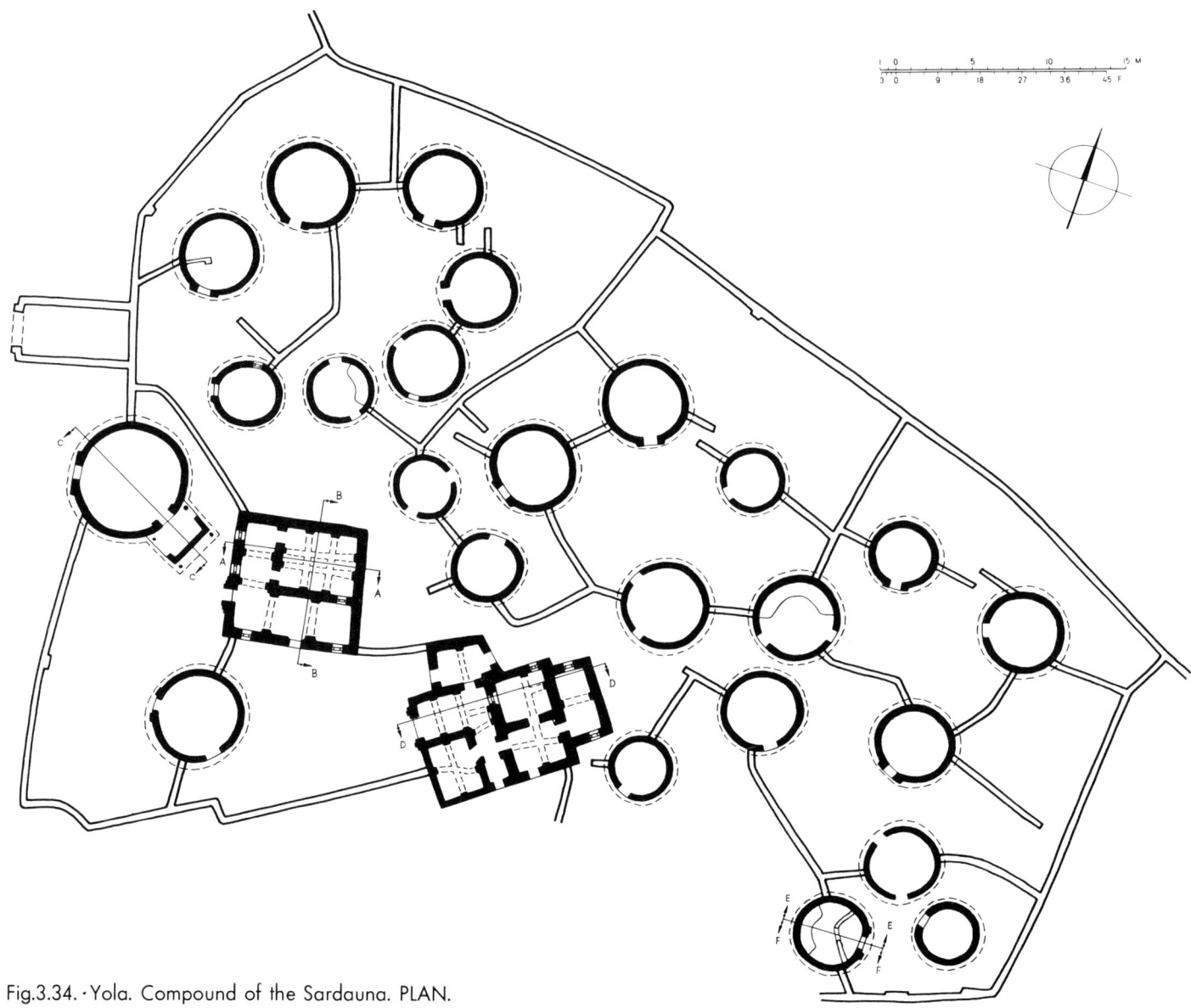

Fig.3.34. · Yola. Compound of the Sardauna. PLAN.

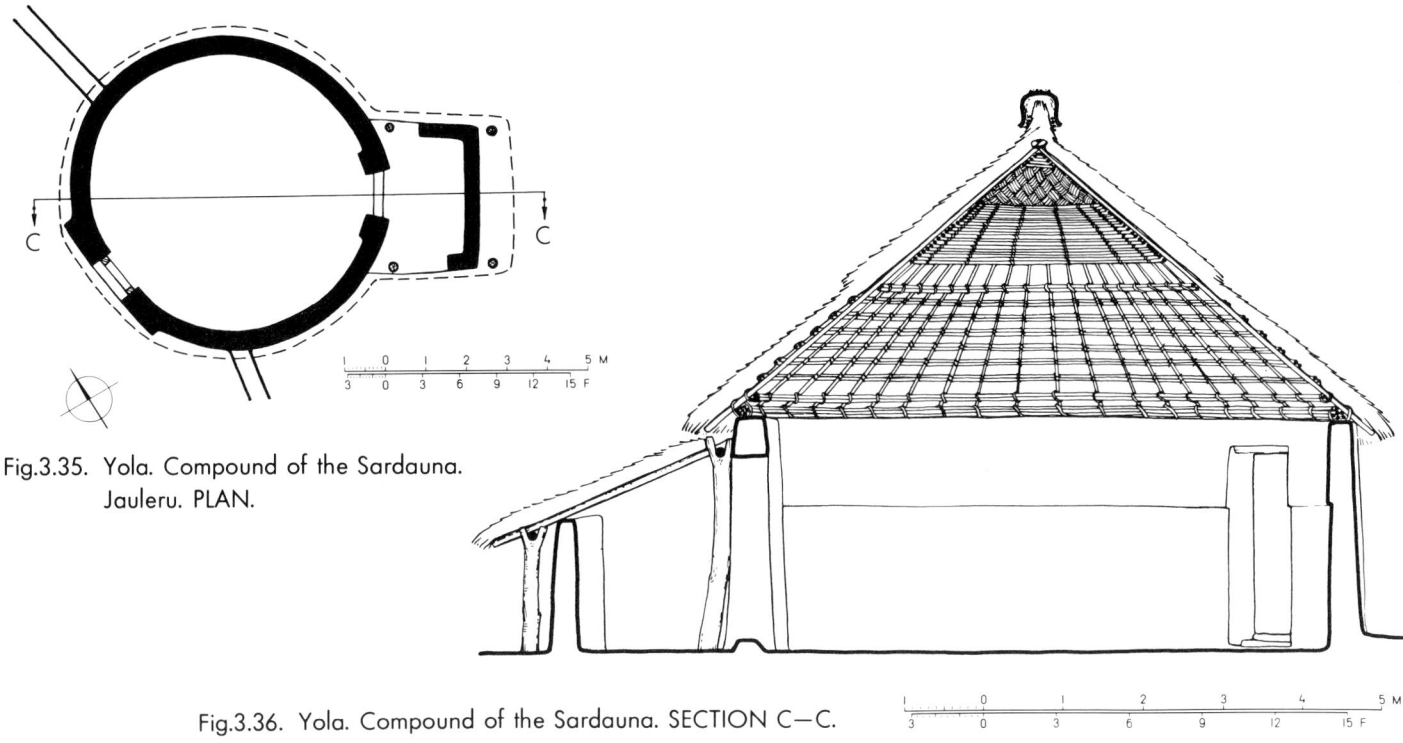

Fig.3.35. Yola. Compound of the Sardauna.
Jauleru. PLAN.

Fig.3.36. Yola. Compound of the Sardauna. SECTION C—C.

Pl.3.13. YOLA. Compound of the Sardauna. The jauleru.

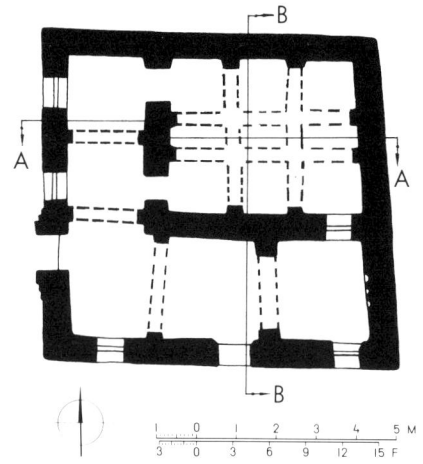

Fig.3.37. Yola. Compound of the Sardauna. Safakare. PLAN.

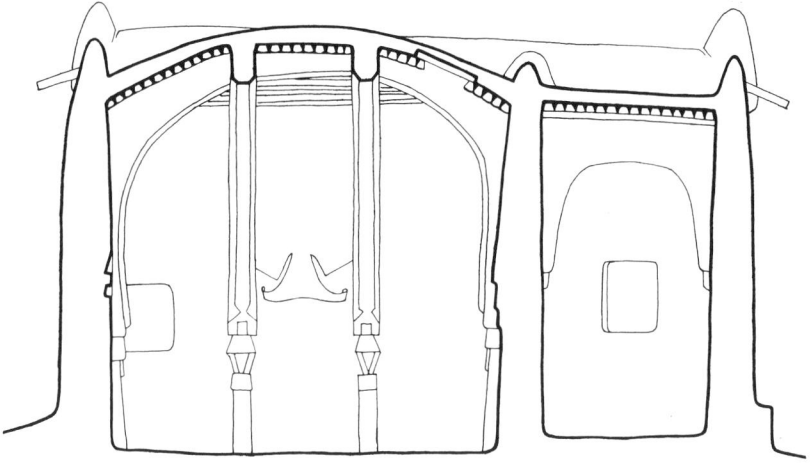

Fig.3.38. Yola. Compound of the Sardauna. SECTION A—A.

Fig.3.39. SECTION B—B.

Two buildings stood in the *babal* courtyard: a *soro* house adjacent to the *jauleru*; and a second *zaure* (*jauleru chaka*). The *soro* was called *safakare* which described not its function but its structure – the building was fireproof, and all its inflammable elements (made from timber and grass) were plastered over. Furthermore it was secure against burglars. It was the sleeping place of the master, and occasionally served as a guest room for important visitors. Its plan was almost square. The entrance door in the W façade led into an L-shaped interior. In the E part of the S arm stood the Sardauna's throne, with his regalia moulded on the back wall (Section B-B). The W arm gave access to a high chamber, covered with a dome, *tuluwa*, supported by two pairs of crossed *baka* arches (*daurin guga – rijiya daya*). (Figs. 3.38 & 3.39).

The N and E walls of *safakare*, facing courtyards built up with minor, circular buildings, were solid and without any openings.

Jauleru chaka was similarly orientated to the entrance

jauleru. The Sardauna received more important guests there and it was the way to the next courtyard, at the E end of which stood the main living *soro*. This was also called *safakare*, because of its fireproof structure, but the plan was more complex. The entrance, as was customary, was in the W wall and as in the first *safakare* it led into an L-shaped interior. Here the similarity ended, and instead of two interiors as in the first building, there were six; two of them, on the N and E, were probably extensions. The architectural conception was simplified: there were semi-circular corbels (*talkamin kasa* in Hausa) in the two rooms shown in Figure 3.41. The interior in the N corner of *soro* was without an elaborate cross arch system *daurin guga* – one of the *baka* supporting the flat *tuluwa* dome was replaced by a triangular arrangement of *azaras* (Figure 3.41, the central room). This unusual solution, although quite simple was an interesting experiment in the search for new form and a new play of light and shadow in the covering of an interior.

Pl.3.14. YOLA. Compound of the Sardauna. South facade of the safakare *building.*

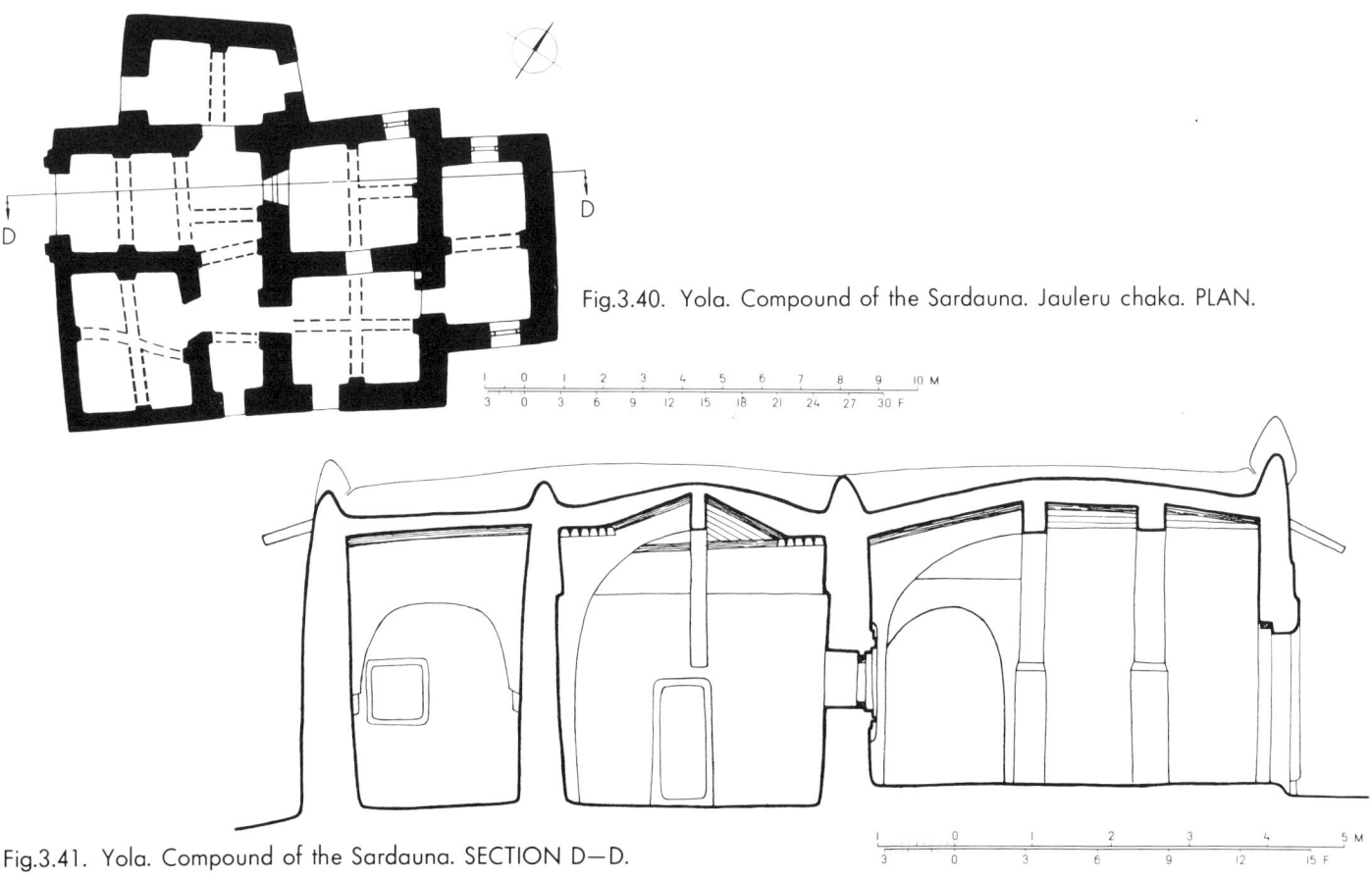

Fig.3.40. Yola. Compound of the Sardauna. Jauleru chaka. PLAN.

Fig.3.41. Yola. Compound of the Sardauna. SECTION D—D.

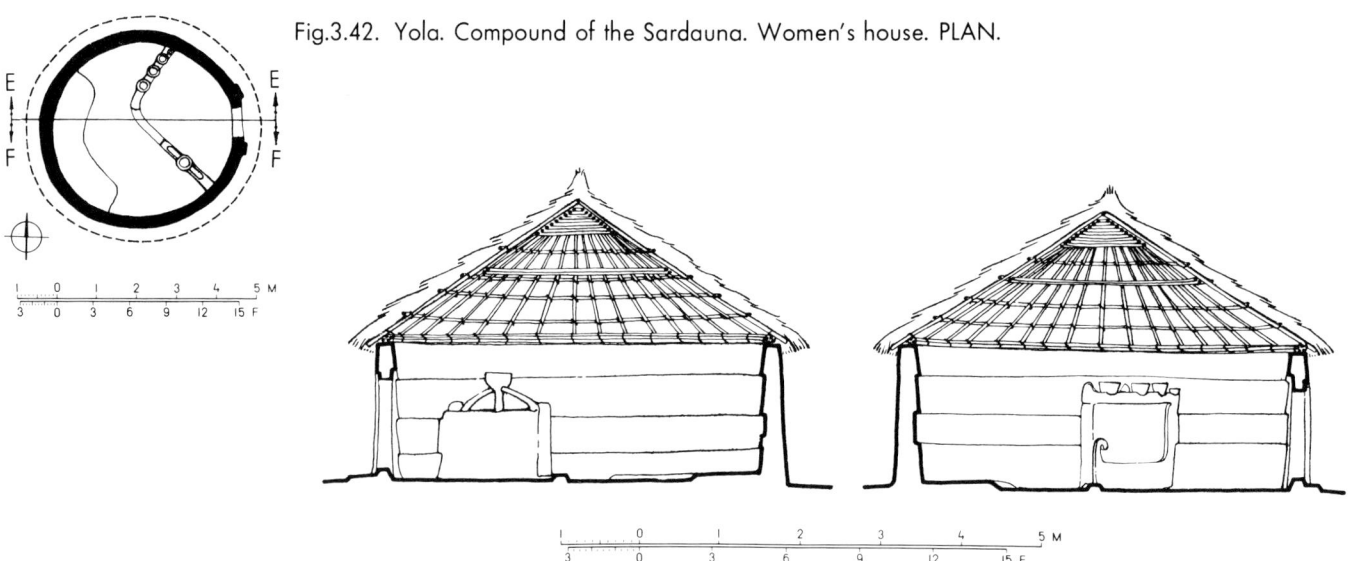

Fig.3.42. Yola. Compound of the Sardauna. Women's house. PLAN.

Figs.3.43, 3.44. Yola. Compound of the Sardauna. SECTIONS E—E, F—F.

Pl.3.15. YOLA. Compound of the Sardauna. Dwellings.

The second part of the Sardauna's compound was divided up into several courtyards by a complex system of partition walls. The majority were reached through their own *jauleru – zauruka* with their typical angled line of entry. Almost invariably there were two more buildings in each courtyard – a living house and a kitchen. Hidden behind a screening wall was a bathroom and toilet. A typical living house is shown in Figures 3.42 – 3.44. The tapering walls were not built from *tubali* but were made in four layers, each accentuated on the inside by being made to protrude slightly in front of the one below. Each layer was allowed to dry for a day before the next was added.

A characteristic element in the interior was two screen walls (*baburum*) on each side of the entrance door. They were decoratively moulded. The one shown in Fig. 3.44 had three small built-in pots (*alabar*) on top. The other screen, shown in Fig. 3.43 had only one pot, but it was set on a stem, which was reinforced with two brackets. *Babarum* concealed the sleeping places, where the women also delivered their babies. At the back of the room was a semi-circular platform, *ngabare*, for storage of clothing and the other possessions of the women. Quite often there was another circular hut, with up to three doors; it had a platform in which were set stone *namugo* for grinding grain.

Pl.3.16 YOLA. Compound of the Sardauna. Jauleru: *detail showing the lower part of the roof construction.*

Pl.3.17. YOLA. Compound of Galadima Aminu. General view.

Pl.3.18. YOLA. Compound of Galadima Aminu. Detail showing forked posts which support a granary.

Compound of Galadima Aminu

The Galadima's house consisted of two large interiors, each covered by a dome, and a low chamber on the S side with a flat roof. The entrance in the W wall led into the more elaborately covered interior, with two crossed *baka* arches. The next room had two arches, set parallel.

The compound contained a number of circular dwellings, with platforms inside for grinding guinea corn and *sorghum*; there were also numerous granaries, *bembe*. All were raised above ground level on forked posts, *noppije*, standing either in concentric circles or in a grid pattern. Horizontal joists (plural: *gafe*; singular: *gafal*) rested in the forks, and on them a strong mat (*malapare*) woven from the thick stems of *iware* grass formed a round platform. The granary proper, circular in plan and covered by a dome, was made on the ground, with the same materials as were used in making the conical roofs. Only when completed was it placed on the platform. It was constructed from *lochi* ribs and coarse *iware* grass matting. The *lochi* were tied together with horizontal rings, *bilordi*, made from bunches of the same *iware* grass. *lochi* and *bilordi* were tightly fastened with *balamji* rope. This inner construction was covered with thatch from the best grass, *titiji bodeji*. There was a circular opening (*damugal* = door) in the apex of the dome. *Damugal* was covered by a lid (*mabbode*) woven from *iware* grass.

Pl.3.19. YOLA. Compound of Galadima Aminu. Granaries in the compound.

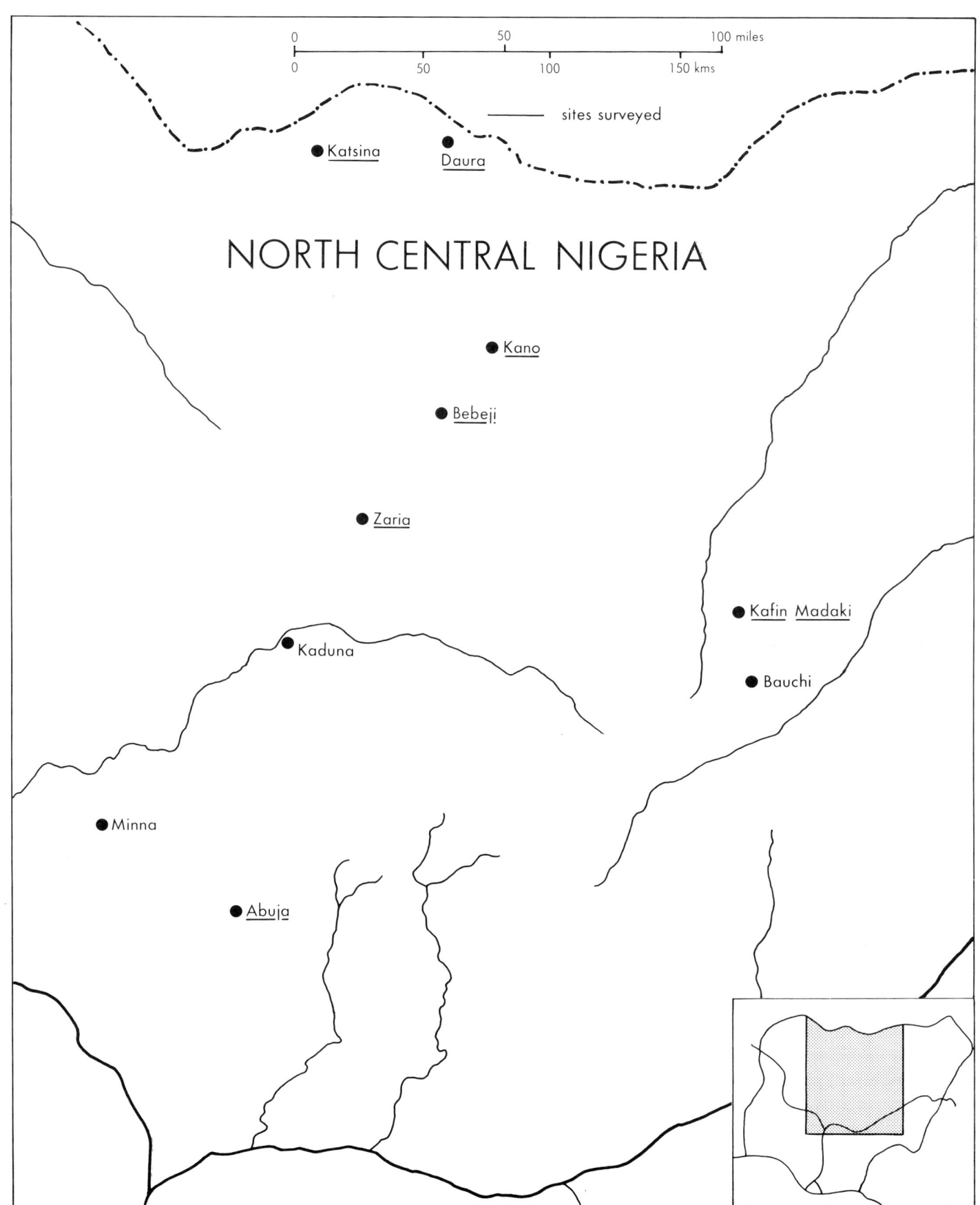

NORTH CENTRAL NIGERIA

sites surveyed

● Katsina   ● Daura

● Kano

● Bebeji

● Zaria

● Kafin Madaki

● Kaduna

● Bauchi

● Minna

● Abuja

4 *Architecture of the Central North*

Kano
Zaria
Katsina

Pl.4.1. KANO. View from the central mosque.

Kano

HISTORICAL BACKGROUND

Tradition maintains that Kano was founded (at the end of the first millenium AD) by ironworkers of the Abagayawa tribe, descendants of the Gaya smith, named Kano,[1] and it seems certain that ironworkers played a vital part in establishing the economic power of this city. There are not sufficient reasons to believe, however, that Kano came into being through such a restricted cause only. Indeed it is conceivable that the foundation of the city was due to a variety of reasons that were both much larger in scope and greater in consequence.

There is no doubt, for instance, that the geographical position of Kano has much to do with the city's development. The organisation of the earliest settlement, which became a nucleus of the future town, was in keeping with patterns commonly adopted all over the world. The pattern is so logical and represents so obvious a basis for the progress of a community, that it became almost a theoretical rule for newly created settlements. First physical security must be obtained, then the organisation of an economy: production and exchange of goods. Finally comes the crowning human achievement, the steady development of the psychical values of the society, still dependent on physical conditions but outside the problems of the domain of matter. The nucleus of a future town was usually created by the erection of a fortified compound on a site possessing a naturally defensive character – say the top of a rocky outcrop, or within the loop of a river or at the confluence of two, occasionally on an island surrounded by water or marshes.

As with every other living organism, the ability to resist attack would not be sufficient for the survival and development if the town. Direct military, or rather tactical values needed to be complemented by strategic opportunities – a condition of future growth. Out of many fortified human settlements only those which were closely linked with the surrounding country and dominated its important lines of communication went through the whole cycle of evolution. Land, sea and river routes served well those who knew how to use them. Travellers, and travelling merchants in the first instance, not only promoted the economic prosperity of their homelands, but were also among the most powerful factors for cultural development. By establishing links with faraway centres of civilisation they permitted foreign trends and achievements to be known, selected and absorbed by their own people. A process of adaptation to their own needs and taste would follow, thus making them in turn adaptable to others. There would be food producers and cloth makers, builders and carpenters, ironworkers and leatherworkers, armourers, artists, musicians. And some of them became merchants, who in time made Kano a commercial centre for local and trans-Saharan trade.

This, of course, was the final phase in the development of many urban societies. In Kano progress was promoted by a particularly auspicious environment. Barbushe, the mythical hero who settled on Dalla Hill and who 'slew elephants with his stick and carried them on his head' – if he ever existed – would be capable not only of great physical feats; he would also be a man of vision, a practical thinker who looked far ahead.

Dalla Hill and the neighbouring Goron Dutse are two lonely peaks rising from a vast area of flat country. They were both easy to defend and therefore fulfilled the primary need for safety, but Dalla probably more so because it was steeper and smaller and thus more manageable by the original, small troop of warriors. Furthermore, it possessed ironstone – a most valuable basis for material development. The acropolis of Dalla had also great strategic possibilities. It was an outpost of the range of hills framing the great plain which extended to the north and east and eventually controlled the trans-Saharan caravan routes at their southern end. The acropolis became a landmark for travellers, a bridgehead to the populous country where merchants could sell their wares, and also a citadel controlling their movements and ensuring their obedience to its ruler.

The Abagayawa period came to a close at the end of the first millenium, and was followed by the Maguzawa epoch, lasting another 500 years. Bagauda was the first ruler of Kano, and from that time there followed the massively increased immigrations of various tribal groups, which anyway had been attracted for many years before. Arab and Berber traders, and Fulani scholars, brought with them Islam, which became the official creed of the kings of Kano from the reign of Muhammad Rumfa (1463-99). During the next three centuries the city further developed culturally, and considerably extended its contacts. Arabs, Kanuri, Berbers and Fulani visited or settled in Kano – and Nupe, Yoruba and Jukun settled permanently within the enlarged city walls. Some of them were scholars and some developed the indispensable settlements of craftsmen and artisans. There were food producers and cloth makers, builders and carpenters, miners, ironworkers and leatherworkers, armourers, artists and musicians. Finally some of them became merchants, who made Kano a commercial centre for local and trans-Saharan trade.

[1] S J Hogben and A H M Kirk-Greene, *The Emirates of Northern Nigeria*, London 1966, p. 184.

Pl.4.2. KANO. View from the central mosque.

In time some of them gradually gained privileges, gathered financial means and increased their influence. In order to defend their city, at this period already prosperous and opulent, and also to emphasise their newly acquired power, the burghers would take an active part in surrounding their city with fortifications. Within the walls there was a mosque in its own square and in close proximity to the Sarki's citadel and to the residences of the leading families. There was also a market place, another major feature of the town – not only the scene of trade and manufacture, but also the centre of the social life of the community.

At this point it is interesting to recall the paragraph of the 'Kano Chronicle' in which the eleven pagan chiefs who are said to be original stock of Kano are listed. They were: Gijigiji the blacksmith, Bugazau the brewer, Hanburki who doctored every sickness, Dabuntunia the watchman of the town at night, Maguji the miner and smelter, Asanni, the forefather of minstrels and chief of the dancers, Bakonyaki the archer (or perhaps the bowmaker?) and finally Awar, who it was said, worked salt. Some of the essential occupations one would expect are not mentioned; nevertheless, it is a fairly compreh-

ensive list of the arts and crafts that were the antecedents, at the earliest period of Kano's growth, of the core of the city's prosperity and culture.

The original area enclosed by fortifications became too confined after a while. More land was needed for the growing population, and was secured by bigger and better fortifications. Immigrants from foreign lands wanted to settle permanently and erected compounds outside the city walls. In due time they were also given the protection of city walls and formed foreign wards attached to the urban community, which had been mostly homogeneous until then. And at this stage, it can be said, the material development of the town was complete.

The Fulani jihad ended the Habe or pre-Fulani dynasties of Kano, and Islam, finally established by the Fulani rulers, became the principal religion of the city. In time the Fulani mixed with their Muslim subjects, and together with the former immigrants, became the present 'urban orientated Muslim collectivity with diverse socio-cultural origins'.[2]

[2] Dr Ahmed Beita Jusuf, *The Development of Ethnic Identity among the Hausa*, Draft paper for the Seminar on Culture in West Africa, 14-20 April 1977.

Gidan Makama

Gidan Makama is one of the oldest buildings of Kano: parts of it date to around 1750 and the tradition of the site goes back even further. Erected as the city mansion of the Makama, one of the highest dignitaries of the emirate, it is situated in the SE corner of the large square in front of the Emir's Palace and at the western end, south side, of the Nassarawa Road. This large artery, in places over 30 metres wide and 2.4 kilometres long connects, through Nassarawa Gate, the two residences of the Emir: one in the city and the other in the suburb of Nassarawa. It also connects two important centres of civil administration: the Provincial Office at the eastern end with the offices of the Native Authority and the City Hall at the west.

Gidan Makama occupied originally an area of circa 15,000 square metres measuring circa 150 metres from east to west and circa 100 metres from north to south. This large compound was divided into three enclosures, each of them entered by a separate, monumental gate-house *zaure*; all the three *zauruka* were set along the road in the northern perimeter wall *garun gida*. Of this original layout the three *zauruka* and two western groups of buildings preserved the traditional earthenwork structure. The eastern section is now replaced by concrete-walled, pan-roofed classrooms and offices of the preparatory school for boys.

The western rooms (adapted for the Kano Museum in 1958) are entered from the westernmost gate. It is circa 4.3 metres high and roughly square in plan with sides measuring approximately 9 metres. Its strongly tapering, earthenwork walls vary much in thickness. The outer wall, in which the door facing the road is set, is a mass of masonry over two metres thick. This is about twice as much as is normally used for two-storeyed buildings and has probably been so designed as to give an impression of strength and opulence. It is worth noting however, that in some old Nigerian buildings excessive thickness of the outer walls results from yearly rendering of their surfaces with new layers of plaster. This process, repeated for decades, added several strata to the original cast and resulted in quite imposing masses of solid masonry. The flat roof of the gatehouse is surrounded by a continuous parapet with thick-set finials on the corners (*zanko*). Another pair of *zankwaye* decorates the top of *gemu*. *Gemu* actually means a beard, and this name is given to a number of structural elements that are corbelled or cantilevered. In this case *gemu* means a slab of masonry projecting from the wall and bracketed over the lintel; it rises up to the *zanko* level and forms a flat canopy above the door (Pl. 4.5). The ceiling of the *zaure* is supported by two heavy rectangular pillars, *al'amudai*, tapering towards the top and headed with capitals that are wider than the pillars and trapezoidal in outline (Pl. 4.9). Since the total effect bears a certain similarity to the pestle used by women for pounding the corn (*tabariya*), this type of pillar is

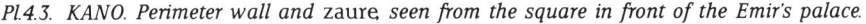

Pl.4.3. KANO. Perimeter wall and zaure, *seen from the square in front of the Emir's palace.*

Fig.4.1. Gidan Makama. PLAN.

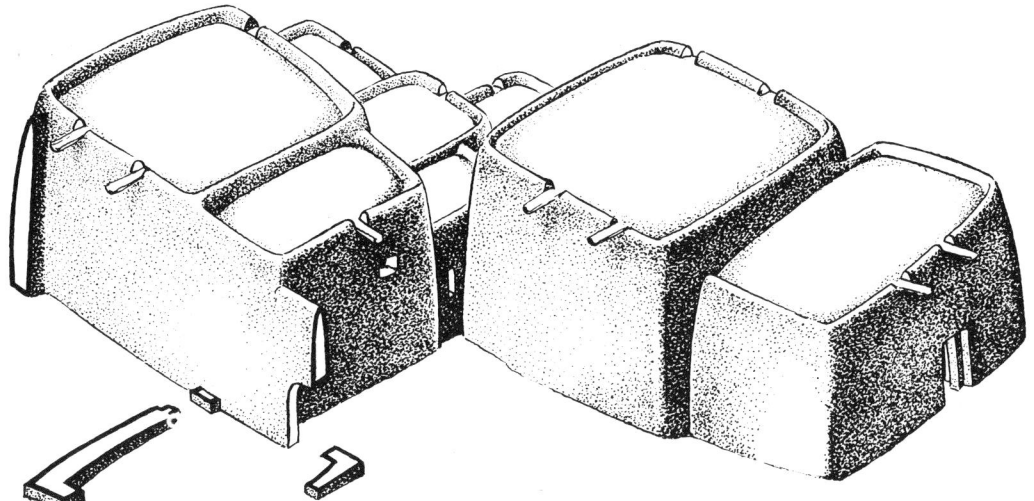

Fig.4.2. Gidan Makama. EXTERNAL ISOMETRIC

called *al'amudi mai tabariya*. The top of each capital is further extended on all four sides by short brackets forming a cross, and made of *azaras* (Pl. 4.8). The brackets of both pillars support the beams (*tauyi*), whose outer ends are laid on the corbels set in the walls. Brackets and corbels carry the beams. Beams (two *azaras* high, eight *azaras* wide) divide the ceiling into six bays (*ciki daya*). The system is devised to lessen the span of the *azaras*; a two metre span between the supports is accepted as the maximum.

The inner door of the gatehouse leads to a small courtyard, *filin kofar gida*, closed on both sides by low walls (*bango*), and at the back by a vestibule of the main cluster of rooms. The first interior is called *soron ajiye takalma*, meaning a building where shoes are put down (by the visitor), or otherwise *soron yara*, a building for the boys, young servants of the Makama who usually slept there. This room, roughly rectangular, about 7 metres wide (EW) and about 4 metres deep (NS), was originally sparsely lit by a couple of narrow windows set high

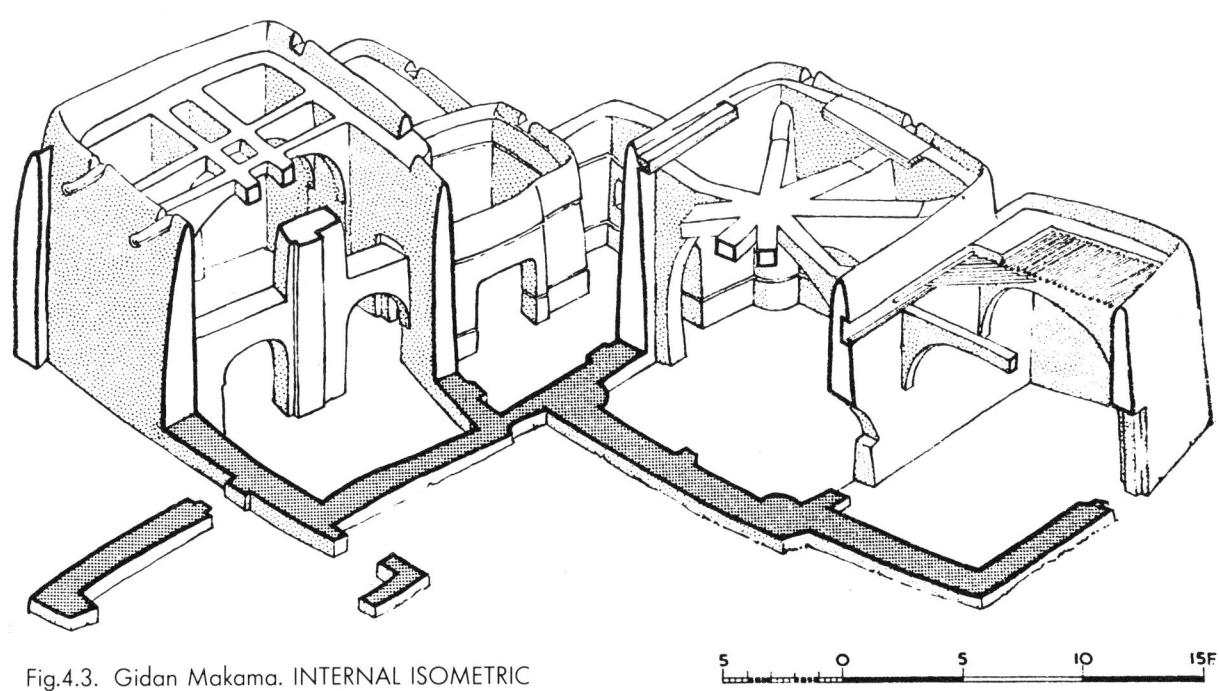

Fig.4.3. Gidan Makama. INTERNAL ISOMETRIC

Pl.4.4. KANO. Gidan Makama. Part of the palace seen from the North East.

in its western wall, sheltered from the eastern winds and rains. The interior had a ceiling of bare *azaras*, laid (EW) on three cross beams, each supported at the walls by quadrantal corbels made of *azaras* and plastered.

A doorless entrance at the east end of the south wall of the vestibule leads to the reception room. The opening is rectangular in its lower part and covered by a semi-circular arch (*kandame*), whose diameter extends about one third of a metre outside each of the jambs. The two small shelves thus formed (*ma'ajin fitila*) are suitable places on which to put oil lamps which are known as *fitila*.

The reception room (*soron fadanci*) was devoted to social occasions — it was here that Makama received his guests, coming to them from the inner apartments of the mansion

where no strangers were admitted. *Soron fadanci* was designed as a rich setting for formal audiences. The skill with which the architect solved the functional and artistic requirements is quite remarkable. He had to provide as large a space as possible, architecturally elaborate and brilliant, giving an unimpaired view of the whole interior. For this reason, and also for the sake of the free movement of visitors, he had to resign from using pillars which add such an air of distinction and monumentality to many Kano interiors. In order to enhance the dignity and wonder, a domed roof was adopted for the *soron fadanci*. The roughly square interior gives an impression of being crowned by four arches: two of them perpendicular, two others set diagonally — a very impressive device. The form of the arches was obtained by coupling

Fig.4.4. Gidan Makama. SECTION B—B.

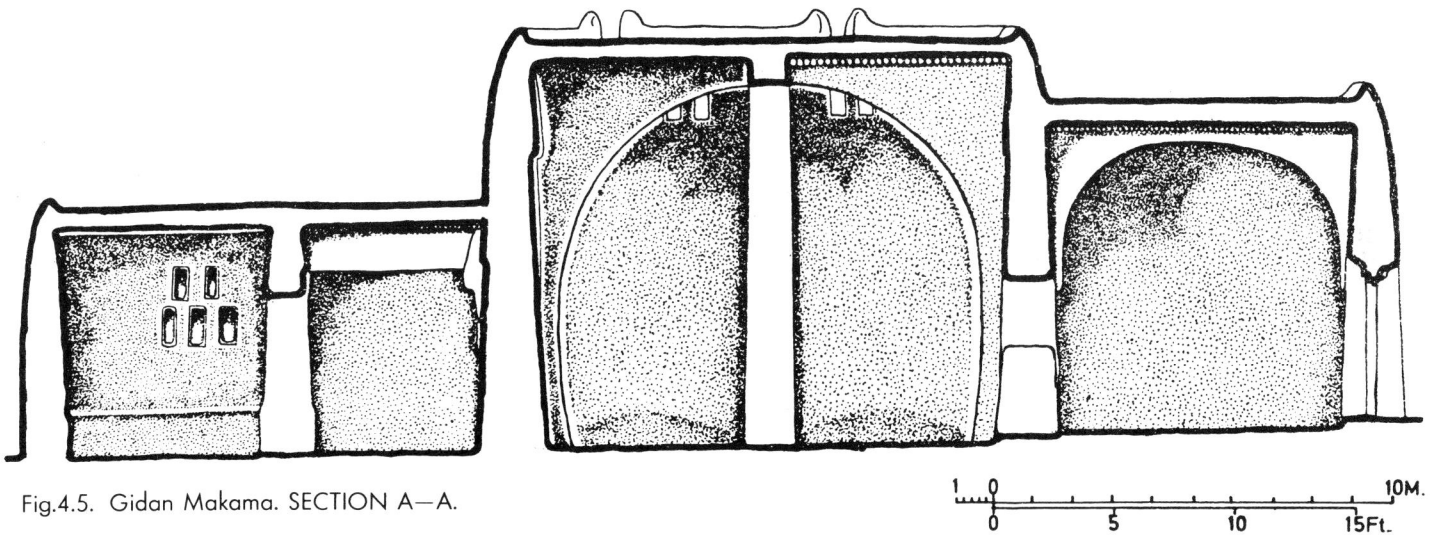

Fig.4.5. Gidan Makama. SECTION A—A.

1 0   10M.

0   5   10   15Ft.

Pl.4.5. KANO. Gidan Makama. Perimeter wall and central zaure.

Fig.4.6. Gidan Makama. *Zaure.*SECTION.

Pl.4.6. KANO. Gidan Makama. Palace interior (see Fig.3).

Pl.4.7. KANO. Gidan Makama. Niche in the zaure, *serving as a shelf for a lamp.*

Pl.4.8. KANO. Gidan Makama. Zaure: *detail of roof construction.*

Pl.4.9. KANO. Gidan Makama. Zaure: *one of the twin pillars supporting the ceiling.*

quadrantal *azara* bracketed beams of the vestibule. The difference is in scale and in the boldness of the configuration. In the vestibule brackets, four layers of reinforcing *azaras* were laid to a height of one metre – here each side of the arch is formed by a consummate system of several superimposed brackets supporting each other and rising from a metre above the floor level up to the central apex six metres in height. To join them together over the optical centre of the room at the properly chosen height and under correct angles obviously required a complete mastery of craftsmanship.

City Merchant's House

Pl.4.10. KANO. City merchant's house, seen from the street.

Pl.4.11. KANO. City merchant's house. Detail of decorated interior walls.

Pl.4.12. KANO. City merchant's house. Detail of decorated interior walls.

Market Stalls

According to the Kano Chronicle, Sarkin Rumfa (Rimfa), 1463-1499, 'the author of twelve innovations in Kano . . . established the Kurmi market',[3] the main market of Kano city. (It replaced the former market of Karabka.) As well as being situated at the intersection of two main thoroughfares, it also formed a nucleus on which all the main city arteries converged.

Clapperton gives a comprehensive description of Kano Market:

'indeed there is no market in Africa so well regulated . . . . particular quarters are appropriated to distinct articles; the smaller wares being set out in booths in the middle, and cattle and bulky commodities . . . in the outskirts . . . The interior of the market is filled with stalls of bamboos, laid out in regular streets; where the most costly wares are sold . . .'[4]

Heinrich Barth also wrote about the regular planning of Kano Market:[50]

'On the northern margin of the Jakara[6] is the market place forming a large quadrangle mostly consisting of sheds built in regular rows of streets; but the westernmost part of it forms the slaughtering place . . . on the northeast side of the sheds is the camel market, where also pack-oxen are sold. The shed where the slaves are sold is at the northwest corner; and thence along the principal street, which traverses the market, is the station of the people who sell firewood . . . The market-place is necessarily much less frequented during the rainy season, when most of the people are busy with the labours of the field. A great part of the market-place during that time is even inundated by the waters of the pond Jakara.'

Unfortunately Barth does not say whether 'stalls of bamboos' as described by Clapperton were replaced during the intervening thirty years by loam and *azara* buildings. Photographs from the beginning of the twentieth century show stalls of an almost monumental character, excellent in their proportions, and covered with rich, moulded geometric decoration.

In 1960 when I carried out a survey with a team from the Department of Antiquities, the majority of these buildings were in a dilapidated condition and nothing was left of the original surface decoration. As often happens in similar circumstances, the damage revealed the inner structure of the buildings and permitted an appreciation of its high constructional values.

A typical stall consisted of two long aisles covered with a flat roof. It was a kind of portico with three parallel rows of strong pillars establishing the two aisles. They were open to each other, and also to the outside by wide inter-columniae along the whole length of the building. The four corners of the building were accentuated by wider pillars, composed of two short walls set at right angles thus, strongly enclosing the body of the building.

The construction of the pillars and of the architraves carried on them, which is different for the inner rows and the outer rows, presents the most impressive device known to me for a Hausa large-spanned flat roof.

The pillars of the inner row were crowned with capitals, the purpose of which was to reduce the span of the beams joining the pillars on the longitudinal axis of the building and also to reduce the span of the *azaras* in the two bays of the ceiling, which were set between the central beam and the external architraves. In both cases the reduction of the span was achieved by a typical application of a *gemu*. The *gemu* of the central beam was not very large but the shape of the beam itself was exactly appropriate, both in its cross-section resembling a T-beam and in its expedient arrangement of the *azara* reinforcement. The reduction of the ceiling span required a double-bracketing of *gemu*, which permitted the placing of the ceiling *azara* on the *tauyi* far out from the pillars. (Figs 4.13 & 4.14)

The two rows of outer, elevation pillars are differently constructed and have a much richer composition. The architrave and the outer façade of the pillars formed a smooth continuous surface, with *gemu* projecting only on top of the inner surface and on both sides of the pillars, parallel to the longitudinal axis of the building. However, as can be seen in Figures 4.7 – 4.12, both the sculptural and structural composition of the architrave and the combination of three *gemus* gave the architect an opportunity for a solution which was not only reliable but aesthetically satisfying. A differentiation was made in the complex carried by the outer pillars: first, a straight beam carrying the slight weight of the parapet and, second, another beam, formed by a series of triple brackets, carrying the ceiling together with the axial beam. The formation of triple brackets backed by the lower part of the architrave created a number of niches of interesting three-dimensional composition with particularly good effect of light and shadow.

The ceiling was laid with tightly-fitting *azaras* set at right angles to the longitudinal axis of the building. Their flat surface was covered with *zana* mats, on which rested the outer layer of the roof made of loam and impregnated with *katsi*. This outer layer was slightly sloped from the axis so that rainwater could flow towards the parapets, into which gutters were set; open conducts leading to the outside were originally without channels or pipes (*indararo*) letting the water run down the façade along semi-circular grooves, presumably waterproofed with *katsi*.

[3] Quoted from *Nigerian Perspectives* by Thomas Hodgkin, p. 89, and from *Sudanese Memoirs* by Palmer.
[4] Denham, Clapperton and Oudney, *Travels*, Captain Clapperton's Narrative, p. 51-3.
[5] H Barth, *Travels*, Vol. I, p. 506.
[6] Jakara – a large pond in the centre of the densely inhabited central area of Kano.

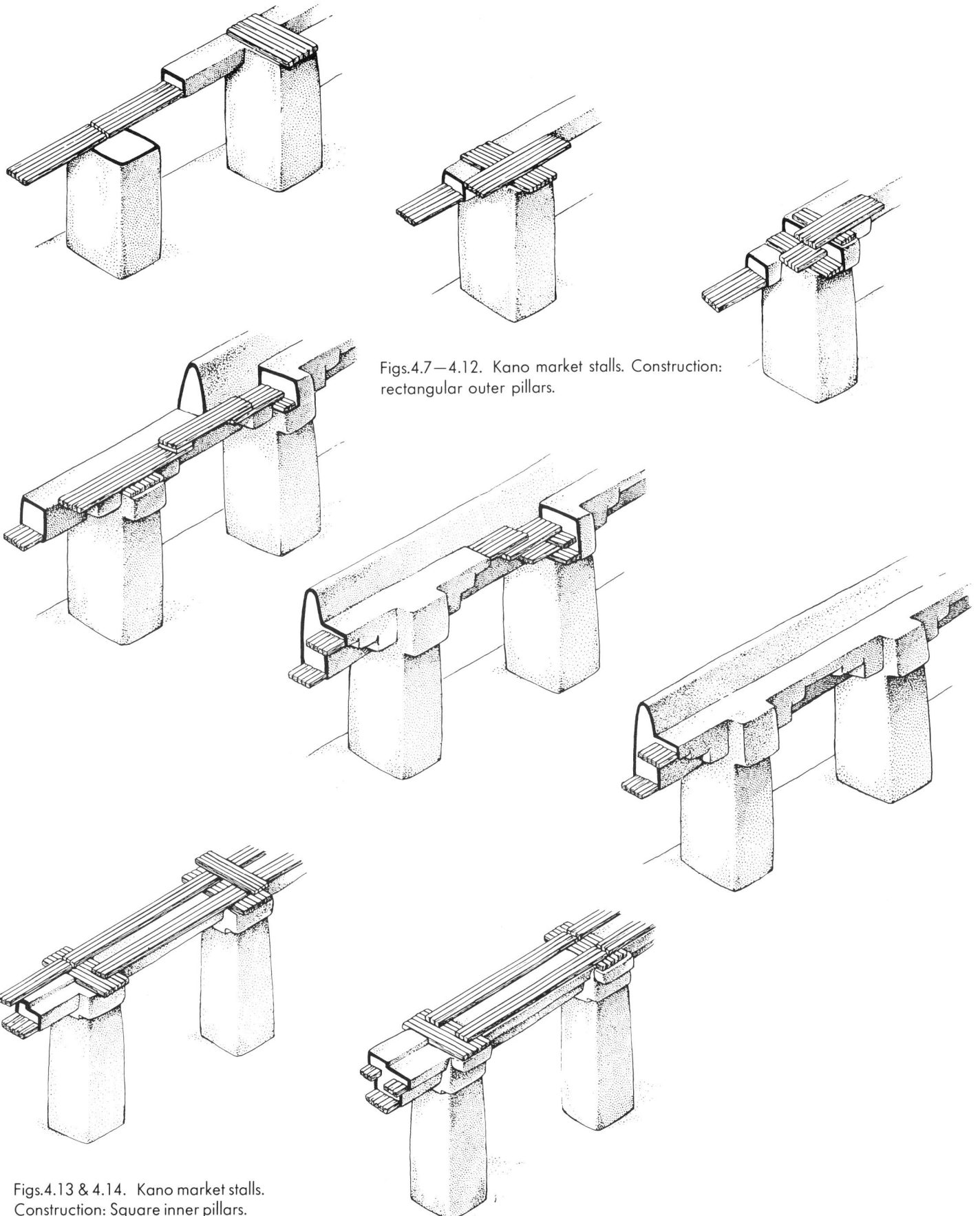

Figs. 4.7—4.12. Kano market stalls. Construction: rectangular outer pillars.

Figs. 4.13 & 4.14. Kano market stalls. Construction: Square inner pillars.

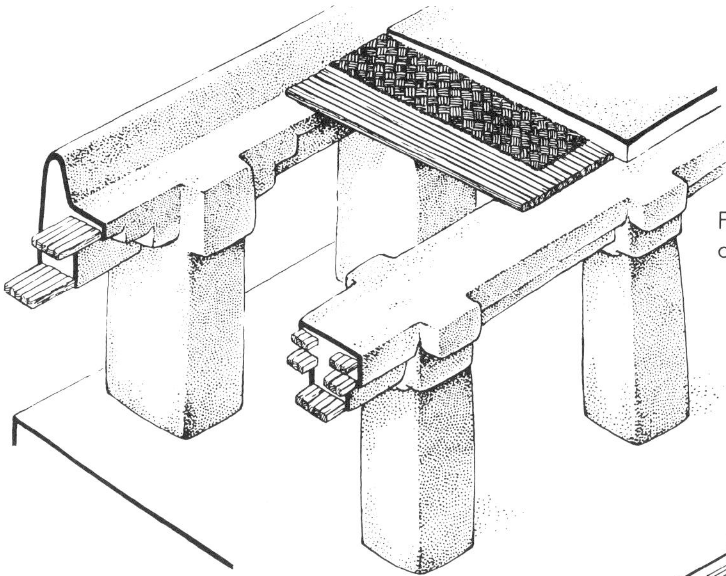

Figs.4.15 & 4.16. Kano market stalls. Construction details, showing outer and inner pillars, with roofing.

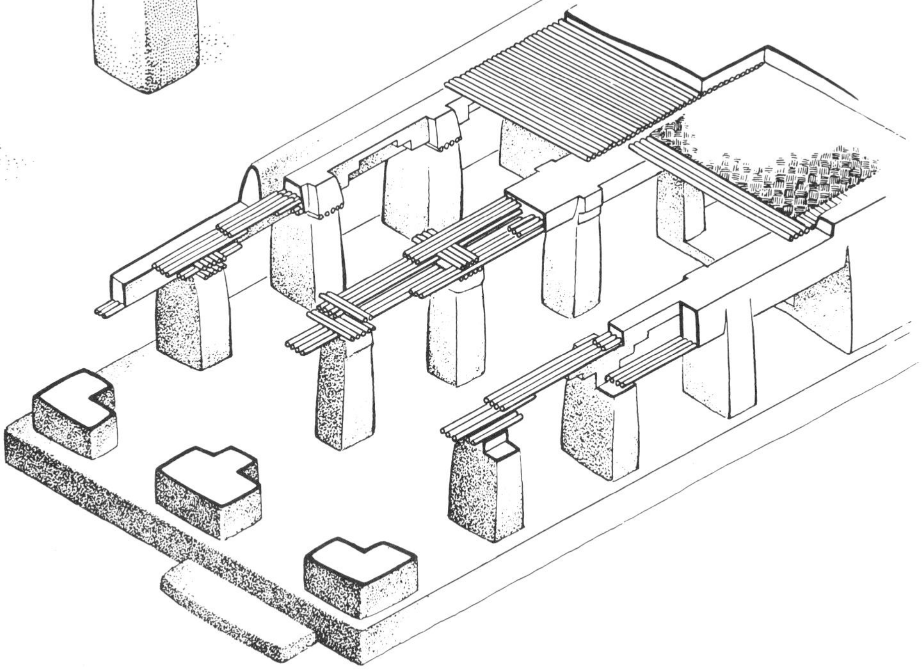

Pl.4.13. KANO. Market stalls. External view.

Pls.4.14 & 4.15. KANO. Market stalls. Internal views.

ZARIA: Structures in the old city in 1965. Photos: courtesy J. Baker.

Zaria

HISTORICAL BACKGROUND

Zaria, one of the seven original Hausa states (the Hausa Bakwai) was founded by Gunguma, the first ruler of Zazzau.[7] Gunguma was the son of Bawo and the grandson of the semi-legendary hero Bayajida, who were both kings of Daura (see Chapter One). Gunguma began a line of sixty Habe kings and queens of Zazzau. The twenty-second ruler, Queen Bakwa of Turunku, moved her people to the foot of Kufena Hill, where the new capital was built.[8]

It was about this time that Zazzau, which previously had been subject to the Gao empire, gained prominence among the Hausa states. Queen Bakwa had two daughters: one was Zaria, whose name was given to the new city, which was built either by her mother or by her. The other daughter, Amina, was thus referred to in the 'Kano Chronicle': 'Queen Amina conquered all the towns as far as Kwararafa and Nupe. Every town paid tribute to her . . . Her conquest extended over thirty four years. [9] The walls of Zaria, as well as those of many other cities, were called *Ganuwar Amina* (Amina's walls). The date of Amina's rule is not reliably established – some authorities give it as the sixteenth century. If this is so it would coincide with the African explorations of Leo Africanus, who wrote his *Description of Africa* in the 1520s, probably after visiting Zaria some ten years earlier.

According to him, at this time Kano paid tribute to Zegzeg, although both kingdoms were vassals of the 'King of Tombuto'.[10]

Of the kingdom of Zegzeg he wrote as follows:

'The inhabitants are rich and have great traffique with other nations. Some part of this kingdom is plains, and the residue mountainous, but the mountaines are extremely cold, and the plaines intolerably hot. And because they can hardly endure the sharpness of winter, they kindle great fires in the midst of their houses, laying the coles thereof under their high bedsteads, and so betaking themselves to sleepe. Their fields abounding in water are exceedingly fruitfull, and their houses are built like the house of the kingdom of Kasena. They had a King of their own in times past, who being sleine by Ischia (as is aforesaid) they have ever since beene subject unto the said Ischia.[11]

About this time Zazzau was converted to Islam, although the date is also given as mid-15th century. According to Uthman dan Fodio, who followed Ahmad Baba ibn Ahmed ibn al-Haji (1553-1627), 'part of Zegzeg' was Muslim country.

In 1804 Muhamman Makau, the last of the Habe kings and queens of Zaria, was driven out and the first Fulani Emir, Mallam Musa, started a series of Fulani dynasties. Some time before the city was moved to its present site, on the left bank of the river Kubani.[12] Abdul Karim (1834-46), the son of Mallam Musa, was offered support in building a great Masallaci Juma'a by the Sultan of Sokoto, who sent his own Babban Gwani, Mallam Kikhaila, to perform the work.

Clapperton gave a description of Zaria in his journal. The town was surrounded by high clay walls within which 'are built a number of little villages and detached houses . . . Near the centre of the wall stands its principal mosque, built of clay, having a minaret about forty or fifty feet high. The principal market is at the south end, inside the walls . . . The house of the governor is north of the great mosque and is surrounded by a high clay wall . . .[13]

Some fifty years later Dr W.B. Baikie spoke of the walls of Zaria being some ten miles in circumference and between sixteen and eighteen feet high. The mosque was 'a large building, 120 feet long, with two domes and a square tower at the north-east ascended by steps'.[14]

In 1963 Zaria still retained a lot of its original character. The main glory of the city, the Masallaci Juma'a, was still intact, and there were only a few alterations in the Emir's palace. Also in its original form was the fine compound of Sarkin Magina. A number of other city houses showed the steady continuation of the decorative treatment of façades, from originally sculptural to increasingly linear designs, concentrating on ingenious and superficially picturesque adornment. To the present writer it resembled, in spirit though not in form, the European treatment of Rococo interiors and occasionally Rococo façades.

It is to be hoped that this is only a short transitional period, which will be followed by a renaissance of the essential nature of Hausa aesthetics and the creation of a modern twentieth century architecture inspired by Zaria's own architectural achievements. It was traditional in spirit but had the basic values of all good architecture: functional planning, making full use of the best contemporary technology available. This was excellently done by Zaria's old master builders and this trend should now be developed, by combining traditional values with twentieth century necessities and possibilities.

---

[7] Zaria was variously referred to as Zazzau, Zazak, Zakzak or Zegzeg (cf. Gazetteer of Zaria Province, E J Arnett, 1920).

[8] S J Hogben and A H M Kirk-Greene, *op cit*, p. 216.

[9] 'ano Chronicle' translated and published by H R Palmer in *Sudanese Memoirs*, Vol. III, p. 107-9.

[10] Thomas Hodgkin, *Nigerian Perspectives*, O.U.P. 1960, p. 102, footnote 2: Timbuktu was actually not the capital, but the major cultural and intellectual centre of the Gao empire.

[11] *Ibid*, ie. al-Hajii Askia Muhammed, otherwise known as Askia the Great, was ruler of the Gao Empire from 1493 to 1528. The text quotes from Leo Africanus, *The History and Description of Africa done into English* by John Pory, ed. Robert Brown, Hakluyt Society, London 1896, ii, pps. 291-4.

[12] S J Hogben and A H M Kirk-Greene, *op cit*, p. 218.

[13] Quoted after S J Hogben and A H M Kirk-Greene, *op cit*, p. 222.

[14] W B Baikie, *Narrative of an Exploring Voyage up the Rivers Kwora and Binue in 1854*, London 1856. Dr Baikie's description does not correspond at all with Mallam Mikhaila's mosque as it was in the 1850s. He could have been referring to the old Zaria mosque, which no longer existed in 1963.

CONSTRUCTION

Building Materials

Building earth (*kasa'n gini*) was dug from pits scatter all over the city. It was generally acknowledged to be very good and was obtainable from any depth. The work was done by labourers hired by the master builder or the person ordering the building. Permission to excavate the building earth was given by the head of the city ward (*mai ungwa*) concerned.

Kasa'n gini was broken into pieces with shovels, watered and puddled underfoot; then it was covered with grass and left for twenty-four hours. Next, horse or donkey manure was added, it was again mixed with water and then worked every day for fourteen days. The building earth thus processed (*kwabe bbiya*) was used to make tubali, mortar and plaster. Before making *tubali* however crushed straw was added – the best kind was called *budu*. Then the *tubali* were left to dry for seven days. Their strength was tested by dropping them from chest height – if they did not crack they were ready for use in building.

The minor cracks in the walls which appeared while they dried were covered with *kashin kaguwa*, made from casts of the *kaguwa* crabs which bury themselves in the river bank. The casts were powdered, sieved, and after water was added and they had been kept for two days, they were applied in a very thin layer. On it next day *buse* was overlaid – this was a solution from very fine earth collected among the rocks by the women.

Walls

The master builder designed the plan of the building, following the instructions of the owner. He plotted the plan on site in the owner's presence, measuring the dimensions by putting one foot close in front of the other; the size depended on the wealth of the master. The plan was outlined with pegs and string, and round buildings were marked out with a string attached to a central peg. Sometimes both the interior and exterior outlines of the walls were marked on the ground; sometimes only the inner outline was marked, and then the number of *tubali* used determined the thickness of the walls. The walls were at least two *tubali* thick; but this number was found only in less important buildings. The thickness of walls was often more than doubled later on by the laying of more *tubali* and plaster on the outside.

Walls were built without foundations. The surface of the ground was so hard that it was thought unwise to perforate it with trenches, as this would produce settlement of the building.

Ceilings and Domes

The simplest ceilings (*shgifa*) were laid in a manner similar to those in Kano (cf. pp. 4.5 & 4.7, isometries p. 4.7).

The main difference in constructing the corbels (*kafa*, cf. Hausa corbels, p. 1.30) was that the overlapping layers of *keffi* (*kafar guga*) rods were not bound in rope as in Kano, but merely counterweighted at their lower ends by the *tubali* in the wall. An additional counterweight of *azaras*, laid above the base of the *keffi* (cf. p. 1.30) was also used, in Zaria as in Kano; it was called *denni* (*masham fidi* in Kano).

Bakan gizos sprang at a height of three *dunguna* (*dungu* means the length of the forearm from the elbow to the end of the closed fist).[15] Perhaps for this reason the bracket which supported the 8 centimetre overhang marking the bottom of the *bakan gizo* was called *dunguna* as well.

The upper parts of the walls from which the *bakan gizos* sprang were often built in overhanging layers. Each overhang was supported by a *denni* running parallel to the face of the wall and embedded in the thickness of two neighbouring *bakuna*.

The panels formed by crossed *bakuna* (*daurin guga*) were filled by several layers of *azaras*. As described on p. 1.40, those laid diagonally (*alwatika*) and superimposed by perpendicular *tauyi* were covered with as many further layers of *azaras* as necessary; all these were called *zubi*. *Asabari* mats were loosely spread over the surface of the *zubi*; the mats were made of thick, strong *iwa* grass, tied together with *rama*[16] or with cord from the *kuka* tree. On top of the *asabari* was put a layer of wet layer of wet building earth, *kwabe-bbiya*, and this was finally waterproofed later. Both flat and domed roofs were waterproofed by the application of various plasters – *katsi, dafar, gashin, jima* and *laso* (cf. p. 1.7 on plasters).

The parapet (*rawani*) surrounding the roof was erected above the outer walls of the building. As a rule it was crowned with *zankwaye* (*zanko*, singular) which were sometimes positioned along their length and were always found at the corners of the building.

The rainwater running from the roof was collected in the gutter which ran along the parapet. It was projected far outside the walls by a number of spouts, *ndororo*; these were made of burnt clay by women potters. Otherwise (especially recently) draining devices were made out of the upper part of

---

[15] Cf. G P Bargery, *op cit*, p. 278.
[16] Cords were made from the bark of the *rama* plant, which was specially planted for the use of Zaria builders.

Pl.4.16. ZARIA. Sarkin Magina's compound. Detail of roof construction (talkamin kasa).

giginya palm trunk, which was split in half and then hollowed out.

There were various ways of supporting the roofs with *bakuna* (cf. paragraph on corbels, p. 1.30) and in addition there was an attractive solution in the form of a frame called *maburgi*. It consisted of two *talkamin kasa* set opposite each other at a distance of up to two metres, with a rectangular panel in between.

Decoration

The interior embellishment was restrained. The aesthetics of the interior apparently relied on good proportions and the harmonious composition of structural elements. Nevertheless there were shallow niches *alkuki* in the walls, sometimes in combinations of two or three. The main ornamentation was concentrated on the *bakuna* and the *bakan gizos*. Their soffits (*yanciki*) were incised horizontally to give a zig-zag cross section (*dagagye*), and this was often combined with simple geometrical patterns – triangles, squares, lozenges and circles. Paint made from light-reflecting mica fragments (*bouze*) emphasised the plasticity of these mouldings.

Openings and Floors

Most of the inner doorways were arched (*kandame*). Rectangular doorways, usually found in the outer walls, were closed by a door. This was hinged in two mortices – the upper one in the lintel, the bottom one in the floor. The pivot was usually of hard wood, and the rest of the door was made from vertical *gongolas*, braced with rails made of *lukuki* plant and fastened together with strips of leather. Such doors provided protection against thieves (*barawon*). They were often set on the inner side of the wall in a shallow niche, *barawon kofar*, and secured by a short chain hasped to the *azara* jamb. On the outside they were often screened with a length of *asabari* mat. Doorways were often flanked by decorative pilasters, *afari*, especially on the outer façades of the buildings.

Floors, as practically everywhere in the country, were laid by women when the building was completed. The ground was carefully levelled, then watered profusely and spread with *tsakuwa* gravel, which was beaten in with mallets. Again as was usual, the work was accompanied by singing and drumming. Two calabashes were used as drums; the lower, larger one was filled with water to give better resonance, and the upper one was used as a cover, and beaten with drumsticks.

Pl.4.17. ZARIA. Sarkin Magina's compound. Zaure entrance.

Compound of Sarkin Magina

Sarkin Magina's house was built by Mallam Sumaila, a descendant of Mallam Mikhaila and the last in the line who enjoyed the honourable title of *Babban Gwani*. He was a wealthy man and erected a splendid residence, which was completed by his son, Mallam Balarbe (died 1961), the first Sarkin Magina of Zaria. Balarbe's son, Mallam Ibrahim, Sarkin Magina, gave permission for a thorough survey of the residence, and provided me with comprehensive information on the building technology of Zaria (cf. pps. 4.20 – 4.21).

The compound, although in general outlines corresponding to the typical planning of well-to-do Hausa residences, carried unmistakably the creative ideas of its designer, both in the general setting of its separate parts and in the lavish decoration of walls and structural elements. This struck one immediately, at the very gatehouse of the residence, which was brilliantly designed to compress within a limited space three main sections, each serving a different purpose, yet communicating in a truly functional way.

The only entrance to the residence, the *zaure* was in the front wall, facing roughly west and the long lane which led to the main market place. As is sometimes to be observed (for instance in Zaria or Kafin Madaki) Sarkin Magina's mosque stands in the immediate vicinity of the *zaure* – in this case at a distance of some nine metres door-to-door.

Pl.4.18. ZARIA. Sarkin Magina's compound. Zaure interior.

The *zaure* (1) (Fig. 4.17) was flanked on the W by a garage (2) and by an inner antechamber (3) on the other side. The front façade, rather restrained in character (Pl. 4.17) hid three excellently composed interiors. The core of the design was, naturally, the domed room where most of Sarkin Magina's visitors were received. The dome had an elaborate *tuluwa* of four *bakan gizos*, ie. eight *bakuna* corbels. Those of the NW, NE and SE sprang from pilasters on the corresponding three walls; those on the SW were carried by two stout pillars standing at a distance of one metre from the W wall. Thus an isolating space (1) was provided between the entrance door and the reception area (2); this tiny antechamber added to the composition-in-depth of the *zaure* and gave access to the (3) composition-in-depth of the *zaure* and gave access (3) south-eastwards to the waiting room (4) and to a passage on the NE leading to the private apartments.

The *zaure* (Fig. 4.19, Section A-A) in spite of its fairly small size had a truly monumental character because of the imaginative partioning of its space and the decoration of *bakan gizos*, which was simple along the *baka* soffits (Pl. 4.18) yet concentrated the attention on the elaborate mouldings at the apex.

The waiting room was domed, and had a simple frame, *baka hudu*, of four corbels; there was small antechamber (5) further NE with a decorative arched door of a type called *fintilla* (ie. having small shelves for lamps) at the back (Section A-A. Pl. 4.20). The further view was screened by a wall, but towards the NW a flat-roofed *soro* led to a household courtyard (A) (Pl. 4.19) with a large *debi*, a circular verandah not unlike the *debi* in the women's quarters of the Emir's palace (p. 5.40).

In the NE corner of courtyard A was a two-roomed house for the male youth of the compound (7). Further NE extended the domain of Sarkin Magina's women; as usual this occupied the major part of the compound. Its centre was an irregular court (D) (Pl. 4.22) surrounded on all four sides by women's houses. Those varied in plan, structure and decoration, and all except one were separated from the perimeter wall by large courtyards, C, E, F, G, H and I.

The façade of the easternmost house (8) linked two stretches of the perimeter wall. Naturally the façade was windowless, but the front room was most lavishly decorated with moulded, geometrical patterns (Section D-D. Fig 4.20). It also had one of the two most agreeably embellished clay bedsteads in this unique compound; it was hollow, and was heated with red embers (Section E-E. Fig. 4.21). The bedroom door was set almost opposite the main entrance. Both rooms

had flat roofs on simple *bakuna*. A little passage led from the front room to a small private courtyard, E.

The house (9) on the NE side of the square was separated from the former house by a fairly wide passage leading to courtyard F. It had three domed rooms of simple construction (cf. Section F-F and G-G) and a square annexe leading to courtyard F and to private courtyard G.

The NE wall was richly moulded in the usual geometrical patterns, with a composition of three niches (*alkuki*) at the mid-height of the wall. The mouldings over the door leading to the mid NE room are especially worth noting – they belong to the same type of three-dimensional patterning, obtained by the overlapping of layers of plaster, as wall applied by Mallam Mikhaila in the Zaria Masallaci.[17]

The E side of the entrance room was formed by the elliptical wall of house 10. This, because of its form and situation, was the focal point of courtyard D. The plan of house 10 resembled rooms 126-127 and 128-130 in the womens' compound of the Emir's palace (cf. p. 000), but its inner formation was, if anything, even more decorative. There was no front verandah, but the living room, *shirayi*, was obviously designed with the greatest care and skill. Its *tuluwa* was adapted to the elliptical outline of the room, in such a way that the two *bakuna* flanking the longitudinal axis of the room crossed at the apex of the dome, and emphasised the position of the two main doors of the interior, the outer and the inner, leading to the *daki* at the back (Section C-C, Fig. 4.24). These *bakuna* produced a special effect, appearing almost like baldachin over the doors. The crosswise *bakuna* were not laid in a straight line but sprang from the centre of the curves delimited by the two former *bakuna*. This was made possible by their corbelled structure. The harmonious convergence of all the corbels above the optical centre of the room proves how completely the builders had mastered their technique. The moulded surround of the door to the *daki*, is shown schematically on Section C-C.

The room contained a hollow, clay bedstead – the most decorative bedstead I ever saw in the country. Using generally known Hausa geometric designs, it was formed as clay tracery openwork, and provided a beautiful finishing touch to this impressive interior.

---

[17] It was also recorded far away in the old houses of Bida.

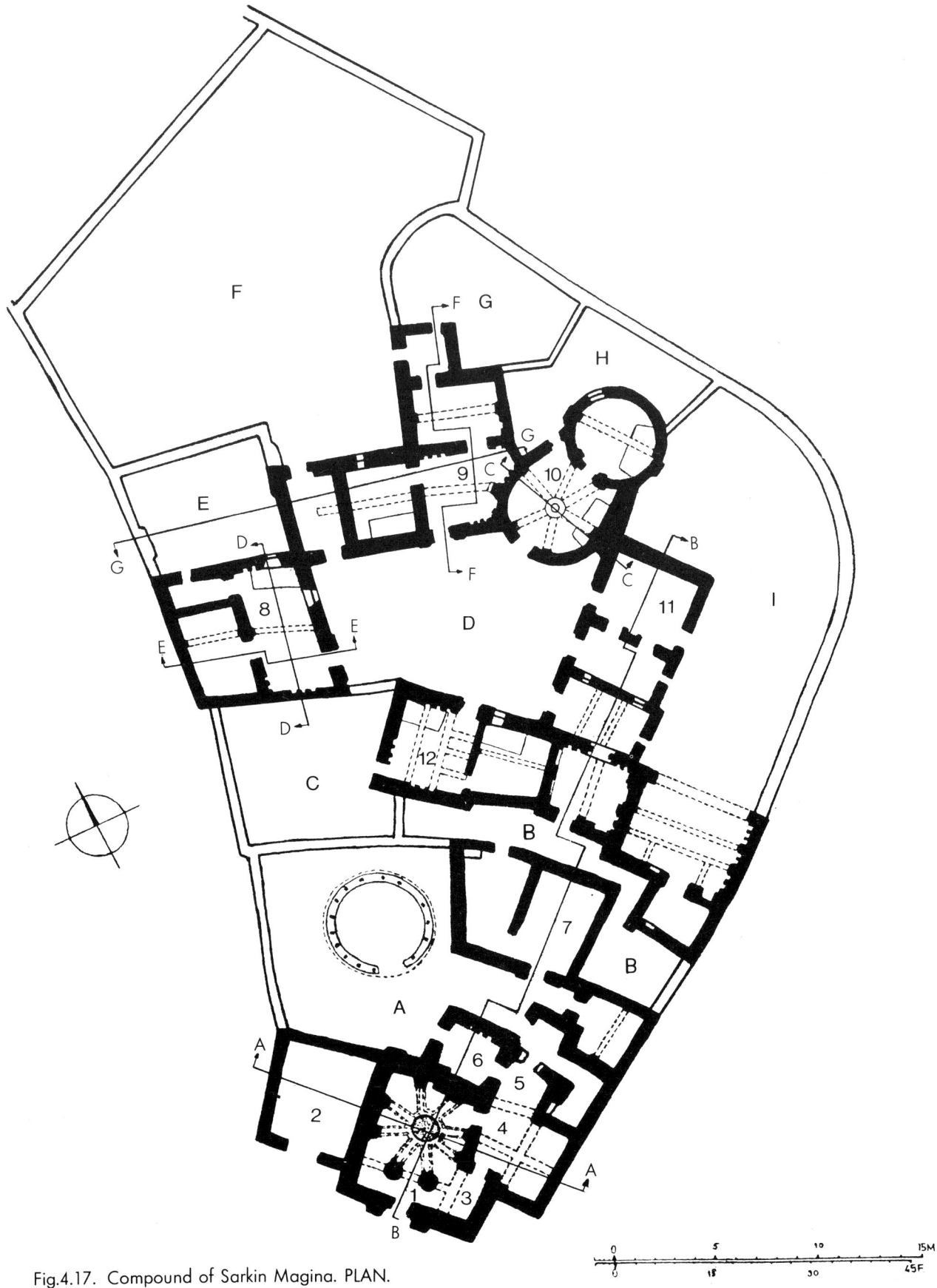

Fig.4.17. Compound of Sarkin Magina. PLAN.

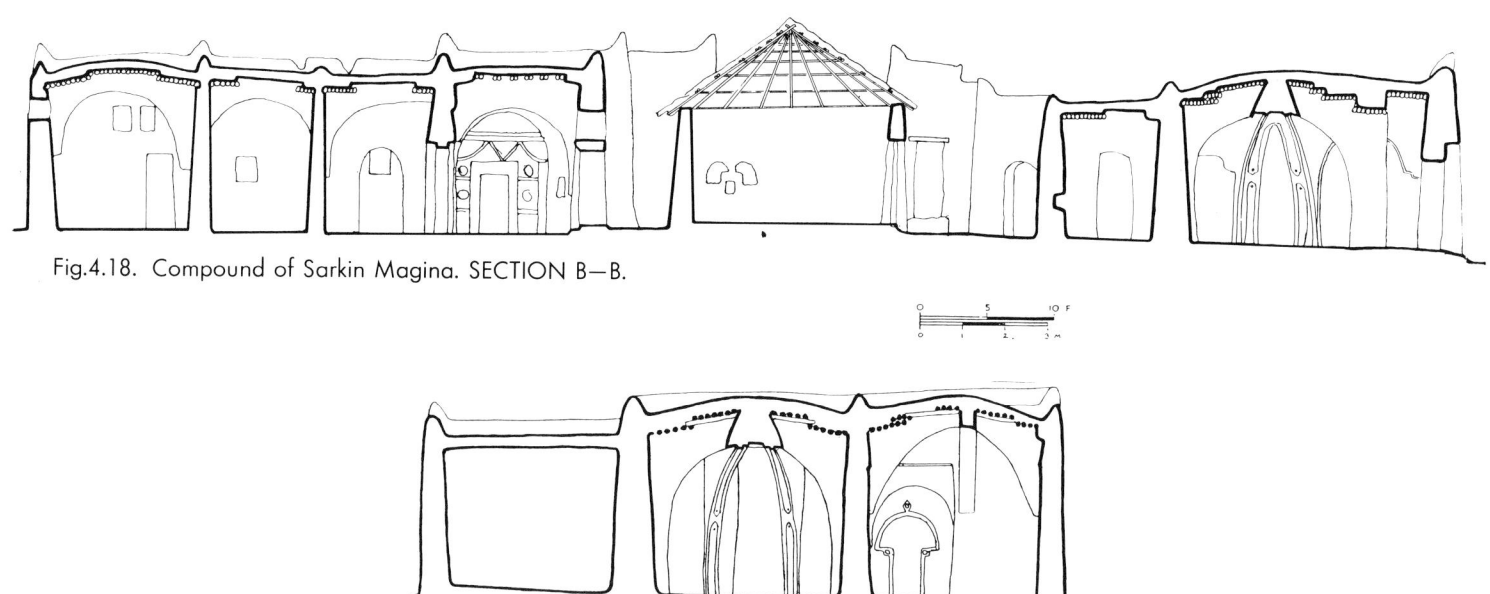

Fig.4.18. Compound of Sarkin Magina. SECTION B—B.

Fig.4.19. Compound of Sarkin Magina. SECTION A—A.

Pl.4.19. ZARIA. Sarkin Magina's compound. Household courtyard, seen from the large circular verandah, debi.

Pl.4.20. ZARIA. Sarkin Magina's compound. Decorative arched door, with two small shelves for lamps.

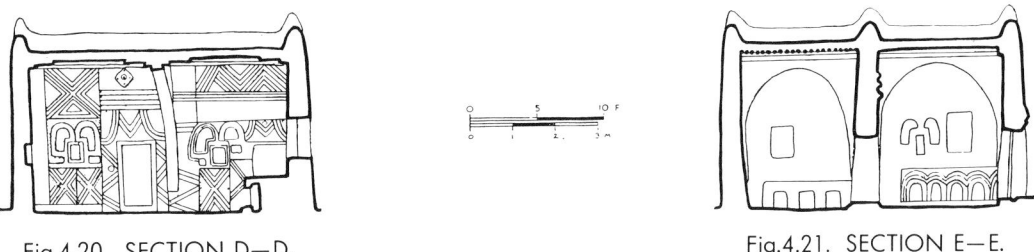

Fig.4.20. SECTION D—D.   Fig.4.21. SECTION E—E.

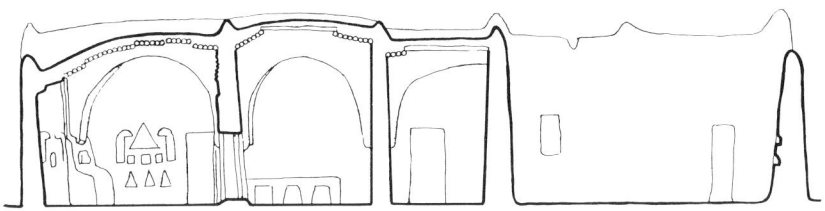

Fig.4.22. Compound of Sarkin Magina. SECTION G—G.

Pl.4.21. ZARIA. Sarkin Magina's compound. Room 8 with clay bed (see Fig.21).

Pl.4.22. ZARIA. Sarkin Magina's compound. Courtyard D.

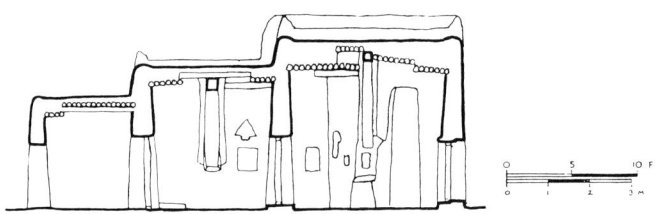

Fig.4.23. Compound of Sarkin Magina. SECTION F—F.

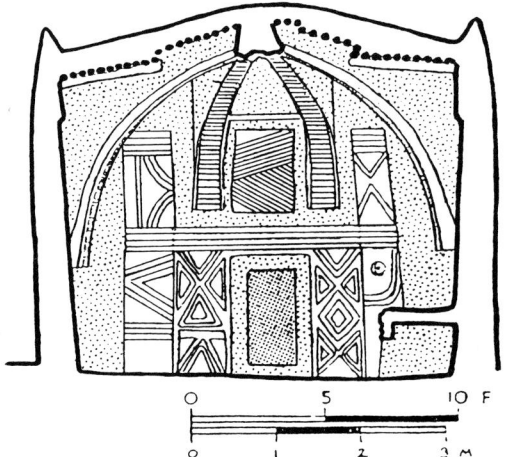

Fig.4.24. Compound of Sarkin Magina. SECTION C—C.

Pl.4.23. ZARIA. Sarkin Magina's compound. Room 10. Detail of domed roof.

Pl.4.24. ZARIA. Sarkin Magina's compound. Room 10. Bedstead, beautifully made in clay tracery openwork.

Katsina
Training College

Pls. 4.25–4.27 KATSINA. Training college. Views.

Nasarawa Palace. Part of the North elevation.

SECULAR ARCHITECTURE OF NORTHERN NIGERIA

5 *Architecture of the Central North, Emirs' Palaces*

Daura
Katsina
Kano
Zaria
Kafin Madaki
Abuja

Pl.5.1. DAURA. Emir's Palace: doorway to the palace.

Daura
Emir's Palace

Daura is commonly accepted as the earliest – the mother – Hausa kingdom. There are numerous versions of the Daura legend, one in the *Girgam* (written record)[1] and the other in *Daura Makas Sariki*.[2]

When surveying Daura palaces I was offered a manuscript, 'Daura History – Memorandum' by M Bukari Musa, Madaki Daura.[3]

There are various opinions about a number of Habe rulers of Daura: 17 queens and 47 kings, or 9 queens and 46 kings.

In the sixteenth century Daura, as well as the six other Hausa *bakwai*, were well established city states, and Daura territories extended far to the north of present-day Nigerian boundaries.[4] During the Fulani conquest, Daura, being apparently surrounded by strong fortifications which could not be taken by storm, was occupied in 1805 only after a long siege. It seems equally apparent that the last Habe ruler of the kingdom, Sarkin Gwari Abdu, lived in a palace reflecting the power and glory of the cradle of the seven Habe kingdoms.

When I was surveying the palace in 1964, I was unable to chronologise any of the various parts of the palace. The buildings were described as 'very old' – which was obvious merely by analysis of their style, and also by recording the numerous alterations in their structure and network of inner communications, when old doors were bricked up and new

passages created. These probably resulted from changes in custom and organisation of royal court ceremonial, made by consecutive rulers. All the same, it is reasonable to presume that most of the original plan of the residence has not changed for several centuries

In 1964, some of the palace was inaccessible, and part of the rest was abandoned and much dilapidated. However, a number of buildings proved the mastery of succeeding generations of Daura builders who created, maintained and occasionally improved the original designs.

Pl.5.2. DAURA. Emir's palace. Detail of the roof construction in kofar zaure.

---

[1] Translated by H R Palmer in *Sudanese Memoirs*, Lagos 1928.

[2] 'Daura Makas Sariki' (Daura snake slayer), translated by E J Arnett, *Journal of the African Society*, IX, 1909-1910.

[3] According to this manuscript, a hero called Najib, who migrated from Egypt to Canaan, had a son, Abdul Dar (Abdurdur) who advanced westwards and then southwards until he came to a suitable place, probably an oasis, and settled. Abdul died there, and then his daughters succeeded him one after another as Magajiya, ie. female successor. These were the well-known nine queens of Daura. The ninth queen, Magajiya Daura, migrated to a new site, called Daura after her. This is the present town, known as Birnin Daura. The old site is now known as Tsofan Birni (old ruins of a walled city); it is about seven miles north of Daura town. The following are the names of the nine queens: Kufuro, Yakumo, Awaiana, Gidirgidir, Inagari, Gamata, Shawata, Sanlamata and Daura. This version seems to be incomplete. There were apparently seventeen Hausa queens of Daura (as listed by J S Hogben and A H M Kirk-Greene in *The Emirates of Northern Nigeria*, London 1966, p. 154). Mallam Bukari Musa narrated in his 'Daura History' the marriage of Daura to Abayajide, known as Bayadidda. He came from Baghdad through Nubia . . . Karen and Bagarmi into Bornu. There he married Magirana, daughter of the ruling Mai, but later had to escape. At length, after further adventures, he arrived in Daura. Here he killed a dangerous snake, Kiala, who was preventing Daura's inhabitants from using the town's well, *kusugu*. Queen Daura 'offered to give Bayajidda half of Daura town, but he refused and asked for her hand instead. She agreed and thus they became wife and husband. Then people began to call Bayajidda a new name, Sare-Kia, later on shortened to Sarki'. The royal couple had a son, Bawo Gari, whose six children became rulers of the further six Hausa states. All seven were named Hausa Bakwai.

[4] Thomas Hodgkin, *Nigerian Perspectives*, Oxford University Press, 1960.

The most impressive building was the *kofar zaure*, the entrance hall. It projected outside the perimeter wall of the residential complex. Its walls were extremely thick – up to 2.8 metres. The structure and three-dimensional design were most imaginative and proved the proficiency of the builders in spatial composition.

The roughly square interior was covered by a flat roof, supported by an elaborate system of four main corbelled arches. These were supplemented by a number of semi-elliptical consoles or cantilevered beams, all reinforced with timber. The main arches, the *bakan gizo*, sprang from eight pillars: the four pillars standing on both sides of the main axis were square; the four along the transverse axis were round. All of them stood independently for only one-third of their height; the upper two thirds of each pillar joined with the walls of the *kofar*, thus forming an extremely powerful system of supports. It could be compared with the structural concept of flying buttresses but set inside, rather than outside the building, and leaving a free passage along the walls all around the *kofar zaure*. This passage could be compared with the ambulatory of a medieval cathedral, to borrow once again from the vocabulary of European gothic. This comparison, it must be emphasised, applies only insofar as each problem was solved by similar thinking on the part of the designers. The structure, form and purpose had no similarity to any European device. (Pls. 5.1 – 5.4.; Figs. 5.2 & 5.3).

From the *kofar zaure* access was provided to the outer courtyard of the palace, *filin kofar gida* (see Plate 5.5). The passage turned at a right angle through a couple of small rooms (2) (Fig. 5.1) to the left and into the open. Such a tortuous passage was in keeping with the common Hausa tendency to screen the inner parts of the residence. This idea was obviously rejected in recent times when a new outer gate was built, piercing the front of the perimeter wall, and giving a direct view of the courtyard. (Plate 5.5).

At the back of the trapezoidal *gida*, flanked with *bango* walls, stood the first entrance hall, called *soron fadanci* ('a place where respects were paid to the Emir') (3). This building was again defined as 'very old', but in 1964 the interior was much modernised. The structure of the *soron* was ambitiously conceived, and often exceeded the technological possibilities of the materials used – the roof of the building collapsed a number of times in the past. The last reconstruction was carried out in 1944 by Sarkin Gini (who on the orders of the Emir guided me around the palace.) He did an excellent job, for in strengthening the framework of the interior he achieved a striking loftiness. In front of the original pillars which carried the main *bakan gizo*'s he added four slender pillars. These were linked in their uppermost part with the original pilasters in a manner resembling the arrangement in the *kofar zaure*. Pairs of the newly erected pillars (*ginchiki*) were joined at the top with transoms shaped like semi-elliptical arches; these were slight in appearance and gave the impression of being a mere decorative fancy, but they strengthened the network carrying the flat roof (Fig. 5.2). Similar arched transoms flanked the central one and the final structural

effect was to provide a beam which tied the pillars with the outside walls of the *soron fadanci* and at the same time reduced the span of the *bakan gizo*.

Soron fadanci led to the slightly larger hall which served as a resting place (*soron hutu*) (4) for the Emir (Pl. 5.10). The crossed *bakan gizo*s of both these interiors should be considered rather as corbelled beams. The corbels were made of four layers of cantilevered *azara* rods, *kafin kafa*, (*azara* rods were called *kemi* in Daura, but were made from the same *giginya* palm as in Kano.) The two corbels were set in opposite walls and then joined together by the last, horizontal layer. Every two consecutive layers of a corbel were bound together with a rope (*kabai*) made from *goriba* (*giginya* palm). Each layer was two *azaras* thick and had three *azaras* in a row. This was a daring arrangement which utilised the strength of the material to its utmost capacity. Realising this, Daura builders decided to combine boldness with caution: they used trestles, set up in the centre of the room, to give support in the place where all the *bakan gizo*s met. This method was never used in Kano or Katsina. Nevertheless, as in other Hausa *soraye*, all the *bakan gizo*s in each room were built simultaneously, in order to reach their peaks at the same time. Once this was done the still fragile points of connection were reinforced by binding further layers of *azara* on top of them. Only then were the trestles removed, leaving the entire floor space free of any vertical supports.

Sarkin Gini, who explained his method of reconstructing the roofs of both *soraye* to me, also provided further information. The building earth (*dendonkwa*) used in the palace construction was of the highest quality in Daura – it was dug from *kofar baru* (*kofar* = gate, *baru* = pit). *Dendonkwa* was mixed with water only once, then grass called *wudu*, which was very soft and shredded small, was used for making *tubali*. *Dendonkwa* to be used for mortar was processed for five to seven days, and mixed with water every day in the usual manner.

Another kind of earth was used for plastering the walls. It was called *gode* or *jungergeri*, was known for its fineness and again was taken from a special pit. It was mixed with *makuba* or *loda*. *Makuba* was made of powdered pods, *loda* of the roots of the same tree. Both, when soaked in water, produced a sticky liquid which had a reddish colour. The *kemi-azara* were usually four to five *kamu* long (*kamu* = a man's forearm). The foundations were dug from 90 centimetres to 120 centimetres deep.

The moulded decoration of pillars and *bakan gizo*s was called *ado*; the same word was used for painted decoration. The small niches for oil lamps were called *alkuki*.

Soron hutu had two doors, one on each side. Both led to adjoining antechambers (*sherai*). The *sherai* (5) to the left was out of bounds to me; the one on the right, in the far corner, had three doors, all giving access to the inner courtyard, *pagacin samiya*. At the back of this stood two buildings. The rectangular *soron* with its two heavy square pillars supporting the roof was used as a schoolroom for the Emir's children and grandchildren (6). To the left of it, a door set in a very thick wall gave access to the inner *sherai* (7) from which there was a turn to the left into *dakin ganawa* (a room of introducing) (8). The room was completely dark and had a complex plan. The entrance from *sherai* was set in a semi-circular recess; another almost symmetrical recess was divided off by a pillar. In front of this separating pillar, a metre away, stood another pillar, reinforced with two pilasters; this divided both recesses from the main interior. To the right was the rostrum for the Emir's throne. Next to it a steel door (Pl. 5.13) separated *dakin ganawa* from a tortuous suite of corridors (9) proceeding to a lofty council chamber (10). Originally this chamber was covered by a roof supported by one full arch combined with a semi-arch. This fairly popular arrangement (Pl. 5.8) collapsed some years ago and was replaced by an enormously thick pillar which spoiled the original composition (Pl. 5 12). To the right of the corridors there was another interior (11), used as a guest room. Nearby a flight of steps (12) led to the upstairs storerooms.

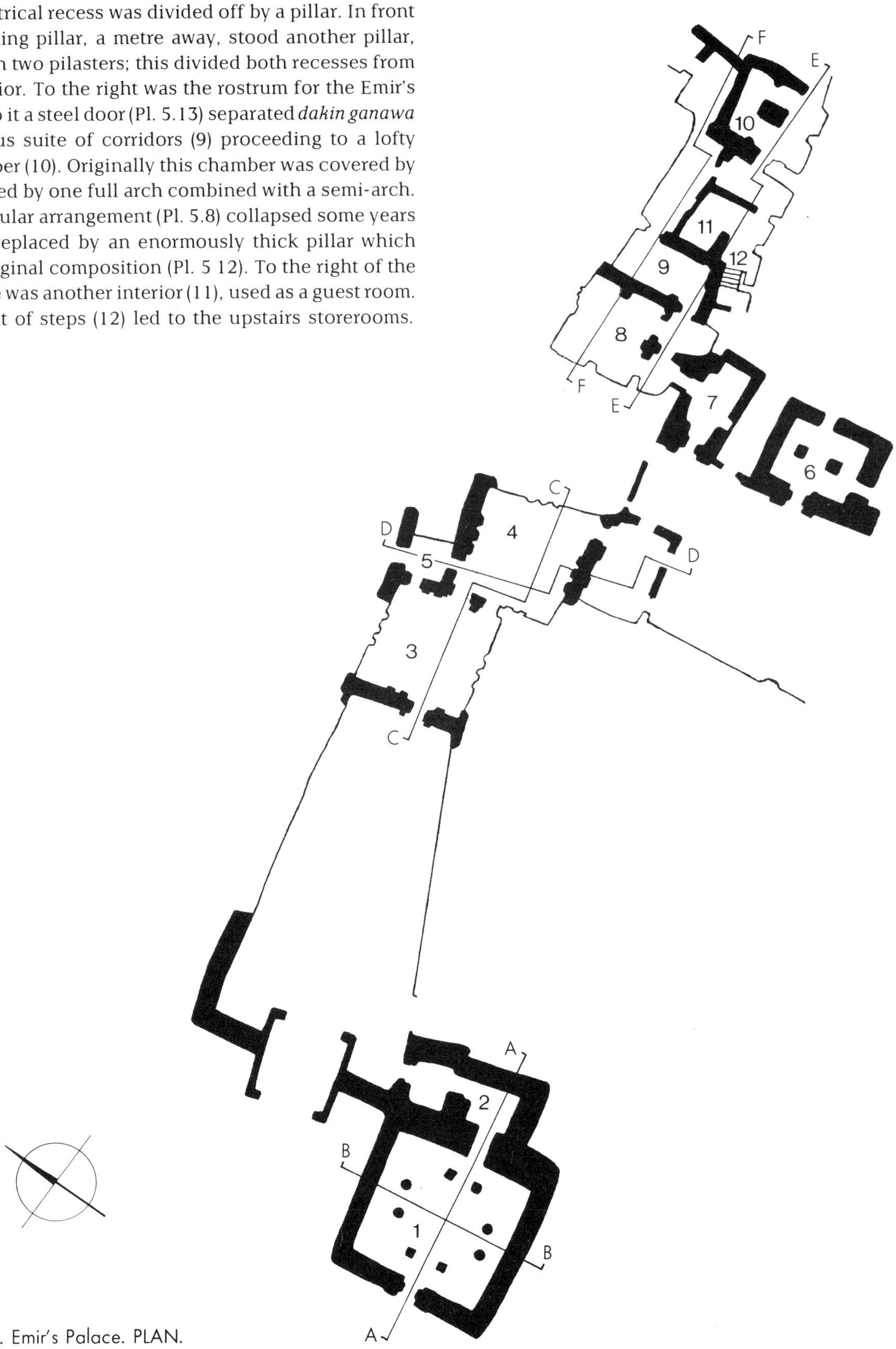

Fig.5.1. Daura. Emir's Palace. PLAN.

Pls.5.3 & 5.4. DAURA. Views of the interior of kofar zaure *(room 1).*

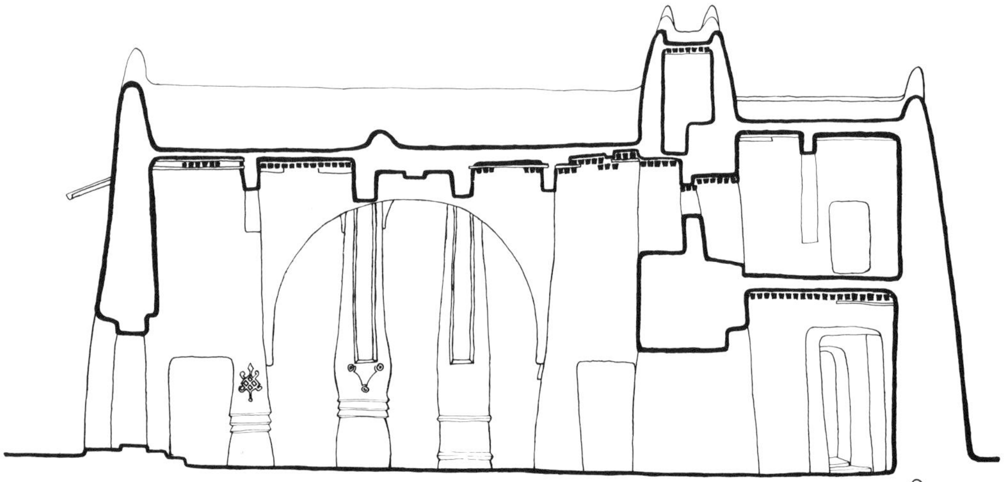

Fig.5.2. Daura. Emir's Palace. SECTION A—A.

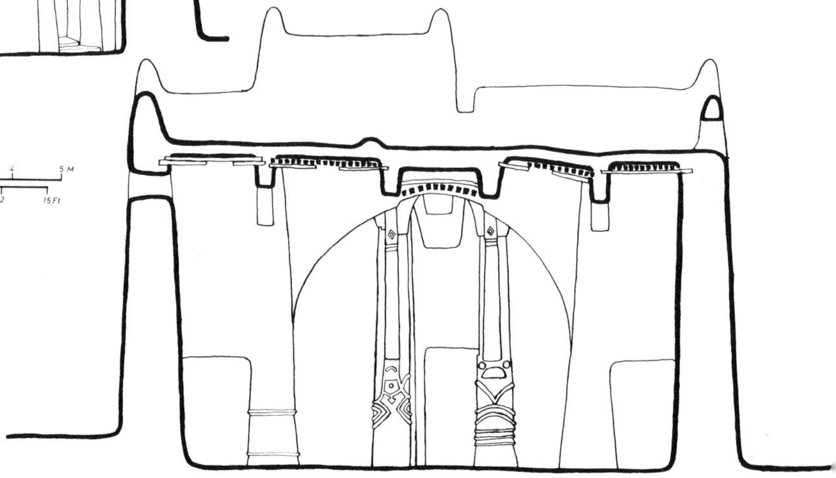

Fig.5.3. Daura. Emir's Palace. SECTION B—B.

Pl. 5.5. DAURA. The Emir's palace. The new gate and the old zaure.

*Pl. 5.6. DAURA. Emir's palace. Filin kofar gida,
the courtyard leading to the first interior of
the palace.*

Pl. 5.7. & 5.8. DAURA. Emir's palace. Soron fadanci *(Room 3), where respects are paid to the Emir.*

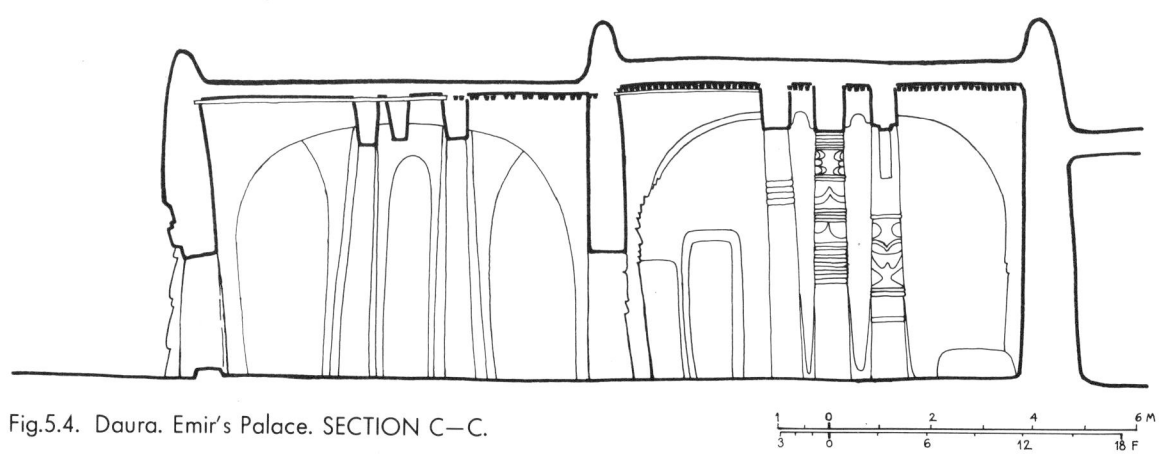

Fig. 5.4. Daura. Emir's Palace. SECTION C—C.

Fig.5.5. Daura. Emir's Palace. SECTION D—D.

Pl.5.9. DAURA. Emir's palace. The inner courtyard of the palace.

Pl.5.10. DAURA. Emir's palace. Soron hutu *(Room 4).*

Pl.5.12. DAURA. Emir's palace. Council chamber (room 10), with heavy central pillar.

Pl.5.11. DAURA. Emir's palace. Dakin ganawa (Room 8), reception room seen from the recess.

Fig.5.6. Daura. Emir's Palace. SECTION E—E.

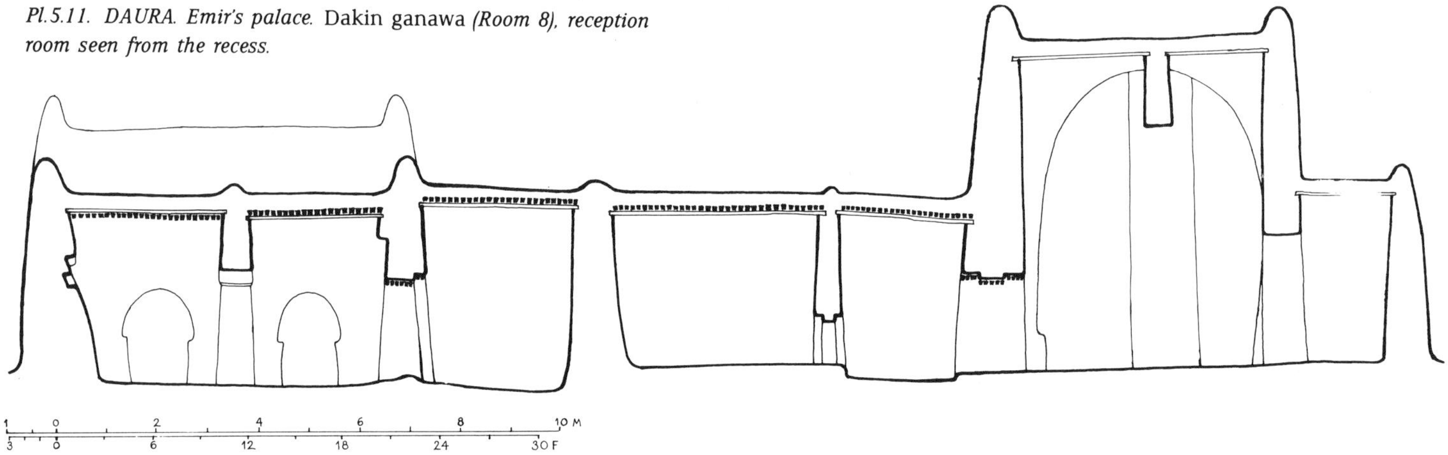

Fig.5.7. Daura. Emir's Palace. SECTION F—F.

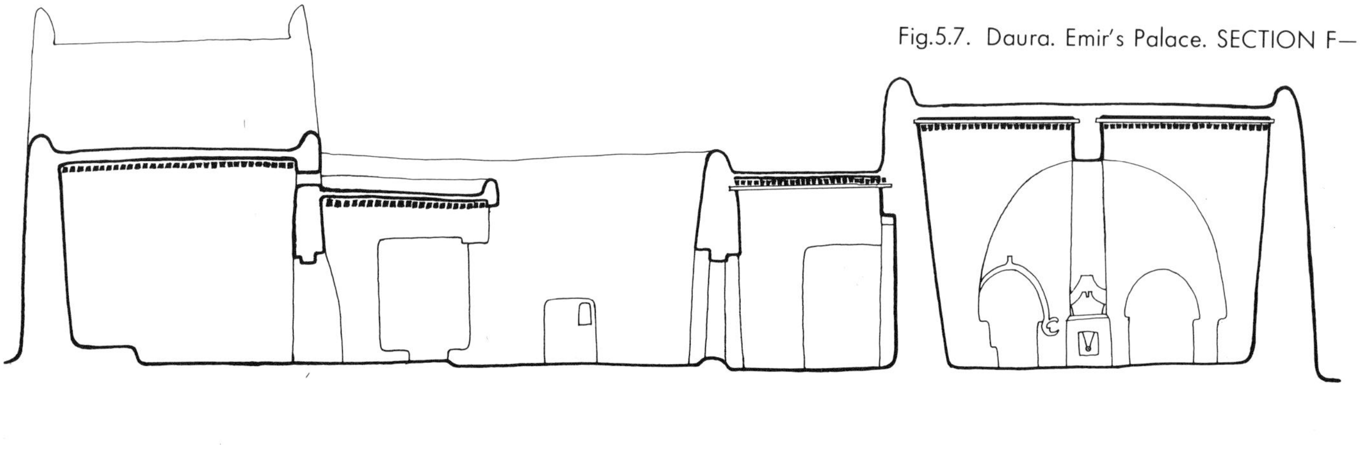

Pl.5.13. DAURA. Emir's palace. Steel door between Room 8 and corridors leading to the council chambers.

Pl.5.14. KATSINA. Emir's palace. Entrance portal to Room 4. West facade of main building.

Katsina
Emir's Palace

It is said that the first Katsina dynasty was founded by Kumayo, grandson of Bayajidda and son of Bawo, around 1100-1240. There is no mention of the building of Katsina palace, but among the ancient insignia of the emirate there is a 'brazen pot' for cooking charms for 'Korau the Invincible', the founder of the second dynasty. This might be a clue in the search. The bronze pot was carried to the council chamber,[5] most probably in the royal palace, and this seems to suggest the period when the residence was already erected. However, Leo Africanus, who visited Katsina at the beginning of the sixteenth century, said nothing about the royal palace and described the city dwellings as 'most forlorn and base cottages'.[6] On the other hand, since the fortifications of the city were commenced in the second half of the sixteenth century it may be assumed that at this time the palace was already erected; probably it was there even earlier, but, as happened in many Hausa cities, it might have been the only

one, or one of the very few, buildings erected in loam masonry. Until the mid-nineteenth century the majority of Hausa city dwellings were circular cornstalk huts, as noted by Barth in Kano and a number of other places – which probably biased Leo Africanus' opinion.

I surveyed the palace in November and December 1959, receiving full support and advice from the Emir of Katsina, Sir Usman Nagogo. The accessible parts were very old, though I could not determine their exact age.

For reasons which I will explain I would venture the opinion that the core of the palace interiors which I studied was erected in the mid-nineteenth century, perhaps using some elements of the original palace. The very large area, *sarari* (open field) occupied by the palace compound (*barga*) had a sizeable square (*kan giwa*) surrounded by Native Authority offices. All the other wards were west of this. The first gate occupied almost the whole width of a tower; this was

[5] Hogben and Kirk-Greene, *op cit*, pp. 156, 157, 158, 181.
[6] Leo Africanus, *The History and Descriptions of Africa Done into English*, by John Pory, 1896, quoted in T L Hodgkin, *Nigerian Perspectives*, O.U.P. 1960, p. 102.

Pls.5.15 & 5.16. KATSINA. Emir's palace. The modern west portico.

Fig.5.8. Katsina. Emir's Palace. PLAN.

a modern building with a flag pole for the Emir's standard over the roof. The tower gate opened onto a long approach to the palace. There was an elongated courtyard with some fairly recent buildings on the north side, and at the end of the north-west/south-east vista stood the palace.

There was a small square in front of the palace, screened to the north-west by a memorial erection with a high wall at the back and a flight of steps leading to a crowning conical finial – an excellent, almost sculptural, composition.

The original façade of the palace was largely hidden behind a modern portico (it was called *layi* – probably meaning waiting room. The front of this portico was divided asymetrically into two groups of pillars and voids – six on the north-west side, three on the south-west. The pillars were rectangular in plan; the voids between them were rectangular in their lower parts, and were covered with semicircular arches (*kandame*) the diameters of which were wider than the voids. In order to balance the composition of the modern façade, a plain wall and a rectangular building were erected at its south-west side. *Layi* was covered with a flat ceiling of *azaras*, supported by flat cantilevered arches. (Pls. 5.15 & 5.16.)

A recess between *layi-layi*, outlined by two convex curves, formed an entrance to the *babban zauri* (or *zauri kofar gida*) separated from two more *zaurukka*, one on each side. These three were the original outer row of interiors and comprised the original façade. Because of their height, the upper part of their walls, with small *kandame* windows, was still visible above the parapet of the portico.

Babban zauri was higher than the other two and its square interior was covered by a dome supported on a system of six *bakan gizo* (Pl. 5.17),[7] three of them springing from opposite walls and the other three crossing them from the other two walls. Thus in the centre a square of ribs was formed, divided into four square panels. The outer corners of this construction were further strengthened by four diagonal corbels springing from the corners of the *zauri*, and the central part of the structure was enriched by a number of short ribs – these were of minor structural importance but formed a four-cornered star at the apex of the dome.

[7] The general definition of a room thus covered was: *zaure mai kafa da tulluwa*, which meant, 'room with an arch and dome'.

Pl.5.17. KATSINA. Emir's palace. Domed roof of zaure *(Room 1).*

The two other *zauri* had much simpler roofs, supported by corbelled beams. At the south-west end of the row of three *zaurukka* stood a fourth one, roofed on a lavish arrangement of eight *bakan gizo*. (Pl. 5.18 & Fig. 5.9)

In the south-east corner of *babban zaure* a door led to the courtyard where the main complex of palace interiors had been erected. This was entered through an inner *zauri*, which had two doors – the one on the north was framed with elaborate mouldings (Pl. 5 14). The interior had a most imaginative composition which made full use of corbelled construction. In the centre of the room stood a massive pillar.

This central pillar, *ginshiki*, was both structurally and aesthetically the true focus of the *zauri* (Pl. 5.19). At a height of about 1.8 metres, ie. above the level of a man's head, four bracketed semi-arches sprang up on each side of the pillar. Those directed E-W were linked with the N-S walls, and the other two joined the apexes of two full *gizo* outlining the N and W quarters of the room. (Figs. 5.11 & 5.12.)

Both bracketed semi-arches and *bakan gizo*s were strongly constructed of four layers, laid in rows of five *azaras*. Contrary to Kano practice the consecutive layers were not fastened with rope. Thus the flat roof of the *zauri* was divided into four square panels in the centre of the room, with two rectangular panels at both its ends. The spans of the panels were reduced in the usual way by placing in each corner a triangle of *azaras* (*taui*) set diagonally, which in turn supported the next layer of *azaras* which ran parallel to the walls. Only then was the top layer of *azaras* (*rufi*) laid, covering the interior. Structurally, as noted above, the central pillar gave firm support to the centre of the *rufi*. At the same time aesthetic satisfaction was provided by the perspective view of the full arch followed by the two central semi-arches, with another full arch completing the composition.

Fig.5.9. Katsina. Emir's Palace. SECTION A—A.

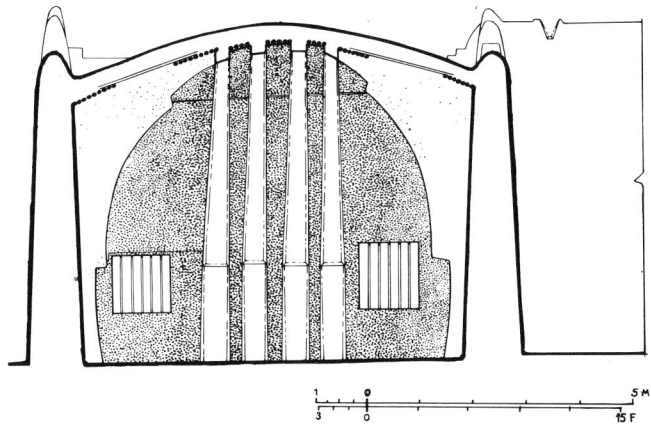

Small rectangular ventilating slits, *taga* (the word used for windows as well), pierced the wall beneath the *rufi*. The architectural effect of the whole was so strikingly impressive that ornamental details were, quite rightly, much restrained, although they were skilfully used to emphasise the structural hub of the framework.

The floor (*dabe, debe*) of building earth was, when hardened, moistened with water, sprinkled with gravel and then beaten with a mallet, *madabi*. When dry the surface was covered with powdered pods of the *Dorowa* tree.

Pl.5.18. KATSINA. Emir's palace. Room 3, with eight bakan gizos,

When surveying the *zauri* I noted the unusual shape of its southern wall – it was concave, and had a niche in the centre. I was told that this was a bricked-up door, leading to the ancient circular throne room (*adudu*) originally the southern-most interior of the palace, but later demolished. I dug out the surface of this site, which permitted me to establish with a fair degree of accuracy the diameter of the room and the thickness of the walls. This I believe indicated the approximate age of the palace. It was almost certainly erected by Habe builders in a local version of the Habe plan. But the first Fulani emir of Katsina, having agreed to the local style of residence, insisted that at least his throne room should have a typical (circular) Fulani plan. When I discussed this possibility, the Emir not only agreed with it but, together with his courtiers, recollected the original furnishings of the throne room. The throne stood not on the axis of the *zauri* but on its SW side, near the wall. The whole eastern semi-circle of wall was lined with benches for the important men of Katsina's community, who sat, according to their rank, near the throne and down towards the north. The door leading to the *zauri* was reserved for the Emir alone, and all the visitors entered by the outer door in the NE part of the room. Between these two doors there was a place for *magayaki* (a titled official at the court) and *sarkin bai* (chief of slaves). The head of the palace guards stood beside the outer door.

Pl.5.19. KATSINA. Emir's palace. Inner zaure. Detail of the central pillar.

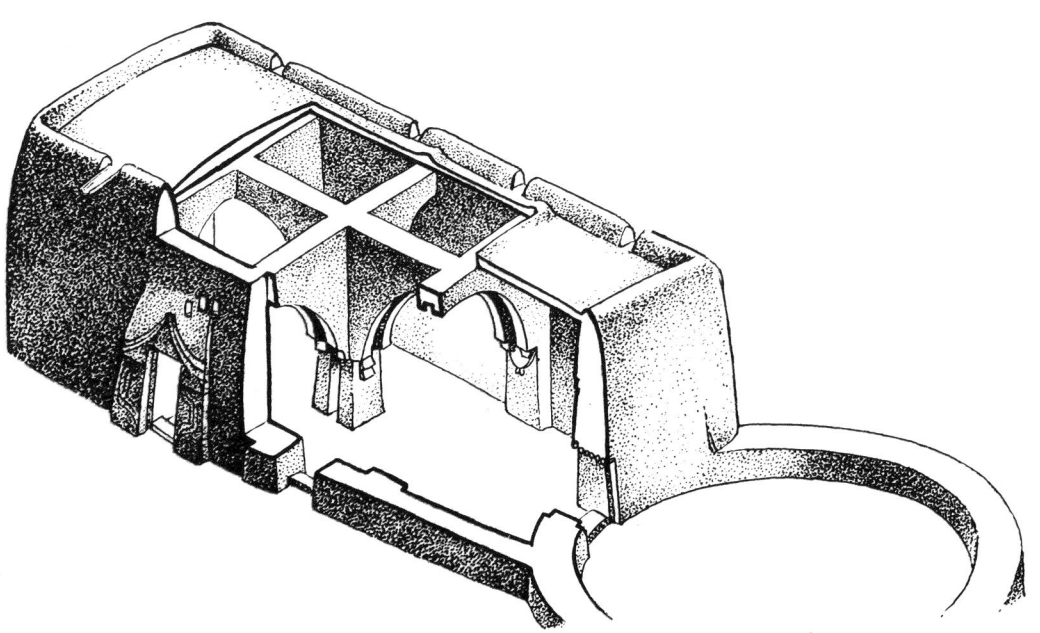

Fig.5.10. Katsina. Emir's Palace. ISOMETRIC.

In the N wall of the *zauri* was a door leading to the rectangular council chamber. Its flat roof, about 1.2 metres higher than the *zauri*, was supported on six crosswise *bakan gizo* (Pl. 5.22). There was another door to the room leading from the inner courtyard, for members of the council, and three large windows on the N wall of the chamber. The Emir's rostrum stood by the E wall which, however, gave the impression of being a later partition. Behind it was thus created a fairly small chamber with only one *bakan gizo*. A door in the very thick E wall gave access to the innermost courtyard where stood a solid square building, the treasure chamber.

In the E wall of the *zauri* there was a strong door made of narrow strips of iron (Pl. 5.20). This led to the Emir's private room, which was covered with a rectangular network of six *bakan gizo* and two crosswise corbelled beams (Pl. 5.21). This room again communicated with the innermost courtyard.

One of the Emir's courtiers, Mallam Yusufu, drew me a little sketch showing the original surroundings of the palace. Within a rectangle of perimeter walls the palace stood as shown and described above, and on its southern side, apparently near the old throne room, was the house of Ajiya ('sitting with the Emir day and night'). To the north of the palace was the abode of *sarkin bai*, and near the north east corner of the compound was that of the *magayiki*.

Pl.5.20 (left). KATSINA. Roof construction of the Emir's private room.

Pl.5.21 (above) & 5.22 (right). Katsina. Emir's palace. Roof construction of the Emir's private room.

Fig.5.11. Katsina. Emir's Palace. SECTION B—B.

Fig.5.12. Katsina. Emir's Palace. SECTION C—C.

Kano
City Palace

Legend says that the first chief of Kano, Barbushe, built his house on Dalla Hill, where he performed religious rites by the sacred shrine-tree, which was surrounded by a wall. Kirk-Greene mentions an old Kano palace which used to stand somewhere to the east of Dalla. Mohammadu Rumfa (1463-99) erected a new palace nearby. The south gate of the older building exists to this day, and leads to the private courtyard through the royal graveyard.[8]

The present palace of the Emir of Kano, still called Gidan Rumfi, very much impressed all the travellers who ever entered it. During the 1920s, this is what we are told by Denham, Clapperton and Oudney's 'Narrative':

'Governor's house (was) 500 or 600 yards from the gate . . . when introduced we had to pass through three coozees or guard houses, the walls of which were covered with shields and the doors guarded by black eunuchs. These coozees were connected by screens of matting cover overhead. The Governor was seated at the entrance of an inner coozee . . .'

And:

'The Governor's residence covers a large space, and resembles a walled village. It even contains a mosque, and several towers three or four storeys high, with windows in the European style, but without glass or framework. It is necessary to pass through two of these towers in order to gain the suite of inner apartments occupied by the Governor.'[9]

Some thirty years later, Heinrich Barth had this to say:

'The palace of the Governor, called 'Fada', 'Lamorde' . . . forms a real labyrinth of courtyards, provided with spacious round huts of audience, built of clay, with a door on each side and connected together by narrow intricate passages . . . We were first conducted to the audience hall of the Ghaladima, who, while living in a separate palace, visits the Fada almost every day, in order to act in his important and influential office as Vizier.'

'(The Governor's and Ghaladima's) . . . apartments were so excessively dark that, coming from a sunny place, it was sometime before I could distinguish anybody. The Governor's hall was very handsome and even stately for this country, and was the more imposing as the rafters supporting the very elevated ceilings were concealed, two lofty arches of clay very neatly polished and ornamented, appearing to support the whole. At the bottom of the apartment were two spacious and highly decorated niches, in one of which the Governor was reposing on a 'Gado', spread with a carpet.'[10]

Colonial Reports from 1902 added the following information: 'The King's Palace . . . consisted of a network of buildings covering an area of 33 acres and surrounded by wall 20 to 30 feet high outside and 15 feet inside . . . in itself no mean citadel.'[11]

In Karl Kumm's book there are a number of valuable photographs of the palace taken at the beginning of the twentieth century. Together with his accompanying text, Kumm's photographs permit an attempt to enlarge upon the descriptions given by former authors. One of the photographs is apparently taken towards the NW (Dalla Hill can be seen on the horizon), from a slight mound in front of the walls of the palace. The southern façade of the outer bulwark contained the entrance gate. The curtain protruded to enclose the gate's recess. There was a moat with a parapeted bridge leading to the doorway in the gate. The photograph seems to indicate that the gateway was similar in plan and form to the standard city gates. The walls flanking the recessed block of the gate had loopholes on both sides, and this probably means that there were banquettes on the inner side of the parapet. The gate iself, again typically, had a loopholed mantelet over the doorway, covering the direct approach to the bridge.

Another valuable photograph in Kumm's book shows an excellent example of a sophisticated ceiling in one of the palace interiors, called an 'audience chamber'. It had twenty corbels, forming ten bakan gizo, and was covered with azaras laid in two directions. At the apex of the dome, azaras were laid horizontally to form a polygon, and beneath it they radiated from the central vertex down to the walls, into which they were set.[12]

More valuable information about the Emir's private apartments is contained in a description of the palace by E D Morel.[13] He begins with a general account of Gidan Rumfi, saying:

'To depict the Emir's residence as a compound built of clay, is, while accurate, to give but an inadequate idea of the imposing character of these structures, the best of which are, with supervision, capable of resisting for centuries the action of the weather. I am probably understating the case when I say that the tall and bulky wall – some fifteen feet in thickness – surrounding the residence encloses five acres . . . Dismounting at the principal entrance, we are escorted through the gateways by several functionaries and emerge into a vast enclosure open to the sky. At its extremity, facing us, is an inner wall and another deep embrassured gateway leading to the state apartments. On our right stands the Emir's private mosque, a building of considerable proportions, but smaller, of course, than the public

---

[8] Hogben and Kirk-Greene, The Emirates of Northern Nigeria, p. 184.
[9] Denham and Clapperton, Narrative . . . 1822, 23, 24, London 1826, p. 43.
[10] H Barth, Travels and Discoveries . . . in the years 1849-55, Vol. II, pps. 103, 104, 105.
[11] Colonial Reports Annual, Northern Nigeria, 1902 (No. 409, p. 87).
[12] Karl Kumm, The Sudan, 1907.
[13] E D Morel, Nigeria, its peoples and problems, London 1911, p. 310-311.

mosque outside the walls . . . we pass through the inner gateway and find ourselves in a broad passage flanked, on either side, by lofty audience chambers whose dimensions it is difficult to gauge in the semi-obscurity . . . At the end of the passage is yet another gateway . . . Crossing a courtyard we enter the outer room of the Emir's private apartments . . .'

The room was about 6-8 metres high and was covered 'with an arched roof supported by a wooden beam on the cantilevered principle . . . Both beams and roof are, like the floor, stained a deep black with the varnish obtained from the shell of the locust bean; a few plates of European manufacture are let into the supporting rafters'.

The walls, constructed from *tubali*, were covered with plaster to which an admixture of mica gave a silvery, glittering appearance. The two doors of the room were of massive planks bound with iron bars, fastened with native nails which were ornamented with large circular brass heads.

The same way of decorating walls with light-reflecting plaster is mentioned by Robinson: 'The king was sitting in a comparatively small room, the walls of which were all silvered over.'[14]

Later, the particles of mica were mixed with yellow dye, which produced not a silver but a golden glint to the surface of the walls. In 1960, on the only occasion when I was able to see the interiors of the palace (during a ceremonial audience) I saw several chambers thus richly ornamented.

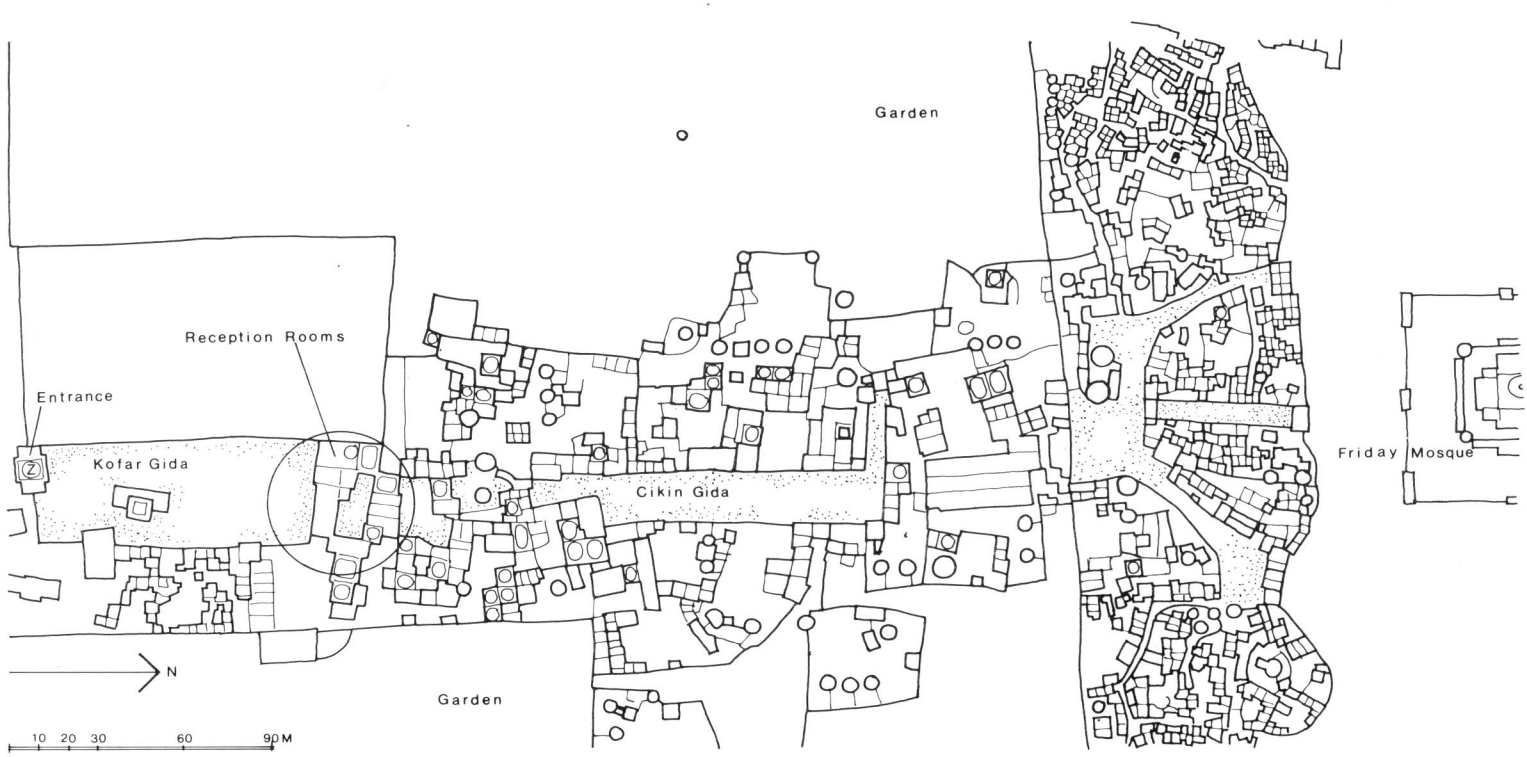

Fig.5.13. Kano. Emir's Palace. PLAN.
courtesy J.C. Moughtin, *Hausa Architecture*, 1985.

[14] C H Robinson, *Hausaland or Fifteen Hundred Miles through the Central Sudan*. New edition, London 1896.

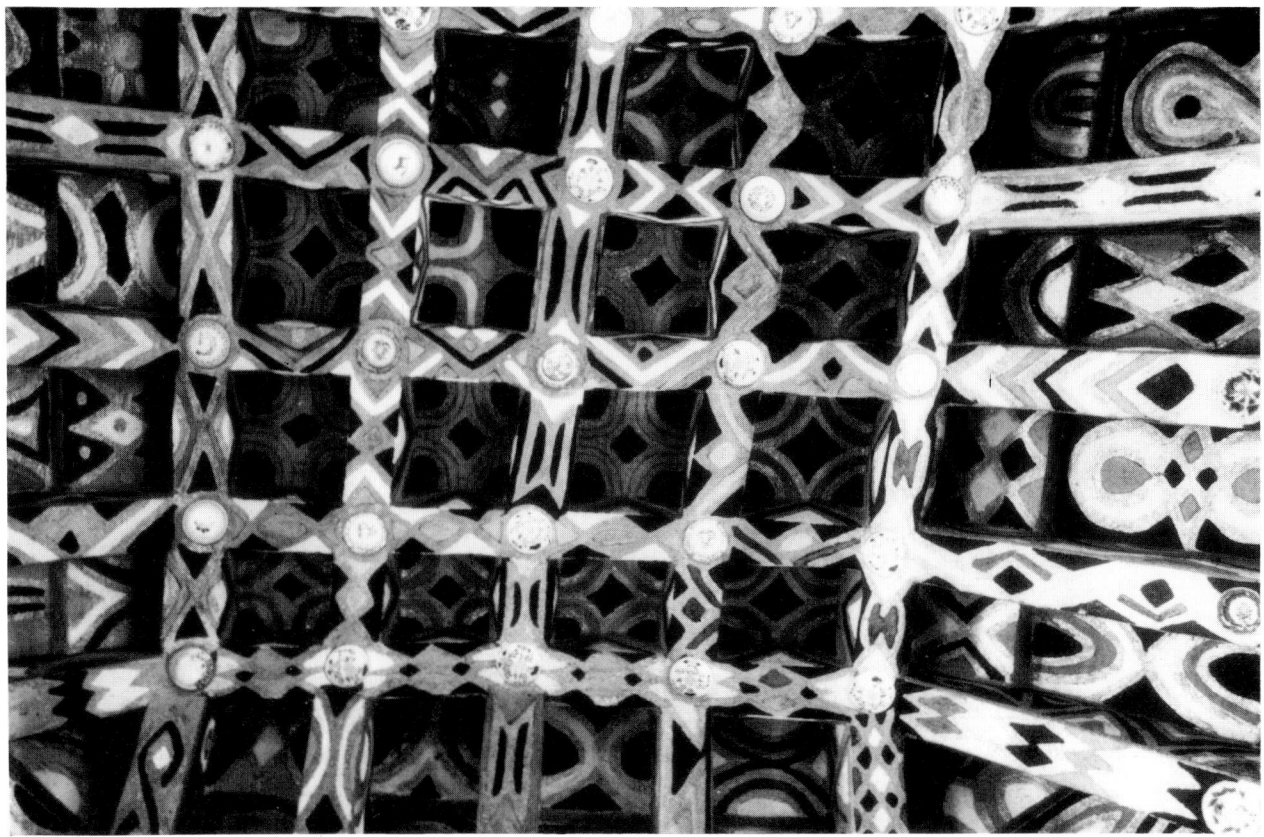

Pls. 5.23 & 5.24. KANO. Emir's Palace. Soron Ingila. Details of roof.

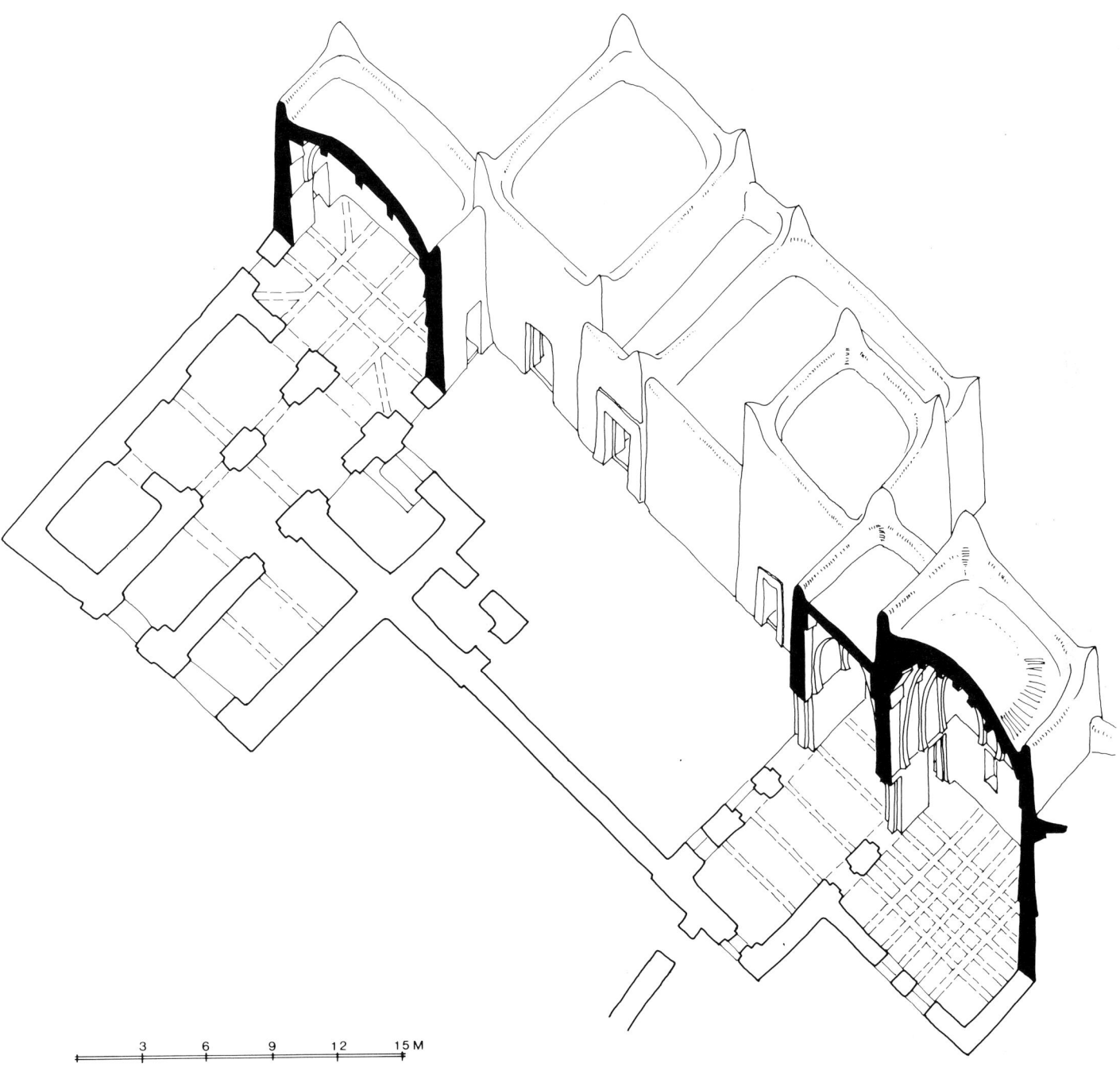

3   6   9   12   15 M

Fig.5.14. Kano. Emir's Palace.

Pls. 5.25 & 5.26. KANO. Emir's Palace. Soron Giwa. Details of roof.

Pl. 5.27. KANO. Emir's Palace. Soron Giwa.

Pl. 5.28. Nasarawa Palace. Outer zaure.

Pl. 5.29. Nasarawa Palace.

Nasarawa Palace

Pl.5.30. Nasarawa Palace.

Fig.5.16. Zaria. Emir's Palace. PLAN.

Zaria
Emir's Palace Compound

The Emir's palace in Zaria[15] stands immediately beside and to the NE of the Masallaci Juma'a. Its entrance gate was on the W edge of a long open space reaching to the main street of the town and the market place nearby. The palace was originally built by Habe rulers who called it Gidan Bakwa.[16] During the following centuries alterations and development of the palace undoubtedly took place. They were carried out by Sarkin Abdul Karim, continued by his son Sarkin Sambo (1879-88) and in the 1930s Sarkin Ibrahim (1924-36) built a new entrance gate, replacing the old one which had stood elsewhere.[17]

Works on the palace were supervised by the sons and grandsons of Babban Gwani Mikhaila. They inherited his honorary title – the last to bear it was Mallam Sumaila, who built a fine family residence (see Ch. 4). His son, Mallam Balarabe (died 1961), was too young in the year of his father's death to inherit his title; consequently he and his descendants, up to Mallam Jibrin in 1963, were called Sarkin Magina.

The character of the old moulded decorations in the palace interiors showed a resemblance to the patterns used in the Masallaci, although the constructions were clearly linked with traditionally popular Habe/Hausa devices. The plan of the great compound was also traditional, with a typical division into the main block of the Emir's residence and courtyards beyond it containing the dispersed dwellings of his wives, concubines and female servants.

A monumental gate led into the entrance courtyard (A) of the palace (Pl. 5.31). The gate comprised three square

[15] Informants: Jihrin, Sarkin Magina; Sarkin Ladane; Mallam Usuman Mani.
[16] Queen Bakwa transferred the capital from Turunku to Zaria, which is perhaps evidence of the ancient foundation of the palace. It must be remembered ,however, that up until recently the word *bakwa* was also used to denote any high ranking, much honoured person.
[17] Informant: Sarkin Ladane, Mallam Usuman Mani.

Pl.5.31. ZARIA. Emir's Palace. Entrance gate.

*Pl.5.32. ZARIA. Emir's Palace.
Roof construction of entrance gate.*

interiors. The central one (2) was entered under an arch and its roof rested on two *bakan gizo*s; it provided access for horsemen and vehicles. The S interior (1) (Pl. 5.32) was formerly a passage for pedestrians; the N interior (3) was an Islamic classroom.

The large forecourt, about 60 metres long and almost 29 metres wide, extended to the W façade of the palace. On the N side was a very large stable yard, in which two large circular stables (10 and 28) were prominent; they housed the Emir's favourite horses. This courtyard was reached through a two-room *soro* (12,13). Its SW corner (B) was partitioned off by an internal wall and its W part contained a small area with five rectangular houses for women (4 to 15), with latrines at the back and a kitchen in the centre. The round building of the head woman (14) stood separately by the *soro* entrance.

From the *soro* the E door led to the second courtyard (C) which was L-shaped. The horse-keeper's house (27) stood near the stable for the Emir's horses (28). Opposite them was a room for young male children, and further to the N were two circular granaries (25,26) and the stable courtyard . This was flanked with boxes and there was a small room for the groom (24) at the end of one row of boxes.

At the end of the N wall of the entrance courtyard (A) was a series of rectangular rooms: a store (14); two garages (15 and 16); and two waiting rooms for palace visitors (17 and 18). The entrance to the palace, according to custom, was in the W façade. This was deformed because it was occupied for half its length by the gates to three garages (38, 39, 40), which overwhelmed the access to the reception hall (37–Figure 5.19). The reception hall was domed, on a frame, *daurin guga*, of eight *kafa*, with a square central panel (*rijia*). A small door in the N wall led to a *soro* (36) serving as an antechamber to courtyard D. A door on the E-W axis led to the waiting room (50), again

domed but with a simple *baka hudu* of two crossed *bakuna* only. From there, still on the E-W axis, two doors opened on to a large *majalisa* or council chamber (perhaps also used as the Emir's court). It was a very impressive room, with a decorative dome on a grid of four N-S and two elaborate E-W *bakan gizo*s. The latter combined the principle of *kafar kasa* (chicken's foot)[18] with an ingenious support for the apex of the dome (Figure 5.19). There were two windows in the N wall filled with modern tracery and a door onto a small internal court, D. *Soro* 35 led to court E. There was a bathroom (34) and three toilets (30, 31, 32). There were more bathrooms and toilets (52 and 59) accessible from the SE corner of the *majalisa*.

In the centre of courtyard E stood a large square guest house for important visitors, but it was completely isolated and accessible only through court F, which was surrounded by a large number of women's dwellings. Near *soro* 35 was a small room for a tailor, and a toilet (33 and 30).

Court F was built up in a rather haphazard way. The buildings and partition walls forming its E boundary separated it from the huge back court, which was filled with a variety of women's quarters. Opposite the entrance from court D was a quadrilateral building containing two dwellings (67 and 68, and 69 and 70). Each consisted of a woman's room preceded by a parlour. Another group of more humble women's dwellings (63 to 66) was situated SW of the former, and there was still another but larger group (71 to 74) to the N of the doorway between courts D and F. There were three more houses (the largest of all) on the E side of court F. One of them had a kitchen (79), and two had front parlours, with two living rooms behind (81 and 82).

---

[18] The word was used because of the similarity to a chicken's foot.

Fig.5.17. Zaria. Emir's Palace.
PARTIAL PLAN.

Fig.5.18. Zaria. Emir's Palace. PARTIAL PLAN

S of the area just described was the main complex of rooms used by the Emir. They were interlaced with passages and small sanitary courtyards. The northernmost row of rooms (37, 50 and 51), referred to above, served the public requirements of the Emirate. This part of the palace can be roughly divided into five almost parallel rows of rooms, each with a different function.

Starting at the westernmost part, the waiting room (50) had a door leading along a covered walkway to an almost square *soro* (47), with doors all round it. One of the two doors in the W wall led to an elongated *soro* (42) and from there to the outside of the compound. Nearby was a tiny dark cubicle (41), described as a room for male children. S of *soro* 42, behind a solid partition wall, was a large bedroom (43) entered from a resting room (44) which had direct access to the outside of the building. There were two other doors: one to the toilet and bathroom (45); and one eastward, to the old *majalisa* (46).

It seems probable that the recent arrangement of the above listed row of rooms was the result of alterations caused by the insertion of three garages (38, 39 and 40). The W façade of rooms (43 and 44) was probably continued northwards until it reached the wall of the present reception hall (37), which projects slightly westwards. Before these alterations were made, it seems reasonable to assume that the block of rooms within the angle of interiors 59, 37 and 44 was, and remains, the centre of the original *gidan bakwa*. Indeed in parts it seems to be the very ancient core, perhaps only slightly altered during centuries past.[9]

The second N-S row of rooms, shown in Fig. 5.20 began with the new *majalisa* (51). As shown in Fig. 5.20, to the S of it is a small, narrow *soro* (49), a passage to a larger, square *soro*, domed with *daurin guga* of eight *kafa* (48). Still further southwards was a larger *soro* (47), domed like the former. At the end of this row of rooms was the rectangular old *majalisa* (46) connected to the Emir's old private apartments on the W (43, 44) and with another *majalisa* (55). (One of these was a council chamber, the other, perhaps, a court house.) North of the latter was yet another *soro* (54) (as shown on E-W Section, Fig. 5.21) called *soro mai*, with a high dome of two crossed *bakan gizos* (*baka hudu*). One of them sprang from floor level, the other from immediately above the E and W doors. Next to *soro mai* was the *jakadiya*'s (female messenger's) apartment; it consisted of a living room (58) and its antechamber (53) from which a passage (used as a toilet) gave access eastwards to the womens' court F.

The *jakadiya*'s living room was the northernmost interior. It was entirely separated from *soro* 57 (Pl. 5.34) which nevertheless in 1963 already belonged to the set of women's apartments. Judging by the decorative treatment of its *maburgi* roof frame, it seems to have been closely linked with Mallam Mikhaila's tradition. A pleasant accent to this very picturesque interior was provided by a flight of steps (Pl. 5.34) leading through a tiny *soro* (56) to a narrow courtyard (G) which gave access to just two interiors, in the corner. 101 was the grave of Emir Janfaru's wife and 104 was the grave of Emir Dalhaji.

Soro 57 was linked through a door in its E wall with a square, lofty *soro* (60), the *kunguni*, ie. the women's reception hall. Its roof frame supporting the dome was rather unusual. Its *bakuna*, springing from floor level, were only slightly bent and ran diagonally up to a height of 4.2 metres; there, rather like large brackets, they supported the central, horizontal *kafin kafa* beam (see Chapter 1, corbel construction). This structure was further strengthened by three N-S beams at the very apex of the dome. The door in the E wall of the *kunguni* opened towards courtyard H, adjoining courtyard I and, still further N, courtyard J, where a narrow passage led to the largest courtyard in the palace (K). It was virtually a compound on its own, and was built up with various houses for palace women and their children. The striking characteristics of practically all of the houses in the women's quarters were the variability of their plan and spatial composition, and the impressive moulded decoration of their interiors and often of their façades.

Pl. 5.33. ZARIA. Emir's Palace. Room 54: Roof construction.

[19] As a suggestion for further research I would risk the assumption that rooms within the outline of interiors 41, 58, 56 and 44 may prove to be the original Habe residence of the *sarkis* of Zazzau. The information that the outer gateway built in 1963 replaced an older gate which stood 'elsewhere' may induce continued study of the subject by Nigerian architectural historians.

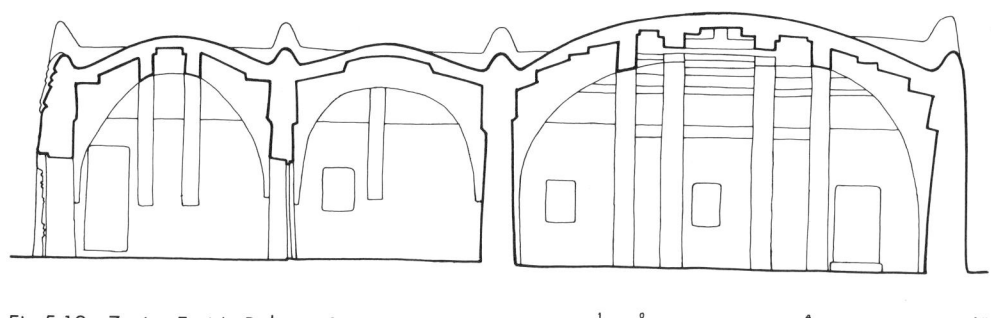

Fig.5.19. Zaria. Emir's Palace. SECTION A—A.

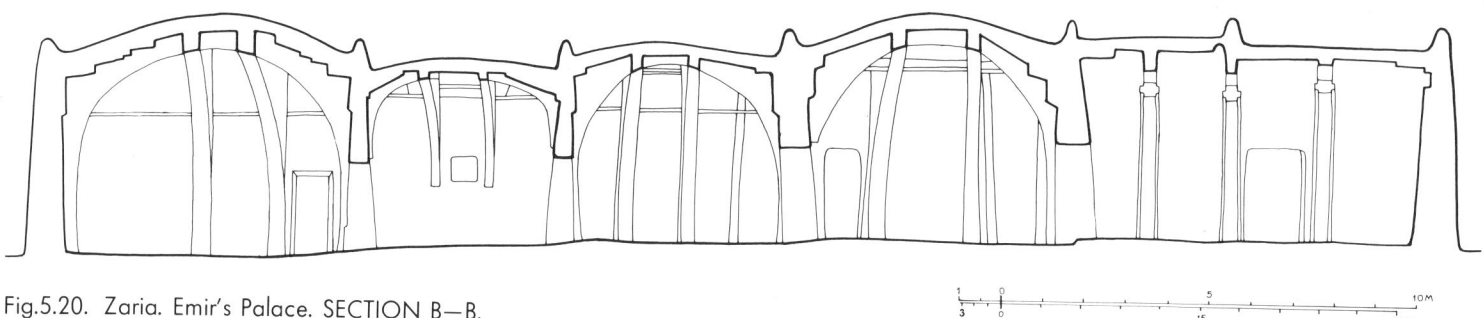

Fig.5.20. Zaria. Emir's Palace. SECTION B—B.

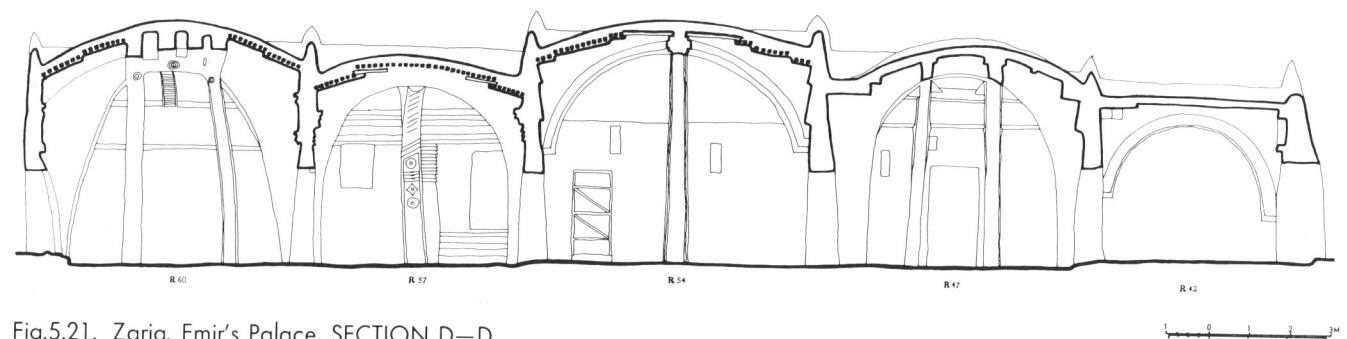

Fig.5.21. Zaria. Emir's Palace. SECTION D—D.

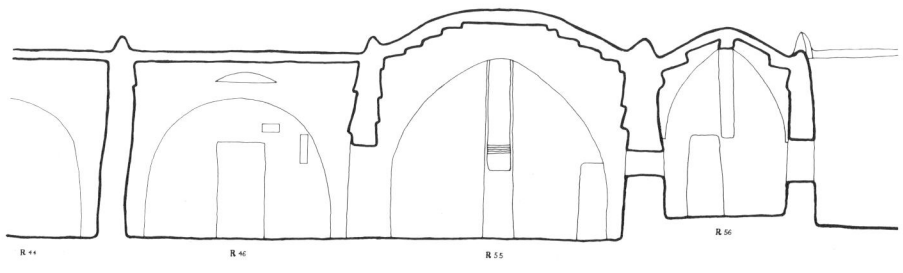

Fig.5.22. Zaria. Emir's Palace. SECTION E—E.

Pl.5.34. ZARIA. Emir's Palace. Roof construction and steps leading to courtyard G.

Pl. 5.35. ZARIA. Emir's Palace. Room 55, majalisa.

Pl.5.36. ZARIA. Emir's Palace. Decorative portal.

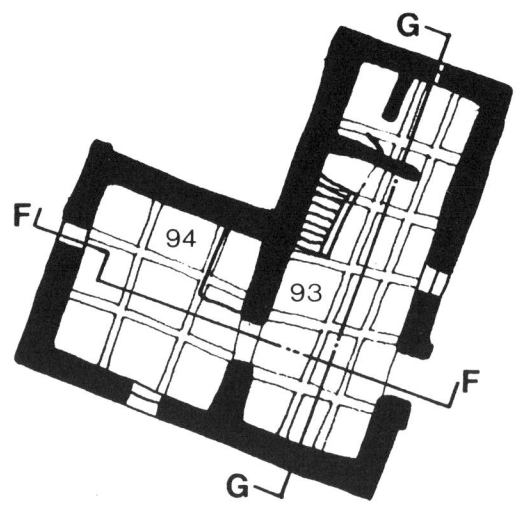

Fig.5.23. Zaria. Emir's Palace.
Women's house, rooms 93—94. PLAN

The westernmost house, roughly on the E-W axis of the compound, and in courtyard K, was a combination of two rooms, arranged, unusually, on two levels (Pl. 5.37). It had an elongated vestibule (93) with an entrance door facing E, and a door opposite which led to a high, domed bedroom (94). The vestibule was designed on two levels, and the roof was supported by a very elongated *daurin guga* of four wells (*rijiya hudu*), which were roughly rectangular in shape (see Fig. 5.23). The southern part of the vestibule served as a parlour; the northern was partly occupied by a staircase leading to a kind of inner balcony, which was separated from the parlour space by a balustrade. Beneath it were two small compartments, a lavatory and a bathroom. The bedroom was separated by a thick wall from another house (75,76), facing W. The bedroom had *daurin guga rijiya daya* and two windows. There was a large clay bed in the NE corner.

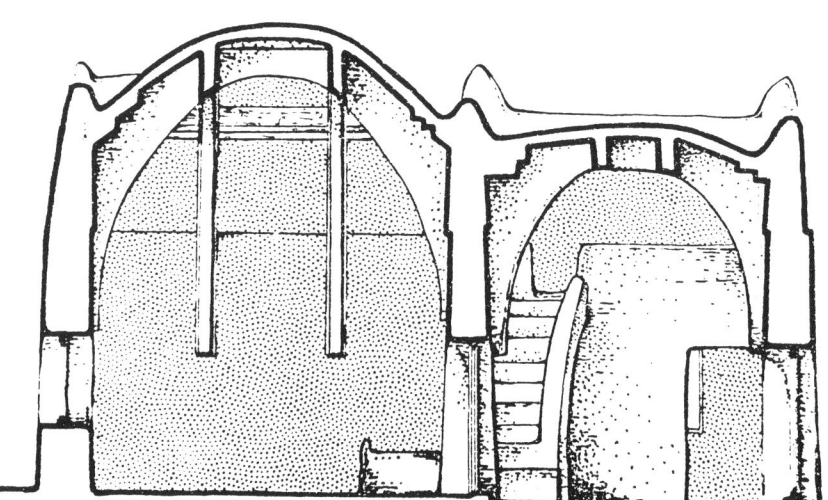

Fig.5.24. Zaria. Emir's Palace.
Women's house, rooms 93—94. SECTION F—F.

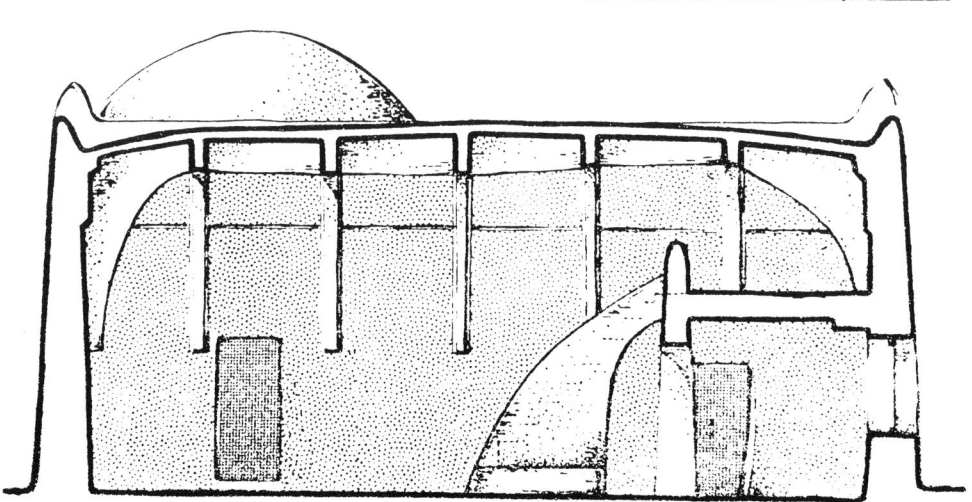

Fig.5.25. Zaria. Emir's Palace.
Women's house, rooms 93—94. SECTION G—G.

Pl.5.37. ZARIA. Emir's Palace. Women's house (Rooms 93/94). Staircase to inner balcony.

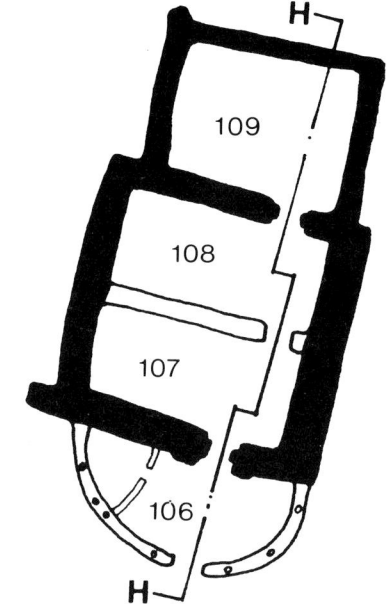

Fig.5.26. Zaria. Emir's Palace.
Women's house, rooms 106–109. PLAN.

Almost opposite this house stood another, with three rectangular interiors (107, 108 and 109). There was a semi-circular verandah in front (106, Pl. 5.38). The verandah was surrounded with a parapet, in which were embedded short forked posts. Purlins made of cornstalks supported the semi-conical thatched roof, which was set against the front wall of a monumental *soro*. Its spacious interior was divided into two rooms (107 and 108), but structurally it formed a single unit. It was square in plan, with a flat roof supported by *baka hudu* (two crossed arches) supported by four pilasters. The partition wall reached to about the height of the pilasters and was pierced by a door, connecting rooms 107 and 108 (Fig. 5.26). There were clay beds, heated from underneath, in both rooms. At the N end of the building was a pit-latrine, which was unroofed (109).

Pl. 5.38. ZARIA. Emir's Palace. Women's house (Rooms 106 - 109). Thatched roof extending to the parapet.

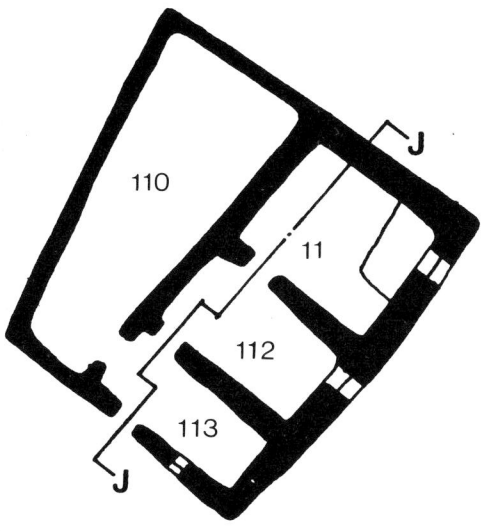

Fig.5.27. Zaria. Emir's Palace.
Women's house, rooms 110–113. PLAN.

The southernmost side of courtyard K was closed by two linked buildings (90) and the two-roomed building (91, 92). The oval-shaped room 90 had a dome supported by two arches (*baka hudu*), one of which rested on a pair of pilasters, while the second sprang from the height of the decorative profile of the wall. The soffits of both *hudu* were moulded with geometric patterns.

To the E was a two-roomed house (111 and 112) with a front verandah (113) (Figs. 5.27 & 5.28); all three spaces were rectangular. The verandah had a side entrance to a spacious latrine and bathing place (110). Room 112 was a parlour, and 111 a bedroom. In 1963 the building was in very poor condition, although its domes were still supported by central *bakuna* which ran along the longitudinal axis of the building.

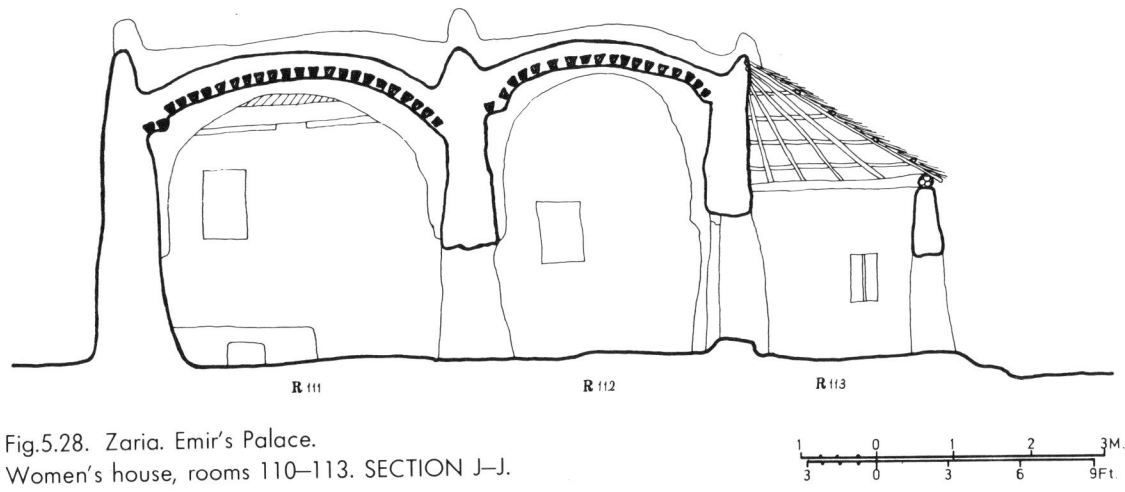

Fig.5.28. Zaria. Emir's Palace.
Women's house, rooms 110–113. SECTION J–J.

Still further to the E stood a house with a particularly imaginative composition (145, 146; Fig. 5.29 & Pls. 5.41, 5.42). The main and only living interior was circular (*shayeshaye*).[20] It had a flat roof resting on a central pillar with a wide capital formed of *azara* brackets set crosswise; they were symmetrical and therefore well balanced. The shaft was not tapered as was usual in Hausa *ginshiki* or *al'amudai*, but was the same thickness from the bottom up to the capital. The shaft was moulded around three *azaras* set vertically into a hollow about 30 centimetres deep. There were two clay beds on both sides of the room, screened from the entrance with low walls (*bari*). The third bed was located in a crescent-shaped annexe (*paparanda*),[21] E of the room. The room and its annexe were connected by a wide aperture, divided in the centre by a massive pillar, with the bed behind it. Continuing the curve of the annexe was the thatched front verandah with its entrance facing S and another bed to the right of it. The doorway to the inner room was flanked by decorative pilasters and covered with an archivolt, furnished with moulded profiles and bosses (Pl. 5.39).

[20] *Shayeshaye* = partaking of one thing.
[21] *Paparanda*: the name given to any ringlike interior surrounding a circular room.

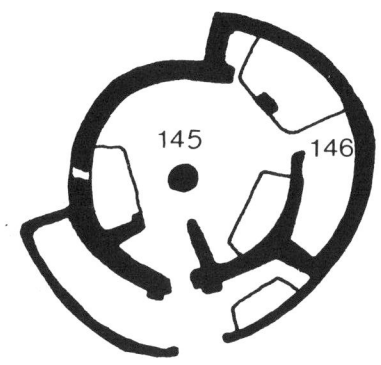

Fig.5.29. Zaria. Emir's Palace.
Women's house, rooms 145–146. PLAN.

Pl. 5.39. ZARIA. Emir's Palace. Women's house (Rooms 145/146). Entrance.

Pl. 5.40. ZARIA. Emir's Palace. Women's house (145/146). Front verandah.

Pls.5.41 5.42. ZARIA. Emir's Palace. Women's house (Rooms 145/146). Exterior views.

Pl.5.43. ZARIA. Emir's Palace. Women's house (Rooms 125 - 127). External view with women's house (Rooms 128 - 130) verandah in the foreground.

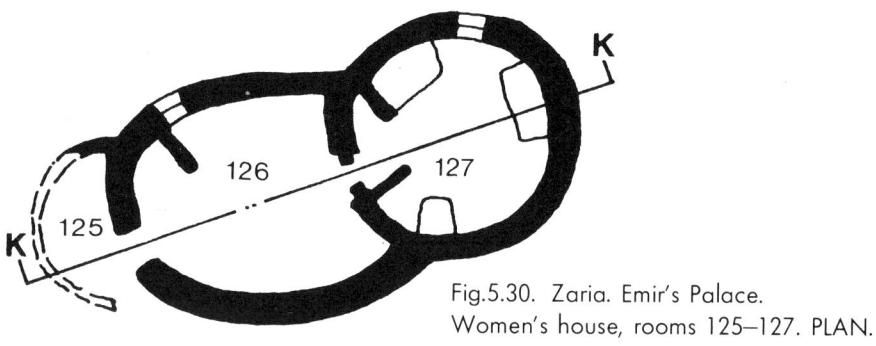

Fig.5.30. Zaria. Emir's Palace.
Women's house, rooms 125–127. PLAN.

Along the E wall of the women's compound stood a row of four houses. The two central ones, large and elaborate, were flanked by two smaller dwellings. They were all entered from the west. The southernmost was rectangular in plan (*tafarfara*) and thatched, and had a parlour (124) with a bedchamber behind (123).

The next house had a front verandah (*kafe*) (125) which in 1963 was badly dilapidated – only the balustrade, holding the original semi-conical thatched roof, remained (Pl. 5.43). Nevertheless the decorative surround of the entrance door leading to the front parlour remained intact. The rectangular aperture was flanked by architraves with a semi-circular low-relief archivolt above – both were enriched with moulded semi-circles and quadrilaterals. The outer room (*shirayi*),

elliptical in plan, was covered with a flat roof on a frame, *daurin guga*, with one (*daya*) panel (*rijiya*) in the centre (Fig. 5.30). In accordance with its name, which actually means a porch to a house, its E part was filled by the curve of the house, or the room proper (*daki*). This was circular in plan, and the entrance from the *shirayi* was richly decorated. Its dome, *tuluwa*, had four *baka*, ie. eight corbels, radiating from the central circular *rijiya*. The structure of the *baka* was simplified, and instead of an elaborate system of overlapping layers of *azara* (see section on corbels, page 1.32), the structure relied on eight conically arranged *azara* beams. Two clay beds, heated from underneath, provided the main items of furnishing in the interior.

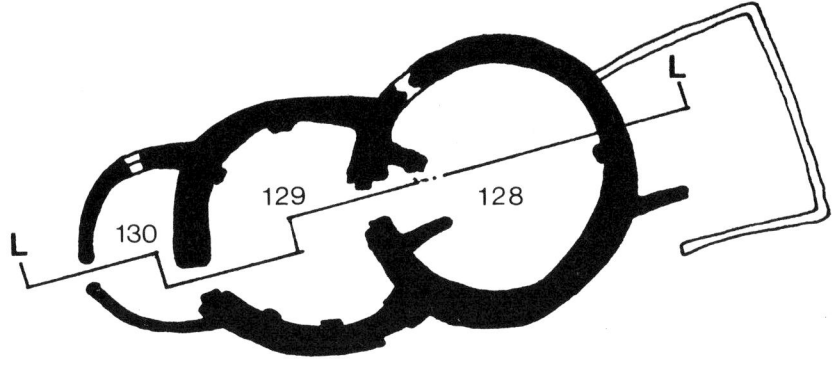

Fig.5.31. Zaria. Emir's Palace.
Women's house, rooms 128–130. PLAN.

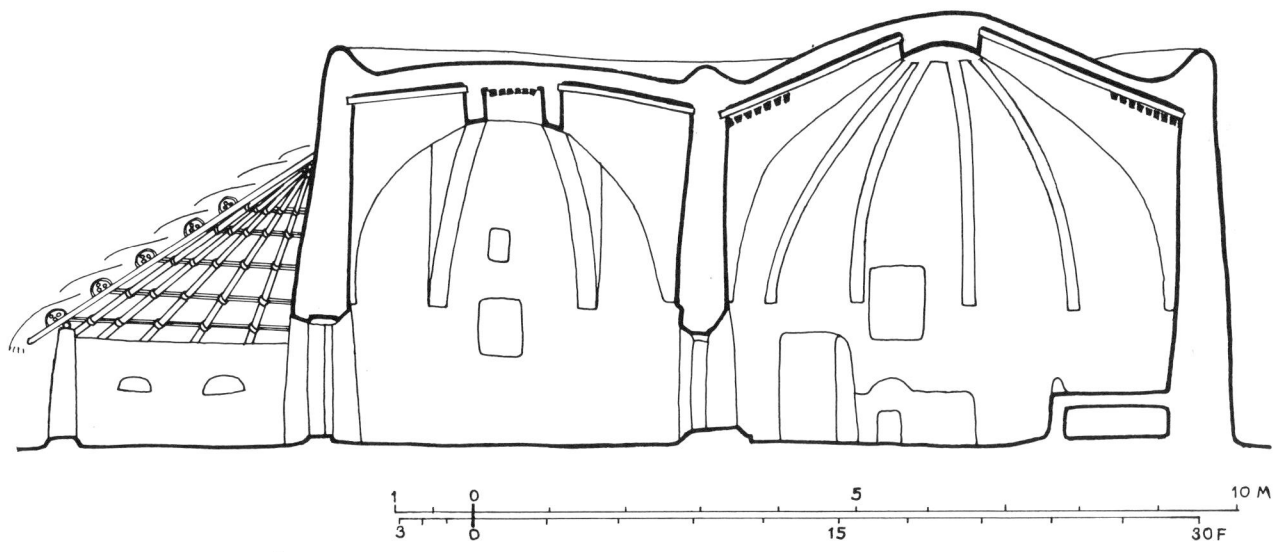

Fig.5.32. Zaria. Emir's Palace.
Women's house, rooms 128–130. SECTION L–L.

The next dwelling in the row resembled the southern one in plan, but was better preserved and more elaborately constructed and decorated. The walls of the *kafe* (verandah) were undamaged, and unlike 106 and 125, the semi-conical roof had a purlin resting directly on the crown of the walls. There were two small arched apertures in the N side of the *kafe* (Fig. 5.32). Both internal doors, leading to room 129 and to room 128 had architraves and archivolts moulded in semi-circles, quadrilaterals, embossed circles and rectangles. The elements of this decoration were more or less the same as in other women's dwellings and in the palace, but the arrangement of patterns varied every time, giving a different character to the whole. *Shirayi* 129 had a slightly domed roof, resting on an unusual frame of one axial *baka*, supported on both sides by pairs of corbels (Figs. 5.31 & 5.32). Here, as in *shirayi* 126, the walls enclosed part of the circumference of the bedchamber, *daki* (128), the entrance door of which was screened on both sides with *bari*. There were three beds inside and a window, facing N as in the preceding example. The domed roof had a frame of twelve *bakuna* corbels, making it one of the richest constructions, used only seldom, even in square interiors (Figs. 5.31, 5.32 & Pl. 5.46).

Pls.5.44 & 5.45. ZARIA. Emir's Palace. (Rooms 128 - 130). Entrances to rooms 129 and 128 respectively.

Pl.5.46. ZARIA. Emir's Palace. Women's house (Rooms 128 - 130). Domed roof of room 128.

Pl.5.47. ZARIA. Emir's Palace. Women's house.(Rooms 128 - 130). External view.

The last building of this eastern row (143, 144), had only two interiors, and together with *soro* 124-123 framed the two larger more sumptuous dwellings. Room 143 combined the function of *kafe* and *shirayi*. It was much lower than the following *daki* (144), which had an unusual plan: a semi-circle, with a flat wall at the back. Like the *soro* at the other end, the building was thatched, but its plan created a picturesque combination of two roofs – semi-conical and hipped (Pls. 5.48 & 5.49). At the front, both roofs were linked with a plaited grass mat (*boto*) with a projecting plaited rib along its centre.

Between the four buildings described above and dwelling 145 extended a small, internal square, with a circular verandah

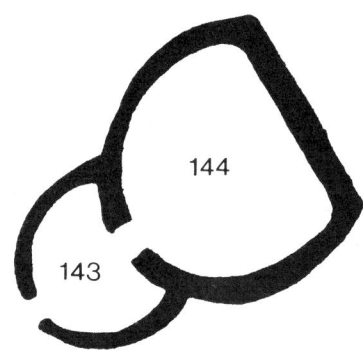

Fig.5.33. Zaria. Emir's Palace.
Women's house, rooms 143–144. PLAN.

(*debi*) in the centre, serving as the common workplace of the women of the compound. It had a loam-built parapet in which a ring of stout *azara* posts was embedded. They were carved into forks at the top (*azara mai gwafa*) and carried a ring of thin *gongola*s and cornstalks (*kara*) bound with *tukke* cord. This circular purlin (*ginia*) was first laid on the ground, as a base for the roof frame. First, four rafters of *gongola* (called *dawaki*) were arranged conically; next another four were placed in between; and the whole was stiffened at the peak by a cone of cornstalks (*kurkudu*). The ends of the rafters were cut to half their thickness, and then bent vertically upwards and tied together to form a bolt. The outer laths (*tanka*) were made partly from split *gongola*s and partly from cornstalks, and also from bunches of grass.(Pl. 5.51)

The thatch, which as usual was of grass mats laid in a spiral, was sewn to the *tanka* with a curved iron needle called jocularly *yaro ba kyuya* (the boy who is not lazy). The uppermost layers of thatch were softened with water and enveloped the rafters of the bolt. The lower part of the pinnacle thus made was about 30 centimetres high and was tightly bound with string. The top of the grass, reinforced with string and shaped into a conical cap, topped the apex of the thatch. The end of the string was inserted with a needle into the centre of the pinnacle. (Plate 5.50)

The palace of Zaria, with the Emir's apartments and the womens' compounds, contained in 1963 a comprehensive collection of excellent and valuable examples of Habe/Hausa architectural designs and structural devices. In fact it represented most of the characteristics of traditional Hausa building art. For the sake of documenting the building tradition of Zazzau the palace should be preserved as one of the most important monuments of Nigerian national culture.

Pl.5.48. ZARIA. Emir's Palace. Women's house. (Rooms 143/144). Building seen from the side.

Pl.5.49. ZARIA. Emir's Palace. Women's house (Rooms 143/144). Building seen from the front.

Pl.5.50. ZARIA. Emir's Palace. Detail of roof showing apex of thatch.

Pl.5.51. ZARIA. Emir's Palace. Household verandah, debi. *Detail of roof construction.*

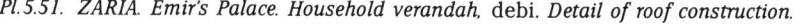

Fig.5.34. Zaria. Emir's Palace. PARTIAL PLAN.

Kafin Madaki
Palace

The town of Kafin Madaki was erected some 45 kilometres N of Bauchi, on the orders of Ibrahim, the ruler of Bauchi and son of the founder of the city, Yakubu, who died in 1845. The walled town was built by Ibrahim's Madaki, whose name was Abdul Kadiri (died 1897), in order to provide a defence (*zaman ribatsi*) against the inroads of the Ningi.[22]

The first monumental building in the centre of the town was the mosque, erected in 1859. The nearby palace, NE of the mosque, was built later.

This magnificent residence should be considered as one of the greatest achievements of Hausa architecture. It is sometimes referred to as Babban Gwani, obviously as an expression of deference to its architect, who was a past master of his art; this is what Babban Gwani means. However, the master of Kafin Madaki should not be identified with another Babban Gwani, Mallam Mikhaila of Zaria, who built the Zaria Masallaci. Certainly nobody in Zaria knew Mikhaila worked in Kafin Madaki. But above all, the structure of the two buildings, even taking their different functions into account, testifies to the entirely different creative individuality of their originators.

Fig.5.35. Kafin Madaki Palace. PLAN.

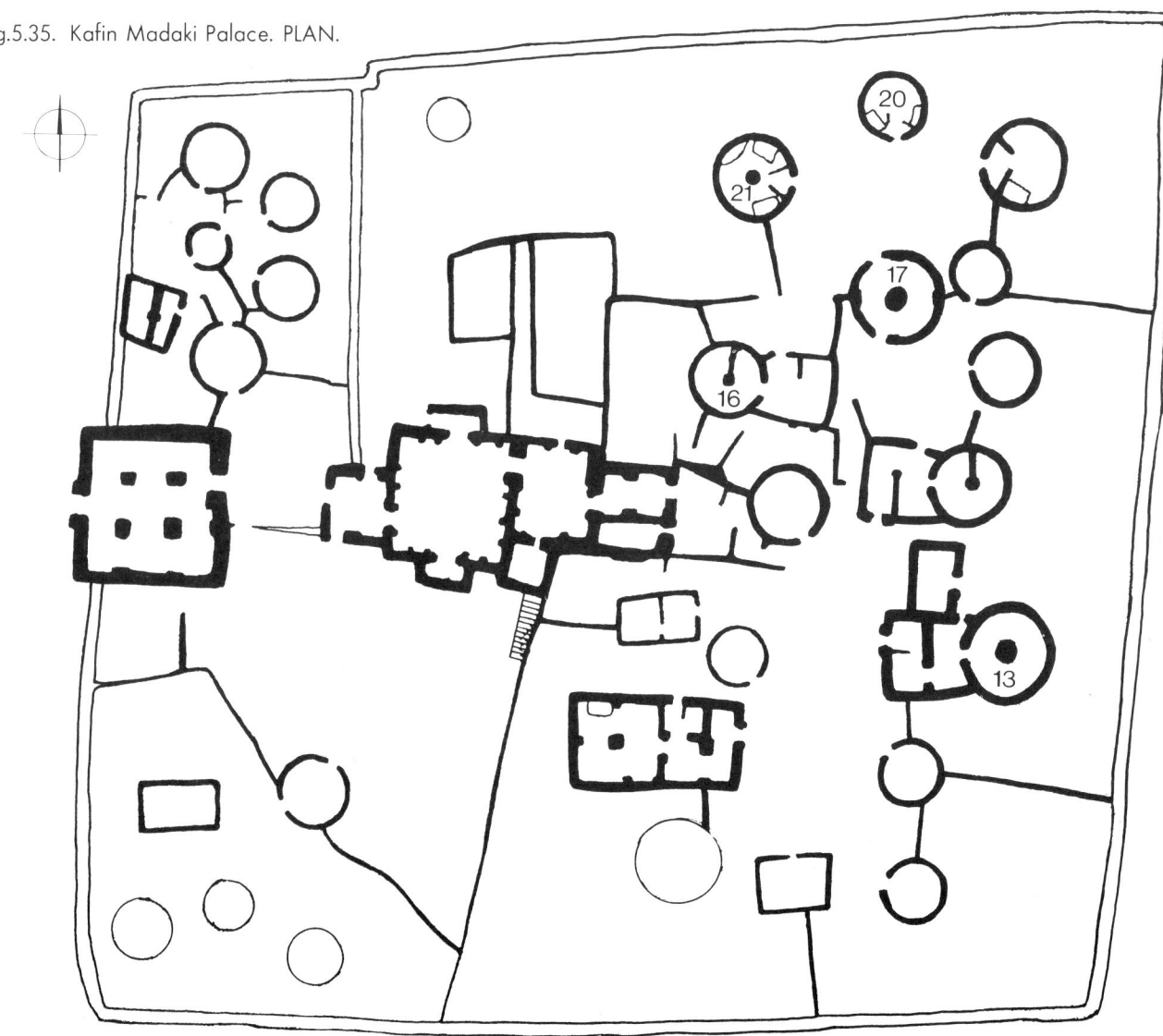

[22] S J Hogben and A H M Kirk-Greene, *The Emirates of Northern Nigeria*, London 1966, Oxford University Press, p. 461.

Pls.5.52 & 5.53. *KAFIN MADAKI. Views from the air.*

The Ciroma of Madaki informed me in 1964 that the builder of the palace worked in Bauchi and then in Kirifi before coming to Kafin Madaki. He also agreed with the accepted date of the starting of the fabric – one year after the Masallaci was built, which would mean 1860. On the other hand, Mallam Ahmadu Jermai, Sarkin Gini of Madaki, maintained that the date was much later, in 1894. At this time the Madaki Abdul Kadiri was still alive and Sarkin Gini was twenty-two years old. It may be that what he remembered (he was ninety-two years old) was one of the numerous restorations which the palace underwent after it was built. The extremely daring structure of the palace and the originality of its spatial composition were bound to require repeated reconstructions – the fate of many of the greatest monuments of architecture, including the Gothic cathedrals of Europe.[23]

The general layout of the palace is typical of the planning of great Hausa residences. There is a *kofar zaure* in the W front, leading to the first courtyard, with the main palace building at the back. Further E extends a large courtyard separated by additional internal walls. It contains the smaller houses of the Madaki's wives and servants, and, there are the not uncommon smaller courtyards on both sides of the *zaure* (ie. to the E and W). (Fig. 5.35 and Pls. 5.52 & 53.)

The main entrance hall, *kofar zaure*, was set in the centre of the front part of the perimeter wall, which surrounded the palace compound in almost rectangular outline. The flat roof was supported by four heavy square pillars (*al'amudai*, Pl. 5.55). In the usual Hausa fashion each pillar was topped by a few crossed layers of *azara*, forming four brackets (Fig. 1.25, Chapter One). These supported the beams (*tauyi*), so that the ceiling was divided into nine bays. The surface of the flat roof was divided by two low parapets, set above the E-W *tauyi* and draining off the rainwater to the outside.

[23] In December 1962, Mr C Duxbury, Department of Antiquities, Superintendent of Monuments, found the roof of the *zaure* of the palace badly damaged, five of the nine bays collapsed, and the remaining four sagging badly. Similarly the roof of the ante-room was about to collapse (Department of Antiquities File T128/C5/B). The most urgent repairs were done almost immediately, and Mallam Baba Galadima of the Department of Antiquities reported in February 1963 that all nine bays of the *zaure* had been reconstructed. On the other hand he found the two bays of the ante-room still in bad condition and cracks and traces of termites over the roof of the main hall. This seems to imply that periodical restorations have taken place during the century the palace has been in existence.

The people of Nigeria owe a debt of gratitude to the Madaki of Bauchi, Alhaji Garba Abubakar, for the loving care with which he protects this great monument of national architecture.

Pl.5.54. KAFIN MADAKI. Kofar zaure.

The interior was called *wurin zuba takalma*, which expressed some of the purposes it served. *Wurin* means a passage to, *zuba* means to pour in or out, and *takalma* means shoe or sandal. It was indeed a place through which guests passed, the more important being met by the Madaki in front of the hall, and then led inside. The visitors left their shoes there, while at night the palace children slept there. The door in the back wall was positioned northwards; it was almost hidden by the *ne al'amudi*, thus hiding the view of the small courtyard beyond. In this courtyard, *filin duka*, boys were punished, and on both sides were entrances to side courtyards. To the N a circular, thatched *zaure* led to a small enclosure in the NW corner of the perimeter walls; it contained the Madaki's armoury (*makamai*) kept in a few small circular buildings, and one rectangular one: *soron ajiya kain-yaki* (store for war equipment). The passage in the S wall of *filin duka* led to the *shamaki* (stables) courtyard, where horses were tied by one foot to low, mushroom-shaped posts.

On the E side of *filin duka* rose the Babban Gwani palace. It consisted of three main blocks of different sizes and heights.

The first room, *soron fadanci*, had a flat ceiling divided into two panels by a N-S corbelled *baka* of considerable dimensions (Fig. 5.37). In *soron fadanci* respectful homage was paid to the Madaki by his visitors, who entered the room one by one. The Madaki's couch stood in the SE niche.

A door in the SW corner gave the Madaki access to the *shamaki* and to his horses; another side-door in the N wall provided entry to the western part of the northern courtyard where there stood a guest house, *masauki*. In the eastern wall there was a portal to the great hall of the palace. This portal, set deep in the thickness of the wall, was flanked by two massive pilasters, which also acted as buttresses, counteracting the oblique pressures of the huge *bakan gizos* in the great hall (Figs. 5.36 & 5.37.)

The great hall of the palace was again called *soron fadanci*, because of its social function; and also *babban gwani*, in appreciation of its architectural merit. Indeed it was a magnificent achievement in the formation of space, as well as a courageous and successful structural conception.[24]

The frame carrying the roof consisted of five main *bakan gizos* which sprang from the E and W walls about 70 centimetres above floor level, and twenty brackets springing from all four walls (Pl. 5.57). The brackets were shaped like large cyma reversa and reached the two outer *bakan gizos*, in a sinuous curve. They gave them support and at the same time reduced the span of the roof beams running E-W which were carried by the *bakan gizos* (Pl. 5.57). In this way the central square of ceiling in *soron babban gwani*, whose floor surface measured about 8 metres square, was only about 4.7 metres square: this was the part in which the E-W beams were supported by *bakan gizos* alone.

Pl.5.55. *KAFIN MADAKI. Interior of the* zaure.

[24] The fact that in 1962 the roofs of both the massive *zaure* and the antechamber had to be reconstructed, while the roof of *soron babban gwani* was found to be structurally sound, proves the reliability of this complex fabric.

Pl.5.56. KAFIN MADAKI. The Babban Gwani Palace. South elevation.

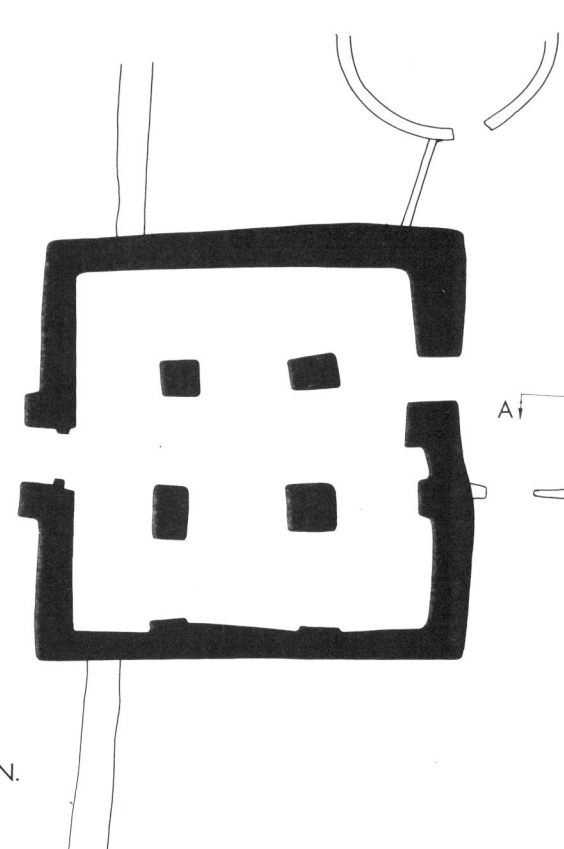

Fig.5.36. Kafin Madaki Palace. PARTIAL PLAN.

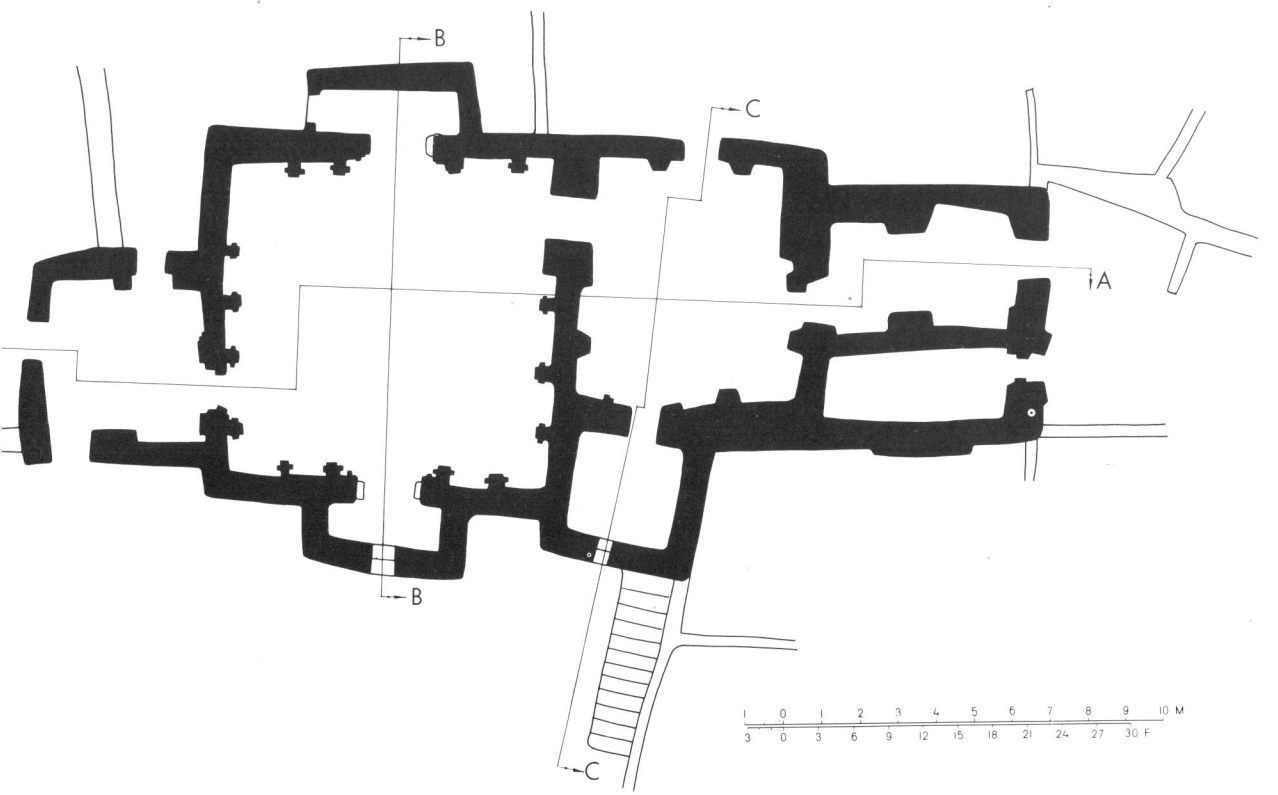

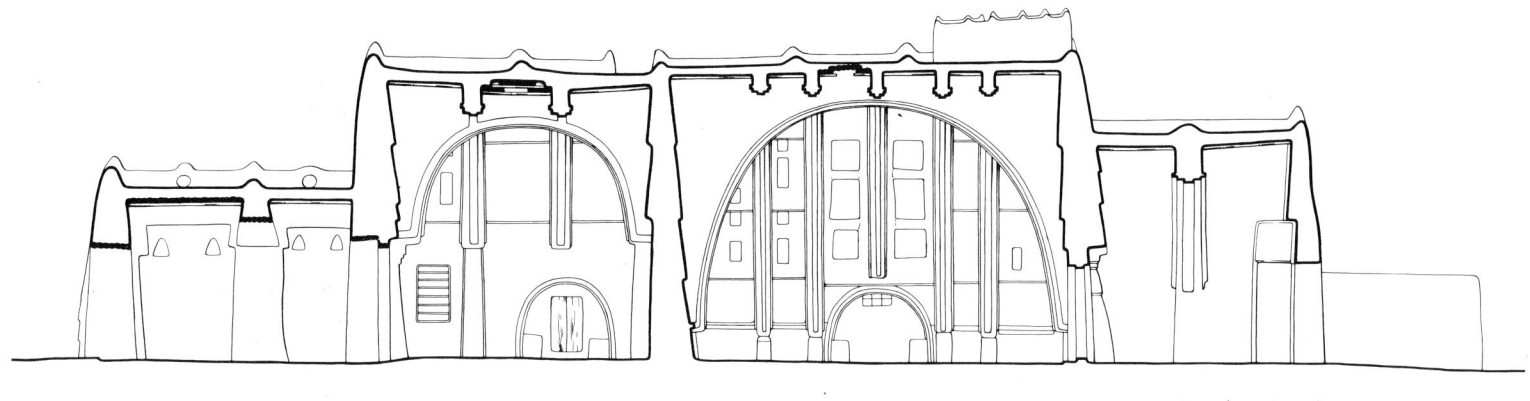

Fig.5.37. Kafin Madaki Palace. SECTION A—A.

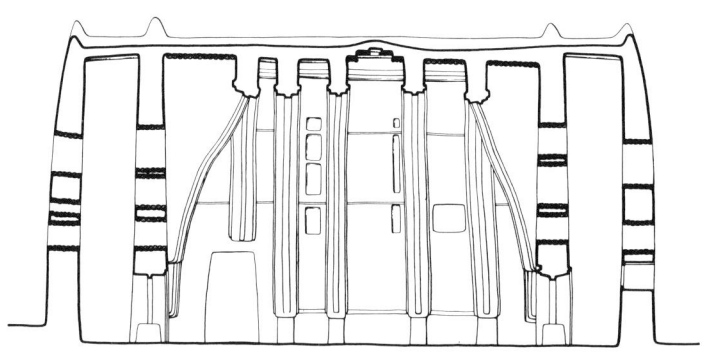

Fig.5.38. Kafin Madaki Palace. SECTION B—B.

Layers of *azaras* were laid on top of the beams, and the waterproof surface of the roof was divided by low parapets into three sections draining the rainwater N and S. Most of the rainpipes were made of wood, but a single ceramic one remained in the S façade of the small *soron fadanci* (Pls. 5.60 & 5.61.)

On each side of *babban gwani* was a rectangular structure about 1.9 x 4.3 metres in plan. The walls were as thick as in the rest of the building, so that their interiors ('pocket' = *aljihu soro*) were considerably reduced; yet their ceilings were as high as that of the main hall. Each was linked to the main hall by an arched doorway on the cross axis of the hall. The walls above them were pierced by three pairs of apertures (*taga*); much smaller apertures pierced the outer walls of these chimney-like interiors (Pl. 5.62). And indeed the S *aljihu* served as a fireplace. The N one however was used as a dining room for important guests, unless, during the dry season, food

was served outside its W door, in *wurin cin abinci*.

There was another *soro* N of the main hall. Its roof support was a simplified version of the former. In the S wall was a wooden door set in an arched niche (Pl. 5 59). Behind it was a small room belonging to a day and night female janitor, *jakadiya madaki*, a woman twenty-five years old, the specially chosen confidante of the Madaki.

The easternmost room of the palace, *soron garki*, was where the shields (singular: *garkuwa*) were stored. The room was rather low, and its roof of azaras and loam was laid on a massive central beam running N-S, which divided the ceiling into two panels. The beam ran across the interior between two heavy pilasters topped with *gemu* brackets. The back courtyard was divided into a number of interlocking enclosures, some of them entered through thatched *zauruka*. There were fifteen dwellings, mostly circular; these formed a comprehensive set of typical small-scale Hausa habitations. (Pls. 5.63–5.66.)

Pl.5.57. KAFIN MADAKI. Soron fadanci: *the great hall showing three* bakan gizos *running E–W.*

Pl.5.58. KAFIN MADAKI. Room 4: East door.

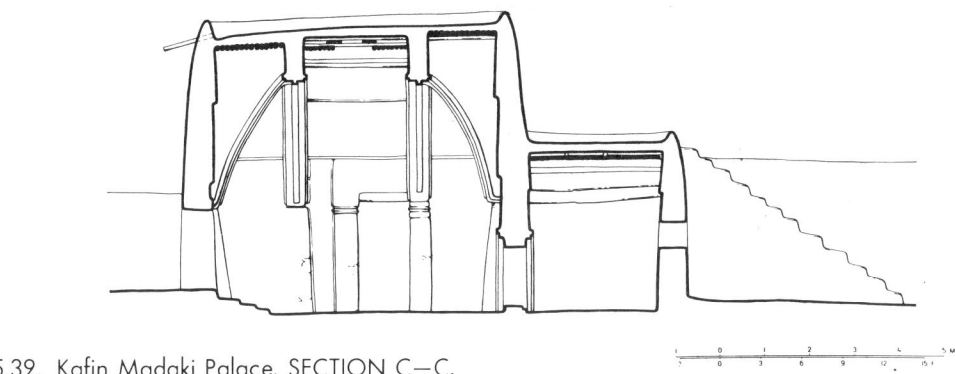

Fig.5.39. Kafin Madaki Palace. SECTION C—C.

Pl.5.59. KAFIN MADAKI. Room 4, adjoining soron fadanci: *arched niche leading to the janitor's room.*

Pl.5.60. KAFIN MADAKI. South elevation of palace, showing clay gutter.

Pl.5.61. KAFIN MADAKI. South elevation, showing wooden gutter.

Pl. 5. 62. KAFIN MADAKI. Detail of South elevation.

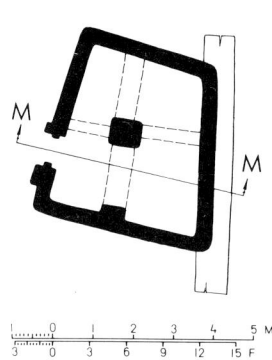

Fig.5.40. Kafin Madaki Palace. *Soron.* PLAN.

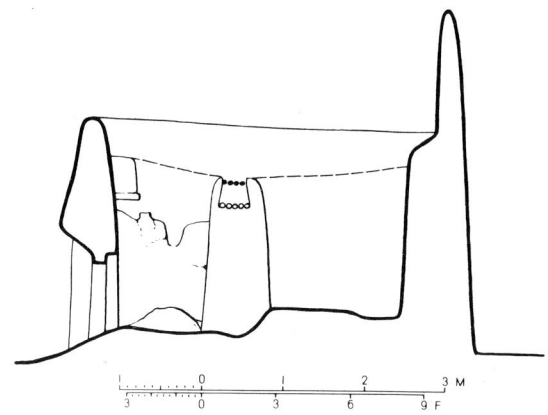

Fig.5.41. Kafin Madaki Palace. *Soron.* SECTION M—M.

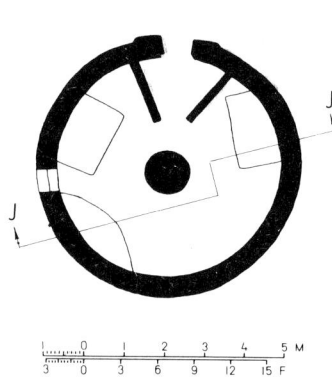

Fig.5.42. Kafin Madaki Palace. House 21. PLAN.

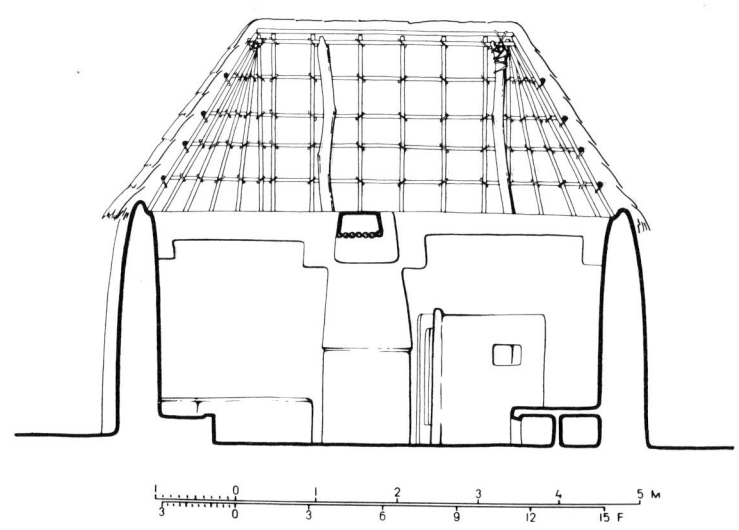

Fig.5.43. Kafin Madaki Palace. House 21. SECTION J—J.

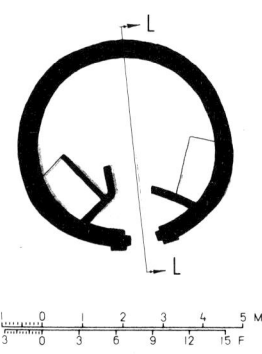

Fig.5.44. Kafin Madaki Palace. House 20. PLAN.

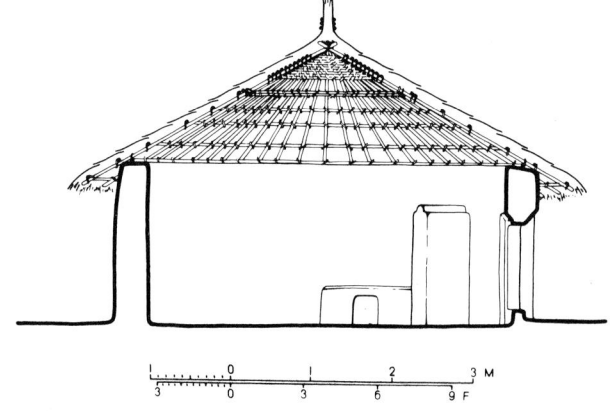

Fig.5.45. Kafin Madaki Palace. House 20. SECTION L—L.

Pl.5.63. KAFIN MADAKI. House 21.

Pl.5.64. KAFIN MADAKI. View North from the roof of the soron: *house and two granaries.*

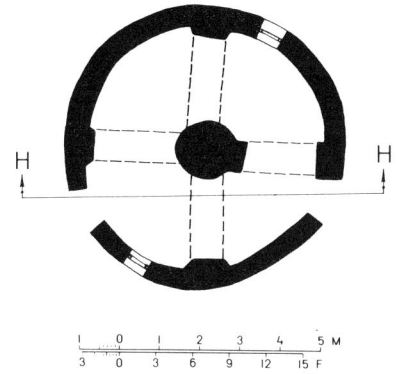

Fig.5.46. Kafin Madaki Palace. House 17. PLAN.

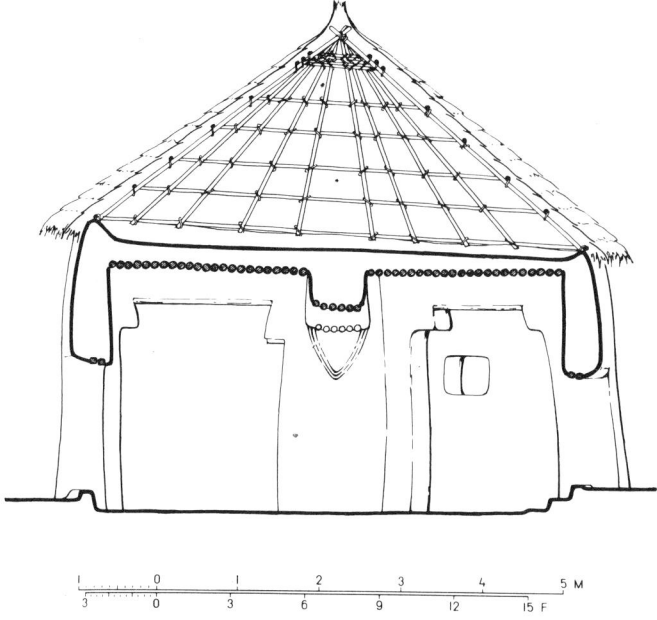

Fig.5.47. Kafin Madaki Palace. House 17. SECTION H—H.

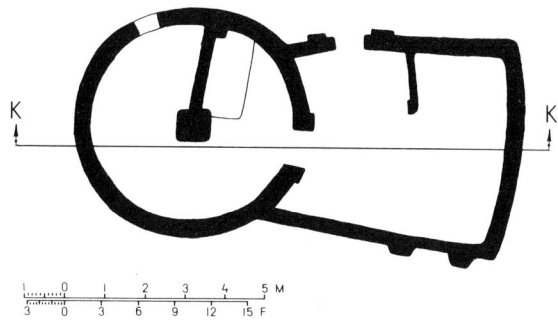

Fig.5.48. Kafin Madaki Palace. House 16. PLAN.

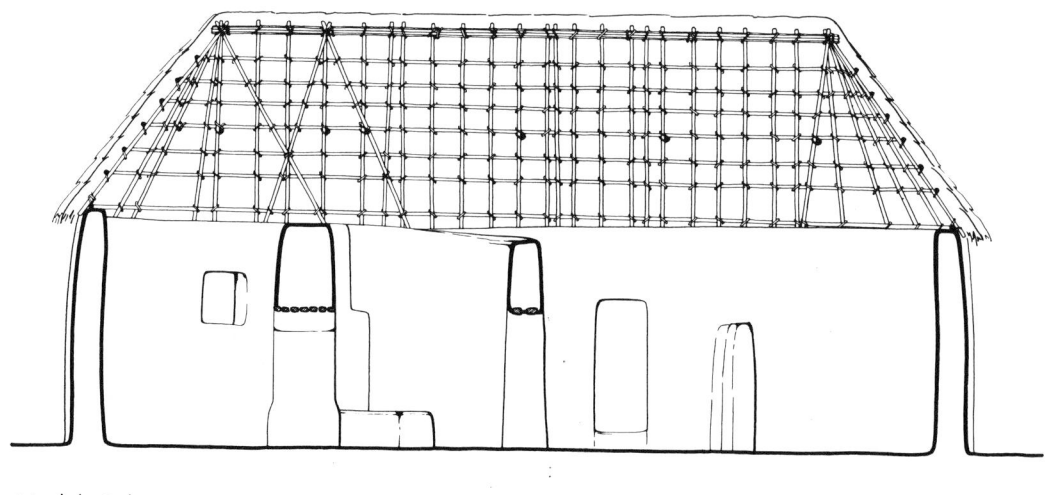

Fig.5.49. Kafin Madaki Palace. House 16. SECTION K—K.

Pl.5.65. KAFIN MADAKI. View N.E. from the roof of the soron.

Pl.5.66. KAFIN MADAKI. View S.E. from the roof of the soron.

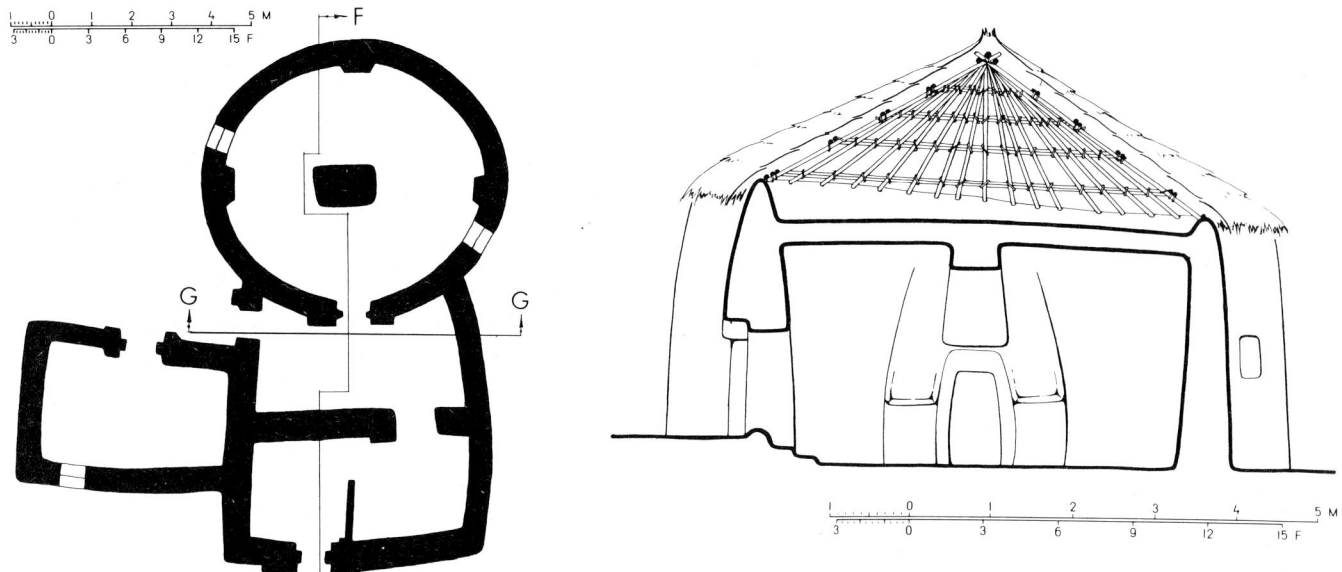

Fig.5.50. Kafin Madaki Palace. House 13. PLAN.

Fig.5.51. Kafin Madaki Palace. House 13. SECTION G—G.

Fig.5.52. Kafin Madaki Palace. House 13. SECTION F—F.

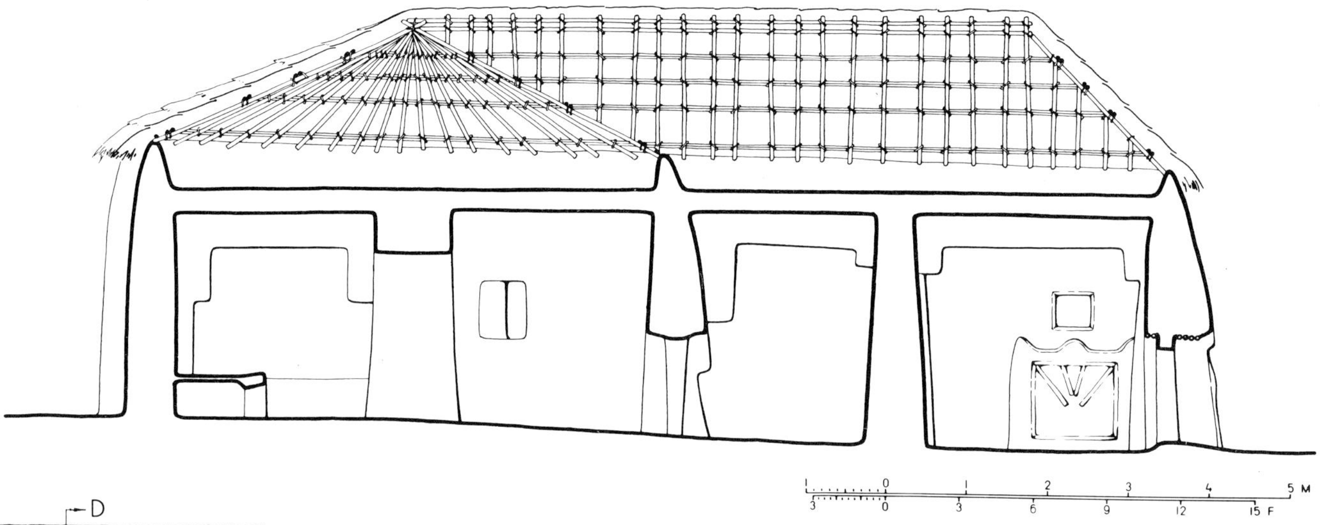

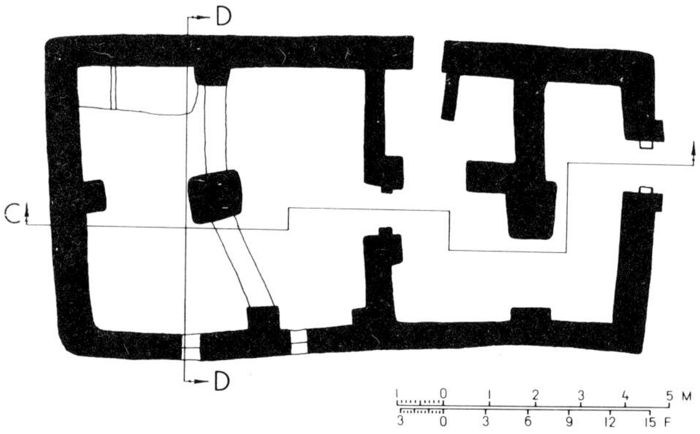

Fig.5.53. Kafin Madaki Palace. House. PLAN.

Fig.5.54. Kafin Madaki Palace. House. SECTION D—D.

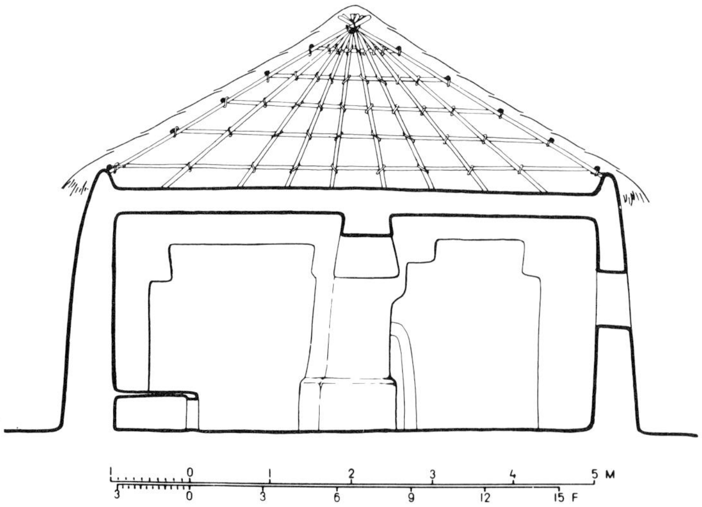

Pl.5.67. *KAFIN MADAKI. Detail of South elevation of the palace.*

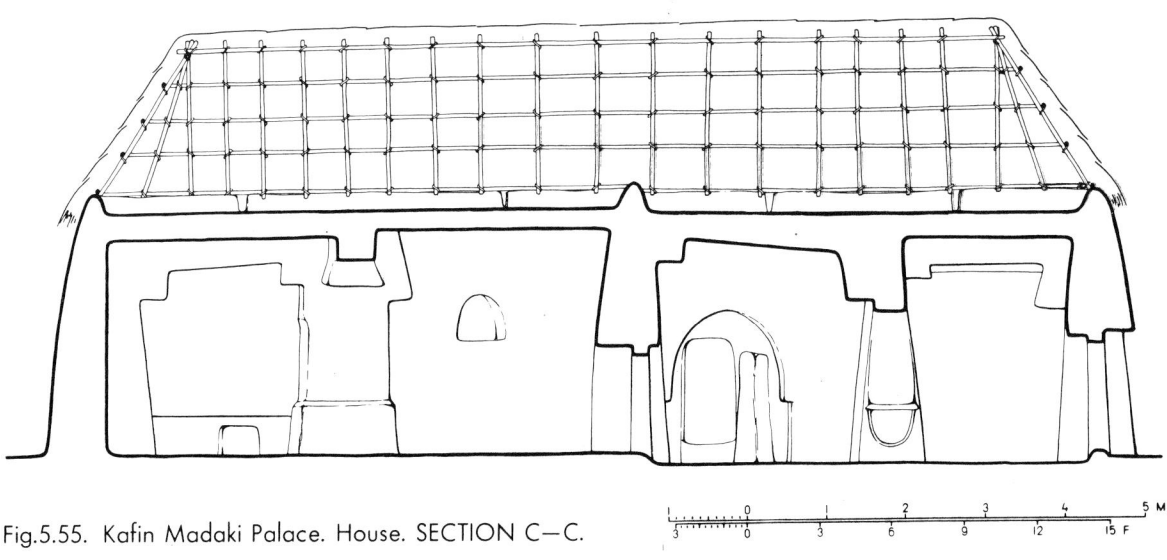

Fig.5.55. Kafin Madaki Palace. House. SECTION C—C.

Pl. 5.68. KAFIN MADAKI AREA. Compound from the air.

Pl.5.69. KAFIN MADAKI AREA. Compound from the air.

Abuja
Emir's Palace

The palace of the Emir of Abuja was by far the most impressive building of the old town: in size, in refinement of plan and in structural quality, which combined various elements of the Abuja school of design.

The fragment of the palace surveyed (Fig. 5.56) drew attention to the two characteristic interiors. At the NE end of the complex there was a circular living room surrounded by a spacious verandah. The room had two doors on the EW axis; they corresponded with the verandah's doorways, although slightly moved sideways from this axis – the usual tendency to protect the view of the private interior. The numerous windows of the verandah provided cross ventilation, while its roof kept the living room in constant shade. The verandah was divided into two parts: the eastern part formed an ante-chamber to the living room, the other part served as a parlour. From there a rectangular passage (an enlarged version of a corridor linking parlour and bedroom of the more opulent women's houses as described above – led to a number of smaller rooms and to a magnificently constructed treasury

chamber, a royal version of a store room *kurukuru*.

The axis of the chamber had an entrance door at the eastern end and a window opposite. Two more windows were set on the NS axis. The massive ceiling rested on two semi-elliptical *bakkuna*, rising at floor level from four thick solid bases. The rods of their corbels projected towards the apex, Abuja method, at an acute angle. They provided the frame for almost pointed *bakkuna* arches. The apex was strongly accentuated by a bulky circular mould, decoratively shaped. The ceiling, formed as a shallow cone, rested on a number of timbers, laid on top of the *bakkuna*. It carried a thick layer of carefully processed loam, very hard and about as strong as the circular walls of the treasury. The crown of the walls supported the frame of a thatched roof.

There were only a few moulded embellishments in the treasure chamber, rightly considered as unnecessary in an interior whose spatial composition, made up of special structural devices, provided an impressive manifestation of Abuja building art.

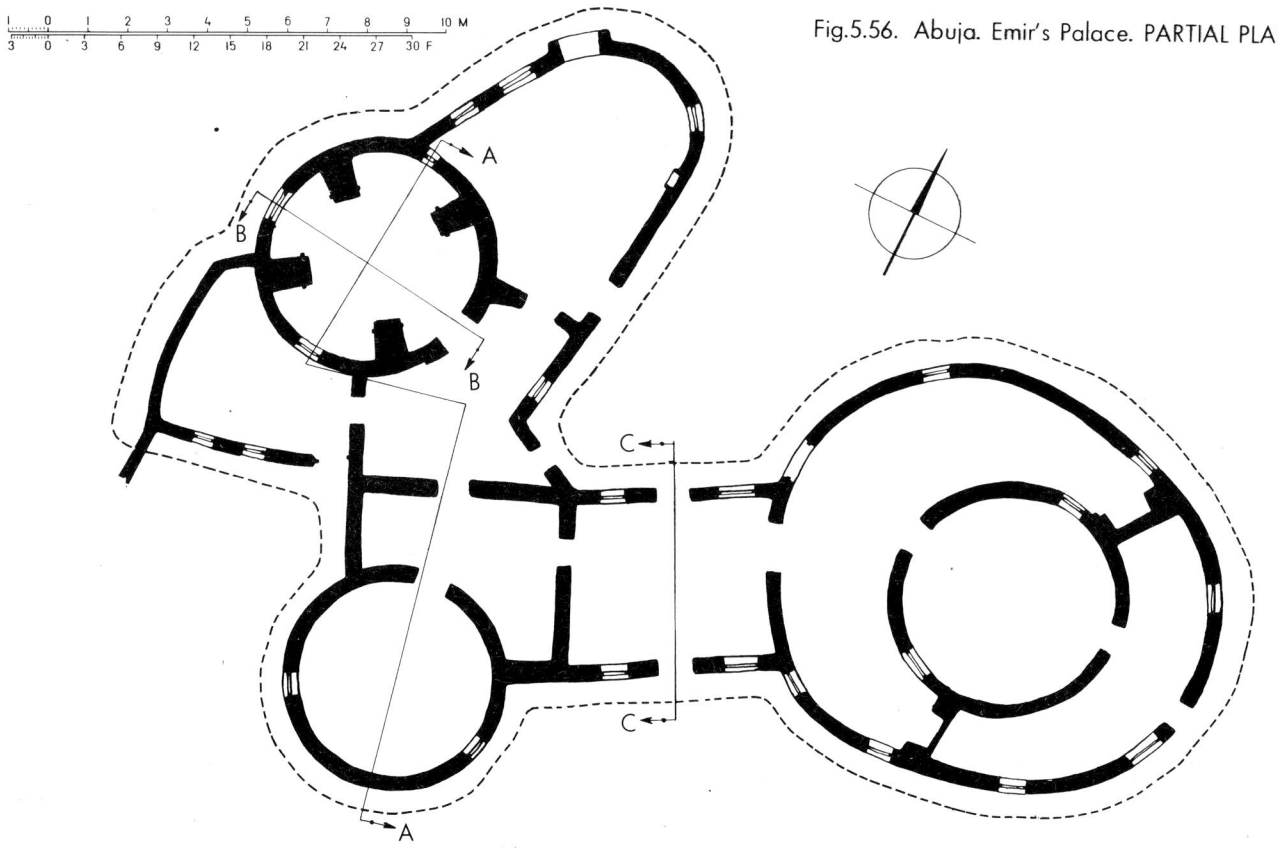

Fig.5.56. Abuja. Emir's Palace. PARTIAL PLAN.

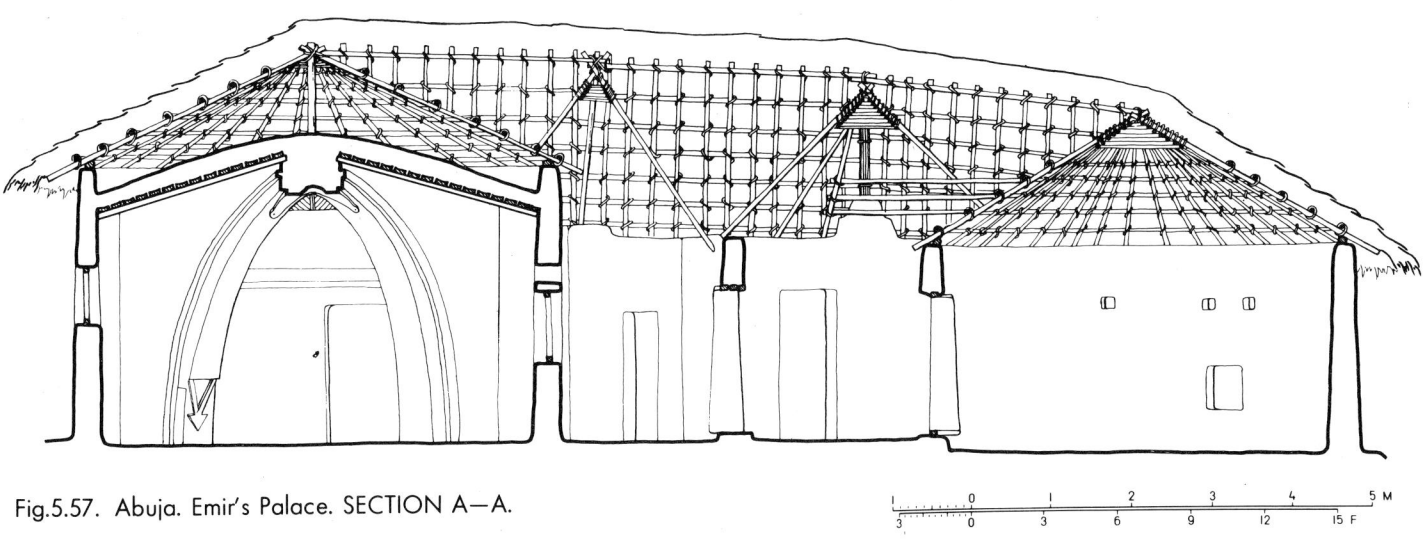

Fig.5.57. Abuja. Emir's Palace. SECTION A—A.

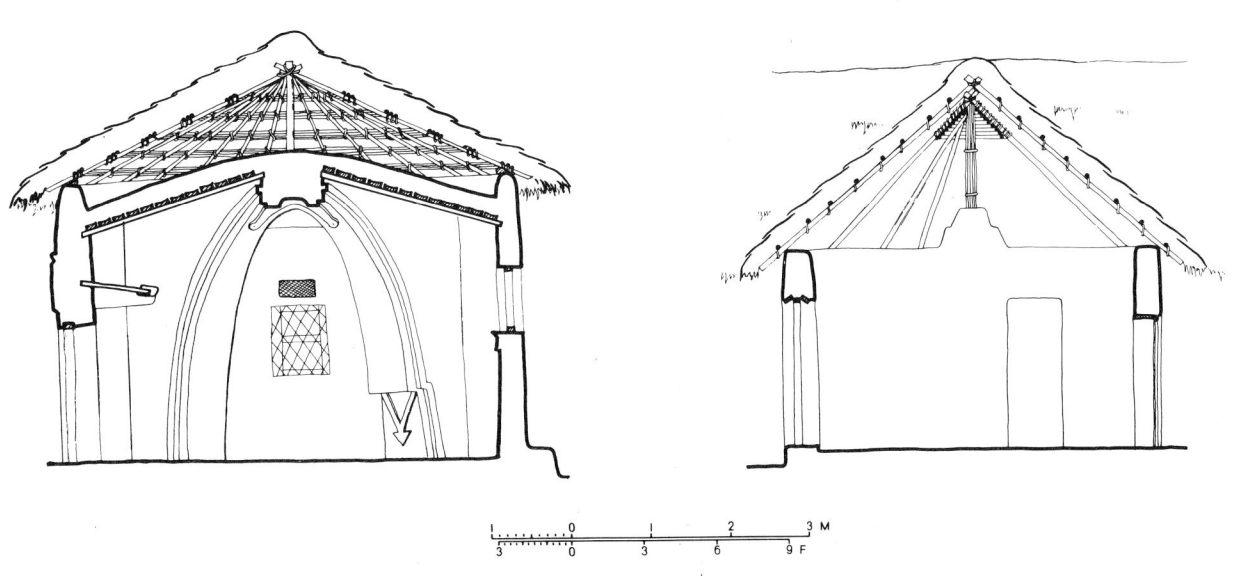

Fig.5.58. Abuja. Emir's Palace. SECTION B—B.

Fig.5.59. Abuja. Emir's Palace. SECTION C—C.

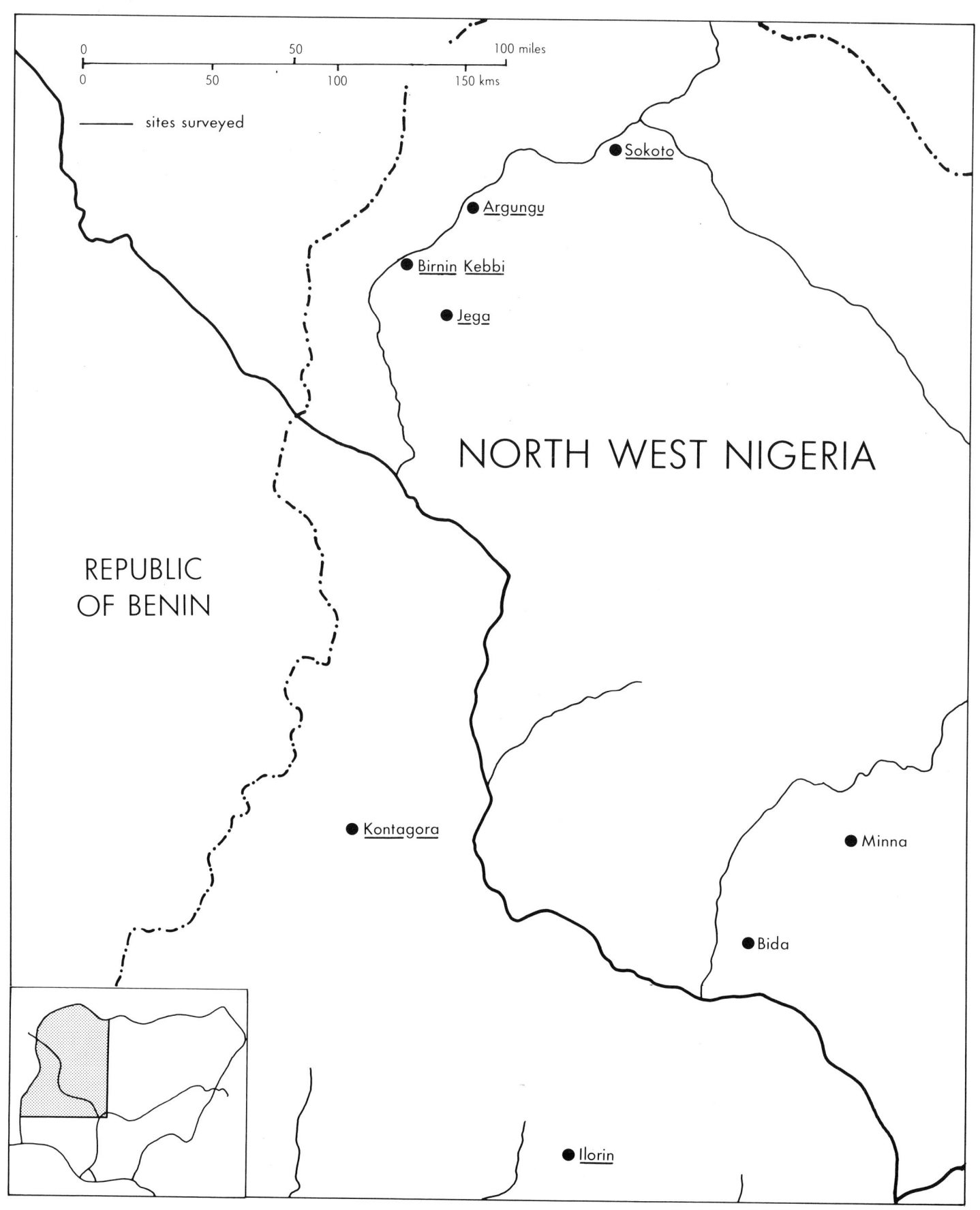

0   50   100 miles

0   50   100   150 kms

—— sites surveyed

●Sokoto

●Argungu

●Birnin Kebbi

●Jega

NORTH WEST NIGERIA

REPUBLIC
OF BENIN

●Kontagora

●Minna

●Bida

●Ilorin

6 *Architecture of the North West*

Sokoto
Argungu
Kontagora
Ilorin

Sokoto

The vizierate of Sokoto was founded *c.* 1809[1] a few years after Shehu Uthman dan Fodio, a member of the Mallam class of Fulani scholars, settled in Sokoto.

The history of modern Sokoto is linked with the immigration of the Fulani people. They consisted of two categories: the nomadic herdsmen and the Fulani Mallam class, whose scholarship earned them respect and positions of rank in many Hausa states. The most famous of them, Uthman dan Fodio, in protest against the oppression of the Habe ruling class and their lack of orthodoxy, proclaimed a jihad, a holy war, to achieve his religious and social ideals. It began with the *hijra*, his flight from his former pupil, Yunfa, Sarkin Gobir, to Gudu, some 60 km. from Sokoto; the date of the *hijra*, 1804, can be accepted as the beginning of the jihad. The revolution spread quickly, gathering an ever increasing force of supporters. The conquest of Zaria, Katsina and Kano began the process of building the Fulani empire. It spread south to a small part of Yorubaland, and east to Adamawa and certain of the Bornu emirates. The Fulani empire was organised as a confederation of self-governing states, a caliphate. It was linked by common social and religious doctrines and by political dependence on the Sarkin Musulmi, which title was first acquired by Shehu Uthman dan Fodio, in 1809.[2] But, a scholar and divine, he left the organisation of the jihad and caliphate to his brother Abdullahi and to his son, Muhammed Bello, who after Shehu's death became the second Sarkin Musulmi and Caliph of Sokoto. He founded the vizierate of Sokoto in 1809 and built the walled city on and around the site of a pagan settlement, whose founder gave his name to the place. It was in Bello's reign that Sokoto was explored for the first time by Europeans. Hugh Clapperton visited the city twice, in 1824, and 1826-7.[3] In March 1824 after an audience with the Sultan, he wrote as follows of his residence:

'In front of it there is a large quadrangle, into which several of the principal streets of the city lead. We passed through three coozees, or guardhouses, without the least detention, and were immediately ushered into the presence of Bello, the second Sultan of the Felatahs. He was seated on a small carpet, between two pillars supporting the roof of a thatched house, not unlike one of our cottages. The walls and pillars were painted blue and white, in the Moorish taste; and on the back wall was sketched a fire-screen, ornamented with a coarse painting of a flower-pot. An armchair, with an iron lamp standing on it, was placed on each side of the screen.'

After his second visit Clapperton gave an account of the city walls, which were over 7 metres high and had a dry ditch in front. Eleven gates gave access to the city, seven of them 'having been built up since the breaking out of the rebellion.' In the journal of his second expedition, he considerably enlarged his former description of the palace:

'The house of the Sultan is surrounded by a clay wall, about 20 ft. high, having two lower tower entrances, one on the east, the other on the west . . . The whole of his house forms, as it were, a little town of itself; for in it there are five square towers, a small mosque, a great number of huts and a garden, besides a house, which consists of a single room, used as the place for his receiving and hearing complaints, receiving visitors, and giving audiences to strangers. This room is nothing more than what we should call in our country a shed. Two large pillars support a beam, or bundle of long rods, plastered over with clay. These support the rafters, which are the branches of the palm tree.'

This description probably refers to the *zaure* of the palace, and there follows on the same page a further account, which appears to be based on hastily collected information.

Further descriptions of Sokoto were published in 1830.[4]

'The hut in which we resided was a round building, about thirty yards in circumference, having so small an entrance that we were obliged to stoop on going into it, and its appearance very much resembled an immense bee-hive. It had no window or other aperture whatever, besides the door-way already alluded to, so that light was admitted only from that channel . . . The hut was enclosed in a square yard, at one end of which the horses were confined, and the camels and another; and sheds were erected close to it, as sleeping apartments for the servants and slaves.

'For the erection of the walls of their huts, the natives use clay and earth, without hair, or any other substance. The mortar is made into

[1] H F C Smith, *Arabic Manuscript . . . on the History of Western Sudan*. Historical Society of Nigeria, Supplement to News Bulletin iii 4, 1959.
[2] S J Hogben, and A H M Kirk Greene, *op cit* p. 367, *passim*.
J B Webster, A A Boahen, A O Idowu, *The Revolutionary years – West Africa since 1800*, London 1971, p. 3, *passim*.
J D Fage, *A History of West Africa*, London 1969, p. 147, *passim*.
E Isichei, *History of West Africa since 1800*, London 1978, p. 18, *passim*.
H F C Smith, *Arabic Manuscript . . . on the History of the Western Sudan*, Historical Society of Nigeria, Supplement to News Bulletin, iii 4, 1959.
D W Macrow, *Sokoto City*, Nigeria Magazine 57/1958, p. 110.
[3] D Denham, H Clapperton, and W Oudney, *Narratives of Travel and Discoveries in Northern and Central Africa, in the years 1822, 1823 and 1824*, London 1826; and H Clapperton, *Journal of a Second Expedition into the Interior of Africa*, London 1829.
[4] R Lander, *1Reports of Captain Clapperton's last Expedition*, London 1830, Vol. II, pps. 58, 59.

round masses, somewhat larger than a skittleball, which being dried and hardened in the sun, are fit for use, and placed in tiers like bricks in England. As soon as the walls are raised to the usual height, the roof is constructed and placed on them; and the interstices between the tiers of balls and the balls themselves being filled up with moistened clay, the whole surface is plastered over with the same material by the hands of the workman which . . . . is his only tool, and the hut is then fit to be inhabited."

The information contained in the two extracts cited above was confirmed in December 1965, when I spent three days exploring the city with the generous and kind support of Sir Ahmadu Bello, Sardauna of Sokoto, and Sarkin Musulmi, Alhaji Abubakar.[5]

The city was built up mostly with circular huts covered with thatch and dome-shaped roof frames. There were also some flat-roofed rectangular buildings, which both structurally and formally resembled Habe-Hausa architecture.

The old Sokoto mosque, described in 1824 by Captain Clapperton, was pulled down and replaced by a new building. The city walls and gates built by Muhammadu Bello were much dilapidated.

The most revered building of the city, to which Muslim pilgrims come from all over the Sudan, was the tomb of Shehu Uthman dan Fodio. It was erected over the site of Shehu's old circular living house, in the centre of which he was buried. The building was a rectangular block, erected in loam and recently covered on the outside with stucco, marble-like tiles, and with green velvet inside. The sarcophagus itself, standing exactly over Shehu's grave, was again in the shape of a rectangular block, overlaid with velvet and with gilded cords at the edges. It became the nucleus of a large burial ground, surrounded on three sides by a wall and on the fourth by a partly arcaded verandah. Within there were numerous graves – some in separate buildings, some surrounded by cemented parapets, elipsoidal in plan and filled with light-coloured sand.

SOKOTO BUILDING MATERIALS

The building earth (*buri* or *turda*) is of poor quality, and was therefore mixed with *laka* clay, which was dried and pounded into greyish powder. *Laka* was dug out of selected pits – the place was easily recognisable since its surface was usually wet. The site where *laka* was found (called *maginan laka*) formed a semicircular belt to the east of the town. The proportion of the mixture was ⅔ *buri* to ⅓ *laka*. To this was added grass (cut with machetes when fresh, crushed by hand when dry). Then the mixture was profusely wetted and stamped underfoot; the process was repeated up to seven times, every three days. The resulting mass (*kasa*) was used only as plaster. The local variation of *tubali* (called *kunku*) was made with *buri* alone and three or four of them were laid in the thickness of the wall. The length of the layer completed, *kasa* was thrown on top of it, (thrown, not pressed, as was noted in Kano). The process was called *damri* (binding). Originally walls had no foundations; shallow foundations, one hand deep, were recently introduced.

HABE-HAUSA TYPE BUILDINGS IN SOKOTO

Rectangular, flat-roofed buildings appeared in Sokoto fairly recently, at the beginning of the twentieth century, and their structure was modelled on the Hausa fashion. Both the flat and domed roofs were similarly erected, on a frame of *azara* corbels, and similar arrangements were made according to the dimensions and proportions of the interior. The *azara*, called *kyami*, had an accepted span of 1.80 metres, but very occasionally reached up to 2.40 metres. Slightly trapezoidal in shape, the *azaras* were laid with the hardest, bark-side, downwards. Sometimes they were used as unplastered beams, laid in twos and threes, the beams 60 to 80 centimetres apart. Acting as joists, they supported the ceiling, which was decoratively laid zigzag fashion between two adjoining beams. The pattern was called *auzun zaki* (lion ribs) and usually the bush paw-paw was used for this purpose.

I was given some local terms for structural elements in the Hausa-type buildings. The thickened upper part of the wall, called *taushi*, was supported on *kemi*, the *azara* beam set between a pair of *bakuna*. The corner *almatika tauyi* (cf. Chapter 1.) were called *bance*. The crossed *bakuna* of the roof were given the name *guga* (actually a net of four cords holding a calabash for pulling water from a well). *Kafar kaza* (called also *talkamin kasa*) – a structure consisting of one whole *baka* with a half-*baka* supporting it at right angles – was named in a more descriptive idiom: *hayin takalme* (binding of a sandal).

[5] I was provided with a group of guides – the Sarkin Magina of Sokoto and three of his eldest master-builders, to whom I am indebted for the information on the Sokoto mosque.

Pls.6.1 & 6.2. SOKOTO. Top and bottom respectively of the rope net covering the thatch on a circular building.

SOKOTO CIRCULAR BUILDINGS

The domed Sokoto roofs over circular buildings were made in a way that was peculiar to the Sokoto area.[6] On top of the walls a circular wall-plate (*giniya*) was laid. It was up to 15 centimetres in diameter, and made from a thick bunch of *gamba* grass (the same species was used to make *zana* mats). It was tied together with plaited strips from the outer skin of cornstalks. The *giniya* was first laid on the ground, and the roof frame was built on it before being raised to the crown of the walls for thatching.

The roof frame had a construction of radially set rafters, also made of cornstalks (*karandaua*); these, once cleaned, were put in the hot ashes of millet leftovers, which prevented decay and altered the original light colour to a burnt sienna. Each rafter was made from a bunch of cornstalks 9–10 centimetres in diameter. Part of the stalks in the bunch were specially pointed, and were stuck into the grass *giniya*. Two or three of the outer cornstalks in the bunch were up to 60 centimetres longer than the rest. Their ends were broken with stones in order to change their stiff, tubular configuration into a number of flexible, flattened laths. These were wrapped around the *giniya*, then placed along the inner surface of the rafter and fastened together; the rafter and both layers of flattened cornstalk were joined with a number of rings, plaited from the skin of cornstalks. In this way the dome of the roof frame was bound strongly to the *giniya* around its circumference. Almost immediately above the uppermost binding two rings were placed, inside and outside the rafters, and tied

together. These bottom rings were made of thin cornstalks (*tanka*) or of millet stalks (*karan keru*). The next ring was usually very tough, made from *kirynya* (*k'irya*)—acacia-like branches, or branches of the *Sabara* shrub. Further up, the rafters were held together with two composite rings (*yabe*) of *tukura* grass; the lowest consisted of three, the topmost of six bunches of grass, set one above the other. The peak of the roof was convex, and covered with *kwando* matting plaited from the twigs of the *gyeza* tree.

Thus completed, the roof frame was covered with *zana* mats, which were tied to the rafters. Finally the thatch was made, from *shibci* grass, sewn into long mats with a single thread and laid in a spiral upwards from the eaves. This thatch was covered with a net (*taushi*) of cords made from the *Kaba* palm. The net was held in place by a strong ring (*mundua*) of rope at its top; the ends of *taushi* were fixed at the bottom of the thatch. The fixture was called *hakori da'ki* (teeth of the hut). The topmost spiral of mats was tightened with rope and trimmed horizontally – then a short shaft was pushed into the peak as an axis for the crest (*tukku*).[7] *Tukku* was made separately on the ground using *shinaka* grass and bound with *rama* coils, painted black with pigment prepared from soot mixed with gum-arabic. When dry, *tukku* was impaled on the central shaft – one more method of securing the top of the roof, which in this case was not conical, but domed.[8] (See Pls. 6.1 & 6.2).

[6] Their shape possibly followed that of the domed huts of the nomadic Fulbe.
[7] *Tukku* means a plait of hair on the crown of the head, and also the crest of a bird (Revd G P Bargery, *op cit*, p. 1051).
[8] Possibly a development of bush-Fulani domed huts.

Compound of Mallam Azika

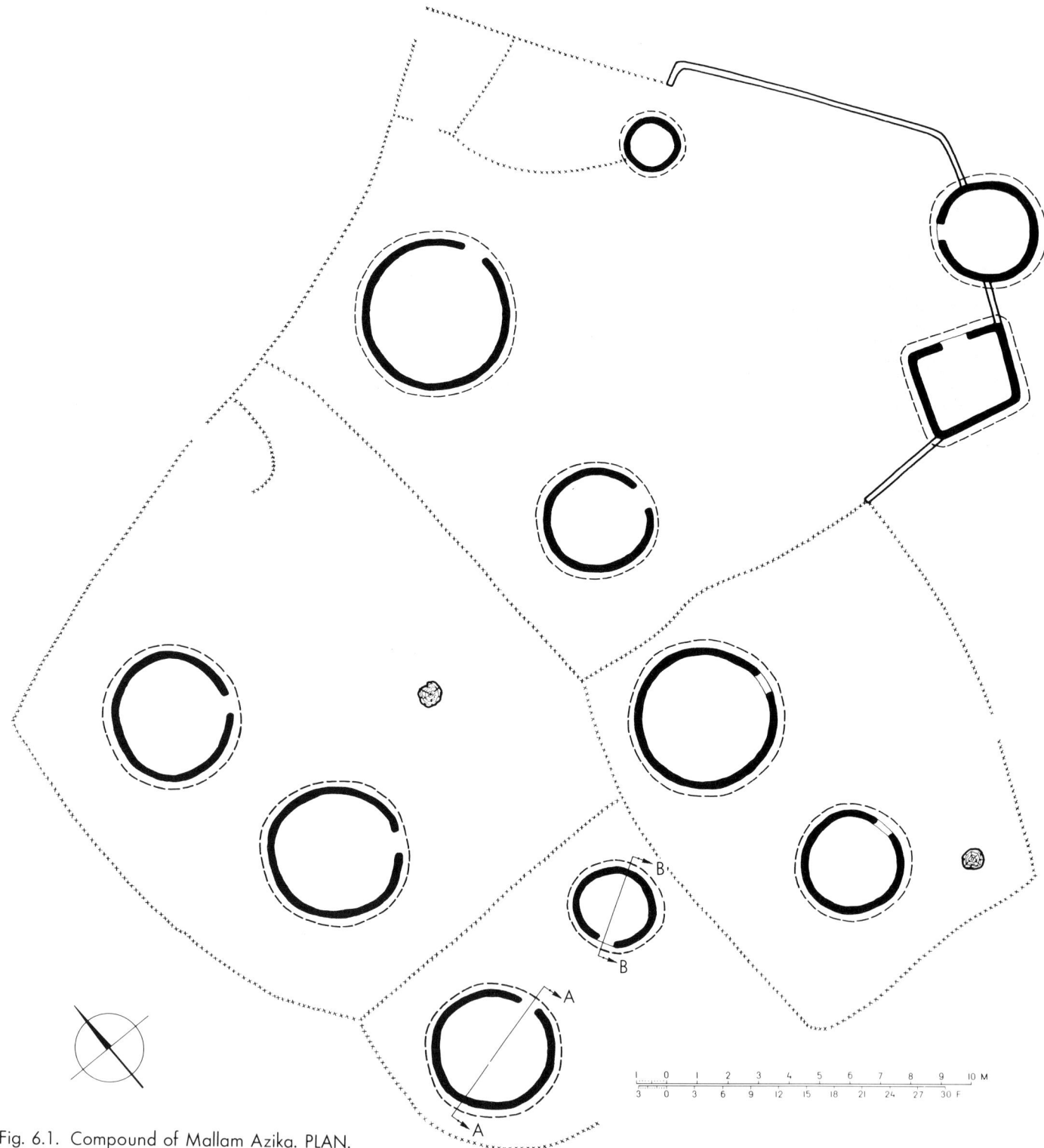

Fig. 6.1. Compound of Mallam Azika. PLAN.

Pl.6.3. SOKOTO. A typical circular building.

Fig. 6.2. Compound of Mallam Azika.
SECTION A—A.

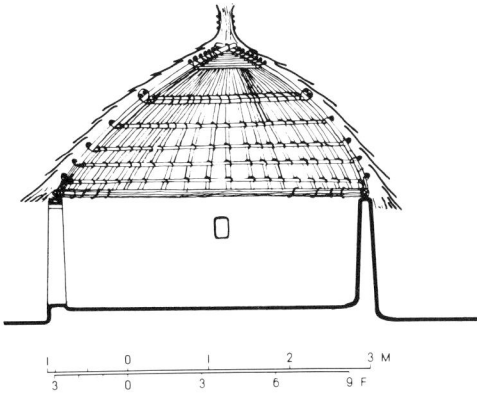

Fig. 6.3. Compound of Mallam Azika.
SECTION B—B.

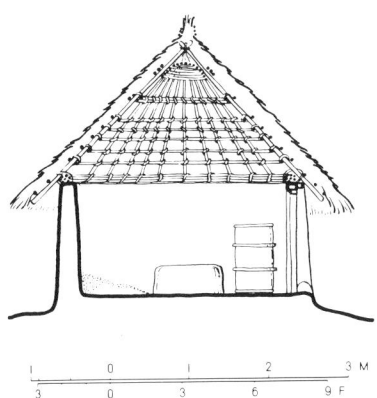

Argungu
Emir's Palace

The palace of the emirs of Argungu dates from 1849 (it was built by the Emir Yakubu Nabame, (1848-54). The *zaure* of the palace is said to have been erected in the mid-eighteenth century.[9] The independent spirit of the Kebbi people, which during the Fulani jihad led them to repulse the attempted conquest of Argungu (where they moved from their former capital, Birnin Kebbi) was also reflected in their cultural and architectural individuality – already discussed in connection with the Argungu Masallaci. (Chapter 2).

The structure of the palace is based on typical Habe/Hausa principles of building craft. The thick walls were erected with *tubali*, the flat roofs were supported by *tauyi* beams and *al'amudi* pillars.

At the same time the spatial composition of the palace compound, when compared with other palaces of the group, displays the same self-reliance on the part of the Argungu master builders as has already been shown in the autonomous design of the Argungu Masallaci.

The basic plan of the compound consists of four rectangular buildings, joined together along three sides of the

[9] J L Oram, *The Kanta Museum, Argungu*, stencilled typescript, N W S History Bureau, Sokoto 1975.

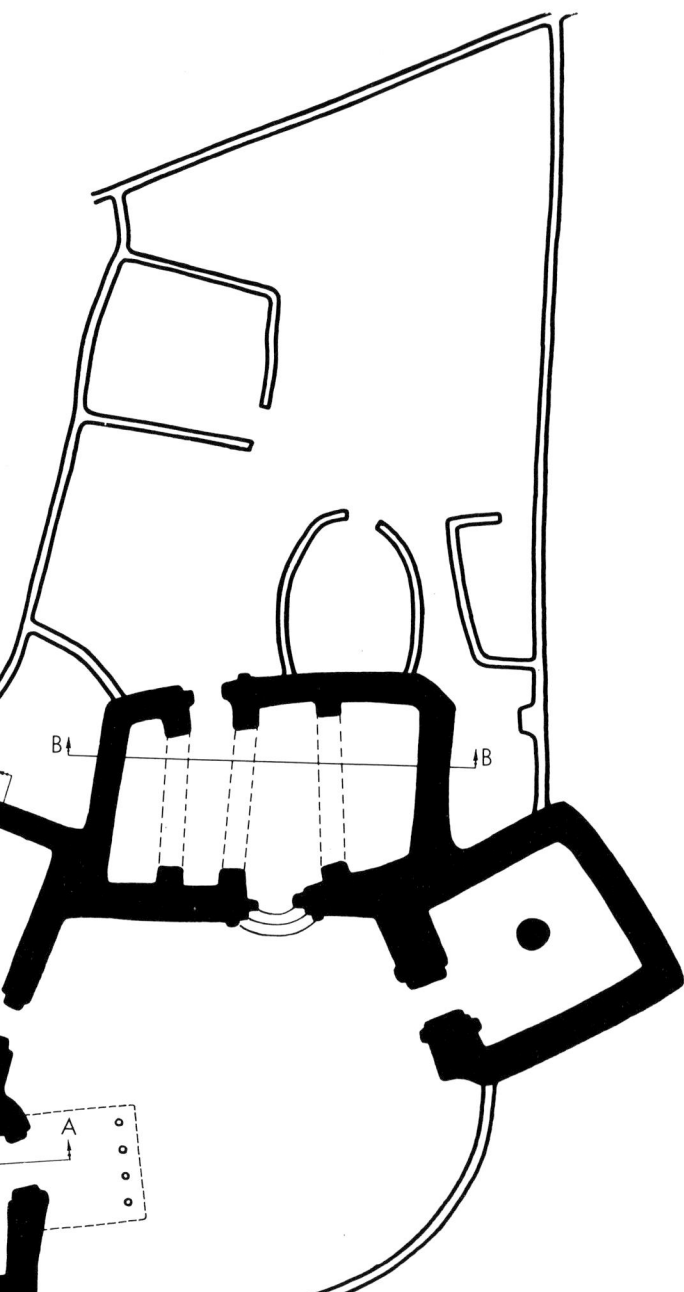

Fig. 6.4. Argungu. Emir's Palace. PLAN.

central courtyard which all the doors face. Thus the courtyard is not only a convenient centre of communication for the four interiors, but also provides a pleasant feeling of seclusion and privacy. It should be noted that the oldest element in the compound, the two-pillared *zaure*, conforms with traditional Habe/Hausa custom, and has its outer doorway orientated to the west.

The compound is extended W and N by two walled, royal graveyards, accessible from two central rooms (see Fig. 6.4.). The inner, E doorway of the *zaure* was protected by a thatched lean-to roof. The *zaure* still serves as the reception room for the Emir. The three other rooms were adapted for the local museum, *Gidan Kayan Al'adun*. It was opened in 1958 and extended by an outer courtyard on the S and E, with two rectangular concrete buildings.

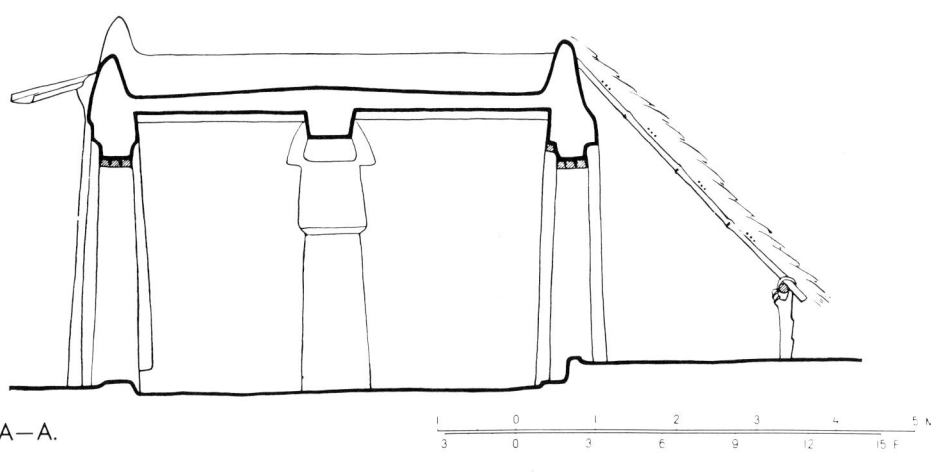

Fig. 6.5. Argungu. Emir's Palace. SECTION A—A.

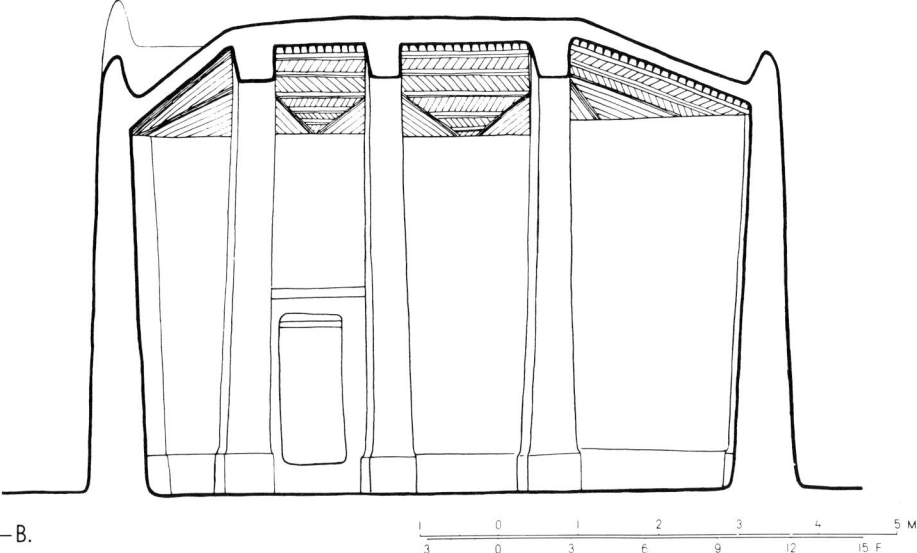

Fig. 6.6. Argungu. Emir's Palace. SECTION B—B.

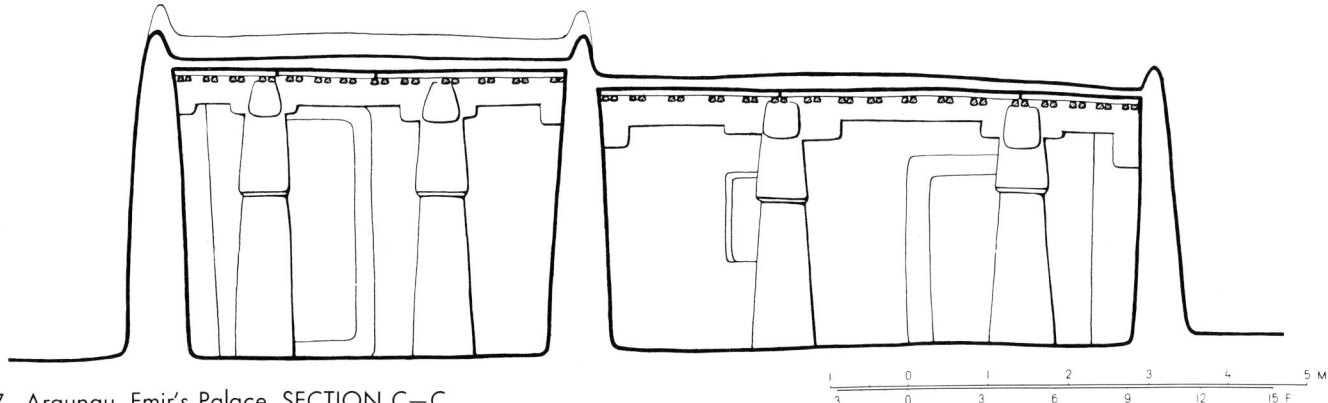

Fig. 6.7. Argungu. Emir's Palace. SECTION C—C.

Compound of Mallam Haruna

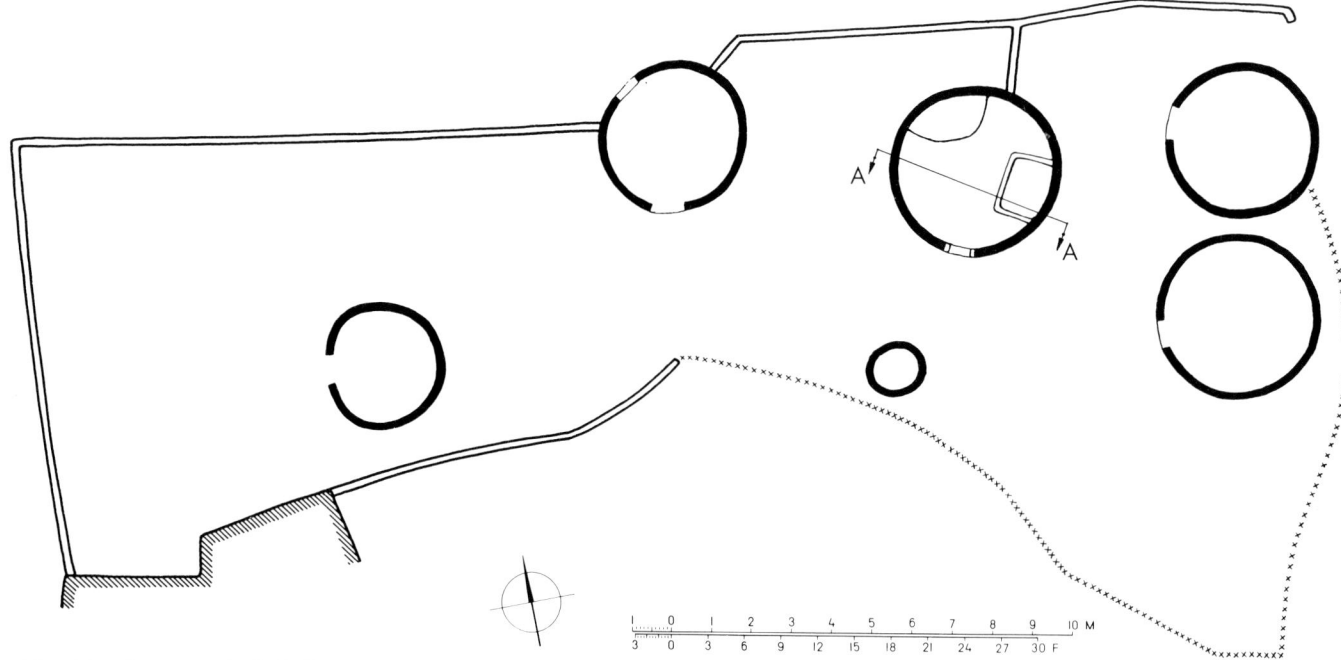

Fig. 6.8. Compound of Mallam Haruna. PLAN.

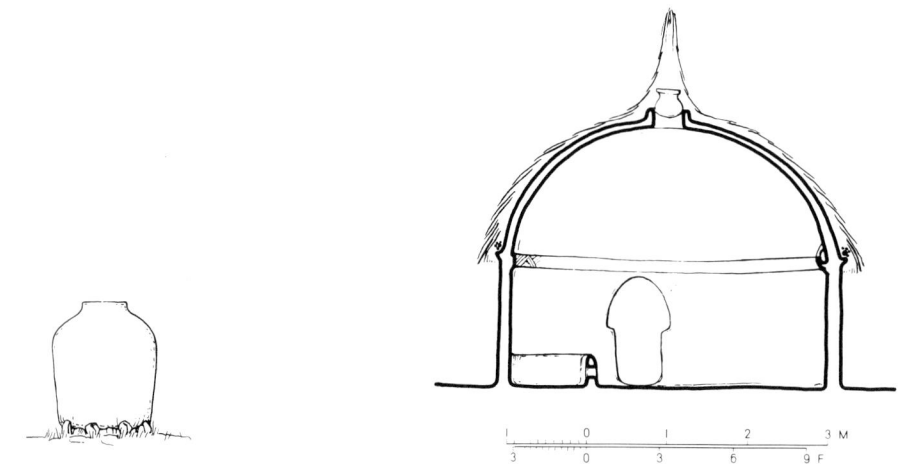

Fig. 6.9. Compound of Mallam
Haruna. Granary. ELEVATION.

Fig. 6.10. Comound of Mallam
Haruna. SECTION A—A.

Compound of Mallam Umaru

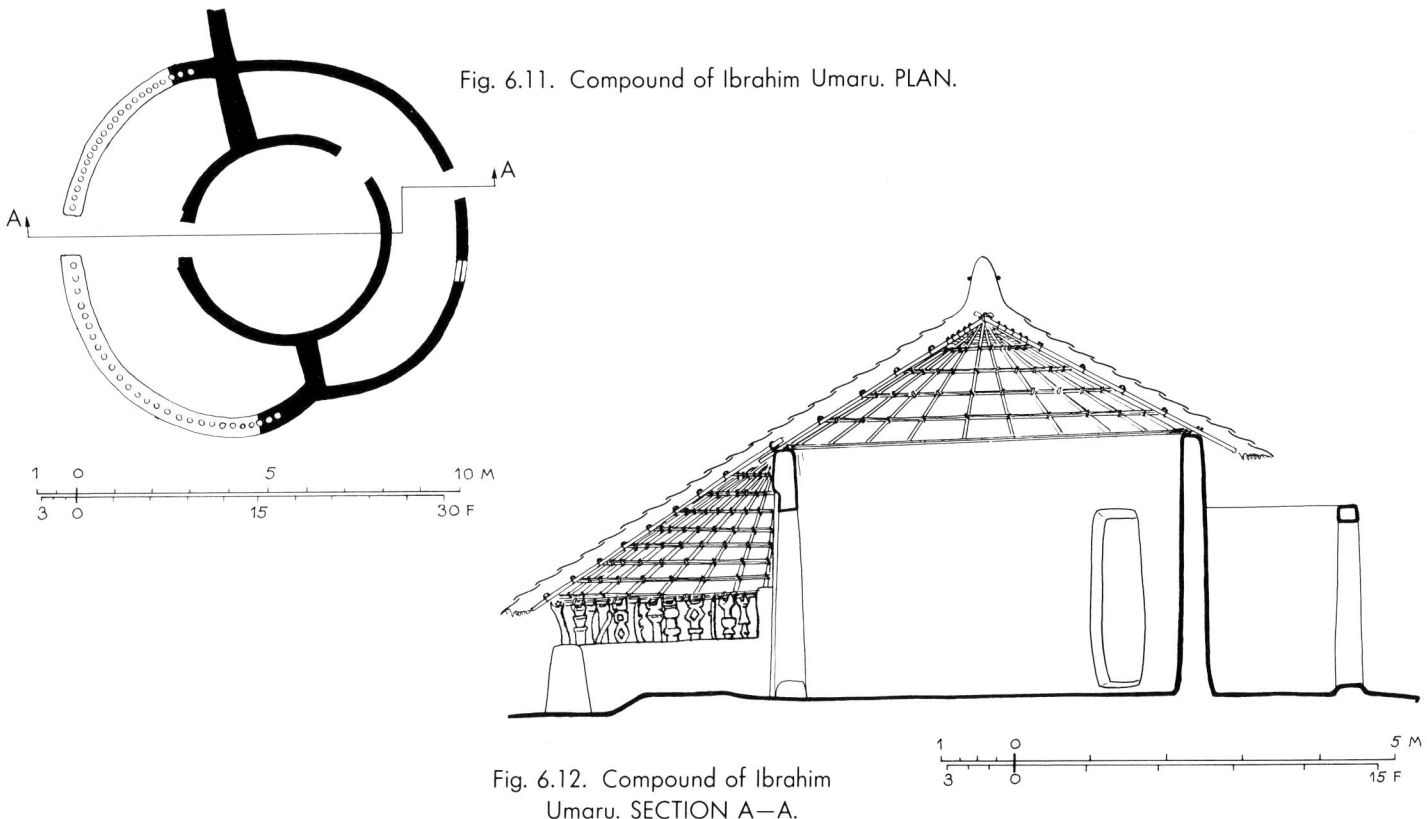

Fig. 6.11. Compound of Ibrahim Umaru. PLAN.

Fig. 6.12. Compound of Ibrahim
Umaru. SECTION A—A.

Compound of Mallam Labo

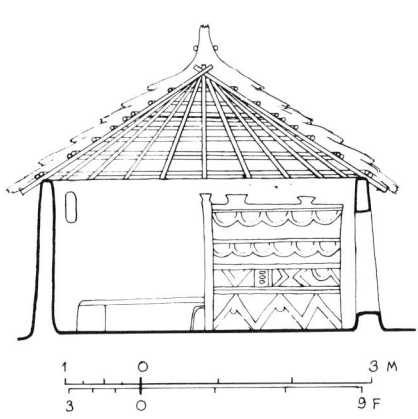

Fig. 6.13. Compound of Mallam Labo.
SECTION.

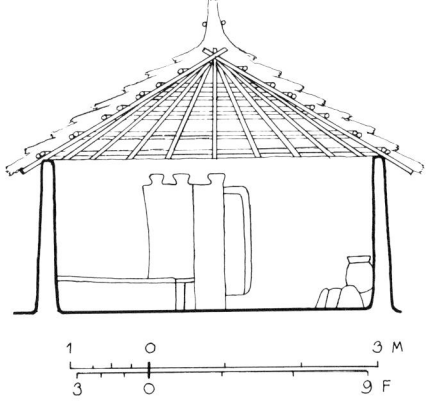

Fig. 6.14. Compound of Mallam Labo.
SECTION.

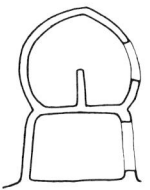

Fig. 6.15. Compound of Mallam Labo.
Granary. SECTION.

Kontagora

Compound of Tanko Dangata

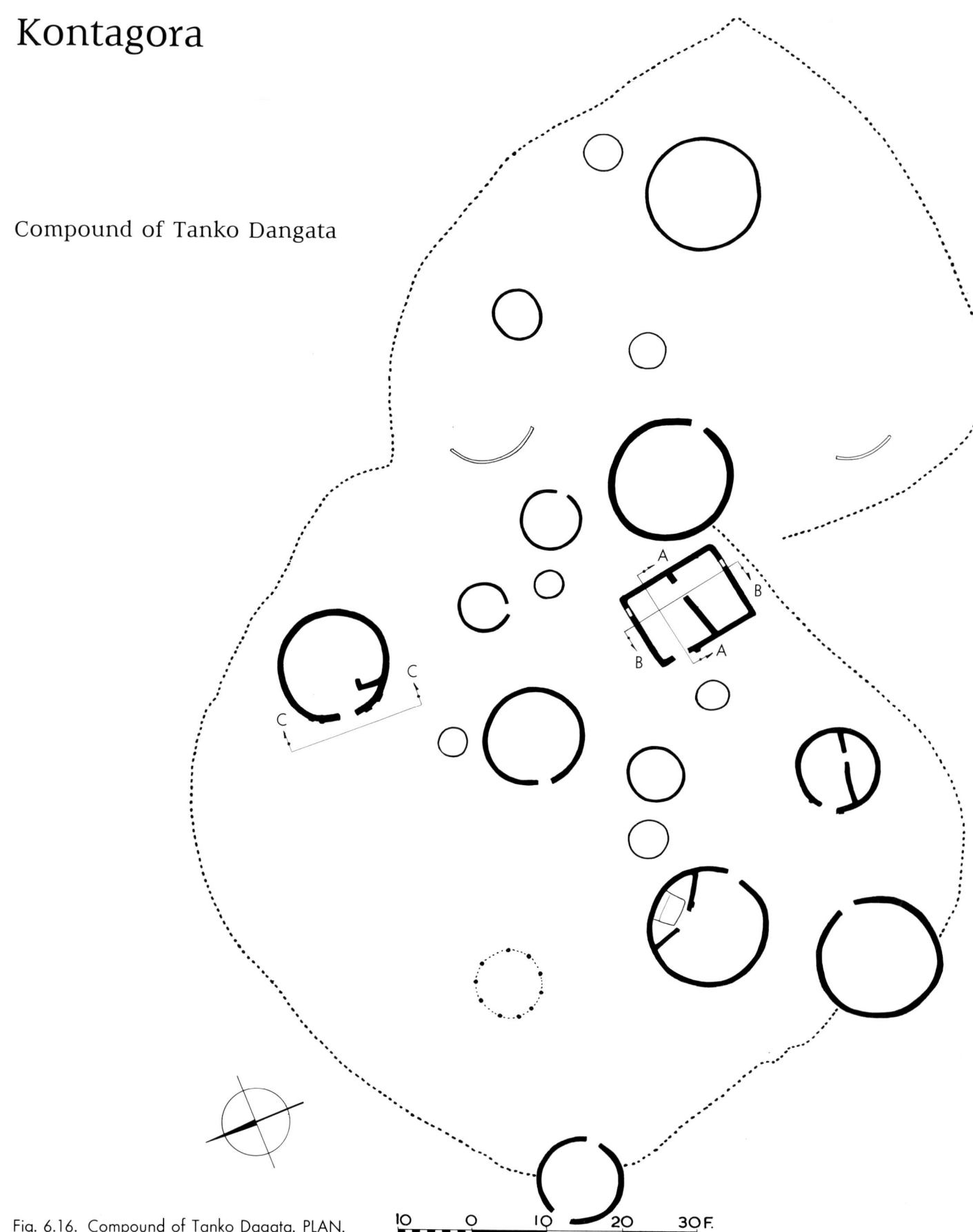

Fig. 6.16. Compound of Tanko Dagata. PLAN.

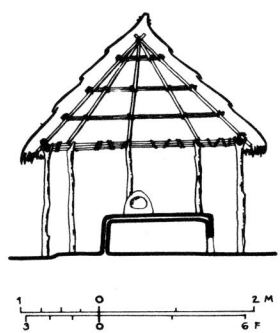

Fig. 6.17. Comound of Tanko Dagata.
SECTION.

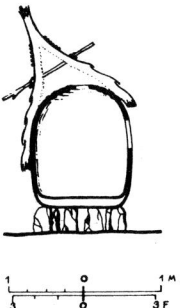

Fig. 6.18. Comound of Tanko Dagata.
Granary. SECTION.

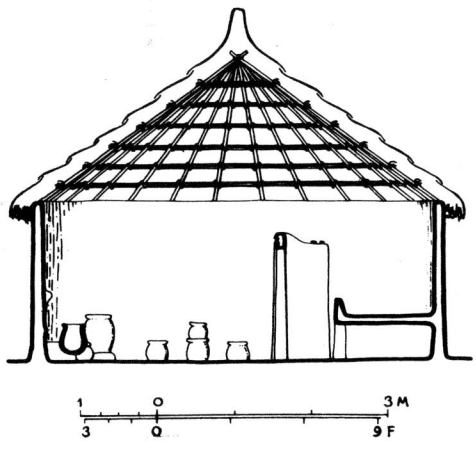

Fig. 6.19. Comound of Tanko Dagata.
SECTION A—A.

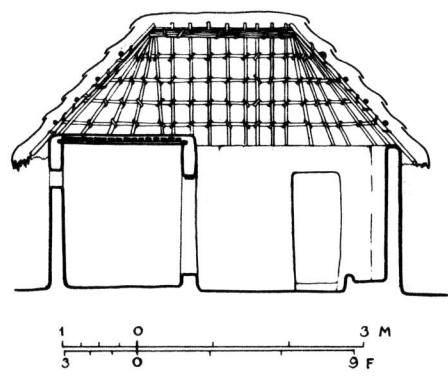

Fig. 6.20. Comound of Tanko Dagata.
SECTION B—B.

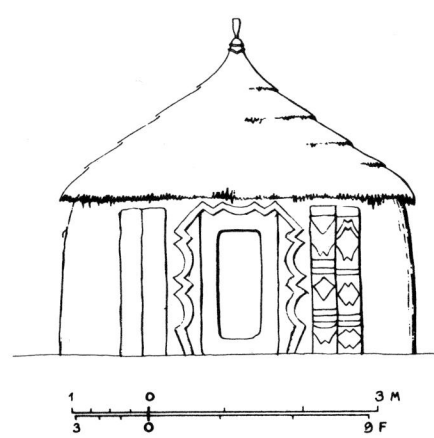

Fig. 6.21. Comound of Tanko Dagata.
ELEVATION C—C.

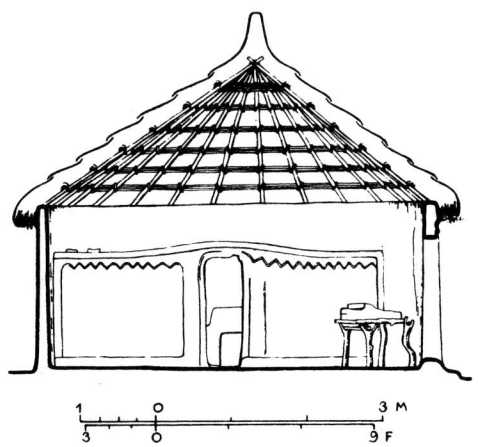

Fig. 6.22. Comound of Tanko Dagata.
SECTION.

Ilorin

Compound of
Mallam Abubaka Daudu

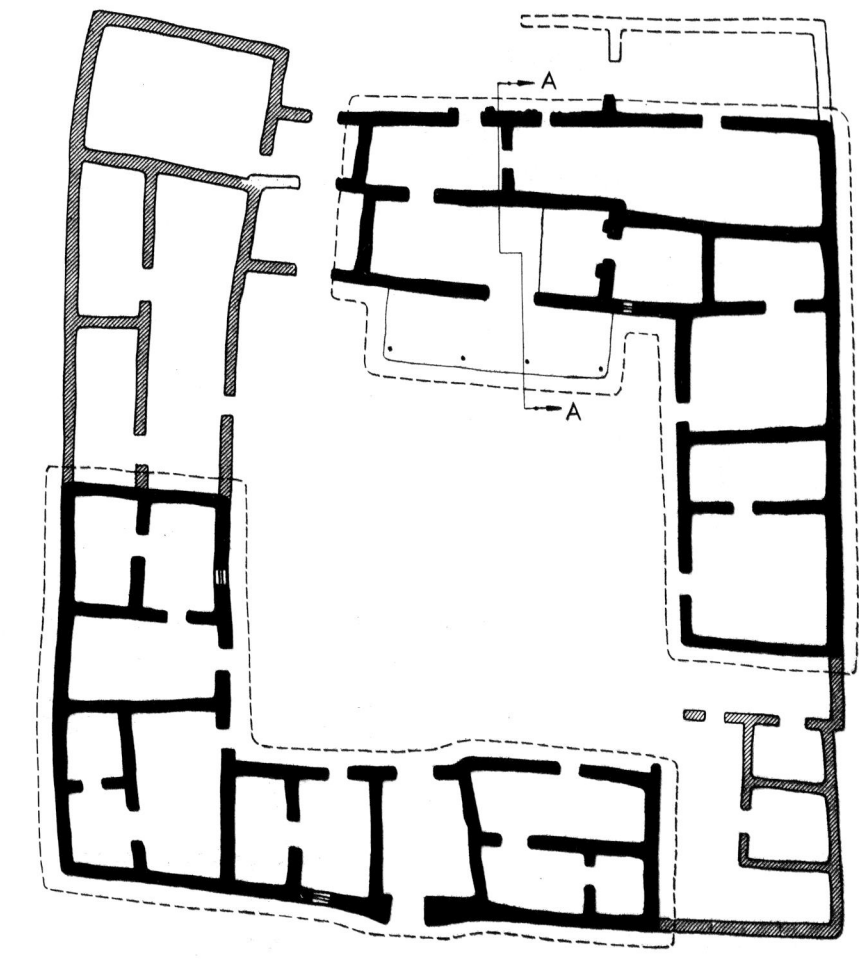

Fig. 6.23. Compound of Mallam Abubakar Daudu. PLAN.

Fig. 6.24. Compound of Mallam Abubakar Daudu. SECTION A—A.

Fig. 6.25. Compound of Mallam Abubakar Daudu. SECTION

Pl.6.4. ILORIN. House of Mallam Abubakar Daudu. The entrance verandah.

Pl.6.5. ILORIN. House of Mallam Abubakar Daudu. Decorative doorway under the verandah.

Pl.6.6. ILORIN. House of Mallam Abubakar Daudu. Detail showing top of forked post.

Pl.6.7. ILORIN. A door.

Pl.6.8. ILORIN. Gegele Street. A blocked-up doorway.

Pl.6.9. ILORIN. Gegele Street. Verandah posts.

Pl.6.10. ILORIN. Carved posts in the square outside the Emir's palace, from which the drums were formerly hung.[10]

[10] Frobenius, *op cit.* p. 118. Photograph of drum in position.

House of Sarkin Galadima

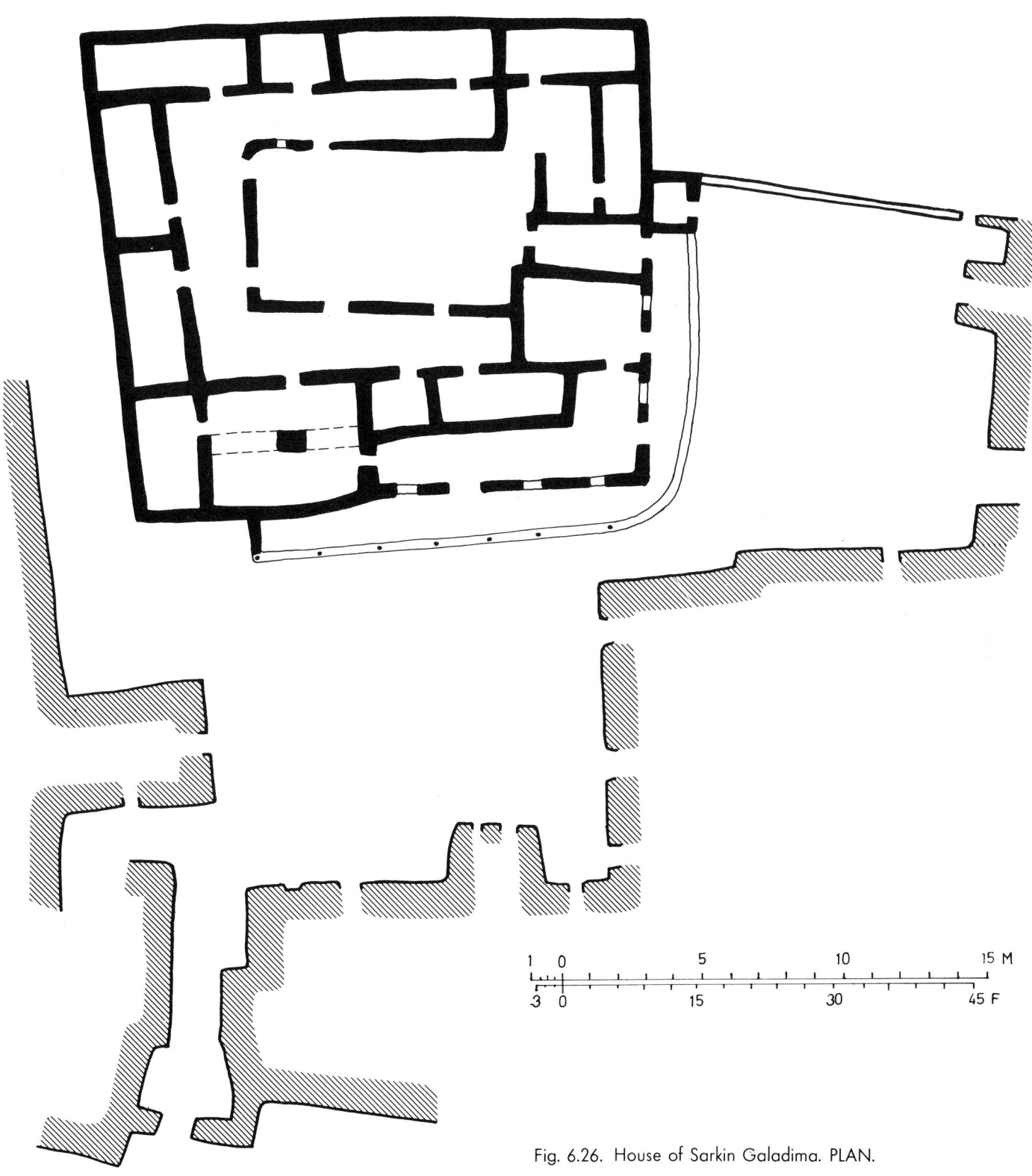

Fig. 6.26. House of Sarkin Galadima. PLAN.

Glossary of building terms

I. Hausa Building Technology

A

al'amudai – pillars that are square in plan

al'amudai mai tabarya – pillar in the shape of a pestle (*tabarya*)

asabari – flexible mats made of *tsaure*

azara – heavy, rigid timbers that are resistant to termites and decay

B

baba – plant from which indigo dye is extracted

babarkiya – deposit formed at the bottom of indigo dye pits, used for *katsi*

bagaruwa – final coat of plaster

baka – uniform plastered arch

bakan gizos – coupled, quadrantal corbels

bakuna – plural of *baka*

bango – labourer laying *tubali* on the wall

biko – *azaras* used for *hadin kafa*

birji – specific earth used for making mortar and *tubali*

buri or turda – *birji* in Sokoto

C

casta – name for cornstalk and grass buildings built by Ngizim tribe, Fika

chafe – plaster made of black earth and *makuba*

cham – stems used for *gofa*

churi – a lump of *birji*, used to make *tubali*

D

dabe, debe – floor

dada kyau – decorative plaster of quartz set in gum arabic

dafara – wild vine plant, gum made from its pounded roots is an ingredient of *laso*

dakwora (Acacia senegal) – the twisted bark of the roots is used to make strong rope

dangarama – threshold of a doorway

datsi – *birji* mixed with grass

daurin guga – apex of crossarched roofs (domes)

deleb – name for male palm tree (Borassus flabellifer)

dogari – outer projecting buttress for strengthening walls, also called *mat-aimkin al'amudi*

doki – strong beams spanning the width of a gate

dorowa – fruit pods of the locust bean tree

dustin kofa – stone socket, pivot for *kafar*

F

fara geza (Combretum micranthum) – plant whose tough stems are used for binding rafters of grass-roofed houses

fitilla – oil lamps

G

gaba – term used to indicate depth of foundations

gashin jima – goat hair and grease scraped from inside of soaked skins, an ingredient of *laso*

gemu – copings which overhang outer door

giama – small tiles of baked clay

giginya – local name for male palm tree (Hausa name *gazari* or *karinkgi-finya*)

ginshiki – pillars that have a cross shaped plan

gizago – verticle planks of doors

gofa – forked poles for supporting roofs

gongola – midribs of *tukuruwa* palm

goriba – dum palm wood

guntun azaras – strengthened timbers

H

hadin kafa – the top layer of cantilevered *azaras* projecting to the centre of a room

I

indararo – rainvalleys chased in the parapets of flat roofs

irongo – roof slab of flat roofs made from a mixture of cow dung and the outer shells of anthills

izara – *azara* in Katsina

J

jan birji – reddish or sanguine coloured earth from Kano

K

kafa – erect, established, set up

kafar – door stile

kafar guga – *azara* rod

kafar rufi – plastered ceiling

kafi – the fixing and securing of rods making arches

kafin kafa – layers of *azara* rods

kahwan karo – supports for *gemu*

kainya or kaiwa (Diospyros mespiliformis) – 'ebony' tree

kandame – semi-circular arch

kasa – mixture of earth and clay, a high quality plaster

kastiya – stems used for *gofa*

katsi – fine, light grey powder made from *babarkiya*

kawo (Afzelia africana) – wood used for planks

kirya – wood for planks

kista – inner layers of the bark of the *kuka* (baobab) tree used to make strong rope

kududdufi – pit from which *birji* is dug

kurna – wood used for rafters

kusa – nails

kyaure – door

kyemmi – *azara* in Sokoto

L

lagara – mats made of reeds

laka – mortar made of light grey clay

laso – type of plaster or waterproof cement

laterite – brittle red clay containing iron or iron oxide

M

ma'ajin fitilla – small shelves formed on top of door jambs

madabi – tool for beating floors

makapa – roofbooms laid crosswise to *mchichi*

makarto – strong wood used for making axe handles

makuba – glutinous fluid made from pounded beans, used in plaster for waterproofing and plastic qualities

marike – saplings used for *gofa*

mariki – iron holding *kafar* in place
mashim fidi short plastered *azaras* laid along axis of wall providing counterweight
mataimaki – helper
matiyade – rails holding *gizago* in position
mchichi – roof booms for flat roofs

R

rawani – continuous parapet surrounding a building at roof level
rufi – ceiling

S

sarka – short chains for closing doors
shuni – extract from *baba*
sombiri – forked post for supporting roofs
soro – room
Sugu – peculiar reed used for making *lagara*
sugu – peculiar reed used for making *lagara*

T

tabarya – pestle used for pounding corn
tauyi – beams
takalmin kasa – crosswise *baka*
Tsaure – strong grass used for *asabari*
tsaure – strong grass used for *asabari*
tubali – sun dried bricks
tuluwa – domed roofs

U

unku – *tubali* in Sokoto

W

walo – raft of thin branches laid on top of *makapa*

Z

zana – matting made from *zana* grass
zanko – parapet finials on the corner of buildings
zaure – entrance gate

2   Muslim Religious Architecture

A

ake ebo – type of wood (Ilorin)

alwala – ritual ablutions
alwatika – triangles (of *azaras*)
ama or **oro** – building earth (Ilorin)
aparum – bamboo (Ilorin)
arewa – north (Zaria)

B

babban alkali – chief judge (Zaria)
babban gwani – supreme expert, the master builder (Zaria)
babban mata kali – flight of steps (Zaria)
balami – cords fastening bunches of cornstalks (Gurin)
banwal – type of wood

D

damatsa – ceiling (Kafin Madaki)
damugal fombina – south doorway (Gurin)
damugal woila – north doorway (Gurin)
danki jodugo – stall for sitting (Gurin)
denni – layers of *azuras*
dungu – short horizontal bracket

E

eke – rafters (Ilorin)

G

gabaruwa – a plant
gafe – crosswise laid joists (Gurin)
gemu – extended brackets
ginin haraba – perimeter wall of a courtyard (Zaria)

H

haraba – courtyard
hasumiya – a minaret (Katsina)
hirange – a wall (Gurin)

I

ira – laths
iraile – wall plates (Ilorin)

K

kakan magina – grandfather of the builders (Zaria)
kofar – entrance gate
kofar taimoko – gaps in the perimeter wall 'assisting gates'
kohe – type of wood
kojole – type of wood
kokobal – type of wood
koriko – grass

kudu – south (Zaria)
kulaje – type of wood

L

ladan – one who chants the call to prayers

M

maburgi – arrangement of corbels (Zaria)
maga takarda – court scribes (Zaria)
magariba – platform from which the call to prayers was chanted (Zaria)
majalisa·na·sharia – a court of justice and law (Zaria)
marmara – laterite (Kafin Madaki)
masallaci – mosque, religious building
mesquid – arabic word for mosque
mihrab – niche used to show direction of Mecca
mimbar – *mihrab* (Gurin)

N

nopije – forked posts (Gurin)

O

orun – bent 'like a bow' (Ilorin)

Q

qibla – point to which Muslims turn at prayer, to Mecca

R

randan rua – large water pots for ritual ablutions (*alwala*)
rufi – ceiling

S

sahu – bays between pillar (Zaria)
sarkin – chief, leader

T

tauyi – beams
toka – woodash
tuluwa – domed roof

U

unguwa bayan – ward where *babban gwani*'s slaves were settled (Zaria)
uwar Masallaci – main hall of the mosque (Zaria)

W

wakili – the district head (Gurin)

wakam – transome (Ilorin)

Y

yamma – west (Zaria)

Z

zaman ribatsi – defensive walled town (Kafin Madaki)
zana – matting made from *zana* grass
zauruka – plural of *zaure*

3 Architecture of the North East

(H) = Hausa (F) = Fika (P) = Potiskum (Y) = Yola

A

alabar – built-in pots on top of *baburum* (Y)
anum – type of wood (P)
apsawu – plant whose bark is used for cord (P)

B

babal – the first courtyard (Y)
baburum – screen walls (Y)
ba'e – plural of *ware* (Y)
bagur – *azaras* (Y)
balamji – rope (Y)
bayi – courtyard (F)
bei mbalu – burial ground (F)
bembe – granaries (Y)
bilori – slender rings of *kawal* (Y)
bodaji – superior type of grass (Y)
boggol – decorative plait of *sodornde* for binding *gangawal* (Y)
bulbul – yellow (Y)
buto – ash (Y)

C

casta – type of hut with cornstalk walls (P)
chaddeje – plural of *sagdere* (Y)
chochodi – type of grass (Y)

D

dai – red (F)
dampara [*makuba* (H)] – extract from the pods of the locust bean tree (Y)
damugal – threshold, door (Y)
dinglis – roof structure based on a ring of cornstalks bundled together (P)

G

gabiwa [*rama* (H)] – string made of bark (P)
gafal – horizontal joists (Y)
gafe – plural of *gafal* (Y)
gafuya – front courtyard of palace (F)
gaga – gateman (Y)
gali – layers (Y)
gangawal – thick ring supporting inside of conical roofs (Y)
ganua – city walls (F)
garu – walls (Y)
gene marori – rice leaves (Y)
gina – layers (P)
gizir – thatching needle (P)
guinear – type of corn (Y)
gusho – stone (Y)

H

hagda – type of wood

I

iware – type of grass (Y)

J

janga – building earth (F & Y)
jangan-dai – red clay (F)
jar – type of wood used for split sticks for roofs (P)
jauleru [*zaure* (H)] – entrance gate (Y)
jauleru chaka – a second gate (Y)
jauliji [*zauruka* (H)] – plural of *jauleru* (Y)
jebbe – servants' house (F)
jember – ashes of burnt stalks of *rama* used for black colouring (Y)
jura – courtyard for wives (F)

K

ka-ka-shaki – building earth – gravel, used for floors (Y)
kalwal [*zana* (H)] – coarse grass (Y)
kofar zaure – gate house (P)
kojole – type of timber used for *noppije* (Y)
kole – thin stems (Y)

L

laka – clay plaster (Y)
lamasal (verb: *lamasol*) – process of finishing the apex of conical roofs (Y)
lochi – *azara* (Y)
lochi-dubbe – *azaras* (Y)

lochi kewe – bamboo sticks (Y)
lope – building earth (Y)
lope yabade – building earth processed for *tubali*

M

mabbode – woven covering for door (Y)
machchube – servant boys (Y)
machchudo – singular of *machchube* (Y)
malapare or **lupare** – a conical basket woven from *uware* (Y)
masaya – chief messenger of the Emir (F)
matira – eating room (F)
matira tinja – gate house (F)
mbedu or **bedel** – a round basketwork mat used for covering the apex of conical roofs, also used for serving food (Y)
molu – grid of horizontal beams (P & Y)
murdaka – rings of *tappo* grass (Y)

N

namugo – stones for grinding corn (Y)
ngabare – semi-circular platform (Y)
nguma – broken pottery (P)
noppije – rafters (Y)

P

pai boni moi – palace (F)
pendele – white chalk (Y)
petila – white (Y)
pilal – ridge beam (Y)
pile – battens for roofs (Y)

R

rama – type of tree (H)
rijiya-daya [*daurin-guga* (H)] – arched cross structure of domes (Y)
riyak – type of hut with wooden frame (P)
rusho – dried and broken grass (F)

S

safakare – a fireproof building (Y)
sagdere – axe (Y)
salam – entrance gate (Y)
sandiram – perimeter wall
segifa [Zaure (H)] – entrance gate (Y)
Sheddu – lumps of plaster (F)
sheddu – lumps of plaster (F)
sibi – waterproof covering (Y)

sodornde – type of grass (Y)
soro – building (P), room (F)
soro minda – room of the royal princes (F)
sudu – circular buildings (Y)

T

tame lope – *tubali* (Y)
tamre lope – singular of *tame lope* (Y)
tappo – type of grass used for thin thread (Y)
tapsar – type of grass (P)
tekkere – ring made of *kalwal* used to rest roofs on (Y)
tika – forked post supporting *dinglis* (P)
tinde damugal – transome (Y)
titiji bodeji – superior type of grass (Y)
titorgal – stick (Y)
torom – termites (P)
tubali – pillar used as a flogging post (not to be confused with Hausa *tubali*) (F)
tuluwa – domed roof (H)

U

ugo – pit from which *janga* was dug (F & Y)
uware – type of grass (Y)

V

vome – short type of grass (Y)

W

ware – long mat made of grass (Y)

Y

yabu – plaster (F)

Z

zonge [adua (H)] – type of tree planted behind graves (F)

4. Architecture of the Central North

A

afari – decorative pilasters flanking doors
alkuki – shallow niches
alwatika – triangles of *azaras*
asabari – flexible mats made of *iwa* grass

B

baka hudu – simple framed dome
bango – walls
barawon – thieves
barawon kofar – door set on the inner side of a wall in a shallow niche
bouze – mica fragments
budu – crushed straw added to *kwabe bbije* to make *tubali*
buse – a solution of very fine earth

C

ciki daya – bays between ceiling beams

D

dafar – type of plaster
dagagye – zig-zag cross sections incised in *yanciki*
daki – back courtyard
debi – circular verandah
denni – layers of *azaras*
dunguna – *dungu* means the length of the forearm from elbow to closed fist, also name for the overhang marking the bottom of *bakan gizos*

F

filin kofar gida – inner door of gatehouse leading to courtyard
fintilla – doorway having shelves for oil lamps

G

garum gida – perimeter wall
gashin – type of plaster
gemu – name given to structural elements that are corbelled or cantilevered

I

iwa – type of grass

J

jima – type of plaster

K

kadame – semi-circular arch
kafa – corbels
kaguwa – crabs
kasa'n gini – building earth
kashin kaguwa – filling for cracks

made from casts of *kaguwa*
katsi – type of plaster
keffi (katar guga) – layers of rods
kuka – type of tree
kwabe bbiya – wet building earth processed to make *tubali*

L

lukuki – plant used for bracing rails

M

ma'ajin fitila – small shelves formed by extended door jambs used for oil lamps
maburgi – framework of *bakuna*
mai ungwa – head of the city ward

N

ndororo – rainwater spouts made of burnt clay

R

rawani – parapet

S

shgifa – simple ceiling
shirayi – living room
soro – room, building
soron ajiye takalma – building where shoes are put down (by visitors)
soron fadanci – reception room
soron yara – building for boys

T

tsakuwa – gravel

Y

yanciki – soffits

Z

zubi – many layers of *azaras* laid on *tauyi*

5. Emir's Palaces

(D) = Daura (K) = Katsina (Z) = Zaria
(A) = Abuja (KM) = Kafin Madaki

A

abagana – type of creeper (A)
ado – moulded decoration of pillars and *bakan gizos* (D)
adudu – throne room (K)
agwan taki – type of shrub used for strong pegs (A)

aljihu – pocket, *aljihu soro* – small room (KM)
alkuki – shallow niches
azara mai gwafa – *azara* with fork carved in the top
azaron – *azaras* (A)

B

babban gwani – building named after the master builder (KM)
babban zauri – entrance gate (K)
baka hudu – two crossed *bakan gizos* (Z)
barga – palace compound (K)
bari – low screening walls (Z)
bayan gida – bathroom and latrine (A)
bayan maraya – type of grass (female gender) (A)
boto – plaited grass mat (Z)

C

ciki gida – courtyard gate (A)

D

dafara – gum made from powdered roots of wild vine plant
daki – bedchamber
dakin ganawa – a room of introducing (D)
dakin nace – singular of *kakuna mata* (A)
dakin samari – boys quarters (A)
daurin guga takwas kafa – crossarched roof of eight *baka*
dawaki – *gongola* (Z)
debi – circular verandah
dendonkwa – building earth (D)

F

filin duka – courtyard where boys were punished (KM)
finim kofar gida – inner door of gatehouse leading to courtyard

G

gado – clay bed
garki – plural of *garkuwa* (KM)
garkuwa – shield (KM)
gemu – structural elements that are corbelled or cantilevered
gida – courtyard (D)
gima – *tuke* plaited in threes (A)
ginia – circular purlin (Z)
gode or jungergeri – earth used for plastering walls (D)

gora – rods used for roof frames (A)

J

jakadiya – female messenger (Z)
jambora – type of grass (male) (A)

K

kabai – rope made from *goriba* (D)
kafa – rods
kafa kasa – structure in the shape of a chicken's foot (Z)
kafe – verandah
kafin kafa – layers of *azara* rods (D)
kafin kafa – horizontal team (Z)
kago – walls (A)
kakuna·mata – wives' houses (A)
kamu – an arm length (D & A)
kamun tanka – rings used as tightening purlins (A)
kangiwa – square within compound (K)
kara – cornstalks (Z)
kashintana – earthworm casts (A)
kemi – *azaras* (D)
kini – secured (A)
kofar baru – pit from which *dendonkwa* was dug (D)
kofar zaure – entrance hall
k0ngo – wooden containers (A)
kuringa or **wagiri** – forest creepers (A)
kurkudu – cone of cornstalks (Z)
kururu – store room (A)

L

laiji – probably means waiting room (K)
lode – *makuba* solution used with *gode* for plaster (D)

M

maburgi – framework for *bakuna*
madabi – mallet for beating floors
madawakin magina and **galadina magina** – builders next in rank to *sarkin magina*
magayaki – titled official at the court (Z)
mai·cinnaki·tanka – specialist in elaborate roof apexes (A)
majalisa – council chamber (Z)
makamai – the Madaki's armoury (KM)
masauki – guest house (KM)
matari – horizontal beam (A)
mate hara – 'helper' rods (A)

mawanka – couch (A)
mruhfu na kasa – hearth (A)
murfu – open air kitchen (A)

P

pagacin samaya – inner courtyard (D)
paparanda – annexe (Z)
parpada – family courtyards (A)

R

ragaya – net of cords (A)
rauno – grass (A)
rijia daya – square central panel of dome based on *daurin guga* (Z)
rijia hudu – elongated *daurin guga* (Z)
rijia biu – *talkamin kafar kasa* (A)
rumbu – granary (A)

S

sara – division or rhythm (A)
sarari – open field (K)
sarkin bai – chief of slaves (K)
sarkin magina – master builder
shamaki – stables (KM)
shayeshaye – circular (Z)
sherai – antechamber (D)
shirayi – living room (Z)
soraye – plural of *soro*
soron ajiya kain·yaki – store for war equipment (KM)
soron fadanci – entrance hall where respects are paid to the emir
soron garki – room where shields were stored (KM)
soron hutu – resting place

T

tafarfara – rectangular in plan (Z)
taga – ventilating slits or windows (K & KM)
taki – measuring unit, a foot (A)
talkamin kafa kasa – elaborate positioning of *bakuna*
tanka – laths (Z)
toka – ashes
tsaiko – rafters (A)
tubali – sun dried bricks
tuke – string made of leaves (A)
tukurjwa – type of plant used for string

U

ungwataki – bush shrub (A)

W

waje – *zaure* (A)

wudu – type of grass mixed with
dendonkwa to make *tubali* (D)
wurin cin abinci – outside area where
food was served (KM)
wurin zuba takalma – interior of
palace, *wurin* = passage to, *zuba* =
pour in or out, *takalma* = shoe or
sandal (KM)

Y

yanta – thatching mats (A)
yaro ba kyuya – 'the boy who is not
lazy' (Z)
yaro ba kyuya – semi-circular iron
needle (A)

Z

zaman ribatsi – walled defensive
town (KM)
zauri – entrance gate, *zaure* (K)
zaurukka – plural of *zauri* (K)

6. Architecture of
the North West

A

auzun zaki – 'lion ribs', name for
decorative zig-zag arrangement of
roof timbers

B

bance – *almatika tauyi* – corner beams
buri or **turda** – building earth

D

damri – process of binding plaster
and building bricks

G

gamba – type of grass
giniya – circular wall plate
guga – crossed *bakuna* of roof
(actually a net of four cords
holding a calabash for pulling
water from a well)
gwandan daji – bush paw paw
gyeza (**geza**) – type of tree

H

hakori da'ki – teeth of the hut, term
for *taushi* net, the ends of which
were tied to the bottom of the
thatch and gave a toothed
appearance.

hayin takalme – *kafar kasa* or *talkamin
kasa*. A structure consisting of one
whole *baka* and a half *baka*
supporting it at right angles –
descriptive idiom meaning the
binding of a sandal.

K

karan keru – millet stalks
karandaua – cornstalks
kemi – *azara* beam set between a pair
of *bakuna*
kirynya (**k'irya**) – acacia-like branches
kunku – local term for *tubali*
kwanda – matting
kyami – *azara*

L

laka – clay

M

magina laka – site where *laka* is
obtained
mundua – ope ring securing top of
taushi

S

sabara – type of shrub
shibci – type of grass
shinaka – type of grass used to make
tukku

T

tanka – thin cornstalks
taushi – net cover to secure thatch
taushi – thick upper part of wall in
Habe/Hausa type buildings
tukku – grass apex of thatch
tukura – type of grass

Y

yabe – rings in circular roof
construction

References

ARNETT, E J
translated from 'Daura Makas Sariki', (Daura Snake
Slayer), *Journal of the African Society*, IX, 1909–1910
BAIKIE, W B
*Narrative of an Exploring Voyage up the Rivers Kwora and
Binue in 1854*, London 1856
BARGERY, Revd G P
A Hausa – English Dictionary, London 1934, pps. 278,
503, 524, 527, 528
BARTH, H
*Travels and Discoveries in North and Central Africa . . . in the
years 1849 – 1855*, London 1857-8, reprint 1965, Vol I
p.506, Vol II pps. 103-105, 485, 490, 501
CLAPPERTON, H
Journal of a Second Expedition into the Interior of Africa,
London 1829
DALDY, A F
Temporary Buildings in Northern Nigeria, Public Works
Department of Northern Nigeria, Technical paper No 10,
1945
DENHAM, D, CLAPPERTON, J and OUDNEY, W
*Narrative of Travels and Discoveries in Northern and Central
Africa in the Years 1822 and 1824*, London 1826, Vol II,
p. 251, Captain Clapperton's Narrative, pps. 43, 51-53.
DANIEL, F de F
Journal of the African Society, XXV, 1925-26, pps. 278-283
ENGERSTROM, Ter
Origin of Pre-Islamic Architecture in West Africa
'Ethos', Vol 24, Stockholm 1959
FAGE, J D
A History of West Africa, London 1969, p. 147
FLETCHER, Sir Bannister Flight
A History of Architecture on the Comparative Method,
London 1943, p. 85
FREEMANTLE, J M
*A History of the Region comprising the Katagum Division
of Kano Province*, Journal of the African Society, 1911.
GRAHAM, C
'Some Sketches of Katsina from the Past', *Nigerian Field*,
Vol XXXIII No 1, 1968, p. 88
HALLAM, W J R
'An Introduction to the History of Bornu', *Nigerian Field*,
XXV No 4, October 1970
HODGKIN, Thomas
Nigerian Perspectives, OUP 1960, pps. 89, 102
HOGBEN, S J and KIRK-GREENE, A H M
The Emirates of Northern Nigeria, London 1966, pps. 82,

156, 157, 158, 181, 184, 216, 222, 223–414, 249–251,
367, 429, & 461
ISICHEI, E
History of West Africa since 1800, London 1978, p.18
JUSUF, Dr Ahmed Beita
The Development of Ethnic Identity among the Hausa, Draft
paper for the Seminar on Culture in West Africa,
14-20 April 1977
KIRK-GREENE, A H M
Adamawa Past and Present, London 1958. In *Nigerian Field*,
Vol XXV No 2, 1960
KUMM, Karl
The Sudan 1907 and *Hausaland to Egypt*
LANDER, R
Reports of Captain Clapperton's last Expedition,
London 1830, Vol II pps. 58, 59
LAVERS, J E
'The History and People of Fika Emirate', *New Nigerian
Special Supplement*, 23 December 1972
'The Bolewa of Fika', *Nigerian Magazine*, No 51, 1956, p. 340
*A Note of Birni Gazargamu and 'Burnt Brick' sites in the
Bornu Caliphate*, paper presented to the 4th Conference
of West African Archaeologist.
LELY, H V
The Useful Trees of Northern Nigeria, London 1925
MACROW, D W
'Sokoto City', *Nigeria Magazine* No 57, 1958, p.110
MEEK, C K
Tribal Studies in Northern Nigeria, Vol 2, London 1931,
pps. 289, 290
MIGEOD, C O
Gazetteer of Yola Province, Lagos 1927
MIGEOD, F W H
Through Nigeria to Lake Chad, London 1924, pps. 266-7
MISCHLISCH, A
Uber die Kulturen in Mittel-Sudan, Berlin 1942
MONTEIL, P L
De Saint Louis à Tripoli par le Lac Tchad, Paris 1895, pps.
248-55
MOREL, E D
Nigeria, its Peoples and Problems, London 1911, pps. 310-11
MOUGHTIN, J C
'The Friday Mosque, Zaria City', *Savanna*, Vol I, No 2,
December 1972 pps. 144, 144A
ORAM, J L
The Kanta Museum, Argungu, stencilled type script, N W S
History Bureau, Sokoto 1975

PALMER, H R
  Sudanese Memoirs, Vol III, Lagos 1928, pps. 107-8
ROBINSON, C H
  *Hausaland or Fifteen Hundred Miles through the Central
  Sudan*, New edition, London 1896
SASSOON, H
  'Birom Blacksmithing' *Nigeria Magazine*, No 74, 1962 pps.
  25-31
SMITH, H F C
  Arabic Manuscript . . . on the History of Western Sudan,
  Historical Society of Nigeria, Supplement to News
  Bulletin iii 4, 1959
SMITH, M G
  The Beginnings of Hausa Society AD 1000 – 1500
  The Historian in Tropical Africa
WEBSTER, J B, BOAHEN, A A and IDOWU, A O
  The Revolutionary Years – West Africa since 1800, London
  1971, p. 3
WILLIAM, G J
  'The Juma'a (Friday) Mosque, Zaria City', *Savanna*, Vol II
  No 1, June 1972, p. 104

  Colonial Report Annual, Northern Nigeria, 1902, No 409 p. 87
  Department of Antiquities File TF 128/C5B
  Department of Antiquities File TF 128/C5B
  The Brief Divan, published by H R Palmer in Bornu
  Sahara Sudan, London 1936
  'An Introduction to the History of Hausaland', *Nigerian
  Field*, Vol XXXI No 1, 1966

PUBLISHERS' NOTE

Acknowledgements are due to the Dean of the Faculty of Architecture, The Technical University of Gdansk, Poland for the extended loan of drawings and plans used in this book. Special mention must be made of Jan Sikora, Janusz Przbyszewski, Elzbieta Dybicka-Brozek, Jacek Popek, Zofia Holowinska, Regina Pernak and Jerzy Doerffer for technical expertise and renderings of the scale drawings, plans and isometric projections published herein.

Thanks are also due to several people for their help and advice during the preparation of the series. Particular mention should be made of Professor Ekpo Eyo, Professor Ade Obayemi, Professor J.C Moughtin, Mr Rene Vesque,and Mr J.F Aloa.

MANAGING EDITOR
Stuart Hamilton

DESIGN AND ART DIRECTION
Stuart Hamilton, Gail Tandy and Edgell Marland.

PHOTOGRAHIC RETOUCHING
Nigel Maudsley

EDITORIAL
Anna Dmochowski, Gayle Hermick, Douglas Warner, Alison Hodge, Yemi Opaleye, and Gail Tandy.

Typeset in Itek Book Face and Futura Light.

Printed and Manufactured in UK by Jolly and Barber Ltd., Rugby